Studies in Behavioral Political Science

Editor: ROBERT PRESTHUS, York University. ☐ This series provides detailed analyses and explanations of empirical research in various sub-fields of political science. Each author describes his theoretical framework, methodological approach, including problems encountered in the analysis, and his substantive findings. In this way the series provides, through concrete examples, a realistic characterization of the behavioral approach, the utility of several of its methods, and the kinds of problems often encountered in such research.

The Judicial Mind Revisited
Psychometric Analysis of Supreme Court Ideology

GLENDON SCHUBERT, University of Hawaii. ☐ Using sophisticated computer techniques, Professor Schubert provides a comprehensive study of the voting behavior of the justices of the Supreme Court, extending from the end of World War II and the chief justiceship of Fred Vinson through that of Earl Warren. In addition to tracing the major changes in the Court's policy-making, he analyzes the ideologies of the justices, individually and collectively, to illustrate how their beliefs concerning public policy influence decisions.

This study is built upon the synthesis and application of the ideas of several leading psychologists; Thurston, Guttman, Eysenck, and Coombs. Throughout the analysis, emphasis is placed upon the methods by which the theory is operationalized and tested.

Summer 1974   192 pp.   10 color photographs
cloth $9.00   paper $4.95

Computer Simulations of Voting Behavior

WILLIAM R. SHAFFER, Purdue University

1972   176 pp.   51 tables
cloth $7.50   paper $2.95

Political Socialization

KENNETH P. LANGTON, University of Michigan

1969   240 pp.   paper $2.95

 OXFORD UNIVERSITY PRESS
200 MADISON AVENUE
NEW YORK, N.Y. 10016

Kindly mention THE ANNALS *when writing to advertisers*

Latin America and the United States
The Changing Political Realities

Julio Cotler and Richard R. Fagen, Editors. It is clear today that the realities of Latin America are changing more rapidly than knowledge about those realities, that Latin America can no longer be understood as merely the shadow cast by the Colossus of the North. In an effort to explore the nature of these political relations, a group of distinguished social scientists present twenty-two papers covering such topics as the politics of the multinational corporation, military elites and military thinking, and the sources of U.S. foreign policy. Paper, $4.95ˣ; cloth, $18.75

The Life of Captain James Cook

J. C. Beaglehole. Captain Cook is the greatest seaman-explorer of all time, a complex genius whose great voyages—extending from the Antarctic regions to the Arctic Circle and from Chile to Indonesia—transformed the world's knowledge of the vast Pacific area. This definitive biography, the culmination of the life's work of the most distinguished historian of Pacific exploration, places Cook in the context of his times and affirms his eminence in the history of maritime discovery. 51 pages of illustrations, 4 in color, and 5 maps. $18.50

 Stanford University Press

VOLUME 413   MAY 1974

THE ANNALS

of The American Academy *of* Political
and Social Science

RICHARD D. LAMBERT, *Editor*

ALAN W. HESTON, *Assistant Editor*

INTEREST GROUPS IN INTERNATIONAL

PERSPECTIVE

Special Editor of This Volume

ROBERT PRESTHUS
University Professor of Political Science
York University
Toronto, Ontario
Canada

PHILADELPHIA

Library of Congress Catalog Card Number 73-89782

International Standard Book Numbers (ISBN)

ISBN 0-87761-177-7, vol. 413, 1974; paper—$3.00
ISBN 0-87761-176-9, vol. 413, 1974; cloth—$4.00

*Issued bimonthly by The American Academy of Political and Social Science at Prince and
Lemon Sts., Lancaster, Pennsylvania 17604. Cost per year: $15.00 paperbound; $20.00
clothbound. Add $1.00 to above rates for membership outside U.S.A. Second-class postage
paid at Lancaster and at additional mailing offices.*

Editorial and Business Offices, 3937 Chestnut Street, Philadelphia, Pennsylvania 19104.

CONTENTS

CONTENTS

SOCIOLOGY

ECONOMICS

PREFACE

Interest groups have become remarkably salient during the past decade, and particularly in a political context.[1] In part, this *risorgimento* reflects the emergence of so-called protest and consumer groups whose ideological fervor and provocative tactics, however disconcerting to governmental elites, have captured the attention of the mass media in most societies. The consequences include a clearer picture of the symbiotic role which interest groups often play in shaping public policy. Various publics have been given a look behind the official apparatus and have come away with a new appreciation of political power and the extent to which policy in major institutional sectors is conditioned by the claims and expectations of articulate private groups. The extent to which the legitimacy and authority of governmental elites can be challenged by political amateurs, often with limited resources, is surely one of the critical experiences of these unsettled times. This has disenchanted many scholars and, perhaps, especially political scientists who have often assumed that the decisive role in policy innovation and formulation lay in the hands of those who command the formal political structure.

Meanwhile, the rhetoric and the reality of participation and community control have brought new attention to the larger social role of interest groups from the standpoint of those who have sponsored group action in the political arena, as well as from those who have been mainly concerned with analyzing group behavior. Those in the latter camp have come to see more clearly, with Emile Durkheim, the French sociologist, the functional need for private groups as a mechanism for holding society together, for explaining Durkheim's primal question: "How is society possible?" Some instrument is required to propel individuals into the social mainstream:

Collective activity is always too complex to be able to be expressed through the single and unique organ of the state. Moreover, the state is too remote from individuals, its relations with them too external and intermittent to penetrate deeply within individual consciences and socialize them. When the state is the only environment in which men can live communal lives, they inevitably lose contact, become detached, and society disintegrates. A nation can only be maintained if, between the state and the individual, there is intercalated a whole series of secondary groups near enough to the individuals to attract

1. Some definition of the term interest group may be useful. Sometimes it is used interchangeably with pressure group. At other times, the latter term is applied to interest groups only in their political role. Some observers distinguish the two, with pressure groups regarded invidiously, while "interest groups" are believed to be fully legitimate. It seems, however, that most interest groups act at one time or another as pressure groups, when they are confronted by governmental actions which are sufficiently critical. To some extent, pressure group is used to characterize groups with whose objectives one disagrees. One man's Picasso is another's pressure. Given the broad compass of the following articles, a rather abstract definition seems desirable, such as: interest groups are collectivities organized around an explicit, aggregate value on behalf of which political claims are made vis-à-vis government, other groups and the public. One is tempted to add some aspect of continuity to this definition, but empirically it is clear that group life is often Darwinian, especially among poverty and consumer groups whose lack of hard political resources often makes their lives precarious and short.

them strongly in their sphere of action and drag them, in this way, into the general torrent of social life.[2]

Today, the new corporatism suggests that political influence involves, above all, collective behavior; the analytical focus has moved away from the traditional, highly individualistic drift seen, for example, in the preoccupation with the conditions of individual electoral choice. As often happens, this shift was inspired by events in the real world,[3] by the crises in the cities, the revolt of youth against traditional authority and the demand for participation. This tide is receding and it is clear that the new groups often lack the focused interest and hard resources which have given producer groups the inside track in interest group politics. Nevertheless, things will not be quite the same again.

The following articles reflect such conditions. Each attempts to provide an insight into the political activities of interest groups in a given culture. Most of them draw heavily upon empirical observation, although differences here are bound to be substantial, given international variations in social science, as well as in intellectual style. Symposia rarely achieve much continuity, and it would be unwise to claim that this one is different. On the other hand, we have tried from the outset to make this volume comparative. Each author was asked to try to set his analysis within four themes: the legitimacy of the group or groups analyzed; their major governmental targets; the tactics used in interacting with political elites; and the effectiveness of their attempts to influence public policy. Although the information required to treat these themes was not available in every case, some useful cross-national continuities do appear.

Political culture provides certain rules of the game within which groups must operate. Weakly legitimated groups tend to use provocative tactics, while those who enjoy normative approval rely upon quiet persuasion, fusing their claims with some larger community interest. The highly integrated role of groups in both parliamentary and presidential systems suggests that theirs is a functional role, regardless of political structure. New protest types of groups, representing previously invisible sectors of society, are appearing in most political cultures; all governments are making explicit concessions to their claims. The pattern of accommodation, however, is atypical, compared with the experience of producer groups, in that government itself must often provide both the resources and the impetus required to make such claims good. On the whole, and despite signal variations in political culture and structure, it seems that interest group politics is probably more similar cross-nationally than it is different.

ROBERT PRESTHUS

2. Emile Durkheim, *The Division of Labor in Society* (New York: Free Press, 1947), p. 28.

3. John Maynard Keynes managed the stock portfolio of King's College in bed each morning before arising; some say he derived from this many of the insights which distinguish his theoretical work. So, too, practical events have given us a clearer view of group behavior.

Interest Groups under a Semipermanent Government Party: The Case of Japan

By TAKESHI ISHIDA

ABSTRACT: Despite frequent changes of name, the conservative party has ruled Japan almost continuously since World War II. During this period a particularly close triangular relationship has developed among government party, bureaucracy and interest groups; organized interests compete with each other in cooperation with their sponsored Diet members and their supporters in the bureaucracy. Since the beginning of the 1960s the tendency towards oligopoly has distributed economic power among organizations unequally, and this has been reflected in greater disparities in political influence among stronger and weaker interest groups. Economically strong interest groups, such as those representing big business, do not exercise pressure overtly, whereas weaker organizations must rely on mass lobbying in order to demonstrate how many votes they can control. Moreover, the more powerful interest groups who do not make their demands public are in a more favorable position in the context of Japanese political culture in which insistence on special interests is not considered legitimate. Business groups, for example, always justify their policies as beneficial for the national economy and for rapid economic growth. Recently, however, this national goal has been called into question because of the increasing pollution of the environment and the growing public resentment against oligopoly.

Takeshi Ishida is Professor of Political Science of the Institute of Social Sciences at the University of Tokyo and a member of the international advisory board for Comparative Political Studies. *He is the author of* Japanese Society, *published by Random House (1971) and ten books in Japanese. He has held a Rockefeller Foundation fellowship grant for study in the United States and has served as a Senior Specialist at the East-West Center in Hawaii.*

1

LET ME begin by mentioning some of the difficulties one has to face in dealing with interest groups in Japan, because these reflect, to a certain extent, the special characteristics of Japanese interest groups. I would like to point out that there is no commonly used word in Japanese equivalent to the term interest group.[1] A direct translation from the English is sometimes used in academic works. The term pressure group, on the other hand, began appearing in newspapers in the late 1950s. Its usage has, however, been restricted solely to the pejorative sense; moreover, it has become less common in recent years.[2]

INTEREST GROUPS VERSUS PRESSURE GROUPS

The term pressure group, as it is used here, refers only to those interest groups which use mass lobbying as a technique to present their demands. Therefore, pressure groups cannot be considered synonymous with interest groups; rather, they represent the weaker

1. Following the definition by Lasswell and Kaplan, I understand the term interest group as: "an interest aggregate organized for the satisfaction of the interests." See, Harold D. Lasswell and Abraham Kaplan, *Power and Society: A Framework for Political Inquiry* (London: Routledge and Kegan Paul, 1952), p. 40.
2. A study of the newspaper coverage of pressure groups in the *Asahi Shimbun*—one of the leading national newspapers—produced the following results: the number of lines dealing with pressure groups was 2,044 in 1957, including a twelve-day series of feature articles; 162 in 1960; 126 in 1964; 1,011 in 1966, including a five-day series of articles; 620 in 1967, in one long Sunday edition article; and 73 in 1970. These figures were obtained from clippings made by the Diet Library covering the period June 1957 to October 1973.

interest groups. As Professor S. E. Finer has so correctly pointed out: "Fuss, noise, mass lobbying and similar demonstrations are often an indication of the failure of an organization to achieve effective Parliamentary relations."[3] The usage of the term has declined largely because, in the context of Japanese political culture, almost no group likes being called a pressure group. Furthermore, there has also been less and less room for pressure groups to be influential in the trend towards oligopoly.

The relative decline in the influence of pressure groups has been accompanied by an upswing in the influence of the stronger interest groups which do not need to employ the technique of mass lobbying to achieve their demands. Unfortunately, however, almost no concrete information is available as to the tactics they employ to exert influence on policy making. There is no regulation, for example, requiring the registration of lobbyists in Japan, and although all political organizations should, according to the law, make their income and expenses public, no one really believes that the figures published represent the actual sums which pass through the hands of these groups. Moreover, a major part of their incomes can be kept secret because of loopholes in the law which allows anonymous donations in the form of membership fees. The facts relating to the activities of the stronger interest groups and their contacts with government have always been kept secret from the public. This poses a dilemma for

3. S. E. Finer, *Anonymous Empire: A Study of Lobby in Great Britain* (London: Pall Mall, 1958), p. 54.

the researcher: if he concentrates on gathering information about the number of people attending mass meetings and the number of petitions being presented to the Diet, he will then restrict his focus to the weaker interest groups. It is the stronger interest groups which form the core of the anonymous empire and which do not conduct their activities in full public view.[4]

While it may be true, in some sense, that in all political systems key interest groups keep their methods of influence on the political process confidential, there is no doubt that this is one of the distinctive features of the more powerful interest groups in Japan. This is true largely for the following reasons: as pointed out earlier, the conservatives have ruled Japan since the war; therefore, they deserve the label of a semipermanent governing party. In these circumstances there has been very little opportunity for any of the opposition parties to come to power. The second reason, largely following from the first, concerns the particular nature of the relationship between governing party, bureaucracy and interest groups. The third factor to be considered is Japanese political culture which does not consider the advancement of special interests as legitimate and which, therefore, encourages behind-the-scenes power plays. A more recent additional factor has been the tendency towards oligopoly which has made the stronger interest groups even more influential, thus increasing the difficulties of obtaining reliable data on interest group activities.

4. The term anonymous empire is borrowed from the title of S. E. Finer's book.

GOVERNMENT PARTY AND INTEREST GROUPS

It is often said that the government party tends to be the party of patronage, whereas the opposition party tends to be the party of principle. Under a semipermanent government party system—such as the one which exists in Japan—this contrast is more noticeable than in other countries where a change in the ruling party often takes place. If one party is successively elected to power, thus consistently restricting the opportunity of opposition parties to gain power, then it is not surprising that the allocation of rewards should come to be monopolized by the ruling group or, more precisely, by its top leaders. In such circumstances it is more profitable for interest groups to have a close relationship with the governing party than with the opposition parties. The organization representing Japanese repatriots after the war, for instance, replaced their socialist chairman with an influential conservative party Diet member named Bamboku Ōno. Later on, one member of Ōno's faction became the Minister of Health and Welfare in charge of repatriation affairs; not surprisingly, the demands of the repatriots group came under more favorable consideration from government.[5]

Another feature of Japanese pressure groups—since they are the least influential of interest groups—is their tendency to depend on government benevolence and to please the governing party in order to obtain more subsidies. Supplying campaign workers for the govern-

5. For more detailed information on this affair, see, Tokyo Shimbun, 12 January 1958.

ment party at election time is one of the most important ways in which they can demonstrate their loyalty. Sometimes they also provide campaign funds, but their donations are much smaller than those given by big business. Although pressure groups occasionally pretend to be antigovernment, it is often simply a gesture on the part of their leaders to impress their rank and file with the tough stand they have taken on an issue. Generally speaking, it is these groups which make concessions to government and to the top leaders of the governing party, because of the latters' power to control the distribution of subsidies.

Only groups such as labor unions —which have been permanently affiliated with the opposition parties in Japan—can afford to be continuously critical of government, but they are not influential at all in the process of decision making. They can, however, exercise indirect influence on government; for example, their demands may become so strident and so potentially disruptive that the government considers it wise to do something for the workers in order to maintain economic stability. External pressure from the International Labour Organization has also been known to force the government to make certain concessions to the unions.[6]

The stronger interest groups, such as those representing big business, do not need to undertake overt pressure activities. They can usually rely on the fact that their donations to the governing party will ensure policy decisions in their favor. Even if they think it necessary to voice their demands, a private word in the ears of the party leaders will usually be sufficient to realize their wishes. Only in exceptional cases will they express their desires publicly. For example, *Keidanren*—the Federation of Economic Organizations— demanded the amalgamation of the conservative parties in 1955, and this took place soon afterwards.

The government party, for its part, must necessarily depend on interest groups to compensate for the lack of a mass-based organization. Although it claimed to have 670,000 registered party members in 1970, it is difficult to believe that this number is an accurate figure of party membership. Generally speaking, party members are limited to Diet members, local assemblymen, mayors and other persons who hold public office. The membership figures are inflated, in part, so that faction leaders within the party can claim more delegates to represent the registered members when the time comes for a vote on an important issue within the party.

In spite of its limited membership the party usually receives more than twenty million votes in a general election. It does so by utilizing the bloc votes of its backing organizations. Each year when the annual party convention is held, the government party invites the representatives of numerous friendly organizations, as such groups are called, to attend. These progovernment party groups include those representing small- and medium-sized enterprises, big business, agricultural cooperatives and religious, youth and women's organizations.[7]

6. For details, see, Ehud Harari, *The Politics of Labor Legislation in Japan: National-International Interaction* (Berkeley, Cal.: University of California Press, 1973).

7. More than two hundred organizations are listed as friendly organizations to be invited to party conventions. The number from each field is as follows: small- and

The absence of a mass organization also makes it difficult for the party to obtain substantial financial support through membership fees or funds collected through party activities. To compensate for this difficulty, the party receives financial contributions from big business groups. A special organization, the *Kokumin Kyōkai*, has been created to channel funds from big business into the party. According to published reports, in 1972, 8,320 million yen, or 87.8 percent of the income of the government party, was made available through this organization.[8] It is sometimes estimated that, in reality, almost twice as much as this amount is given to the party. However, it is impossible to know the exact figure, because both the party and big business do not make such information public; moreover, contributions frequently take the form of handouts to faction leaders and other individual candidates. Business groups do contribute some funds to the opposition, but these are merely token contributions to ensure that their interests will not

be ignored in the event that the socialists come to power.

Since their financial support plays such a vital role in maintaining the conservative party in power, big business finds it easy to exert influence on policy decisions. It receives its rewards in terms of concessions to big business interests. Interests on bank deposits and share dividends, for instance, are more lightly taxed in comparison with other sources of government revenue, thus unfairly placing the burden of tax on the shoulders of salary earners. To cite another example, when the budget came up for decision in 1970, the top leaders of the party were asked to visit the leaders of *Keidanren* who demanded a reduction in the percentage of corporation tax; their wish was granted.[9]

IMPORTANCE OF THE BUREAUCRACY

The weakness of party organization also contributes to the importance and maintenance of the bureaucracy, which used to be at the center of power in prewar days. Since the beginning of the cabinet system only about one-sixth of all prime ministers have had no bureaucratic career. Even now, one fourth of the Diet members of the government party are ex-bureaucrats.[10]

Because the party also lacks sufficient staff for policy planning, the bureaucracy often plays an important role in the actual process of decision making. Standing committees in the Diet are formed in

medium-sized enterprises forty-nine; economic—big business—organizations five; local government nine; agriculture thirty-one; fisheries nine; religion six; education and culture twenty-one; labor eight; social welfare forty-nine; youth twenty-four; and women seventeen. In relation to the last two, the revision of the Social Education Act in 1959 is important. Prior to this reform the occupation authorities did not allow the government to subsidize youth and womens organizations which, they maintained, should be independent of government. A revision of the law made it possible for them to receive subsidies from government, and in this way the government party could establish so-called friendly relations with these organizations. For details, see, Takeshi Ishida, *Gendai Soshikiron* (Tokyo: Iwanami, 1961), pp. 176–177, 179.

8. *Asahi Shimbun*, 31 July 1973.

9. Asahi Shimbunsha, ed., *Jimintō* (Tokyo: Asahi Shimbunsha, 1970), p. 163.

10. In 1970 there were 79 ex-bureaucrats out of a total of 486 in the House of Representatives, and 55 out of a total of 250 in the House of Councillors. See, ibid., p. 121.

such a way that each committee corresponds to a ministry. In these committees Diet members—who were once high-ranking officials in the ministry—play an important role, cooperating with the incumbent bureaucrats. For instance, the Diet members try to pass bills drafted by their ex-ministry, and the party also asks the bureaucracy to draft bills in favor of the party through the ex-bureaucrats from the ministry.

The weakness of its grass-roots organization also makes it difficult for the party to recruit good candidates from among party activists; thus, it must often "import" candidates from the bureaucracy to stand in the elections. Having served in government, these imported candidates naturally have sufficient educational background and experience; they also have the added advantage of being able to command the bloc votes of interest groups operating within the field previously under their supervision.

One typical example of this took place in 1969 during the general election.[11] The successful candidate had, in his previous post as vice-minister of labor, built many new buildings for the Public Employment Security Office and other Labor Department offices in his constituency. As a result of his efforts, laborers engaged on unemployment relief work realized that it would be more in their interest to vote for this candidate. In this case the workers had their own labor union affiliated with the Socialist Party. The Socialist candidate expected to receive the bloc vote from the union as he had in past elections, but rather than give the latter their support, the workers who be-

longed to the branch of the union in the constituency of the former vice-minister supported him, instead. Former vice-ministers in the Ministry of Construction have also been elected on the support of groups in the construction industry. A former director of the forestry agency was also successful in being elected because of bloc votes cast by the interest groups related to forestry.

Weaker interest groups can also demonstrate their loyalty to a ministry by supporting an ex-bureaucrat from the relevant ministry. Another means of establishing a good relationship is to ask retired, high ranking bureaucrats to serve as executive members of a group. For this reason it is frequently very difficult to distinguish semigovernmental organizations from interest groups, because so many of the weaker interest groups are subsidized by the relevant ministries and become, in fact, auxilliary organizations working on behalf of the ministries, propagating and helping to execute their policies. It was once reported that the Ministry of Agriculture and Forestry had two hundred and twenty related organizations, sixty of which were subsidized.[12] A reduction in the number of such organizations has often been proposed without success by the government.[13]

In the case of stronger interest

11. Reported in ibid., p. 15.

12. *Tokyo Shimbun*, 11 January 1958.

13. In the late 1950s the Administration Management Agency proposed, without success, that 174 such organizations should be abolished. At the time 303 organizations were investigated, and 63 were found to be receiving subsidies amounting to a total of 1,240 million yen. Furthermore, 174 of them had executives who came from the related ministries. See, Kanryōsei Kenkyūkai, ed., *Kanryō* (Tokyo: San'ichi Shobō, 1959), p. 130.

groups, such as those among big business, dependence on the bureaucracy is much smaller. In fact, they can often control bureaucracy for their own benefit. Even big business, however, is careful to maintain friendly relations with the bureaucracy. For this reason many large industrial corporations invite ex-bureaucrats from the Ministry of International Trade and Industry (MITI) to serve as executives, and banks ask officials from the Ministry of Finance to fill the same type of position. Moreover, ex-bureaucrats who have moved into business circles can maintain friendly relations with their former colleagues who have become Diet members. Through these personal ties, the triangular relationship among the government party, the bureaucracy and big business is maintained.

Knowing well the close relationship between the semipermanent government party and big business, those in the bureaucracy usually view the latter's interests rather favorably. This particular attitude can be seen in the bureaucratic techniques employed to weaken the restrictions imposed by antitrust laws. The relaxation of antitrust laws began at the end of the 1950s; however, evasions of the anti-monopoly legislation, even beyond the degree permitted by the revised law, were made possible by bureaucratic interpretations of the law.

On the other hand, working hard for the interests of weaker interest groups is also profitable for bureaucrats. Success in obtaining subsidies for groups under their influence means an increase in their prestige, where prestige is decided by the amount of money they can control. In addition, friendly relationships with interest groups may secure an executive position with one of the groups for a bureaucrat upon his retirement or may open up the possibility of running for election with the support of a particular interest group or groups.

The one exception to this general rule is the relationship between the Ministry of Health and Welfare and the Japan Medical Association, which is a relatively strong interest group. In this case, the association has more than three hundred sponsored Diet members and is, therefore, strong enough to exert influence directly on the top leaders of the government party. The ministry, on the other hand, is relatively less influential compared to other government ministries. In addition, interest groups in the field under the supervision of the Ministry of Health and Welfare—hospital and pharmacist groups, for example—compete and sometimes even conflict with the Medical Association. The association is, however, an exceptional case in terms of its relationship with the bureaucracy.

INTEREST GROUP TACTICS AND LEGITIMACY

The system of close interlinkages among the government party, bureaucracy and interest groups is closely related to the particular style of interest group behavior characteristic of Japan. Interest groups do not typically exert influence on the legislature and executive from the outside. Rather, they compete with each other in cooperation with their sponsored Diet members, particularly those in the government party, and their supporters in the relevant ministry or bureau. Competition among these political combines of interest groups, bureaucrats and sponsored Diet members has become intense since the late 1950s.

Moreover, the increasing disparities in the distribution of influence among the stronger and weaker interest groups, which became more evident in the process toward oligopoly in the 1960s, has made competition among the weaker interest groups even more serious than it was earlier. In January of every year, when the budget decision comes round, the relatively less expensive hotels in the city center of Tokyo become packed with petitioners and lobbyists from the various localities. They were once reported to have numbered not less than 10,000.[14] These lobbyists, on the advice of their contacts in the bureaucracy and their sponsored Diet members, exert pressure on the top echelon of the government party and the Ministry of Finance. When, for example, the bill concerning the establishment of a special finance corporation for barber shops, public baths, restaurants, laundries and similar businesses was passed in 1967, the interest groups representing these various enterprises—claiming to control 15 million votes—held a mass meeting of more than 10,000 in a park close to the Diet and invited about 200 Diet members to work on their behalf. The Ministry of Health and Welfare also gave them its support, and when the finance corporation in question was actually established, the former vice-minister of health and welfare became its chief director.[15]

The competition among local governments during the formulation of the budget decision is also serious. Governors, mayors and local assemblymen come to Tokyo and busy themselves with petitioning the relevant ministries, the Ministry of Finance and the Diet members from their constituencies. They frequently ask for bridges, roads and railroads to be built in their local areas. In one instance, it was reported that a group of approximately 300 persons, including the governor and local assemblymen, had come to Tokyo for this purpose.[16]

It is also a well-known fact that every year agricultural cooperatives and other organizations undertake a strong mass-based campaign with the aim of increasing the price of rice that the government pays to the farmers. They present millions of petitions and hold mass meetings of hundreds of thousands of people, to which many Diet members are invited.[17]

As mentioned before, strong interest groups, such as those representing big business, do not need to exert influence publicly as they have sufficient reason to believe that the government and governing party cannot afford to ignore their interests. What they say in public, for instance, when *Keidanren* or *Nikeiren*—Japan Federation of Employers Associations—hold their annual meetings, is usually restricted to general statements on such matters as the state of national education, the need for strengthening the national economy in the face of competition from other highly developed countries or the need to strengthen the self-defense forces.

14. For example, see, *Asahi Shimbun*, 13 January 1970.

15. For details, see, *Asahi Shimbun*, 8 June 1967; and Shimbunsha, *Jimintō*, p. 137.

16. *Asahi Shimbun*, 13 January 1970.

17. In 1964, for example, the number of petitions amounted to 4.5 million, and the number of people who attended the meeting was 150,000. Asahi Janaru, ed., *Nihon no Kyodai Soshiki* (Tokyo: Keisō Shobō, 1966), pp. 176–177.

Of course, these public causes mask their own private interests: the creation of a well-qualified and obedient labor force; the strengthening of cartels to reduce excessive domestic competition among industries; and the development of the munitions industries.

In addition to their sheer economic strength, this particular strategy of phrasing special interests in terms of the national good puts big business groups in a better position in the context of Japanese political culture, where the insistence on special interests is hardly regarded as legitimate. One may argue that it is a valid technique employed by interest groups everywhere to justify their demands as beneficial to the public interest, but in Japan this tendency is more pronounced than in many other countries which do not have the legacy of a monolithic emperor system. In fact, the present importance of bureaucracy in Japan is partly the result of the heritage of the emperor system, in which bureaucracy was the core of imperial rule and the loyalty of the political parties which represented sectional interests was, therefore, regarded as suspect.

It is not surprising, then, that against the background of Japanese political culture, the term interest group is rarely used and that the term pressure group is not popular. This is true even among pressure groups, who prefer to avoid labelling themselves with such a term. The one exception to this was the Political Federation of Japanese Small Businesses which defined itself as a pressure group, but which survived only for several years in the late 1950s and early 1960s.

CHANGING PUBLIC ATTITUDES TOWARD LOBBYING

Recently, a slight change has been noticeable in attitudes towards pressure groups. This can largely be attributed to two factors: one is the change in value orientation which has taken place as a result of the change of generations; the other is the increased awareness of, and resentment against, established oligopoly. According to a public opinion poll of 1970, 51.9 percent of those asked about their opinion of the petitions and lobbying activities of pressure groups answered affirmatively. That is, the respondents either strongly supported this type of activity—8.1 percent—or said that it was an inevitable trend—43.8 percent. In 1973, the percent of those who replied affirmatively to the same question increased slightly—53 percent.[18] There is no comparable data available concerning the popular attitude towards pressure groups in the 1950s. However, judging from the critical tone of newspaper editorials appearing during this period, one can guess that popular opinion has become more favorably disposed towards such groups.[19]

Since the late 1950s, when the term pressure group began appearing in newspapers, the economic situation in Japan has undergone rapid change. Among the various changes which have taken place, one of the most important has been the number of corporate mergers—exemplified by the

18. *Sankei Shimbun*, 24 January 1970, and 12 January 1973.
19. One example of a critical editorial had the title "The Pressure Groups Should Be Controlled"; *Asahi Shimbun*, 1 June 1957.

merger between the Fuji and Yawata Iron and Steel companies, which created the second largest iron and steel company in the world.[20] Corporate mergers have resulted in a state of oligopoly, but they have been legitimized by such national goals as an increase in Japan's economic power in terms of gross national product (GNP) and a more powerful position in the world economy.

The emergence of consumer interest groups, which has been a recent trend in many developed societies, has also been evident in Japan, where it has been inspired by increased public resentment against big business. The problem of defective manufactured products—exemplified by the marketing of powdered milk containing arsenic—and the problem of pollution have made many citizens feel the necessity of tackling these problems and have inspired them to form their own groups. These groups—large in number, but usually small in size—are not yet strong enough to influence policy making. They do represent, however, a new trend which may become more significant in the future.

It is worth mentioning here that

in June and July of 1973 *Keidanren*, which is often labelled as the headquarters of big business, but which has never before been publicly criticized, was the target of rallies protesting pollution and big business's "economic invasion" of Japan's Asian neighbors. In the light of this criticism, *Keidanren* emphasized the social responsibility of big business at its general meeting of 1973 and agreed to hold meetings with leaders of labor unions. These did not prove to be very fruitful, but they do indicate changing attitudes on the part of big business.

It is impossible to predict whether, in the future, a new pattern of interest group behavior will replace the old. Of course, if the trend towards increased support for the opposition parties—which has gradually been taking place—makes the possibility of changing the government a real one, then the pattern of interaction among interest groups, bureaucracy and political parties may change from that which I have described. It is too early, however, to say whether or not, or how soon, a change in the governing party may take place. As long as the present conservative party stays in power, the activities of interest groups will follow their customary pattern, possibly, with a few variations here and there.

20. For more detailed information concerning corporate mergers, see, Takeshi Ishida, *Japanese Society* (New York: Random House, 1971), p. 98.

Human Rights and Amnesty International

By HARRY M. SCOBLE AND LAURIE S. WISEBERG

ABSTRACT: This is a descriptive, analytical treatment of international human-rights nongovernmental organizations. A typology of human-rights groups is developed. Threats to human and political rights are analyzed. Following a brief description of Amnesty International as a new type of noneconomic interest group in world politics, the article focuses explicitly on three practical political— yet, also, social-scientific—problems: (1) the legitimacy of human-rights organizations; (2) the selection of targets and of tactics, including prepolitical resource-generating tactics; and, especially, (3) the problems entailed in evaluating the impact, if any, of interest group activities. The last, which questions the efficiency of translation of activity into access and then influence, opens up another discrete question: whether and how the group evaluates its own goals, structure and tactics. This evaluation suggests that Amnesty International has measurable impact on the defense of human and political rights.

Harry M. Scoble was educated at Williams College and Yale University and has taught at the Universities of Wisconsin and California. Scoble teaches American politics and is currently Visiting Professor of Political Science at the College of Urban Sciences of the University of Illinois at Chicago Circle. He has published several articles and a book, Ideology and Electoral Action, on domestic interest groups.

Laurie S. Wiseberg received her doctoral degree from the University of California at Los Angeles. She has taught at University College Swansea and Ahmadu Bello University in Nigeria, where she also conducted field research on the politics of international relief organizations in the Nigerian Civil War. Wiseberg is Assistant Professor in Political Science at the University of Illinois at Chicago Circle, teaching primarily international politics.

The present study has grown out of a 1967 faculty research grant from the Social Science Research Council for exploratory research on democratic values. However, we alone are responsible for the directions taken and the conclusions reached.

THE political interest groups examined in this article are international human-rights nongovernmental organizations. We were not directly concerned with the United Nations (UN) Commission on Human Rights or other international governmental human-rights organizations even though these—like public bureaucracies in national and subnational governments—may at times be usefully conceived of as political interest groups. Human rights is a broad, constantly changing concept which we take to include the following irreducible minima: (1) physical security—that is, a right to life; (2) freedom of religion; and (3) the combined political rights of association, communication and other peaceful opinion-transmission processes to one's rulers. Organizations involved in recent transnational conflicts over human rights include: World Moslem Congress, International Commission of Jurists, International Movement for Fraternal Union among Races and People, United Auto Workers (United States-Canada), International Committee of the Red Cross, Law Association for Asia and the Western Pacific (LAWASIA), International League for the Rights of Man, United World Federalists, National Civil Liberties Union (Britain), Committee on Society, Development and Peace (SODEPAX), Christian Care, *Confédération Mondiale* and Amnesty International (AI).

ANALYTICAL OVERVIEW

From this lengthy, yet only partial, listing of human-rights organizations, we have selected Amnesty International for detailed examination. Amnesty—as are all organizations on the list and many more

which could logically be included—is first to be characterized as nongovernmental, international and permanent. Being nongovernmental, all such organizations lack the sufficient monopoly of force over their own members—in matters such as taxation, criminal justice and military-national service—which conceptually distinguishes all governmental institutions. Even so, the term nongovernmental has multiple meanings—that is, the public versus private dichotomy is less than absolute. Nongovernmental groups, in fact, range from: (1) those which have been created by government initiative—for example, the United States Department of Commerce organized the creation of the United States Chamber of Commerce—through (2) those which are encouraged by government—for example, via tax-exempt status in the case of religious, educational and charitable organizations—(3) those which are permitted by government—that is, those which are private and legal—to (4) those which are private, secret and illegal—for example, the Minutemen, the post-1968 Weathermen or the Black Liberation Army. Amnesty International falls clearly into the second category.

The label international embraces a multitude of logical possibilities; for, the particular organization may be international with regard to its membership, located in two or more nations; its tactics, operating across one or more national boundaries; its selected targets, a bi- or multinational organ or the political elites or masses of two or more nations; or some combination of these. It is relevant to note further that international ought not automatically be assumed to constitute the mutually exclusive opposite of internal or domestic, any more than it makes sense in the 1970s to conceive of foreign versus domestic policy as a rigid dichotomy. By employing the above definition of international, it will become evident that Amnesty qualifies on each of the three counts.

Amnesty is also a permanent group. Among classificatory typologies in the study of political interest groups it is conventional to draw a distinction between permanent organizations and ad hoc coalitions, which are often temporary clusters of permanent organizations. The latter—for example, the International Committee to Investigate United States Crimes in Indochina, which opened hearings in Copenhagen in late 1972—constitute temporary alliances created around an event which those allies seek to convert into an issue in furtherance of one or more interests. The range of tactics available in such a situation is usually limited, and collective action normally requires more bargaining and exchange transactions, including log-rolling among formal decision makers, than is true of permanent organizations with more enduring interests.

However, to distinguish an issue coalition from an interest organization is only part of the problem; for, organizations—of the sort initially listed—ought also to be categorized in terms of whether they maintain an exclusive focus on human and political rights or whether this focus is nonexclusive, often secondary. As should be evident from the names, the list contains many organizations—particularly of religious bodies, but also of labor unions—which get dragged into politics reluctantly, because either their own members or staff find themselves in trouble with governmental authorities.

By contrast, Amnesty is both different and unique: it is the sole organization on the list whose goals and intentional activities eliminate or significantly reduce precisely those conflicts which the other organizations and isolated individuals have with constituted governments. There is an apposite domestic parallel here: the Anti-Defamation League of B'nai B'rith (ADL) and the American Jewish Committee (AJC) work to protect and advance the interests of Jews in America; Mexican American Legal Defense and Education Fund (MALDEF) works for Mexican Americans; the American Medical Association (AMA), for doctors; the National Association for the Advancement of Colored People (NAACP), for Negroes; and so on. However, the only national group which works to keep the United States political process open to all such political interest groups is the American Civil Liberties Union (ACLU). In this sense, AI ought to be conceived of as an international ACLU.

To the extent that it is nongovernmental, international and permanent, Amnesty is similar to many other groups; however, we begin to see AI's uniqueness if, in addition to its exclusive concern for human rights, we note that the organization should be further characterized by the descriptive labels consumer, protest and elitist.

First, the designation consumer implies that the only relevant opposite is an economic-producer group. Yet, this is an empirical question which should not be foreclosed by fiat: some groups may, in fact, be both. Even those which act in terms of a vested, economic-producer interest may actually serve consumer interests; mass media in the United States provide a case in point. In this sense, Amnesty International is interested in both the consumption of freedom and the production of political repression. However—as distinct from consumers of private-sector goods, of private-sector services or of public-sector goods—Amnesty, itself, is not a direct consumer; rather, it seeks to represent consumers of governmental services that are negative, chilling and repressive. As an international consumer group Amnesty may be usefully contrasted with both traditional economic-producer interest groups—for example, the National Association of Manufacturers (NAM) or the Organization of Petroleum Exporting Countries (OPEC)—and traditional mass-membership groups—for example, the Roman Catholic Church, the International Typographers' Union and the New Democratic Party of Canada. The political power of the former rests on strategic control of liquid or raw wealth; that of the latter depends upon sheer numbers which can be massed in opinion-electoral processes and in nonelectoral political situations. Amnesty—with 32,000 dues-paying members in some sixty nations and an annual budget of about $500,000—has little or either of these two prime resources for politics; however, as will be shown, AI has been quite effective in gaining access to, and influence with, governmental elites.

Secondly, the term protest need not necessarily refer only to the massive numbers of persons mobilized for political action nor to direct action creation of creative disorder or civil disobedience toward authorities—tactics associated in the United States with the civil rights movement and with the trade union and feminine suffrage movements earlier. The concept of protest does refer to felt moral indignation in reaction to some action

by governmental authorities; and the protest is communicated substantively and symbolically, but certainly nonelectorally—since an electoral process is either nonexistent or meaningless. Human-rights organizations generally, and Amnesty in particular, are primarily defensive of designated others, but necessarily of themselves, as well. In reaction to attempted repression by government(s) they generate a protest intended to change the repressive behavior of target authorities either through shame—that is, appeal to internalized norms—or by damaging their reputation in the eyes of relevant others—for example, the internal populace, politico-military allies, trading partners, the international business investment community or the World Bank.

Finally, human-rights protest groups, such as Amnesty, are not mass groups even though they seek to protect the interests of largely unknowing or perhaps uncaring masses. Indeed, they are elitist in several important senses. Their officers and contributing members are primarily upper-middle-class professionals, with both communications skills and discretionary income to devote to world politics, their own mass base is itself a tiny minority drawn from among the world's affluent who are also ideologically inclined on human and political rights issues. They are often run as managerial catalyst operations avoiding line operations themselves, but instead stimulating other organizations to act in the latters' own best interests. Their prime tactics are generally elitist, directly tree-topping with public authorities or working indirectly through other elites who control the serious and quality media to which governmental elites are attentive, in order to persuade them to reverse their underlings or themselves—that is, to become humane again, to revert to decency—or to put pressure on other repressive governmental elites —that is, to take a stand in the name of decency, humanity. In this sense the broad function of international human-rights organizations is to preserve the possibility for a genuine counter-elite to exist and function in a given political system.

Amnesty International is again both unique and theoretically interesting because most political interest groups represent the elite stratum—in terms of power, wealth, income or other valued achievement—of their particular socioeconomic segment. While Amnesty is similar to most other interest groups in its middle class membership and reliance on elitist tactics and techniques, it differs from almost all other organizations in its defense of temporary underdogs, permanent minorities and the powerless the world over.

THREATS TO HUMAN RIGHTS

At a different level of analysis, the need for a protective association, such as Amnesty International, can be indicated by reference to two factors, one a long term behavioral characteristic of power holders and the other a more recent, secular trend. First, for some five hundred years national governments—even those which profess to be most democratic—have been always, everywhere and easily tempted to repress internal opposition, by equating dissent with disloyalty which national security interests compel the elite to crush. Secondly, modern technologies pro-

vide an increasingly awesome capacity for effectuating the repressive motives of the political elite. Thus, hardening of state control over its own citizenry may be seen in technological advances such as the following: (1) internal propaganda; (2) governmental monopolistic control of both the source and the flow of public affairs information, including both old-fashioned censorship and new-fashioned classification, such as that dictated by national security imperatives; (3) refinements in techniques of physical torture—for example, the Greek falanga, the Brazilian pau de arara, Russian injections and tranquilizers to cure political schizophrenia or cattle prods and Mitrione vests made in America—including developments in medical science to keep the victim alive and conscious longer; (4) improvements in psychological torture techniques—for example, electroshock, sleep deprivation, noise bombardment and sensory deprivation chambers; (5) the emergence of the new social science of behavior modification— that is, the psychochemical control of human behavior and the psychosurgical elimination of socially unacceptable behavior, including political thought and verbalized opinion; (6) the perfection of miniaturized electronic surveillance equipment—much of it invented and produced by United States business corporations for economic espionage and sabotage, but now adapted to political ends; and, finally, (7) the development of military and police information systems for the storage and rapid retrieval of the individual's identity and political biography.

Amnesty and other human-rights organizations are necessary because the individual is threatened not only by his own government, but by the emergence of multinational business corporations, as well. Neither of these power institutions is as yet effectively checked by international government or world law. The growth of monopurpose multinationals threatens the human and political rights of individuals both within and outside the organizations, because they combine economic motive and the bureaucratic form to achieve it—that is, they combine both low social ethics and high repressive capacity. Furthermore, the larger multinationals seem either to dominate the smaller nations directly or to have inordinate influence over both domestic and foreign actions of the larger nations; the behavior of International Telephone and Telegraph (ITT), Kennecott Copper and other United States corporations towards Allende's Chile is only the most recent example.

If the emergent multinationals are not effectively subject to national legislation, they are even less subject to the United Nations or regional international governmental organizations (IGOs). This is so for two stark reasons: first, both regional and world IGOs are, in practice, simply the creatures of the strongest national government(s) within them. This has been historically true; it will remain true for the foreseeable future, in part because of the second reason: the residual strength of national sovereignty and national loyalties. To expand this latter point briefly, no international law exists which is self-executing—that is, which creates a monitoring and enforcement bureaucracy with a vested interest in defense of its mandate, with positive rewards and negative sanctions to coerce compliance and with direct operating control, rather

than control only through member nations, over individuals, including heads of state and members of governments.

Furthermore, human-rights IGOs —for example, the UN Commission on Human Rights is an appropriate model—constitute no effective check on the dehumanizing tendencies of either multinational corporations or member states for two additional reasons. International governmental agencies concerned with human rights are passive; they cannot initiate action—that is, the UN commission does not possess even the limited power to subpoena witnesses and documents, as does the United States Civil Rights Commission. More speculatively, even if this were not so, the nature of the recruitment process is such that passivity would probably result in any event. That is, the personnel who staff IGOs—human-rights or general purpose—are, in the main, permanent civil servants, including former foreign service officers from the United States, international lawyers and professional economists; it is suggested that these occupational types or personalities are not noted for an active, assertive dedication to human, and especially political, rights.

AMNESTY INTERNATIONAL

Much of what Amnesty does—and what its members think—has been implied by the introductory analysis. Here, we wish to add several points. The organization was created in 1961 by a London attorney outraged by the lack of legal defense for university students jailed for their peaceful protests by the Salazar regime in Portugal. The original intent was a less-than-year-long public campaign for amnesty for all these political prisoners. The campaign peaked, as is traditional, during the Christmas season; the appeal became one for the granting of executive clemency.

The need for continuing organization soon became evident, and from this emerged an organization which carefully researches investigations cases—that is, instances alleging the detention or imprisonment of a person solely for his or her beliefs. From these Amnesty selects a smaller number of adoption cases in which it is evident that the victim did not advocate or use violence. These cases are assigned to working groups of AI members of a different nationality from that of the prisoner. The working group then employs all legitimate means to secure the release of the prisoner, while also often raising support money for him and his family. Furthermore, to maintain balance— that is, to avoid cross-fire from cold warriors—the international organization selects one urgent case from the free, the Communist bloc and the "Third" worlds each month for special postcard campaigns by members.

Members do more than make financial contributions. Where interaction is feasible, they also work in and through small groups, of which there are more than 1,200. Their geographic-national concentration is as follows: West Germany has the largest membership—some 500 groups; Sweden has 200; Britain, 140; the Netherlands, 135; the United States, 60; Denmark, 48; Australia, 31; Norway, 24; Austria, 22; and France, 18 groups.

The groups are organized into national sections which, because membership is voluntary, have considerable autonomy. The national sections are apportioned delegate votes for the annual international council meeting which has both constituent and regular legislative functions—that is, those concerning AI statutes, policy making and budgeting. During the period between the annual assemblies an eight-member International Executive Committee meets at least once a month. Finally, for day-to-day administration there is an International Secretariat located in London and headed by a secretary general whose fulltime staff provides the basic research and the ancillary intraorganizational services required by the national sections and internal groups.

The main weapon of Amnesty is words: research and communication, education and propaganda— for example, documentation on Greece submitted to the Council of Europe; a forty-page inquiry into torture and political repression in Brazil, introduced to the Organization of American States (OAS); a more recent thirty-six-page study of the prisons of Franco's Spain; subsidization of the English-language publication of the Soviet *samizdat*, *Chronicle of Current Events*, produced inside Russia until mid-1972 by dissident Soviet intellectuals who insisted that their 1936 Constitution should mean something. Words, primarily negative words— for, which political elite is moved to change its behavior by praise?

In slightly more than a decade Amnesty's words have gained increasing weight. We note that Amnesty International was granted consultative status by the United Nations, the Council of Europe and, more recently, by both the Organization of African Unity and the OAS. Consultative status is actually a two-fold process. For the private organization, it means gaining some of the stamp of officiality which we associate with government. For the IGO, it is equally functional in that it permits coopting additional private resources to supplement inadequate public resources, such as drawing on the research department of AI. In the case of post-1967 Greece, AI research provided the data presented before the European Commission on Human Rights which, in turn, forced Greece to resign from the Council of Europe in 1968 in order to avoid the predicted overwhelming vote of expulsion. Other details concerning Amnesty will be provided as we turn to analysis of this political interest group in terms of the intellectual and practical political problems of legitimacy, targets, tactics and effectiveness.

LEGITIMACY

The question of the legitimacy of the group(s) being analyzed permits several alternative perspectives—legitimacy in terms of: (1) the group's own image of itself; (2) the particular nation-state, meaning its laws and elite, in which the headquarters of the group is geographically and legally located; (3) the international legal system; (4) the observer-analyst's own articulated perspective. Amnesty International—and all its human-rights allies—is clearly legitimate according to each of the first three criteria; the fourth is redundant, here.

It is relevant to note that the concept of legitimacy is both procedural and substantive. Most American interest group theorists—particularly David B. Truman, who has probably had the greatest impact on the thinking of political scientists—put the problem of legitimacy in procedural terms only. Truman asserts that in order to be effective a political interest group must be perceived—he never specifies by whom, but presumably he means by the political elite—as conforming to the rules of the game; thus, most groups go through the motions of adhering to the democratic mold in matters of internal government. Yet, in practice the legitimacy of opposed individual actors and other political groups is evaluated in a dual fashion, that is, in terms of their stated or imputed ends, quite apart from their adopted methods. Furthermore, "the rules of the game" is as fuzzy as the civic culture or national character. Truman's concept represents an intellectual era of defensive concern for a concept of democracy limited to legalistic due process. Even at this level one finds sufficient empirical evidence of elite violations of its own rules to raise serious doubts about the utility of this concept as an operationalization of legitimacy.

POLITICAL TARGETS AND TACTICS

The targets of Amnesty International are both public and private, but they tend to be elites in either case. That is, Amnesty directs its activities—most of which can be summed up as research and communication—to governmental elites, both national and international; to other organized groups, such as jurists, lawyers, union leaders and political parties; and particularly to the quality and mass media. A major target is thus the attentive publics—that is, approximately the top fifteen percent of any electorate which tends to be continuously attentive, interested and involved in, and informed about, political affairs—but not the mass public, even in Britain, Western Europe or the United States.

Analyses of political interest groups usually distinguish between tree-topping tactics which are aimed at elites and grass-rooting tactics which seek to mobilize and polarize part or all of the mass; they also normally divide the communication of the particular group interest into direct, as against indirect, lobbying —here defined in the broadest sense. To some extent the direct-indirect dimension and that of tree-tops-grass-roots overlap and coincide, but not entirely. For example, the milk producers meeting with President Nixon in the Cabinet Room was both tree-topping and direct; however, lobbying of United States Supreme Court justices, which by judicial norms must be indirect—for example, placement of their clerks and publishing in the best law journals—is, nonetheless, tree-topping.

The functional significance of these distinctions lies in (1) whether the interest group seeks to change elite behavior in a specific situation, such as a pending human-rights issue in Chile and the reaction of the UN and the United States to repression by the military there, or (2) whether it seeks to change the sociopolitical environment—the attitudes and opinions of a public or an electorate such that any political elite will have to act in a predetermined, pro-human-rights manner in all such situations. Most permanent organizations—and Amnesty has now deliberately become permanent—soon develop both of these short run and long term goals; most, thus, engage in all of the above tactics. However, because of currently limited resources, any interest group is likely to designate primary, secondary and, perhaps, tertiary targets and tactics.

As a further consideration of tactics, it may prove useful to introduce a new distinction: that between zero-order and first-order activities. For instance, most discussions essentially cover only manifestly political tactics, which we term first-order; thus, group tactics of a resource-generating nature are ignored. The latter, zero-order activities, may be thought of as prepolitical; they are instrumental preconditions to political actions directed toward some one or more specified collective goals.

Most studies of pressure-groups take more or less sophisticated note of the importance of professional public relations (PR) for successful political action—electoral, as well as nonelectoral. Some of the better studies advance one step further, noting that modern political life involves intransitive circular processes; the image of systematic feedback loops may be invoked. Thus, action—even if initially only verbal —creates publicity; publicity creates support; support creates action; and so on, through the cycle of Myrdalian cumulative causation. However, even the most sophisticated research fails to introduce a clear distinction between those group actions which are primarily resource-generating as contrasted with those which are primarily resource-applying.

This distinction becomes particularly sharp, theoretically interesting and functional in the case of Amnesty International. To generate resources the organization engages in a variety of conventional pressure-group activities, for example: soliciting dues—$15 annually—and binding members to itself via newsletters. Both the international and the large national sections publish newsletters; they are informative, generally well-written and unemotional, although focused on highly emotional subjects. The vast majority of interest groups simply stop at this point: the average member is essentially a legal fiction—desired as an annual donor, used as a counter—and that is all. Amnesty differs significantly, for the organization clearly expects active participation beyond mere financial contributions. To facilitate this outcome, it attempts to locate all new members in a small group and helps to create a new group if there is no existing one convenient to the new member. These groups, which vary in size from three to twenty members, meet once a month in a nonsocial, informal business session. At these meetings members report on their activities of the past month, express their preferences for allocation of future work loads and engage in cooperative planning.

Amnesty did not invent the small group as the building block of larger scale organization; it does, however, effectively make use of the small group. Two functions of this organizational structure may be briefly characterized. Negatively, the small group functions as a device to screen out various unwanted types from membership, for example, those who are emotionally unbalanced by the politics of murder and torture or those who have a partisan-ideological obsession beyond commitment to the democratic process. Positively, and most importantly, locating the member in a small-group context provides significant social support for the attitudes, opinions and actions of that member. Social support is especially important in situations, such as Amnesty's, where the individual holds political views which have a high probability of being judged deviant by the average member of the geo-graphical-statistical community in which the former happens to live. The social support supplied by an interacting small group strengthens both conviction and the practical acting out of these commitments. Amnesty's employment of a small group basis of organization has a multiplier effect upon the political significance of a member.

By contrast, the modal noneconomic interest uses its member in a strictly limited fashion. Ralph Nader's Public Citizen and, especially, John Gardner's Common Cause are relevant. The 200,000 souls claimed last year to have contributed at least $15 to Common Cause have provided the budget for some useful law suits—particularly those concerning electoral contributions and spending—for some press releases and, perhaps, also for Mr. Gardner's presidential ambitions. Yet, the member of Common Cause is a statistic, an IBM card, an addressograph plate and little more.

It may be useful to state two additional speculations. First, the target predetermines the tactics which can be employed; or, alternatively, the social background of leaders and members, their ideology, their skills, expertise and strategic control of information needed by formal decision makers —all internal group characteristics —predetermine the tactics which will be available and can be employed. These, in turn, limit the potential targets of the group. In actuality targets and tactics are inseparable, although they may initially be logically or analytically separable—which is to say, it is impossible to consider one without the other. This suggests that targets and tactics are simply different facets of the same transactional behavior, which is the group acting toward one or more of its goals.

Even so, we may surmise that the primary targets of human-rights groups such as Amnesty are both national and international governmental elites. The editors and columnists of the *New York Times,* for example, are of secondary importance; furthermore, they are important only to the extent that they are read by those with the power and authority to act in human-rights situations. International government is largely controlled by an internationalized upper-middle class—individuals from secure, high status family backgrounds who were thus able to obtain superior higher education, foreign travel and language skills, in addition to high level practical experience in, for example, national government, quality law firms or top business corporations. This international elite must consequently be approached with dignity and protocol; it is not to be stampeded or demagogued. Even if Amnesty International's membership were numerous, geographically concentrated and of lower-middle and working class status, it could not effectively make use of the various street-politics tactics which characterized the United States civil rights, poverty and anti-Vietnam protests of 1960–1970, because the costs—in terms of the predicted negative reaction of the international elite—would be perceived as excessive. The formal political arena in which a group seeks to operate thus acts as a constraint on the group, but the constraint arises not so much from formalistic factors, such as institutional structure, as from personnel recruitment processes.

National governmental elites who can abolish capital punishment, torture and solitary confinement present a second set of barriers to, or channels for, the activities of the human-rights organization. National political elites, whether Western-democratic—and, thus, drawn from the very best elements of the given society—Eastern-democratic—and, thus, drawn from the true working class—or Third World —military or bureaucratic bourgeoisie—have a tremendous capacity to lose touch with their own societies. They so surround themselves with the services, the material gadgets and other privileges of power that they effectively insulate themselves from their own masses. National elites thus find it difficult, if not impossible, to believe that indigenous discontent and political dissidence is, in fact, genuine, localized, legitimate and, perhaps especially, not funded by some conspiratorial external enemy.

Such natural elite suspicions make Amnesty's chosen tasks especially difficult. If it moves too hastily or crudely, it merely supplies the missing evidence that the imprisoned victim was indeed linked to an externally based conspiracy, because the mind-set of national elites is attuned to the self-confirming hypothesis. However, if Amnesty moves too slowly, the victim may die in prison, may be executed or may be driven by torture to suicide. As a further example of these imperatives, when AI involves its membership in direct letter-writing campaigns to appeal for the public trial of a detainee or for the release of a convicted prisoner of conscience, it provides the members with the specific relevant details of international and domestic law; it provides the appropriate correct title, address and so on in the language of the elite addressee; and it repeatedly enjoins "politely worded" communications. However, the constraint on externally based interest group operations is, in this case also, far more sociological and psychological than it is political or structural. This greater relative significance of informal processes, compared with formal structures, becomes even more evident when we examine the problem of group effectiveness in translating activity into access and, then, influence.

The Problem of Effectiveness

In interest group theory, group effectiveness is treated as a function of both the characteristics of the group, itself, and the characteristics of the environment within which it engages in goal-directed activities. Despite the theory, most interest group literature consists of little more than hyperfactual historical case-studies of discrete groups and their great battles won and lost. The effectiveness of the selected group is either not treated at all— on the unarticulated assumption that the group must be effective because it survived long enough to come to the attention of the interested political historian—or it is treated in a nonsystematic manner which simplistically equates activity with impact. We shall focus on a single question: how does the group itself appraise its own activities?

Routine self-evaluation

Almost all political interest groups, especially newly formed ones, make use of a peculiarly Western concept: growth as the primary yardstick for appraising their own past behavior. In this, Amnesty International is no excep-

tion. Since its inception it has published satisfied reports on a variety of growth statistics: membership, now more than 32,000; nationalities of members, now more than 60; functioning small groups within nations, more than 1,200; budget, more than $500,000; annual relief disbursements to prisoners-detainees or their families, more than $230,000; full time staff in the London-based International Secretariat, more than 50; annual number of possible political-prisoner cases investigated, more than 2,000; total number of adopted prisoners of conscience which were released, more than 5,000; number and range of current activities, such as progress toward a current goal of more than one million signatures on a petition for the abolition of torture, directed to UN Secretary General Waldheim and intended to strengthen the 1948 UN Declaration of Human Rights.

Regarding this first criterion, the analyst would point out that the publication by an organization of satisfying growth-statistics is, at best, only negative proof of potential effectiveness, not of effectiveness, itself. This requires amplification. First, if an organization does not— especially if it refuses to—publish internal statistics, then it probably has stopped growing, meaning it has probably already peaked in efficiency. It may survive as a letterhead, a salary for an executive director, a physical location and furnishings; however, it does not do anything. Second, no one knows how much an organization should grow in order to increase its potential efficiency. That is, one can conceive of several alternative baselines (1) the past record—in terms of members, budget and so on—of the organization, itself; (2) changes over an identical time interval for both the organization and either the nation in which it is located or the entire world with regard to population or gross national product; or (3) changes over an identical time period for both the given organization and its nearest functional competitor(s) on these same two measures. Each measure yields quite different results.

The first measure is most commonly employed, especially in the United States; yet, it is the least meaningful, particularly if one considers the fact that there ought to be a discount rate applied against the data on any new organization for the simple reason that growth from nothing to something will necessarily be a vast percentagized rate. By these tests, which are far more stringent than any known political interest group applies to itself, we can say only that the new organization known as Amnesty International continues to grow in those prime resources which have universally proven to be preconditions to effective political action.

Self-evaluation: a second level

But Amnesty does not leave the problem of self-evaluation at this level, thus, differing significantly from the public behavior of most other political interest groups. Although one must leave the apparent safety of quantitative data for softer forms of evidence, such as cases and anecdotes, we may introduce this second level of organizational introspection by asking of all political groups whether they make a serious, rigorous and periodic effort to appraise their past and continuing activities. For most groups the answer is a silent negative; for some few the answer not only is positive, but the organization also publishes

the bases and results of such self-inquiry. Amnesty is one of these exceptional cases. Since about 1965 the organization has systematically reviewed both its goals and the adaption of its form—institutional structure—and its functions—tactics—to those ends.

Concerning its goal of worldwide protection of freedom of conscience and free speech, in 1971 the International Council of AI determined to broaden its operational definition of a conscientious objector (CO) to include so-called unconditionalists—that is, those who refuse the CO designation, since their governments attach the condition that they accept alternative national service; this action followed a similar expansion by a world religious ecumenical congress in 1970. In 1971, also, Amnesty determined to expand its efforts in the United States to include persons imprisoned for political activities performed for reasons linked with their ethnicity. Both of these moves had the effect—and, probably, the intent—of making AI far more relevant to the United States situation. One infers probable intent from an internal crisis in 1967. At that time· the British founder of AI, Peter Benenson, made charges to the effect that the British Secret Service had infiltrated the International Executive Committee and that the Central Intelligence Agency (CIA) controlled the International Commission of Jurists—a body with which AI had cooperated on a number of political prisoner cases and of which AI's number-two man, Sean McBride, was a member. Benenson was, in turn, accused of having accepted British government funds to help finance AI's relief operations in Rhodesia, which in 1965 had announced its unilateral declaration of independence. The conflict was resolved through a process which might best be termed the routinization of charisma. The founder was forced out and replaced by a neutral Scandinavian, Martin J. Ennals, to serve as secretary general; the various charges were investigated and were found unsubstantiated; and the new secretary general was instructed to work more closely with the national sections, to create a more efficient structure and to work to improve both fund raising and distribution. Shortly thereafter, the International Executive Committee achieved coordination with, and integration of, the various national sections. Until 1968 the stronger sections had often acted independently in sending their own nationals on missions abroad, both for fact finding in the field and for secret negotiations with the heads of repressive regimes.

In 1972—and, perhaps, an issue more fundamental to Amnesty's goals—delegates to the international council in Utrecht questioned the desirability of retaining AI's original statutory restriction on the organization's sponsorship of prisoners-detainees: that persons could only be adopted "provided that they have not used or advocated violence." As of this writing, AI has not yet resolved this thorny philosophical and practical political problem, which was stimulated partly by the Berrigan Baltimore draft protest case. In 1972 the annual assembly instructed the International Secretariat that governmental assertions that a prisoner had used or advocated violence were not to bind AI: "Such an assertion should be considered valid only if it has been proved in a fair and public trial." It simultaneously recommended to the International Executive Committee that a special commission be created both to study the problems of retaining or eliminating the violence clause and to formulate a legal definition of the term political prisoner.

AI's structure has also been subjected to periodic reexamination, apart from the structural changes resulting from the 1967 crisis. In 1972, for example, the fifth international council meeting at Utrecht agreed to place an item on the 1973 agenda concerning the feasibility of legislating a maximum for the annual financial contribution which any national section could make to the budget and operations of the international organization; this specifically raised the question of effective control of Amnesty International by West Germany or the United States, since the national sections are assessed levies on the basis of national per capita income.

A second issue of structure arose in 1972, but has not yet been resolved: within the larger national sections there are both regular member working groups—the normal molecule of organizational structure—and also specialist groups—of biochemists only, physicists only or psychiatrists. Since experts tend to be more loyal to their professions than to specific political principles or to humanity in general, such groups frequently generate friction within the organization. This has been a problem particularly for the West German section.

A third and final problem of structure which surfaced in 1972 centered around the fact that the organization is based on the most affluent members of the most affluent societies of the free world, which has consequences for its perspective. For example, the research department of the International

Secretariat includes no person who specializes in repression in Western Europe or North America. With rare self-consciousness, the annual international assembly suggested to the International Executive Committee that it initiate sustained contact with institutions or individual citizens in one or more countries of both the socialist bloc and the Third World with a view towards mutual protection of human rights in general and free speech in particular.

Amnesty's tactics are also subject to review. In 1972, for example, a spokesman for the West Germans questioned the efficiency of the monthly postcard campaign in behalf of three balanced urgent cases. The implicit question was whether this constituted an inefficient overconcentration of scarce resources. As of late 1973, the campaign has been mobilized in behalf of some 250 individuals of whom it is claimed that 115, located in 40 different countries, won release. Consequently, the issue was referred to the research department for review. At the same time the Italian section raised questions about the original limitation against intranational activities, whereby, for example, in the Vietnam era significant United States CO cases were the action-concern of Swiss Amnesty and others, but not of the United States section. The problem of tactical balance is also a recurring issue. Members of the West German section noted two problems of apparent lack of balance in 1971-1972: (1) the adoption of 350 Spanish prisoners, but only 30 in the German Democratic Republic; and (2) AI involvement in CO cases in South Vietnam, the United States, Israel, Spain, Portugal, France, the Federal Republic of Germany, Norway and even Switzerland, but: "Are we to

believe this problem does not exist in Socialist countries?" The short run answer—implied by Ennals' response—is that an organization such as Amnesty depends heavily on volunteered research and that the volunteers come already equipped with both interests and ideology. Furthermore, research, itself—as Amnesty proves—is an effective form of political pressure. Even so, short run imbalances in political rights cases should not prove a long term problem; if Amnesty is truly international, the national sections will perform a watch dog function on one another and the organization, itself, will thus operate with a built-in self-correcting mechanism.

A final consideration of tactics is evident in the annual report for 1972-1973 of the British section, which notes that deadly serious political purposes require not only flexibility and a willingness to experiment, but also that they can be undertaken with humor and even love. The British report that to publicize "Prisoner of Conscience" Week nationally:

In addition to the traditional activities . . . many new and creative ventures were successfully undertaken by groups, including theatrical presentations, a balloon race, poetry readings, a fund-raising "eat-in," a wreath-laying ceremony at a war memorial to the "living dead," film shows, a Festival of Peace, public exhibitions, and a badminton marathon.

Perhaps rarest of all in interest group behavior was item forty-two in the report and decisions of the Fifth International Council Meeting instructing the International Secretariat: "to collect and publish important negative and positive statements about Amnesty International in order to stress its impartiality." This was done in 1973.

The publication is revealing: Erwin Griswold, then United States solicitor general, was "rather puzzled" by Swiss interest in United States citizen Larry Cleveland Vann, imprisoned for refusing military service; South African whites objected to Amnesty's interest in the forced resettlement of black Africans, while Amnesty "apparently condoned or shrugged off" the concurrent murders of 80,000 blacks in the Sudan; the South Vietnamese insisted that their political prisoners, variously estimated at between 100,000 and 200,000 by United States reporters, are "a purely internal matter"; the Indonesian Army newspaper termed Amnesty "a front organization of the new left"; a British regional newspaper thought Amnesty "monstrously misguided" for its support of a man given a two-year prison term for possession of pro-Irish Republican Army leaflets. Spokesmen for Portugal, Ghana, Greece, Honduras, East Germany and Brazil, among others, reacted with equally predictable denials and stereotypic labelling of Amnesty as "our ideological opposite."

In summary, Amnesty is far more rationally introspective than most political interest groups—or most that have been studied systematically. In its flexibility of both form and function, new changes are introduced in a controlled, natural, experimental manner providing further evaluative feedback to the organization. The organization has even been willing to go outside itself—to a British consultancy firm —for advice on the method of evaluating priorities in decision making at the International Secretariat level. In short, the first twelve years of life of this organization indicate a rare, increasing, yet, healthy—nonobsessive—concern for the effectiveness of its activities.

Interest Groups in Sweden

By Nils Elvander

ABSTRACT: Sweden has perhaps the strongest system of interest groups in the world. All important groups belong to a few peak organizations with a very high membership percentage. This system, developed continuously from the end of the nineteenth century, is characterized by bargaining among organizations and the institutionalization of their political influence. The peak associations are highly centralized with a hierarchical power structure, which has caused problems of internal democracy. Their political influence is based mainly on economic and personal resources and on their position in the decision-making process. Influence is exerted through various channels, ranging from informal contacts with decision makers to public propaganda campaigns. The latter, however, seem less effective than information based upon facts. Group influence is expressed mainly in the preparatory stages—through representation on investigative commissions and so-called *remiss* comments on commission reports—and at the executive stage in the agencies. The least significant target is Parliament, although contacts are maintained with the parliamentary groups of the parties. The only association having intimate organizational and ideological links with a party is the Swedish Federation of Trade Unions (LO), which has the strongest influence of all groups, because of its large membership and ties with the ruling Social-Democratic Party. The other associations have all declared their political neutrality, but this is not to say that they do not take a position on controversial political issues. Thus, the Central Association of Salaried Employees (TCO) has increased its influence considerably since World War II by taking an active part in such issues.

Nils Elvander is Professor of Political Science at the University of Uppsala. He is the author of Harald Hjärne och konservatismen: Konservativ idédebatt i Sverige 1865–1922 *(Harald Hjärne and Conservatism: Conservative Ideological Debate in Sweden, 1865–1922),* Intresseorganisationerna i dagens Sverige *(Interest Organizations in Sweden Today) and* Svensk skattepolitik 1945–1970: En studie i partiers och organisationers funktioner *(The Politics of Taxation in Sweden 1945–1970: A Study of the Functions of Political Parties and Interest Organizations).*

27

IN SWEDEN'S strongly developed associational system each interested group has its own association. These associations relate in many ways both to their members and externally to society. They intervene at all levels in the decision-making process and exercise, in this way, considerable political influence. From this it follows that the Swedish associational system provides an unusually rich area for research. It is obviously impossible to cover all aspects of the subject in a short article; thus, this can be but a short summary of some of the main points.[1]

First, one ought to define more closely the concept of interest associations. Here, the concept covers only the so-called top associations; it has not been possible to deal with the many national unions and local branches from which the top associations are built. Furthermore, I have defined the concept interest organization as an organized group whose activity is dominated by material interests; in consequence, I have ignored certain so-called popular movements and promotional groups which have a strongly idealistic, nonmaterial element in their aims. The top associations dealt with here are concerned with: workers and salaried employees, private trade and industry, consumer cooperatives, agriculture and housing markets.

The most important source materials consist of interviews with cabinet ministers, party leaders and members of the Riksdag (Parliament) and with persons in a leading position within the associations, themselves. Minutes, annual reports and printed publications from the associations, committee memoranda, paliamentary publications and debates in the press have also been examined. I have not considered it necessary to supply notes on this source material.

DEVELOPMENT OF THE ASSOCIATIONAL SYSTEM

Certain common features can be discerned in the origin and development of the associations. The first stage was the creation of local societies in the middle or end of the nineteenth century. Thereafter, countrywide unions or branch organizations were usually built up; finally—in most cases not until the twentieth century—came the creation of the large top associations. A series of unsuccessful attempts often preceeded the final form of the association. Older, more unsuitable organizational forms were cast aside until a viable structure, which had withstood the hard test of the early break-through period, emerged. Experience gained in this way showed the necessity for the centralization of power in strong head organizations; the consequent internal power shift is the most striking feature of development during the twentieth century.

Apart from the experience gained during these early break-through years, the concentrational tendency can be explained by the law of counterbalancing forces. The foundation of *Landsorganisationen* (LO)—the Swedish Trade Union Federation—in 1898 was followed by *Svenska Arbetsgivareföreningen* (SAF)—the Swedish Employers Association—in 1902. The foundation of *Kooperativa Förbundet* (KF)—the Swedish Cooperative

---

1. For a more complete account of interest group behavior in Sweden, see, Nils Elvander, *Interest Organizations in Sweden Today* (Lund: Gleerups, 1969).

Union's Wholesale Society—in 1899 was, in part, an answer to the attempts since the 1880s to create an association of individual traders: an answer which, in its turn, brought forth new and more consolidated top associations in the retail and wholesale trades in about 1920. *Sveriges Fastighetsägareförbund* (1914)—the Swedish Real Estate Owners Association—was faced with its counterpart on the housing market, *Sveriges Hyresgästers Riksförbund* (1923)—the Swedish Tenants National Association. Another important reason for the uniform and, in the main, harmonious development which characterizes the Swedish associational system is that all the top associations, except for LO, declared and maintained political party neutrality from the beginning. Sweden has nearly completely avoided the splitting along ideological lines which in many other countries has plagued and weakened associational life.

Parallel with this concentration and shift of power to the top associations, there has been, on the part of certain associations, a marked change in their relationship with their opposite number in the associational world: a development from open, hard conflict to negotiations in orderly form, directly or indirectly sanctioned by the state. The best example of this is the so-called Saltsjöbaden agreement between LO and SAF in 1938, which laid the foundation for peace on the Swedish labor market. A similar development is found in the history of the relationship of popular associations to the state and political life: from struggle, agitation and mutual mistrust to negotiations and trustful, institutionalized cooperation. This change had already begun before the victory of political democracy in 1918, but was first brought to bear with full force between the wars. This can be illustrated by the fact that associations during the Second World War—in contrast with what happened during the First—were well represented on all emergency commissions. They were trusted with important administrative tasks in the areas of trade and supply; state legislation in general was enacted only after consultation with the associations.

STRUCTURE OF THE ASSOCIATIONS

After the Second World War the associational system underwent a powerful expansion and consolidation. To a certain extent this can be traced in the strong increase in membership. LO's membership has grown from 1.1 million in 1945 to 1.8 million in 1972. The most noticeable expansion is that of the salaried employees associations, which were founded considerably later than those of the workers. The two leading top associations were founded at the end of the war: *Tjänstemännens Centralorganisation* (TCO)—the Central Salaried Employees Organization—representing salaried employees in the lower and middle grades in both public and private sectors of the economy and *Sveriges Akademikers Centralorganisation* (SACO)—the Central Organization of Swedish Professional Workers—which is the federation of publicly and privately employed university- and highschool-educated salaried employees. TCO's and SACO's membership figures have grown from 200,000 and 15,000 in 1945 to 800,000 and 120,000 in 1972, respectively.

Even KF and the Swedish Tenants National Association can show a strong increase in membership. The farmers associations, which some years ago were grouped into a single top association, *Lantbrukarnas Riksförbund* (LRF)—the Farmers National Association—show, on the other hand, a reduced or stagnating membership due to a receding population base. The same applies to certain associations in trade and industry. Here, the reason is a continuous process of concentration, creating fewer and bigger company units.

Today, Sweden probably has the world's strongest associational system when measured by percentage of membership within those areas covered by the top associations. In the area covered by LO the percentage is nearly 95 percent; TCO covers over 90 percent of the publicly employed and 70 percent of the privately employed; and about 70 percent of all university- and highschool-educated professional workers are affiliated to SACO. Even in the private trading sector and in agriculture the percentage within associations is very high—on the average, about 70 percent.

One of the reasons for this unparalleled strength is that most associations for employees in industry are built upon the so-called vertical principle, also called the industrial union principle. This implies that the union shall include all employees in the same place of work or in all companies of a particular branch of industry. At the beginning LO was built up of professional unions—that is, all workers in the same profession, regardless of the place of work—but by about 1910 LO had committed itself to the industrial union principle. Since then, most national unions have followed suit; today over 80 percent of union members are organized into industrial unions.

When compared to the United States and England where craft unions dominate, the contrast is striking. The Swedish union movement has, through its principle of organization, achieved a high level of adherence and solidarity at the expense of separating interests; this followed the fact that the employers associations were also built upon industrial union lines and that they had a strong position. In the world of the salaried employees associations the picture is more divided. TCO is organized both vertically and horizontally, which has caused strains on unity and a certain amount of seccession in the last few years. SACO is completely built upon the horizontal principle: a university degree is a qualification for membership.

Concerning the associations' decision-making machinery, one can say that in general the formal structure gives the power to the members' representatives in congress, which is the highest decision-making agency, or to the body of representatives, which is in some associations the highest decision-making agency between congresses. However, the actual power structure—considerably more pointed than the formal—is concentrated in the leading members of the board and in the officials in the secretariat. Normally, the balance of power is held between the association's administrative chairman and its managing director, but there are examples of the director being the association's "strongman." Within some top associations —for example, LO—both posts are filled by the same person, who naturally has a very strong position.

In the last few years this internal

concentration of power, above all within the big popular associations, has become the subject of critical public debate and has attracted attention within the associations, themselves. It is not so much the concentration of power in the hands of a few that has been criticized, but the other side of the picture: the powerlessness and apathy of the members and their elected representatives. The problem has not been made easier by a tendency to centralize within the associations.

The result is that many small, local branches with direct membership democracy are being run together into bigger units completely built up on representative democratic principles. These consolidations are an attempt to satisfy members' demands for more efficient service through permanent officials. Even on the national union level there is centralization into fewer and bigger units; in addition, certain top associations are planning amalgamation. This tendency—which runs parallel to, and is partly the result of, the rationalization and centralization of the whole economy— creates difficult problems for internal democracy within the associations. There is a greater distance between the members and their representatives, and the day-to-day work is taken over by full time officials who rely greatly on the passive trust of the membership.

A further aspect of the current structure of the associational system in Sweden ought to be mentioned: namely, the strong tendency for cooperation among top associations. Naturally, division and tension does occur, mainly in the salaried employees labor market. However, the world of the Swedish associations has been characterized more by cooperation than by opposition

and conflict. Especially noteworthy is the close cooperation between LO and SAF, which developed after the Saltsjöbaden talks, in the form of agreements and a succession of combined committees. Many important questions on the labor market have been solved by their agreements, which either replaced state legislation or complemented it. The most important example is, of course, the Saltsjöbaden agreement, itself. This is the so-called basic agreement on principles for a peaceful solution of controversial issues in wage disputes, which up until now has staved off the threat of state intervention in the private wage market. Even questions of industrial welfare, study during working hours, vocational training and industrial democracy have been wholly or partially solved through negotiations between LO and SAF. It must be emphasized that this cooperation has continued even during the last few years, despite the considerably harsher climate in the central wage negotiations between LO and SAF. This is a good witness to the stability and strong identity of values which exist in Swedish political culture.

INTEREST ORGANIZATIONS IN THE POLITICAL DECISION-MAKING PROCESS

Political influence is the central theme in the following outline of the relationship of associations to government and the political parties. This phrase is used instead of the loaded expression political pressure. Neither is the word power used in connection with the associations, since power should be seen as a special aspect of influence. The concept of political influence is given a broad definition: influence on the decisions of governmental institutions, including administrative agencies, in all questions affecting the associations. When the aim is influence on decisions that are political in the real sense, I shall use the expression influence in political respects. If one speaks of an association's influence, one must make clear that this is something with several dimensions and that it depends on many factors. One must distinguish between two types of influence which can be called (1) basic influence and (2) variable influence.[2]

Basic influence means the continuous influence which the association has due to its place in the political system, independent of its action in a given situation. This influence is created partly by the association's own resources for political action—political resources —and partly by its relationship to the political and institutional environment. The political resources of an association include its ideological relationship to the parties and its general prestige, the number of its members and what they represent, its organizational efficiency and internal cohesion and, finally, the economic and intellectual resources controlled by the leadership. The scope of an association's political resources is naturally something which it can affect to a certain extent—for example, through membership re-

cruitment, internal organizational work, the extension of its investigative resources and its public relations (PR) activity. But this is work on a long term basis; it cannot give results on a day-to-day level. One can therefore say that an association's political resources in a particular situation are of a given size.

This also applies to the other component of basic influence: the associations's position in the political and institutional environment. Environment in this case means partly the relationships of political power and partly the state's decision-making structure—that is, the governmental and party system, the distribution of power in the administration and the decisional framework of the organs of state. Here, one should also take into account the possible dependence of the opposite party in the state on the association when it comes to information and participation in the policies of the government. If the association can supply information which governmental institutions have difficulty in getting elsewhere and if government needs the association's active participation in order to carry out its own policies, this can give the association considerable basic influence.

To take LO as an example: its large political resources in Sweden today can be brought to bear under favorable conditions. Social Democracy has held political power for a long time; we have a strong one-party government and a divided opposition. LO is represented on commissions and in administration and has a decisive role to play in decisions on all questions which have a bearing on its interests. The government is in certain respects dependent on information and assistance from LO, and—as can other associations

2. Among others, see, Elvander, "Intressegruppers politiska inflytande," *Sociologisk Forskning* 2 (1965); Robert Presthus, *Elites in the Policy Process* (New York: Cambridge University Press, 1974); Harry Eckstein, *Pressure Group Politics* (London: Allen and Unwin, 1960); Joseph La Palombara, *Interest Groups in Italian Politics* (Princeton, N.J.: Princeton University Press, 1964).

—LO can also make use of the positive attitude of the public to the associational system. But it is evident that the associations can in general affect these factors only in the long term. It is certainly true that LO, through its cooperation with Social-democracy, can sometimes affect the political balance of power in a direct and tangible way, thereby increasing its own basic influence. This is, however, exceptional; it does not vitiate the main thesis that the political and institutional environment cannot be directly and immediately affected by associational action.

An association's variable influence is, in contrast to its basic influence, a product of its action in a particular situation. The weight of such influence depends on the actual situation and the association's methods of using it. In the main, variable influence operates in two different ways: one is for the association to go directly to the decision-making authority and lay before it material which, through its objective and informative content, can make an impression on the decision-makers. This is an emanation of that part of the basic influence created by the association's research resources. The other way to exercise variable influence is for the association, either directly or indirectly, to arouse public opinion on the question by propaganda of different kinds.

With a certain amount of simplification, this mobilization of public opinion can, in turn, be divided into two main types. First, one finds a more limited formation of opinion which essentially tends to coincide with the communications that are presented to the decision-making bodies. In general,

these are geared to a narrow circle of molders of public opinion: politicians, government officials and their representatives. Second, in particular situations a simplified propaganda is used, aimed directly at the general public, which can be more accurately termed agitation. This can take the form of mass meetings, mass distribution of propaganda material and public statements combined with meetings and lobbying. Which of these different methods of exercising variable influence is used—or which combination of them—depends partly on the situation and partly on the resources to which the association has access. But the choice of method also affects, to a certain extent, the scope of the variable influence; different methods can produce different degrees of effect.

The association makes its influence felt at all stages in the decision-making process. Sometimes the association takes the initiative in raising a new question, usually through a combination of official intervention in a debate, lobbying and informal contacts. As a rule, these contacts are made with government departments or administrative agencies or, more seldom, with the parliamentary parties in the form of suggestions for a motion.

In larger questions the government usually appoints a study commission, which afterwards operates with relative independence. For a long time it has been the rule that associations are represented on commissions which deal with questions involving their own interests. Representation in this case means that either the association, itself, suggests members or approves one of the names suggested by the ministry. The former method has been most common in the last few years—a token of the strong and accepted position of the associations. When the study commission is formed it usually gets a directive from the government. Here, under certain conditions, the association has the possibility of control or influence, usually through lobbying or informal contacts or, in exceptional cases, through taking part in the ministry's consideration of alternative directives. Even if an association does not have a representative on a commission, it nevertheless has several ways to make its views known. It can write spontaneously to the commission; it can, on its own or the commission's initiative, be called to discussions or hearings; it can be invited to appoint an expert, which is often a substitute for representation; and it can receive questionnaires or requests for preliminary suggestions from the commission concerning questions of detail.

The commission stage in the decision-making process is critical from the associations' point of view. Representation on the commission gives them an opportunity to affect the handling of a question at an early stage, which is often crucial for the final form of the decision. The involvement of the associations is also advantageous to the government. It gains contact with opinion within the groups concerned, access to worthwhile expertise and a certain guarantee that measures in which the associations were involved at the early formative stage will receive loyal acceptance.

During the last ten to fifteen years, however, certain tendencies have appeared in the commission system which suggest a reduction in the influence of the associations. Their representation on these commissions has shown a marked decline, and so has that of the political parties. The relative proportion of government officials has risen from 41 percent during 1945–1954 to 60 percent during 1955–1967. This development can be interpreted as a sign of the continuous concentration of power into the hands of the government and state bureaucracy at the expense of the Opposition's and the associations' influence in the commission system. The government has gained a tighter grip on the commissions, and they have become still more integrated with the civil administration. There has also been a tendency in the last few years to set up committees within the ministries or civil service, instead of official independent commissions.[3]

When a commission finishes its work, it submits its report to the appropriate ministry, which in turn sends it for consideration to the concerned administrative authorities and associations. These return their submitted comments—*remiss* comments—to the ministry, which compiles them and presents a summary together with the commission's report on the government bill. As a rule, the associations regard the submitted comment as an important way to bring up their viewpoints—particularly in those cases where they have not been represented on the commission. If they have been forgotten, they are particularly anxious to make their comments and to have measures referred to them for consideration. They often cooperate with related associations—sometimes, even with the civil service—

3. Hans Meijer, "Bureaucracy and Policy Formulation in Sweden," *Scandinavian Political Studies* 4 (1969), pp. 103–116.

with the intention of giving the comment further weight.

Another way to increase the effect of the comment is to follow it up by lobbying and by informal contacts within the ministries. Such action is, however, infrequent and not especially effective. More commonly, the associations' viewpoints are brought out in parliamentary motions in connection with the bill, either on the initiative of the associations or individual members of the Riksdag. In general, the associations consider the effect of the submitted comment to be strongest in questions where they are directly involved and can be reckoned to be expert, whereas the possibility of influencing large political questions is extremely small. In the case of LO—which cooperates closely with the Social Democratic Party and the government—the opposite is true.

It is already clear that the associations have considerable contact with the ministries in connection with initiatives, commissions and submitted comments. Other forms of contact occur during day-to-day work and on special occasions. They vary from daily telephone conversations with ministry officials to discussions with the government on important political questions. Certain associations in trade and industry have the highest frequency of contacts, due to their especially intimate relations with the ministries of trade and foreign affairs in connection with nonpolitical, foreign trade questions. KF and LO have a relatively low frequency, since they have a strong political position—that is, a large basic influence—and, therefore, do not need to make themselves felt so often. In addition, LO has a direct

channel to the government through regular monthly discussions. Concerning the form of these continuous contacts, it can generally be said that informal contacts of different kinds predominate. A gradual deformalization has occurred since the war. With the exception of a couple of small associations, Swedish associations form an establishment in which everyone knows everyone else and all associations have access to government and ministries.

THE EFFECTIVENESS OF INTEREST GROUP ASSOCIATIONS

How deeply does the influence of the associations make itself felt in the ministerial decision-making process? In general, one can say that it comes in at a preliminary stage in the preparatory work and, in some cases, also in the combined work between two or more ministries. It never reaches the combined drafting stage when the whole government takes up its final attitude to the proposal and other important matters. There is rarely participation in the final formation of legislation—with certain exceptions in those cases where negotiation occurred between the associations and representatives of the state before the actual ministerial draft. In certain cases the associations can have a more direct and tangible effect on the contents of the bill. They are sometimes given the opportunity to take a part in the proof reading of the bill and the regulations in order to check that the previously agreed clauses have been properly incorporated in the text.

Such negotiating situations have occurred more or less frequently in two areas—namely, the pay and terms of employment of civil servants and the farm price reviews. In the former area, however, as a result of the civil servants' gaining independent negotiating and strike rights in 1966, the greater part of the negotiating machinery on the government side has been moved from the ministry to a special civil service department. Agricultural negotiations have, as a rule, been dealt with by an administrative agency. However, sometimes the government has been directly involved and has negotiated with the associations itself. Apart from these two areas there have been isolated cases in which the government has made negotiated agreements with certain associations as part of its attempt to achieve economic stability. Some examples of such agreements follow.

In 1942 and 1948–1949 the government reached agreement with the employees—trade and industrial —and agricultural associations on a temporary wage and price stop in an attempt to halt inflation. Since then there have been no stabilization agreements; the government has respected the desire of the organizations for no intervention. On several occasions during the 1950s the government made so-called voluntary agreements with different trade associations. These agreements—which, as a rule, came in connection with the policies of stabilization during the Korean war inflation—were an alternative or complement to economic controls through legislation. The government preferred this method because it could rely on more loyal cooperation from the associations, since they had been allowed to be directly involved in the detailed formulation of the regulations.

The system also had advantages for the associations, as it made for smoother application in practice. Yet, the voluntary nature of these agreements was dubious, since the government always had the alternative of using legislation as a pressure. In this way the voluntary agreements have often had a more compelling nature than the ordinary stabilization agreements. In the main, voluntary agreements ceased by the end of the 1950s, which one can see as a sign of the increased strength of the government's position. The government no longer depends as heavily on the cooperation of the associations to further its economic policies; the result is that the basic influence of the trade associations has declined.

Another form of contact between the government and the associations has been the Harpsund conferences, which were held once or twice a year from 1955 to 1963. The prime minister invited representatives from trade and industry, LO, TCO, KF and, sometimes, other associations to his residence at Harpsund for informal talks on topical questions. No agreements were ever signed—on the insistence of the Opposition parties— but sometimes a mutual understanding, a kind of unspoken agreement, was reached. Harpsund played an important role in discussions on Sweden's relations with the European Economic Community (EEC) at the beginning of the 1960s. It worked as a kind of contact point between the government and the economy, whereby a number of misunderstandings were

4. Among others, see, Grant McConnell, *Private Power and American Democracy* (New York: A. A. Knopf, 1966).

resolved and a certain degree of mutual understanding was reached. During this time, however, the Harpsund conferences had no great importance as a channel for group influence on government.

The same applies to the so-called planning councils which were established in different ministries with representatives from, among others, the affected associations. The most important is the Economic Planning Council in the Ministry of Finance, which became a substitute for the regular Harpsund conferences. This body has only an advisory capacity and serves, above all, as a center for discussions and the dissemination of information. Direct informal contacts with the ministries and government are of considerably greater importance than the conferences and planning councils; this applies to an even greater extent to individual representatives for big industry and the banks. Because of internal opposition of interests and too little authority over their members, among other things, the trade and industrial associations cannot deploy the whole of their basic influence against the government or, if one prefers, the power which lies in the big companies and banks.

The reason for discontinuing the Harpsund conferences was, in part, that they came under sharp attack from the nonsocialist parties. They felt shut out and argued that the Riksdag was being set aside and presented with the *fait accompli* of covert agreements. Bertil Ohlin, leader of the Liberal Party, coined the phrase "Harpsund democracy" to describe a form of government which, according to him, was characterized by an overpowerful government, a powerless Parlia-

ment and unjustifiably strong associations, which directly influenced the government. It is clear that the above description suffers from a good deal of exaggeration. Yet, it is not difficult to understand the critics when one considers the role of the Riksdag. One could point to the negotiated agreements between the government and the civil servants and agricultural associations still being made at that time which were in practice completely or nearly completely binding on the Riksdag.

The associations are well aware that the fulcrum of political power lies with the government and not with the Riksdag. At the same time nearly all the top associations have a strong representation—not to say overrepresentation—in the Riksdag, for most of them have one or more leading spokesmen among its members. However, this sort of contact, in general occurring with individual members of the Riksdag or with party groups—in the form of informal talks, motions, letters to committees and informational activity—has, for most associations, only marginal importance as a channel of political influence.

The decisions of the government and Riksdag are carried out by an independent executive, unique to Sweden and Finland. The independence of this executive is still a reality, despite the present concentration of power in the hands of the government. Since legislation in a modern, complicated state takes the form of a general framework, the independent executive has a strong influence on the formation of the regulations which comprise the laws. In practice, the real content of the laws lies in these detailed instructions. In turn, this gives the associations the opportunity of affecting the final detailing and carrying out of the political decision. This they can do, partly by directly contacting the service departments and county governments. However, the executive is not only concerned with the application of ready-made decisions. It also has an initiating, preparing and planning function, to such an extent that, for instance, *Arbetsmarknadsstyrelsen*—the labor market board—virtually plays the role of a ministry. Naturally, it is of great importance for the associations if they can also affect these functions and thereby exert political influence.

Interest organizations are represented on the boards of a large number of central agencies. From the government's view, the motive for this representation is the same as in the case of the commissions. From the view of the associations, the right to partake in decisions and to gain insight into questions which they consider vital are important assets of such representation. There is usually a high degree of unity among representatives of the associations and other members of these boards. The civil service also functions as an agent of compromise. The continuous contacts between the administrative authorities and the associations naturally have a greater frequency and informality than those with the ministries. In certain cases these intimate contacts can develop into that which has been called a client relationship between authority and association.

Trade, industrial and agricultural associations had a stronger position in the administration during the Second World War than they have today. They were actively involved in the emergency administration; at a time when the state's agricultural administration was scarcely developed, the agricultural associations commanded good investigative resources and gained a strong influence on the formation of agricultural regulations. After the war the trade and industrial associations quickly lost their strong position, because of the wind-up of the emergency administration and the hardening of their political opposition to the Social Democratic government. Agricultural associations, on the other hand, retained a very strong basic influence during the greater part of the 1950s. This was partly due to the fact that the administrative decision-making structure and the agricultural price system were in their favor. More important, however, was the favorable political climate created by the governmental coalition—1951 to 1957—between the Social Democrats and the Farmers Party—at that time still a purely agrarian party. During the 1960s the agricultural lobby lost its strong political position; as a result, their resources and position on the administrative plane has been relatively weakened, whereas the influence of the state has increased. The associations have tried to reverse this process in the agricultural price reviews and the political decisions of the last few years by intensive propaganda campaigns. It seems to be a rule that when basic influence wanes, variable influence is brought to bear strongly in the form of agitation.

To summarize this account of the influence of the associations on the political decision-making process: one can say that it is at its strongest in the preparatory and executive phases—committee, submitted comment and administration. It is at its weakest in the formal decision phase—that is, the government and especially the Riksdag. Most associations try to reach the government as the focus of political power. However, few are granted this direct form of influence. Influence on the government is mostly brought to bear through committees and submitted comments. The administration is also an important field for indirect influence on the government; the associations can have a considerable effect on the executive functions of the administration. For most associations the Riksdag is the least effective and least used road to political influence.

INTEREST GROUP ORGANIZATIONS AND THE POLITICAL PARTIES

The influence of the associations on the political system is not only channelled directly to the decision makers in the organs of state, but also indirectly through the parties. Certain parties, due to social ties, are nearer to certain associations than others. Election statistics and information on the relationship of Riksdag members with the associations suggest that: the Moderate Party—the Conservatives—has most in common with the associations of trade and industry, agriculture and the upper echelons of the salaried employees; this party has more contacts in the Riksdag than any other party. The Centre Party—before 1957, the Farmers Party—has most contact with the agricultural associations, the Social Democrats, with the workers and lower salaried employees associations; while the Peoples Party—the liberals—probably has the widest, though far from the most frequent, contacts with the associations. Contact

between the associations and the parties takes place mostly on the level of the Riksdag. With the exception of LO, the associations avoid any kind of involvement with the national party organizations as a result of their party-political neutrality. On the other hand, the political parties often turn to the associations for information.

The only association which has continuous and intimate relations with a political party is LO. The regular contacts between LO and the Social Democratic Party have already been mentioned. LO is also strongly represented in the Social-Democratic group in the Riksdag and in the party's central committee. Very important cooperation between LO and the Social-Democrats takes place in such temporary institutions as propaganda committees, combined committees and planning commissions. Through these channels, among others, LO has effected a strong, often excessive, influence on the Social Democratic Party and government, primarily in labor market and economic policies. This cooperation is even closer on a regional and local level, which can mean that an individual union can make a decision which links the entire membership to the local Social Democratic Party organization. This has great importance for the party's finances; it has been calculated that 75 percent of party members joined in this way. In addition, LO and the unions directly contribute several million crowns to the party's election fund. This has its counterpart in the contribution of individual companies to the nonsocialist parties; on the other hand, the politically neutral top associations contribute nothing to party finances.

Another form of contact between the associations and parties occurs during the nomination of candidates for Riksdag and county elections. During early periods attempts to influence party nominations were a central activity of the associations. At the end of the 1940s, for example, TCO directed appeals to the four biggest parties requesting them to work for the nomination of TCO-affiliated officials. Such methods are unnecessary today, since the association has grown so strong and salaried employees have become a large voting group. Pressure for the nomination of candidates takes place only within the party, where different organized groups attempt to win representation.

Neutrality vis-a-vis parties maintained by all associations except LO implies that the association operates from the basis of the interests of its own group rather than from that of any particular party. This does not mean that the association refrains from taking a stand on any controversial party-political question affecting its own interests. Certain associations, especially TCO, had interpreted this neutrality principle rather strictly. Since their increase in size and importance, they found that their sphere of interest covered nearly the whole register of domestic politics. They felt that refusing to engage in important issues simply because these questions were a subject of controversy between the parties would be tantamount to neglecting their members' interests.

One can ask, however, whether or not this change in the interpretation of party-political neutrality after the war was a result of the general political development or the consolidation of the associa-

tional system. It is clear that neutrality can be interpreted differently during different periods and that certain associations can have a preference for one or more of the parties. Trade and industrial associations, for example, generally have the same attitude towards economic-political questions as the non-socialist parties. Yet—with the exception of sharp attacks on the government's policies just after the war and the struggle over the supplementary pension reform at the end of the 1950s—they have refused to identify themselves with the policies of the Opposition. During the 1960s these associations drew nearer the government and sought to establish a tentative level of cooperation—also the desire of the government. One can say that their neutrality has become more real and credible. However, the balance is unstable; it is easily upset by shifts in government policy, especially in the balance of power between government and Opposition.

SACO has also freed itself from its earlier involvement with the non-socialist Opposition, but—after the open conflict over teachers' wages in 1966—relations with the government have worsened again. TCO has always held a strictly neutral line, which has not stopped the suspicions of the nonsocialist press; a prominent Social Democrat held the post of director from 1945 to 1961. A change of personnel silenced the critics.

The interests of agricultural associations and their members lie near those of the Centre Party—Farmers Party. During the 1940s there was an unsuccessful attempt by the Farmers Party to infiltrate the *Lantbruksförbundet*—Farmers Cooperative Association—and the post of chairman was held by leading Farmers Party politicians. Since then, the neutrality of the agricultural associations has been strictly observed. In summary, it can be said that most associations have, since the war, increasingly observed the principle of party-political neutrality.

THE ROLE OF INTEREST GROUP ORGANIZATIONS IN THE POLITICAL SYSTEM

This section will summarize the principle points concerning the influence of the associations and their role in the political system. First, it ought to be pointed out that the basic influence on all fronts of the large wage earners associations —LO, TCO and SACO—has grown since the last war. The same applies to the popular associations on the housing market. On the other hand, the political influence of the agricultural organizations and the trade and industrial associations has diminished. The latter have, however, experienced a limited increase in influence in the last few years on an administrative level in technical, nonpolitical questions. Many indications suggest that the associations with the strongest influence in Sweden today are LO, TCO, KF and a couple of trade and industrial associations, especially SAF. There is no doubt, however, that in all respects LO has the strongest influence.

One must also consider the components of political influence—or, in other words, the factors which a politician considers when he takes a position regarding the needs of an association. One can summarize the attitudes of the interviewed politicians and association representatives in the following way. An important element in the basic influence of an association is its level of representativeness, which includes the authority of the leadership over the members. Also important is the association's potential in the maximalization of votes —either because of its size or because it is a marginal voting group, regardless of size. TCO and the craft and small industry associations are examples. Another important factor is the ideological solidarity which might exist among associations and one or more parties in the government. LO is the best example, but one can also point to the strong position of the agricultural associations during earlier coalition years.

Of less importance are what one might term factors of participation and information. These have had reduced importance since the war and the wind-up of the emergency administration. As a rule, these factors are only meaningful in questions of technical detail. The institutions of government seldom have such a strong need for the participation and information of the associations that these gain a key position and, therefore, power. Given this, in the areas where actual negotiations take place with state institutions—and not merely understandings of a nonbinding nature—associations can use their basic influence as power in the form of sanctions or the credible threat of sanctions. This has occurred in connection with agricultural negotiations in the 1940s and wage negotiations between the state and SACO in 1966 and 1971. However, this is unusual. The normal behavior of the associations is to rely on convincing arguments and to refrain from threats and heavy pressure.

Here we find ourselves in the sphere of variable influence. It is the unanimous opinion of those interviewed—confirmed by other material—that the most important tactics are the presentation of information and argument directly to the decision-making institutions or limited activation of public opinion. Agitation is of relatively little importance. It can sometimes be a reinforcing factor, but always in the short term; if overdone or not followed up, it can have a reverse effect. The established and forward-looking associations try as much as possible to back up their arguments with facts. Since the war many of them have built up their own research organizations so that demands, ideas and concrete suggestions for reform can be presented with solidly backed arguments. In conjunction, associations also try to show that their needs are compatible with, and serve the interest of, society. This ambition should not be interpreted as merely tactical. It can well have a sincere intent and a kind of maturing effect; the associations become more and more inclined to see their own sphere of interest as part of the whole.

The dominance of objectivity and the reduced importance of agitation is a sign that, to a growing extent, associations adapt their conduct to certain rules of the game in official life. The rules are that an association—apart from the negotiating situation—shall express its influence only on an advisory plane directed at the preparatory and administrative levels, and not aimed directly at the government and Riksdag's decision-making apparatus. This influence shall be brought to bear by means of persuasion through convincing argument, not through threats, blackmail or heavy pressure. The association which breaks these rules runs the risk of damaging its reputation and, hence, reducing its basic influence.

To a great extent the associations fulfill their functions in an efficient, and from the point of view of the general public, worthwhile way. Yet, there is a risk especially bound up with their aggregation and expert functions: that the contacts between the associations and the state institutions will be removed from any official and political control; a risk of a fraternity of experts, tending to technocratize questions of political values. This is the seed of truth lying at the bottom of the criticism of "Harpsund democracy," criticism that in varying intensity continued during the 1960s and 1970s, both from the non-socialist Opposition and the new left.

There have been discussions in Opposition circles of constitutional regulation of the relations between the associations and the state. This would involve, for example, representation of the Opposition on planning boards or a strengthening of the position of the Riksdag in relation to the associations and government. But it was concluded that these measures were unlikely to make any real improvement in the situation. The best guarantee against misuse of the influence of the associations is probably a lively official debate and a unification of the divisions which have split the Opposition for so long—something for which only the Opposition, itself, can be responsible.

Finally, there is good reason to ask whether Sweden has a corporate political system. Gunnar Heckscher, in his pioneering work, *The State and the Associations,* launched the phrase "free corporatism" to describe a system which, in his opinion, is characterized by far-reaching cooperation between the state and the associations. This operates not only in the form of public activity with official authorities, but also in private combinations and cooperation between associations with opposing interests in an attempt to combat state interference. Heckscher's perspective was dominated by the Saltsjöbaden negotiations and the associations' active involvement in agricultural regulations and war-time administration.

Some of his observations are still valid, but a good deal has changed since then. With the exception of agriculture and wage disputes in the civil service, negotiated settlements between the state and the associations have been replaced by informal non-binding agreements. Within these two negotiating areas, the government is no longer one of the negotiating parties. The responsibility of the associations for administrative functions has nearly ceased, even in the area of agricultural regulations. To call the relationship between the state and the associations "free corporatism" is a question of taste; to my mind, the phrase is somewhat misleading.

The most important point is that the associations—apart from the two previously mentioned cases— have primarily an advisory position. That is not to say, however, that their basic influence has declined; the influence of certain associations has increased. What is undeniable is that the power of the government has strongly increased. This expansion of power has, for example, had a diminishing effect on the influence of the trade and industrial associations. It is the relative importance of the Opposition parties and their position in the Riksdag which has declined most drastically. Between the wars and immediately after the last war, the leading Opposition parties were involved in discussions of all important questions, and during the war they were part of the national coalition government. After the break-up of the coalition in 1957 the Opposition parties have been largely excluded from direct political influence. Apart from the Opposition, the government and the Social-Democratic party stand as the power center, and it is clear that favored associations, to a certain extent, share in this power. Participation in power is perhaps no longer visible in corporative form, but it is there all the same. Some of the big associations, in particular LO, have such a strong basic influence that they have no need to mobilize their variable influence, since the government typically anticipates their wishes.

Interest Group Lobbying: Canada and the United States

By ROBERT PRESTHUS

ABSTRACT: Political theory usually assumes that interest groups play an essential role in democratic polities, providing an instrument through which the individual may participate to some extent in the making of public policy. Such groups synthesize, express and provide technical and ideological support for collective social demands which provide critical inputs into the political subsystem. Despite these contributions, interest groups are often regarded as both normatively and operationally marginal. Using cross-national survey data on interest group lobbying, the present study shows that group activities are common in two political systems. Regardless of variations in political culture and political structure and despite variations in group legitimacy and the intensity of lobbying, groups play a critical linkage role, bringing into concert the private and public sectors of North American society.

Robert Presthus is well known for his work in political and organizational behavior. Editor of Administrative Science Quarterly for a decade, he is also a member of the editorial boards of Theory and Decision and the Comparative Politics Series and editor of the series Behavioral Studies in Political Science. His books include The Organizational Society (1962), Men at the Top: A Study in Community Power (1964), Elite Accommodation in Canadian Politics (1973) and Elites in the Policy Process (1974). University Professor of Political Science at York University, he is presently on leave as Visiting Professor of Politics at Sussex and Göteborg Universities.

This article is a revised version of a chapter included in Professor Presthus' Elites in the Policy Process (New York: Cambridge University Press, 1974). The data reported here are from a comparative study of interest group influence in the policy-making process, based upon random samples of legislators, senior officials and interest group directors in Ottawa, Quebec, Ontario and British Columbia and in Washington, D.C., Michigan, Louisiana and Washington. Professor Presthus is greatly indebted to the Canada Council for funding the study.

THE political behavior of interest groups often includes direct, personal attempts to influence governmental elites. Although such activities are usually called lobbying, the term is variously defined and considerably affected by the norms of any given political culture. In Canada lobbying is often regarded pejoratively as the attempt to sell influence on behalf of a private company, often on the basis of connections made during previous service in government. In the minds of governmental elites, the representations of interest group directors and their agents are apparently of a different order. Among Americans, lobbying is much more broadly defined as virtually any attempt to influence public policy, not only within government but among other groups and the public, as well. Its legitimacy is rarely questioned—among political elites, at least—provided certain rules of the game are followed.

POLITICAL CULTURE AND ATTITUDES TOWARD LOBBYING

These inapposite views of a practice which is common in both political systems reflect certain cross-national differences regarding the nature of society, relationships between private groups and the state, the structure of authority and the role of political elites. The survival in Canada of certain puritan residues and the tenuous emergence of a critical scholarship concerning interest group politics tend to reinforce these conditions.[1] One useful

1. Perhaps there is something about Anglo-Saxon political culture and parliamentary systems which explains this condition, since it was not until 1955 that the first article on British interest groups appeared. W. J. M. MacKenzie, "Pressure Groups: the Conceptual Framework," *Political Studies* 3 (October 1955), pp. 247–255.

way of conceptualizing such differences is in terms of a consensual model—Canada—versus a conflict model—United States—of social theory. English Canada inherited from Britain an organic, corporatist social philosophy in which the role of private groups is equally legitimate as that of government and equally essential to wise policy making. From Confederation onward, the often invidious dichotomy which Americans have made between government and society has rarely appeared. Government has obviously been put to the service of private groups in both systems, but in Canada the process has been more positively legitimated.

Essentially collectivist, corporatism is a conception of society in which government freely delegates many of its functions, and much of its largesse, to private groups which enjoy both normative and functional legitimacy in the political system. In this appreciation, collective goals are usually seen as prior to those of any discrete individual or interest. Government is not regarded as some alien apparatus requiring constant surveillance by outsiders, but instead the usual expectation is that political elites will generally act in the larger community interest. Because interest groups and their agents are integral parts of the system, lobbying is not required to ensure that government does its duty. Instead, political elites enjoy a legitimacy and autonomy rarely experienced in the individualistic, American milieu where a historic fear of government and a highly pragmatic ethic have meant that groups are expected to compete in advancing their disparate interests. In Canada citizens tend to believe in a transcendental public interest, while in the United

States, this honorific condition is defined as the outcome of the clash among opposing private interests.

The sympathetic reception which corporatism ensures for Canadian groups, however, is challenged by other pervasive values. Deferential patterns of authority—the Old Tory conception of leadership—in which leaders in every sphere enjoy considerable autonomy and an elitist philosophy of higher education tend to inhibit political participation generally, including that of interest groups.[2] The parliamentary system, which represents in some sense the crystallization of such norms, lodges decisive power in some fifteen to twenty ministers whose critical role is rivalled by that of only a few senior bureaucrats. Even back-benchers are largely excluded from policy determination. It is not surprising, then, that Canadian politics is a system in which the ordinary citizen "gives full power of attorney to a small committee each four years or so, well knowing that virtually nothing he can do in the interval will have much effect on the group to whom he has given his blank check."[3]

THE STRUCTURE OF INTEREST GROUP LOBBYING

Comparative research indicates that these opposing conceptions have only a limited impact upon the operational demands of the Canadian political system for *corps intermediaries* which can not only "drag the individual into the torrent of social life,"[4] but enable the political system to synthesize the various interests, expectations and expertise existing among the great institutional sectors of society. Although some observers have concluded that American interest groups and lobbyists are not very effective politically, it seems probable that their role in bringing together so-called private and public spheres is a necessary element in any complex society. Our data suggest, moreover, that such groups are often effective in the narrower sense of exerting lobbying influence in discrete issues. Certainly, legislators who interact continually with them believe they are effective. Forty percent of our American sample ($N = 249$) maintain that "lobbyists have too much influence in state legislatures." Precisely two-thirds of them attest to having been influenced either "frequently" or "occasionally" to the extent of "coming to agree with the position" advocated by a lobbyist. Insofar as legitimacy and interaction are a condition of influence, we find that four-fifths of these politicians trust lobbyists "all or most of the time," while a similar proportion interacts with lobbyists "frequently"—that is, twice a week or more. Canadian members of Parliament (MPs) tend to rank lower on these dimensions, but—as subsequent tables will suggest—they behave similarly.

Before comparing legislators, it may be useful to indicate the cross-national pattern of interest group lobbying. In order to ease any ambivalence which directors

2. For an analysis of Canadian political culture, see, Robert Presthus, *Elite Accommodation in Canadian Politics* (New York: Cambridge University Press, 1973), chap. 1.

3. A. R. Lower, *Canadians in the Making* (Toronto: University of Toronto Press, 1958), p. 281.

4. Emile Durkheim, *The Division of Labor in Society* (New York: Free Press, 1947), p. 28.

might feel toward the question, we put the item in a neutral form: "Some observers believe it is fairly common for groups to engage men with special knowledge and contacts to represent their organizations on matters of special importance. Has your organization ever done this?" We indicated that such assistance might have included legal aid, public relations advice and fund-raising activities. Responses are presented in table 1.

It appears that lobbying among Canadian groups is considerably less frequent than it is among American groups. Some one-third—compared with almost sixty percent among Americans—indicate that they have engaged lobbyists at one time or another. Whereas business groups rank highest in Canada, welfare groups are at the top in the United States, followed by labor and business. Some question is raised about this conclusion, however, by the distribution for legal aid, which may often be a form of lobbying. For example, when a lawyer prepares an *ex parte* brief for a legislative committee his activity may reasonably be defined as lobbying. The Canadian data provide some evidence of the extent to which legal aid may actually represent one or another form of lobbying. One category of lobbying refers to the function performed by the individual hired by the group, the other to his occupational role. As table 1 indicates, 62 groups employed lawyers under the first category, yet, a total of 92 individuals—not shown—were defined occupationally as lawyers. If we assume that the 30 lawyers who were not providing legal services were engaged in direct lobbying, the total proportion of individuals employed in a

TABLE 1

INTEREST GROUP USE OF LOBBYISTS AND OTHER SERVICES

PROPORTION USING EACH SERVICE (%)

SERVICE	Business		Labor		Professional Educational		Welfare		Altruistic*		All Groups	
	United States	Canada	United States	Canada	United States	Canada	United States	Canada	United States	Canada	United States	Canada
Lobbying	61	41	63	32	57	28	77	30	42	30	(153) 59	(64) 32
Legal	11	28	21	49	17	26	8	15	30	13	(41) 16	(62) 30
Financial	23	13	11	11	15	22	8	18	11	31	(36) 14	(30) 19
Publicity	4	9	—	—	14	8	—	18	3	9	(14) 6	(16) 9
Other	1	7	5	8	6	17	8	19	13	17	(13) 5	(28) 14
Number	(75)	(46)	(56)	(37)	(66)	(48)	(13)	(33)	(25)	(36)		

* Because the N's in each category are too small for generalization, we have again combined ethnic, religious, fraternal-service and social-recreational types under the heading of altruistic groups; professional and educational groups have also been merged.

lobbying role increases to about 40 percent for the Canadian sample.

Some further evidence of the extent of cross-national lobbying is provided by a case study item which asked directors to list the types of help they had enlisted in working toward some important goal. Among American directors—numbering 358—who had used such special assistance, fully three-fourths had hired a lobbyist. Among their Canadian peers—numbering 200—exactly the same proportion had done so.

These data involved only hired lobbyists. When we asked directors about the extent to which they themselves lobby, we find that about 70 percent in both samples lobby from time to time. Such combined information indicates that lobbying is fairly common among both sets of directors, but that American respondents are somewhat more likely to rely upon this tactic.

BUREAUCRATIC PERCEPTIONS OF LOBBYING EFFECTIVENESS

A condition bearing directly upon lobbying effectiveness—when the term is broadly defined—involves the extent to which senior officials believe interest groups play an important role in policy making in their agencies. Such cohesion can be measured by a scale of items, as presented in table 2. Cross-nationally one-quarter of high-level officials (N = 445) declare that relevant groups are "an integral part" of policy making in their agency. Another 35 percent indicate that the "assumed reaction of relevant groups is noted" in making such policy, while the remaining 40 percent consign groups to only a marginal role. It is often maintained that groups are more effective at the state, rather than the federal, level.[5] These data provide some evidence for the generalization, although among the American regions only Louisiana shows a marked variation in this regard. Another bit of evidence is useful. When officials are asked to rank the effectiveness of groups in agency policy making using another criterion, 45 and 31 percent of Washington and Louisiana respondents say they are "highly significant," compared with 23 and 17 percent for Michigan and Washington, D.C., respectively.

Our research indicates that the legitimacy imputed to groups is highly and positively associated with the influence which officials impute to groups. The four American regions reveal similar gradients

5. Lester Milbrath, *The Washington Lobbyist* (Chicago, Ill.: Rand McNally, 1967), p. 302.

TABLE 2

SALIENCE OF INTEREST GROUPS TO AGENCIES, IN A GENERAL POLICY CONTEXT

RELATIONSHIP	PROPORTION IN EACH CATEGORY (%)									
	D.C.	Ottawa	Louisiana	Quebec	Michigan	Ontario	Washington	British Columbia	United States	Canada
Integral part of agency	17	16	37	25	18	33	21	30	23	26
Assumed reaction noted	31	35	33	47	38	26	41	26	37	34
One among many factors	44	41	25	9	36	37	32	44	34	33
Little or no effect	8	8	6	19	8	4	5	1	7	8
Number	(87)	(87)	(52)	(32)	(50)	(46)	(56)	(35)	(245)	(200)

in this respect: half of the officials in Washington and Louisiana rank groups as being "highly legitimate," compared with 38 percent for federal, and only 26 percent for Michigan, officials. Among legislators, however, this relationship is much weaker. Explanations probably include the fact that group interactions with officials are more functionally specific and client-oriented, compared with those among legislators.

THE EFFECTIVENESS OF LOBBYING

We saw that lobbying is the most common among several kinds of assistance used by interest groups. The vital question is the effectiveness of this activity. Careful observers have concluded that neither lobbying nor interest groups are very effective at the federal level in the United States.[6] On the other hand, there is considerable evidence to the contrary.[7] Our research tends to support the view that such groups and their agents can play a decisive role under some conditions. Certainly, interaction between directors and political elites is continuous, and most governmental elites in our sample maintain that groups play a salient role.[8]

6. Among others, see, Milbrath, *Washington Lobbyists*, p. 354; Raymond Bauer, I. Pool and L. Dexter, *American Business and Public Policy* (New York: Atherton, 1967), pp. 111, 334, 340.

7. See, for example, Grant McConnell, *Private Power and American Democracy* (New York: Knopf, 1966), p. 339; Robert Brady, *Business As A System of Power* (New York: Columbia University Press, 1943); Robert Engler, *The Politics of Oil* (Chicago, Ill.: University of Chicago Press, 1967).

8. One piece of ad hoc evidence from a senior official in the federal Bureau of Manpower and Budget is germane: "Any smart bureaucrat in Washington knows you don't any longer make any policy move without checking with the public interest groups. They have developed highly specialized and

One rough index of lobbying effectiveness is provided by comparing outcomes in the case study issue between groups who employed lobbyists and those who did not. Among 265 American directors who did, 53 percent achieved either "complete" or "mainly" levels of success, compared with 44 percent of those who did not. More systematic evidence is provided by an item regarding the extent to which governmental elites indicate that they have been influenced by lobbyists. The footnote to table 3 indicates the item and the scale used in determining the cross-national distribution.

The association is strongly positive and statistically significant. The data show that the largest proportion of both Canadian and American respondents interact at the highest level of frequency— that is, twice a week or more— and that such interaction culminates in a high level of influence as experienced in direct personal contact with lobbyists. It is clear also that, although Canadian elites rank lower than their American peers on interaction, they are very similar regarding the influence they attribute to lobbyists. Indeed, at the low level of interaction, their responses are strikingly more consistent with the expected theoretical drift, which assumes that lobbyist influence increases with interaction.

Given the comparatively greater influence of officials in the parliamentary system and the attending weaker influence of MP's, one would expect some cross-national

effective analytic programs so they know what's going on. They have their eyes and ears open across town so they know who's thinking what. They have beautiful relations with Congress and very effective lobbies. If you really want to get something done, you go to them."

TABLE 3
PERSONAL CONTACT WITH LOBBYISTS AND INFLUENCE: LEGISLATORS AND BUREAUCRATS

INFLUENCE*	FREQUENCY OF INTERACTION (%)							
	High		Medium		Low		Number	
	United States	Can-ada	United States	Can-ada	United States	Can-ada	United States	Can-ada
High	50	52	48	38	11	15	(201)	(161)
Medium	39	35	35	40	50	22	(184)	(164)
Low	11	13	18	22	39	63	(77)	(52)
Number	(291)	(202)	(101)	(144)	(70)	(131)	(462)	(477)

NOTES: *American sample:* χ^2 = .0001; K's tau b = .23; Gamma = .38. *Canadian sample:* χ^2 significant at .0001; K's tau b = .23; Gamma = .33.

* This index of influence is designed by weighting each level of lobbyist influence; assigning one point for "coming to question one's position" as a result of a lobbyist's appeal; two points for "changing one's position toward that advocated by the lobbyist"; and three points for "coming to agree with his position on an issue." A temporal factor was also included, depending upon whether each of these results had occurred "frequently," "occasionally" or only "seldom or rarely."

variation along these lines; our findings—not shown—indicate that this is so. Just over half of American legislators, compared with only one-quarter of Canadian, rank at the high level of experienced influence. Among officials the distribution indicates that one-third of respondents in both systems rank at the high level.

COMPARATIVE LOBBYING EFFECTIVENESS AMONG GROUPS

Another perspective of lobbying effectiveness is provided by tracing the extent to which directors believe they have been effective in their attempts to influence legislators and officials through personal contacts. Here we are looking at lobbying from the vantage point of those attempting to bring influence to bear on policy making. The same item is used as in the previous table. Although they are subjective, it is worth noting that such perceptions have operational effects. As I. W. Thomas once said: "If men define situations as real, they are real in their consequences." If directors believe their attempts at influence are effective, we may assume that—in a kind of self-confirming prophecy—they will actually have greater impact. Table 4 presents the cross-national distribution.

The data indicate that lobbying is seen to be less effective in the parliamentary system. Canadian directors rank lower on perceived effectiveness in every context, except for altruistic groups, where the number is so small—seven—that little weight can be placed upon the evidence. Canadian labor's weak position compared with that of United States labor is particularly evident. This condition is explicit in evidence regarding legitimacy wherein only 8 percent of labor directors in our Canadian sample, compared with one-quarter of business directors, believe that legislators approve their efforts to influence governmental policy. Among their American peers, however, fully 80 percent—compared

TABLE 4

LOBBYING EFFECTIVENESS AMONG INTEREST GROUPS, UNITED STATES AND CANADA

PROPORTION OF EFFECTIVENESS BY TYPE OF GROUP (%)

EFFECTIVENESS*	Business		Professional Educational		Labor		Welfare		Altruistic		Number	
	United States	Canada	United States	Canada	United States	Canada	United States	Canada	United States	Canada	United States	Canada
High	70	33	59	24	48	16	38	18	25	57	(215)	(35)
Medium	20	29	24	32	30	37	35	39	25	29	(99)	(45)
Low	10	38	18	45	22	47	28	43	50	14	(86)	(70)
Number	(121)	(34)	(114)	(38)	(79)	(19)	(29)	(28)	(57)	(7)	(400)	(150)

NOTES: *American sample:* χ^2 significant at .0001; Gamma = .22. *Canadian sample:* χ^2 = significant at .08; Gamma = −.11.
* Effectiveness is based upon the weighted index of lobbying influence for the combined legislative and bureaucratic sample.

with 82 percent of business directors—believe that legislators regard their attempts to influence them as legitimate "all or most of the time."

Such variations probably reflect differences in public attitudes toward labor in the two societies. More recent industrialization in Canada—attended by the fact that only one-third of her labor force is unionized, compared with about 45 percent in the United States—is probably a factor. In addition, American labor also benefits from the more egalitarian social values existing in the United States, compared with the antiegalitarian tendencies often attributed to Canada.[9] Such tendencies are manifest in Canadian public opinion polls, which for the past two decades have shown that only one-fifth of Canadian adults believe that labor should play an active role in politics. Moreover, the pervasiveness of this opinion is shown by the fact that the proportion of union members who share this view is only marginally lower.[10]

Other aspects of table 4 suggest that business and professional educational groups in the United States enjoy the greatest effectiveness, as measured here. Insofar as shared values and occupational backgrounds provide a productive basis for accommodation between governmental and private elites, the fact that American and Canadian legislatures are manned mainly by businessmen and lawyers may underlie this condition. It is interest-

9. See, for example, John Porter, *The Vertical Mosaic* (Toronto: University of Toronto Press, 1965); and his "Canadian National Character," *Cultural Affairs* 5 (Spring 1969), pp. 46–50.

10. See polls dated 30 November 1955, 12 March 1960 and 26 July 1967.

ing in this regard that no other Western nation approaches Canada and the United States in the high proportion of lawyers in their national parliaments. In the Canadian milieu the differences among groups are just under the significance criterion usually used—that is, .05. Nevertheless, business and professional educational groups rank at the top of the scale, although in every case—except altruistic groups—the distribution clusters at the low point of the scale.

The explanation for the dramatic cross-national variation found here probably lies in the different conditions of group access in the two systems. The parliamentary system, as noted, tends to lodge power in the cabinet and senior bureaucracy. A tradition of official secrecy exists which also inhibits interaction. Even back-benchers, who are integral parts of the constitutional system, have little influence in policy making. Yet, the evidence suggests that it is not only access into the system which presents the major problem for Canadian lobbyists, but the difficulty of achieving their goals despite the opportunity to be heard. For many groups it seems that access tends to be ritualistic rather than operationally decisive. Even though the functional need for interest group participation is patent in Canada, the generalist tradition and the concentration of power in the cabinet and high bureaucracy tend to blunt this common requisite of modern government. As a result, directors are likely to perceive themselves as being less efficacious than their American counterparts who enjoy a political environment which is both structurally and normatively more sympathetic.

COMPARATIVE POLITICAL RESOURCES OF DIRECTORS

We are generalizing here, however, from the entire cross-national sample. When directors are differentiated according to their political resources, and the association between resources and effectiveness is determined, it becomes clear that some one-quarter to one-third of groups in both systems monopolize political access and effectiveness. First, it is useful to indicate the comparative distribution of directors' resources, by group and cross-nationally. Table 5 presents the evidence.

It is clear that business, professional educational and welfare directors enjoy the greatest amount of political resources. Socioeconomic status—based upon education and occupation—felt legitimacy, access to governmental elites, income, membership in three-or-more voluntary groups and perceived lobbying influence, all find business directors ranking equally or higher than others. Professional—that is, law, medicine, dentistry—and educational directors rank next on most of these dimensions, followed closely by welfare directors.[11] Altruistic and labor directors rank significantly lower on most counts. The salient point, however, is the difference such patterns make for political effectiveness. Table 6 throws some light on this question. In order to meet the caveat that

11. The welfare category in this research included directors of both public and private social welfare groups, including such well-financed charity groups as the United Fund and the American Cancer Society. This fact probably explains, in part, the high ranking of welfare directors on several of these dimensions.

TABLE 5

COMPARATIVE SOCIOECONOMIC AND PSYCHOPOLITICAL RESOURCES OF DIRECTORS

PROPORTION RANKING HIGH* (%)

RESOURCE	Business		Labor		Professional Educational		Welfare		Altruistic†		All Groups	
	United States	Canada	United States	Canada	United States	Canada	United States	Canada	United States	Canada	United States	Canada
A. SOCIOECONOMIC												
SES	84	76	38	30	92	86	90	81	76	58	78	66
Experience	29	21	40	24	15	15	30	16	19	18	25	19
Income	84	58	50	18	65	38	52	30	35	12	62	31
Membership	67	57	40	30	67	60	63	50	53	33	60	46
Access	70	31	54	13	63	21	63	18	40	16	58	20
B. PSYCHOPOLITICAL												
Legitimacy	61	44	32	24	52	44	58	43	44	47	49	40
Cooperative ethic	90	72	81	58	88	67	86	70	80	61	86	66
Commitment	48	43	39	22	49	38	46	52	41	47	45	40
Persuasiveness	70	36	48	16	59	28	38	18	25	3	48	20

* High = SES, based upon education and occupation, levels I and II, using Hollingshead index, *Social Class and Mental Illness;* income, $15,000 and over; experience, ten years or more as director; membership, three or more voluntary groups; interaction with governmental elites frequently—twice a week or more. Regarding psychopolitical resources, high refers to the following conditions: legitimacy, the proportion ranking "always" regarding perceptions of legislators' approval of their group; cooperative ethic, rejection of the proposition that legislators are "competitors in a struggle to shape public policy"; commitment, proportion of members "intensely" identified with the group's goals; persuasiveness, proportion ranking at the "high" level on a weighted index designed according to the influence each director felt he had exerted over governmental elites through lobbying.

† These are so-called "noneconomic" groups, including ethnic, religious, fraternal and recreational types.

TABLE 6
POLITICAL ACTIVISM, DIRECTORS' RESOURCES AND GROUP EFFECTIVENESS

EFFECTIVENESS*	COMPARATIVE DISTRIBUTION OF POLITICAL ACTIVISM (%)					
	High		Medium		Low	
	United States (246)	Canada (105)	United States (44)	Canada (47)	United States (39)	Canada (58)
High	80	67	74	67	57	36
Medium	17	28	24	19	38	43
Low	3	4	3	14	5	21
Number	(153)	(57)	(72)	(28)	(21)	(20)

EFFECTIVENESS*	COMPARATIVE DISTRIBUTION OF DIRECTOR'S RESOURCES (%)					
	High		Medium		Low	
	United States	Canada	United States	Canada	United States	Canada
High	41	36	15	17	11	23
Medium	46	55	54	67	33	69
Low	14	9	31	17	56	8
Number	(22)	(22)	(14)	(12)	(8)	(13)

NOTES: *American sample:* χ^2 = not significant at .05; K's tau b = .13; .36; and .36, respectively; Gamma = .27; .54; and .58, respectively. *Canadian sample:* χ^2 = significant at .05; K's tau b = .9; .11; and −.18, respectively; Gamma = .33; .19; and −.18, respectively.

* Index based on lobbying effectiveness.

some groups with important resources do not use them, we have controlled for political activism—defined as the frequency with which directors attempt to influence governmental elites.

Although the association is not significant, the American distribution is nicely linear in the expected direction. Four-fifths of those directors who rank high on both political activism and resources—compared with only one-quarter of those who rank low on activism but high on resources—also rank high on effectiveness. The strong correlations, especially in the low sector of the table, indicate that the variables used to test the relationship are appropriate. The dramatic cross-national variation in the proportions of directors in the high activism category is noteworthy.

Turning to the Canadian sample, the association is statistically significant and positive in the high and medium sectors of the table, although not as regular as among the American group. Two-thirds of those directors who rank high on activism and resources—compared with only 17 percent of those who rank low on activism, but high on resources—also rank high on effectiveness. The correlation, however, becomes negative in the low sector, in striking contrast to the American distribution where gamma was a very strong .58. In general, then, we can say that, while political activism often has an important intervening effect, the variation in directors' resources shown in table 5 seems to have a decisive impact on political effectiveness when measured by the amount of success that directors believe they have achieved in influencing government elites. On the whole the relationship is much stronger among American directors, reflecting in part the effects of political structure and political culture—more favorable to lobbying in the American context.

SELECTIVITY AND LOBBYING EFFECTIVENESS

In addition to the advantages they gain simply by being highly active, it may be that such directors augment their effectiveness by focusing to a greater extent than their less active peers upon more rewarding activities. At the same time, the fact that the association among activism, resources and effectiveness is not always as positive as expected may mean that some less active directors are more selective in their political activities. Some kind of equalizer effect may partially explain the inconclusive relationships found earlier. Table 7 provides a test of this possibility using the group service designated as "most important" by directors, again controlling for activism.

The data suggest that highly active directors do indeed focus more intensely upon providing information on bills to legislators. Two-thirds of American, and 45 percent

of highly active Canadian, directors rank high on this service—compared with only 30 and 11 percent, respectively, among those who rank low. The differences are strongly significant for both samples, and the correlation values are high, especially for the Canadian sample.

It is clear from the comparative data that Canadian directors tend to be less selective in their lobbying activities. Even though Canadian MP's rank information on bills and issues as the most important group service, the overwhelming majority of directors rank low on this activity. In part this is a built-in structural condition, in that backbenchers are not always privy to the details of forthcoming legislation. On the other hand, since MP's value such information so highly, directors are missing a bet by not devoting more of their time to it.

Following the hunch that active groups are more likely to provide rewarding services, one would also expect American legislators to rank receiving information on bills as the most valuable group service. When this is checked, we find that the largest single proportion of them—one-half—do rank this service as most valuable. On the other

TABLE 7

POLITICAL ACTIVISM AND VALUATION OF SERVICES TO LEGISLATORS

TIME SPENT INFORMING LEGISLATORS ABOUT BILLS	POLITICAL ACTIVISM (%)					
	High		Medium		Low	
	United States	Can-ada	United States	Can-ada	United States	Can-ada
High	64	45	40	22	30	11
Medium	20	11	40	30	40	10
Low	17	44	20	49	30	78
Number	(160)	(33)	(211)	(120)	(300)	(402)

NOTES: *American sample:* $\chi^2 = .0006$; K's tau $b = .21$; Gamma $= .33$. *Canadian sample:* $\chi^2 = .0006$; K's tau $b = .29$; Gamma $= .49$.

hand, the finding also suggests one reason that the relationship among activism, resources and effectiveness was so inconclusive in one of the earlier tables: some directors may spend relatively little time in political interaction, but such time may be devoted mainly to providing information to legislators.

A final indication of comparative group effectiveness is provided by an analysis of case study outcomes, differentiated by types of groups. A caveat is required here in that this evidence is based upon a single issue in the political life of these groups, in which their respective goals probably varied considerably in difficulty. Cross-nationally, professional, business and welfare groups rank highest on this effectiveness scale. Variation among all groups is statistically significant in the United States, but not in Canada. Labor, as suggested earlier, ranks very low, along with educational groups. Canadian labor groups are much less effective than their American counterparts. This ranking is dramatically opposed to the high effectiveness attributed to labor by governmental elites, especially in the United States where fully 60 percent of all legislators placed labor groups at the top of the scale, with professional groups a remote second—with one-quarter. Canadian labor directors appear to be more accurate in their perception of labor's role, since only 8 percent indicate that they believe legislators regard labor's attempts to influence them as legitimate, compared with fully 80 percent in the United Staes. It is clear that ideology shapes such perceptions, since the largest proportion of business directors in the United States rank labor as "most powerful," while the largest proportion of labor directors rank business as "most powerful."

CONCLUSIONS

This brief survey of comparative interest group lobbying suggests that political culture and structure have some impact upon the effectiveness of group efforts to influence governmental policy. Even though the functional need for group participation in policy making ultimately proves decisive, it seems clear that certain Canadian norms inhibit group participation in the political system. Corporatism nourishes group legitimacy and a positive view of government, but it manifests itself at times in the assumption that political elites will act in the community interest without much need for group surveillance. Deferential patterns of authority reinforce this quasi-participative ethic by delegating considerable autonomy to governmental elites.[12] Meanwhile, the elitist cast of higher education inhibits the emergence of articulate countervailing authority structures.[13] Parliamentary structure has similar effects, lodging decisive political influence in a small minority of elected officials, reinforced by a talented higher bureaucracy which tends to monopolize information through its cooptation of alternative sources of knowledge in the universities. Parliamentary committees, which might have provided a counterpoise, are relatively undeveloped. Despite such barriers to a lively group politics, interaction between governmental and group elites is pervasive; the former

12. For evidence regarding Canada's quasi-participative political culture, see, Presthus, *Canadian Politics*, chap. 2.
13. Porter, *Vertical Mosaic*, p. 371.

have a generally positive view of group utility and legitimacy; lobbying is the most common among several aids that directors enlist in supporting their claims; and some one-quarter to one-third of all groups are highly active politically.

In the United States the system of interest group politics is more fully developed. Explanations include a more participative political culture; the separation-of-powers apparatus which provides more, and more effective, points of group access; and greater wealth and occupational differentiation which encourage a more intensive and well-supported interest group structure. As a result, lobbying activities are more common and group effectiveness seems to be generally higher, particularly regarding business and welfare groups. Although labor is only marginally effective in the American system,[14] it is clearly more effective than its Canadian counterpart. American directors tend to have more political resources, which apparently rest

upon a generally higher level of felt political efficacy. Since several of their hard resources—for example, directors' education and occupation, experience, age, organization—are often no greater than those of Canadian directors, one must attribute this condition to cultural differences, including American optimism, contrasted with the somewhat pessimistic strain apparent in Canadian thought and literature.

---

14. This judgment requires qualification. Perhaps it is more accurate to say that American labor's effectiveness rests mainly in electoral politics, which does not necessarily pay off in issue-by-issue effectiveness between elections. An example is the well-known disenchantment of the AFL-CIO with Richard Nixon's price and wage policy, despite labor's electoral support. Insofar as it is true that parties are primarily concerned with winning elections, leaving substantive issues to be fought out ad hoc, this distinction may be useful. In the immediate context, of course, our conclusion about labor's marginal effectiveness is based upon the criterion used in the study reported here—that is, the success of labor directors in case study issues.

Interests and Institutions in the Netherlands: An Assessment by the People and by Parliament

By Hans Daalder and Galen A. Irwin

ABSTRACT: This article analyzes the background of the very dense and highly institutionalized network of interest groups in the Netherlands. This well-integrated system has recently come under some strain, as a large number of new action groups have sprung up next to the political parties and the older, more established interest groups. On the basis of surveys among members of the Dutch Parliaments in 1968 and 1972 and with a cross-section of the population in 1972, the article analyzes the relative influence—both actual and desired—which members of Parliament and the population ascribe to cabinet ministers, expert members of Parliament, civil servants and party executives; to the more important economic interest groups of employers, workers, farmers and retailers; to the churches; and to voters, action groups, newspapers, radio and television and public opinion polls.

Hans Daalder is Professor of Political Science at the University of Leiden. Previously, he taught at the University of Amsterdam and the Institute of Social Studies in' The Hague. He has been a Fellow at the Center for Advanced Study in the Behavioral Sciences in Stanford, California (1966–1967) and at the Netherlands Institute for Advanced Study in the Social Sciences and Humanities (1972–1973). His major publications are in the field of European comparative politics.

Galen A. Irwin is Senior Lecturer at the University of Leiden. After receiving his Ph.D. from Florida State University, he taught at the University of Iowa. Dr. Irwin was a Fellow at the Netherlands Institute for Advanced Study in the Social Sciences and Humanities in 1972–1973.

This article was conceived when Professor Daalder and Dr. Irwin were Fellows of the Netherlands Institute for Advanced Study, Wassenaar, in 1972–1973. The data come from: (1) a study of the Dutch Parliament undertaken in 1968 with the support of a grant from the Netherlands Association for the Advancement of Pure Scientific Research (ZWO) and (2) from a mass survey and a survey among members of Parliament undertaken in 1972 as part of a wider international study of political representation. The latter study has been supported by the National Science Foundation in the United States, as well as by ZWO. The authors gladly acknowledge the considerable amount of work contributed by Sonja Hubée-Boonzaaijer, Jan Verhoef, Warren Miller, Jan Kooiman, Philip Stouthard, Felix Heunks and Jacques Thomassen in the preparation and execution of these two projects.

A HIGH level of formal interest group activity has been the inevitable concomitant of an increasingly activist state in an otherwise free society. Everywhere in the Western world the borderlines between state and society became increasingly blurred as industrialization took place and as government began to take increasingly specific actions to regulate the course of industrialization and its consequences. The growing relevance of state measures for private interests stimulated the latter to organize, to seek specific favors and to resist possibly adverse government actions. As the organization of one group often provoked the organization of countergroups, a myriad of social organizations have sprung up with increasingly complex relations to one another and to sections of the government bureaucracy. In the course of this development, society has become more heavily institutionalized and government, more diversified. These developments are not particular to the Netherlands.

THE STRONG INSTITUTIONALIZATION OF INTEREST GROUP POLITICS IN THE NETHERLANDS

In a comparative perspective the Netherlands have a very dense network of interest group organizations,[1] and these have highly institutionalized forms of access to the various organs of government.[2] A

variety of factors may account for this situation. The Netherlands is geographically a small country, which is very densely populated. Some 13,500,000 persons live pressed together on a land surface roughly the size of the state of Maryland. The short physical distances facilitate easy access to the seat of government in The Hague and increase the mutual visibility of like-oriented, as well as antagonistic, groups. The population, itself, is sufficiently large and heterogeneous to provide the basis for the organization of a large number of groups.

The political culture of the Netherlands has long been favorable to the view that politics is largely about the mutual adjustment of interests. Pluralism has ancient roots. In the loosely structured Republic of the Seven United Provinces, which existed from about 1579 to 1795, the Dutch elites learned of necessity about the politics of accommodation.[3] Ever since, there has been a distrust of strongly centralized political power, an emphasis on a collegial style of governing, a belief in proportionality rather than in simple majority decisions and great stress on the need to leave separate groups alone as much as possible.

These ancient traditions were reinforced by the development in the

---

1. See the data in Galen A. Irwin and Henk A. A. Molleman, "Political Participation in The Netherlands" (mimeographed, Wassenaar/Leiden), pp. 14 ff.

2. The most easily accessible sources in English are: Hans Daalder, "The Netherlands: Opposition in a Segmented Society," in *Political Oppositions in Western Democracies*, ed. Robert A. Dahl (New Haven, Conn.: Yale University Press, 1966), pp.

188–236; P. E. Kraemer, *The Societal State*, (Meppel: J. A. Boom en Zoon, 1966); Johan Goudsblom, *Dutch Society* (New York: Random House, 1967); Arend Lijphart, *The Politics of Accomodation: Pluralism and Democracy in The Netherlands* (Berkeley, Cal.: University of California Press, 1968); and John P. Windmuller, *Labor Relations in The Netherlands* (Ithaca, N.Y.: Cornell University Press, 1969).

3. This quote refers to the title of Arend Lijphart's study on Dutch politics referred to in note 2.

nineteenth and twentieth century of a system of strongly articulated minority subcultures which sought to organize their section of society from a particular ideological perspective. Calvinists, Catholics and, to a lesser extent, Socialists and Liberals formed powerful social organizations of their own which were gradually extended beyond church and party into all sectors of social life. This process of ideological segmentation—known in Dutch as *verzuiling*, which literally means pillarization—multiplied the number of active interest groups in any given social area. Separate schools, health centers and social welfare organizations were established for groups adhering to a particular belief system, and so were trade unions, employers' organizations, small businessmen's and retailers' associations and farmers' organizations. The process of ideological separatism has also been extended to the mass media, including radio and television. Since the organizations of a particular type shared many common interests, they usually developed patterns of— formal or informal—confederal cooperation among themselves. Nevertheless, no matter how strong the cooperation might be, the postulate of social autonomy has remained very strong. Through the collective weight of this plurality of organizations, the Dutch state became to some extent a common denominator—that is, a neutral and shared instrument of government through which the different ideological groups promoted their common interests. An equitable distribution of subsidies allows each group to go its own way on the basis of common standards.

This form of social organization was buttressed by the establish-ment of a system of parties based on the particular ideologies: (1) three religious parties—the Catholic People's Party, the Antirevolutionary Party and the Christian-Historical Union, the latter two both Calvinist—and (2) two non-religious parties—the Labour Party and the Liberal Party which represented, respectively, the non-religious left and right. As each of these parties consciously sought to represent the diverse social interests within their own ideological world, such interests have had a relatively secure access to the centers of legitimate decision making.

The representation of interest groups in the political system has been facilitated further by a number of constitutional factors in the Dutch political system. Since the arrival of general suffrage in 1917, elections have been organized strictly on the basis of party lists. Such a list system gives central party organs a strong voice in the rank ordering of candidates for election to Parliament. They have often nominated candidates who were associated with the more articulate interest groups in their own subculture so as to make their list more attractive to members of these groups. Because of the presence of many political parties, Dutch cabinets are inevitably coalition cabinets. These are formed after a delicate weighting of program demands, departmental portfolios and political personnel. The arduous process of constructing a coalition cabinet therefore gives interests an excellent opportunity to pose specific claims. There has been a considerable reluctance to establish specific clientele departments; however, within departments of government, political undersecretaries are being appointed in increasing numbers to oversee particular policies which happen to be dear to articulate groups in society.

The Dutch bureaucracy also offers many points of access. Its structure has traditionally been fairly loose. Although appointments and decisions on tenure and promotion are based on the merit principle, there is no central recruitment of civil servants based on competitive examinations. Each department, and even some of the more important sections within it, tend to recruit staff ad hoc. Although formal and informal codes prescribe a certain detachment of bureaucratic personnel from overly direct personal involvement with interest groups, bureaucratic specialization has forged strong informal links among specialized groups and subsections of the bureaucracy.

Finally, a more formal system of advisory bodies has sprung up which contributes strongly to the institutionalized access of interest groups to government. Such bodies are generally of mixed composition: they combine officials, independent academic experts and representatives of interest groups in a council which offers advice either on the request of the government or on its own initiative. Their variety and number is great, and their place in the system of policy making is secure. Advisory agencies of this type provide a constant flow of information. They guarantee high level access for groups and make government decisions more legitimate to them. Without them, government would falter.

THE RECENT REACTION AGAINST ROUTINE INSTITUTION-ALIZATION

This routinized pattern of interest group institutionalization has re-cently come under a certain strain. The prevailing accommodationist style has been supplemented, and occasionally supplanted, by direct pressure methods of more loosely structured groups. This new development is rooted in a number of factors.

Institutionalization, itself, meets with the dangers of success. As long as groups had to fight for recognition—as Catholics and Calvinists did for separate schools or Socialists for workers' rights—there was enthusiasm and easy identification. Routinized institutionalized policy making does not retain such an emotional hold, even though its collective impact on society may be larger than it was in the days of more militant contestation.

Recent social developments create new problems to which there is no immediate answer through institutionalization. There are many forgotten groups: the elderly; widows; the small shopkeepers or small farmers; the city poor, who may be the object of government services; and voluntary bodies who cannot organize themselves as easily. There is a definite reorientation in attitudes towards economic growth: while the phenomenon of growth is taken for granted, there is more debate on its negative aspects, as its positive benefits seem guaranteed. A host of ad hoc groups have sprung up in defense of the environment and in opposition to further industrialization and suburban sprawl. Television has brought the world into Dutch living rooms, and a large number of groups have come to plead for a reorientation of foreign policy in regard to the North Atlantic Treaty Organization (NATO) or to the third world, as well as for a reappraisal of all sorts of domestic problems.

There are now many thousands of such so-called action groups in the Netherlands. Their weak organizational base results in a high mortality rate among them. However, this is more than compensated for by the birth of new groups of the same type.[4]

The impact of these ad hoc groups is enhanced by a number of other factors. They often engage in flamboyant actions, such as demonstrations and occupation of university buildings, factories or even foreign consulates. They tend to direct their activities partly with an eye on the mass media, especially on television which lends itself more easily to the reporting of dramatized events than of the more complex issues of institutionalized politics. Direct action tactics have often proven a short cut to success. Learning from this example, more established groups have also occasionally resorted to this type of agitation, thus straining the more traditional accommodational style which characterized Dutch politics.

To some extent these developments have led to a reversal in the relation between parties and interest groups. At one time the position of parties was so securely established that all groups found it profitable to work through them. Now that direct actions have proven equally or more successful, even the more traditional institutionalized groups—such as trade unions, farmers' organizations and also the once fairly party-tied news media—find it profitable to go their separate ways. Whereas groups once courted parties, parties now often court groups—frequently, a rather pathetic pursuit.

This in turn has increased the volatility of the system, since neither voters nor party activists are as sure as they once were on the stand of parties. This factor has contributed to a process of fragmentation in the Dutch party system. Besides the five established parties and a number of smaller older dissident parties—such as the Communists and a few dissident Calvinist parties—a number of new political parties have sprung up. Although none of them has yet established a stable clientele of its own, movements such as the Pacifist-Socialist Party, Peasant Party, Democrats '66—a radical party which split off from the left-wing of the religious parties (PPR)—and Democratic Socialists '70—a dissident right-wing splinter from the socialist Labour Party—have collectively reduced the aggregate strength of the main system parties, particularly of the larger religious parties.[5] This in turn has destroyed the assumptions of the stable coalition politics of the five main system parties. A new plebiscitary style in politics poses a challenge to the habitual politics of accommodation.[6]

5. The total strength of the five main system parties declined from a high of 91.6 percent to a low point of 71.9 percent in 1971. At the time of the 1972 survey the distribution of the 150 seats in the Lower House of the Dutch Parliament was as follows—parties ranked from left to right: Communist Party, 6; Pacifist Socialist Party, 2; Radical Party, 2; Labour Party, 39; Democrats '66, 11; *Catholic People's Party*, 35; *Antirevolutionary Party*, 13; *Democratic Socialists '70*, 8; *Christian Historical Union*, 10; *Liberal Party (VVD)*, 16; and a further 8 seats for five right wing splinter groups. The governing parties at that time are those printed in italics.

6. Notably, the parties of the left have sought deliberately to force a polarization of politics at the expense of the religious parties by demanding that coalitions should be formed before, rather than after, an elec-

4. See, H. A. A. Molleman, "Who Are the Activists?" *Sociologica Neerlandica* 9 (1973).

In this state of flux it is important to investigate how members of Parliament and how the population at large see the relative influence on parliamentary decisions of the main actors of contemporary politics. How, in other words, do they see the relative position of ministers, members of Parliament and officials; of the main institutionalized interest groups of employers, workers, farmers and small retailers; and of the chief alternative instruments of political opinion—that is, ad hoc action groups, the mass media and public opinion surveys? What is their view on existing degrees of influence, and what changes—if any—would they like to see come about in their relative position to one another? We can present some material on this subject from two surveys conducted among members of Parliament (MPs), undertaken in 1968 and in 1972, and from a survey among a cross-section of the Dutch population conducted in 1972.

SOME SURVEY RESULTS CONCERNING INTEREST GROUPS

The 1968 findings

In several ways the 1968 study conducted among the members of the Dutch Lower House was exploratory in regard to interest groups;[7] as such, it included several open-ended questions along with some closed questions. One sees in table 1 that MPs feel that

interest groups are highly influential. More than three-fourths feel that interest groups have very much influence—or rather much—upon both governmental policy and upon the decisions taken in Parliament. Evaluation of the influence of interest groups on parties is regarded as somewhat less certain, with slightly more than one-fourth answering: "it depends."

When asked to indicate which three groups in the Netherlands were the most powerful, the MPs consistently mentioned the organized economic interests. More than 80 percent mentioned the trade unions; approximately 35 percent, banks and big business; about the same percentage, the employees; and some 45 percent, the farmers. All other groups were mentioned only sporadically.

Having influence or being powerful has both positive and negative aspects which are not properly accounted for if one asks only if groups are influential or which groups are the most influential. Members were also asked to mention which groups they felt were too influential and which had too little influence. More than 40 percent could not think of any group which had too much influence. The groups which were mentioned most often were again the economic interest groups: farmers, 31 percent; trade unions, 25 percent; industry and employers, 16 percent. These figures are considerably lower than those for the question of which were the most powerful groups and indicate that there are a relatively large number of MPs who apparently are satisfied with the influence which those groups exercise in fact.

On the other hand, approximately one-fourth of the members could

tion; thus, voters could give an actual mandate rather than apportion votes among parties which remain free to coalesce or not to coalesce after an election.

7. Any later references to opinions expressed by the members of Parliament refer to opinions of members of the Lower House only.

TABLE 1

DEGREE OF INFLUENCE OF INTEREST GROUPS AS VIEWED BY
MEMBERS OF THE DUTCH LOWER HOUSE, 1968*

	INFLUENCE ON PARLIAMENTARY DECISIONS (%)	INFLUENCE ON GOVERNMENT POLICY (%)	INFLUENCE ON POLITICAL PARTIES (%)
Very much or rather much influence	85.8	77.3	54.6
Fairly little or very little influence	10.0	15.6	16.3
No influence	0.7	1.4	0.7
It depends	3.5	3.5	26.2
No reply	—	2.1	2.1

NOTES: N = 141.

not mention a group which they felt had too little influence. For those who did mention one or more such groups, there were no groups which were consistently mentioned. The highest percentages were for the elderly—27 percent—and retailers —20 percent—whereas all other groups—including the relatively unorganized intellectuals, consumers, youth, the poor, people with inadequate housing and invalids, as well as the organized employers and labor unions—were named by less than 10 percent of the members.

Judged together, one does not get the impression that the members were particularly concerned about the position of interest groups in the system. There would appear to be considerable agreement on which groups are influential. There was no widespread feeling in 1968 that particular groups were either too influential or had too little power. The rather positive attitude toward interest groups is emphasized in the response to the direct question of whether Parliament would work better if it were possible to exclude interest groups from the Chamber. Only 30.5 percent—mainly concentrated among the secular parties on both sides of the spectrum—thought that this would be so. Some 27 percent thought it would make little difference, and 35.5 percent—in particular, Catholics and Calvinists— thought Parliament would be the poorer for it.

Despite these close connections, most members of Parliament do not regard themselves as representatives of groups. Only 28 percent responded positively when asked whether they regarded themselves as group representatives; however, when asked about the group which they felt they represented, their answers centered around poorly organized ones—such as the aged, consumers or persons with inadequate housing—rather than the more institutionalized interest groups. This may seem to be in conflict with what has been said concerning the relationship between the parties and some groups and with the organizational affiliations which the members had in the past or still had at the time of the interview. That these were not mentioned is indicative of both the picture members have of themselves and the one they wish to portray. This picture is not one of a delegate for powerful groups, but of a trustee of the public interest. If the interests of a group are to be promoted, they wish to decide this for themselves as free agents and not as earmarked representatives.

The 1972 findings

Based to a certain extent upon these findings from the 1968 survey of Parliament, the 1972 study attempted to gain somewhat more specific information about the influence of interest groups. The two studies differ in at least five ways. First, instead of limiting the evaluation of interest groups to the members of Parliament, similar questions were administered to a sample of the adult Dutch population. Second, rather than relying upon spontaneously mentioned groups, a list of fourteen specific sources of group influence was drawn up: cabinet ministers, expert members of Parliament,[8] civil servants,[9] party executives, churches, labor unions, employers' organizations, farmers' organizations, retailers' organizations, action groups, radio and television, newspapers, public opinion polls and voters. Third, the object of influence was specified to be the decisions taken in the Lower Chamber of the Parliament—that is, as opposed to political decisions in the Netherlands in general. Fourth, the respondents were asked to rate separately the amount of influence which

each group ought to have and how much it actually did have. Finally, these ratings were given on the basis of a seven point scale ranging from 1, for very little influence, to 7, for very much influence. Thus, it was possible for respondents to rate all groups high or low, since they were not asked simply to rank the order of the fourteen groups.[10] Figure 1 presents these ratings.

The rating of governmental actors

Rated at or near the top in all cases—both in terms of actual and desired influence—are the formal governmental institutions of cabinet ministers, members of Parliament and the civil servants. However, there are some differences of preferences and ordering. Although members of Parliament feel that the experts within their midst have considerable influence on matters involving their speciality, they do not seem to feel that this is enough. Cabinet ministers are felt to have even more influence than expert MPs—apparently a fact which is somewhat resented, since the desired average is considerably lower. One should, of course, remember that the question did not refer to policy making in general, but to the influence of cabinet members upon decisions taken in the Lower House. Interestingly, this opinion is shared by the population who also feel that cabinet ministers have more

8. This reference differed somewhat in the mass and parliamentary questionnaires. For members of Parliament the reference was to those members of the various parties who function as experts on various substantive subjects. For the general population the reference was simply to "other members of Parliament."

9. This was limited to those top level, career members of the civil service who may be important in policy formulation.

10. At this point we should add that the use of averages can be misleading if one does not know something about the frequency distribution of the values, themselves—for example, a U-shaped distribution which produces an average in the middle. We have examined the distributions and are convinced that in these instances the average does indicate a central point around which the values cluster.

FIGURE 1

EVALUATION BY PARLIAMENT AND POPULATION OF ACTUAL AND
DESIRED INFLUENCE OF INTEREST GROUPS

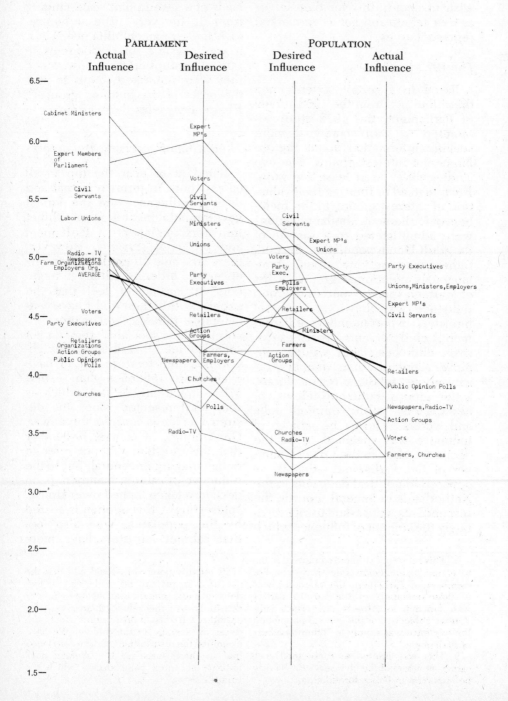

influence than they should.[11] Within the Parliament members of opposition parties oppose the influence of ministers more than the governmental parties. From all of this it is difficult to determine whether there is a general plea for a more independent Parliament or merely a desire that others get into the influential positions. Undoubtedly, both aspects are present to some extent.

The rating of the chief institutionalized groups

A second bloc is formed by what we have called institutionalized interest groups. These include labor unions, employers' organizations, farmers' organizations and the organizations of retailers and small businessmen. All but retailers are ranked by the members of Parliament as above average in actual influence. They see the organizations of retailers as having considerably less influence and, indeed, less influence than they should have. The others, they feel, have more influence than they should have, albeit the farmers' organizations and employers' organizations more so than the labor unions.

This picture of institutionalized interest groups is somewhat different for the population. They agree that the labor unions and the employers' organizations have considerable influence; in fact, they rate them as high as the formal governmental institutions. This is about equal to the average desired level for employers, but somewhat lower than the average desired level for unions. As do members of Parliament, they feel that retailers' organizations are shortchanged. The greatest difference between the population and the MPs for any of these fourteen items concerns the farmers' organizations. Parliament felt that farmers had influence equal to the employers, which was more than either should have. Although the population is in complete agreement with the MPs about how much influence farmers' organizations should have, they regard the actual influence of the farmers as far too small, unlike the members of Parliament who find their influence much too great.

In summarizing these findings concerning formal governmental institutions and institutionalized interest groups, one can add another distinction between Parliament and population. Although members of Parliament ranked both formal institutions and institutionalized interest groups higher, the former were clearly ranked as more influential than the latter. In other words, although labor, employers and farmers were influential, they were regarded as less influential and, therefore, presumably under control of the governmental apparatus. This distinction is not made as clearly by the population. The population accords no significant difference in average influence level to cabinet ministers, expert MPs, the civil service, the labor unions and the employers' organizations, and it puts only the executive of the various political parties somewhat above these groups. There is more than a strong suspicion that they regard the political parties, the government, Parliament, the

11. A similar finding has also been reported for the attitudes of high level civil service officials. See, Samuel J. Eldersveld, Sonja Hubée-Boonzaaijer and Jan Kooiman, "Elite Perceptions of the Political Process in the Netherlands—Looked at in Comparative Perspective" (Paper delivered at the Ninth World Congress of the International Political Science Association, Montreal, Canada, 1973).

bureaucracy and the dominant economic interest groups as a somewhat undifferentiated influential mass—that is, as the people who are running things. Among these, they probably would not mind if the bureaucracy, Parliament and the unions were somewhat more influential and the cabinet, somewhat less so.

The influence of voters and agencies of public opinion

In looking at the middle columns of who ought to have influence, one notes that the second highest average for the Parliament and fourth for the population are the voters. This is far greater influence than either feels the voters actually have on the decisions taken in the Lower House. How crucial is this feeling? On the one hand, this finding might be dismissed easily by pointing out that hardly anyone in a democratic country would argue that the voters should have less influence. On the other hand, the question is not so simple in this case; for, the actual influence of the voters is ranked below the average line by the members of Parliament and at almost the bottom by the population. This suggests that the population feels a considerable gap between the influence of voters and both the institutions of government and the institutionalized interest groups. One could possibly conclude that Parliament and population express a certain implicit criticism of the accommodational style which characterized Dutch politics in the past and that both would like a more immediate impact of electoral will. Some of the background for this development has been described earlier.

At the same time, the essential problem of how to give substance to this undifferentiated electoral will remains. Clearly, the population does not feel that it is exhaustively represented by the large economic interest groups which have been drawn so directly into the mechanism of government, although the level of their influence is not strongly contested. How, then, do Parliament and the population react to three other more informal channels which offer information about the wishes of voters: the mass media, public opinion polls and action groups?

In asking about the mass media separate questions were put for radio and television, on the one hand, and newspapers, on the other. Both are seen as very influential by the members of Parliament—at the same level as farmers and employers—but are accorded very much less influence by the population. Both regard the influence of the mass media as being greater than it should be, with clear signs of resentment on the part of members of Parliament. In fact, except for newspapers in the case of MPs, the mass media items have the lowest averages of desired influence both for the population and Parliament. This is perhaps even more surprising when one recalls that respondents were not asked to rank the order of items from 1 to 14, but they could have assigned a high desired influence to all items. Nevertheless, on a seven point scale the average desired influence for these mass media items in the population is only 3.25 and only slightly higher for members of Parliament. Evidently, both Parliament and population do not regard the mass media to be as much the keepers of the public will and conscience as journalists would like.

A major development for gauging public opinion is the sample survey or poll. Whereas the journalist often must rely upon his own experience and intuition to measure the public pulse, a well-designed survey can probably do so more accurately. Polling has become highly popular in the Netherlands, with polls being taken on all varieties of subjects and with the reports often widely disseminated through television and newspapers. Neither the members of Parliament nor the population feel that public opinion polls have much actual influence on the decisions of the Parliament. However, they do disagree sharply as to whether this is proper. Members of Parliament rate opinion polls rather low in desired influence, averaging only slightly above radio and television. This is still lower than the—not very high—average for the influence which they feel polls actually have. The pattern for the population is exactly opposite. Public opinion polls are felt, on the average, to have considerably less influence than they actually do have. The average for desired influence is roughly equivalent to that for voters and party executives. This conjunction of items for the population would hardly seem to be an accident.

The population seems to equate polls which measure their opinions with an expression of electoral will. The members of Parliament take a different view. They assign great weight to voters, but little weight to public opinion polls. Polls are undoubtedly seen more as noncommittal, as possibly superficial expressions of opinions which may offer little guidance for translation into direct policy decisions on complex public issues. Other evidence in our surveys revealed that Dutch MPs regard their role of representative very much as one of trustee for the public rather than of its delegate.[12]

Finally, action groups may be a source for determining the will of the voters. As yet, neither Parliament nor population seems to feel that such groups have very much influence. Parliament would rate this influence slightly higher than the population. Both, however, express themselves favorably towards a somewhat greater influence of such groups. The higher place accorded to the institutionalized interest groups suggests at the same time that both Parliament and population regard the role of such action groups as complementary, rather than as alternative, to the present system of highly institutionalized politics.

No inventory of interest groups in the Netherlands would be complete without examining the influence of the churches. Religion has long played an important role in the social and political life of the Netherlands, both directly and as an organizational principle for parties and interest groups which are divided along religious lines. In view of this, it might come as a surprise that both Parliament and the population accord very low actual influence to the churches and, on the whole, are well satisfied that this is so. However, there is somewhat more disagreement regarding the influence of

12. See, Hans Daalder and Jerrold G. Rusk, "Perceptions of Party in the Dutch Parliament," in *Comparative Legislative Behavior*, ed. Samuel C. Patterson and John Wahlke (New York: John Wiley and Sons, 1972), p. 156 ff.

churches than for some of the other items.

PARTIES AND VIEWS OF INTEREST GROUPS

The use of averages in the previous section should not cloud the fact that there is variance about these averages. Some of this difference is readily explainable in terms of the political philosophy of the respondent. This can be seen by comparing the averages for various political groupings. For reasons of space we cannot present the figures, but must summarize our findings in words. Parliament has been divided into the three left-oriented parties which were in opposition at the time of the survey—Labour, Radicals and Democrats '66—the religious governing parties—Catholics, Anti-revolutionaries and Christian-His-toricals—and two secular government parties—Liberal and Democratic-Socialists '70 (DS '70). Due to a coding error, DS '70 voters were not included for the population. A separate group was added for nonvoters. These parties fall along two dimensions: a left-right dimension ranging from the left progressive parties to the right secular parties, with the religious parties in the middle; and a religious-secular dimension. These two dimensions have implications for the way both Parliament and the population view the actual and desired influence of the groups.[13]

The first important finding is that there is remarkable agreement across the parties—both with the population and the Parliament—concerning the degree of influence that groups do have. This suggests that the reputational method of

searching for influence of interest groups bears fruit in our case. The only major exception to this agreement concerns the appropriate clientele groups of employers and labor unions. The left parties see the unions with which they are themselves in strong sympathy as having less influence than do the religious and liberal parties. Alternatively, they regard the influence of the employers as being higher compared with the governmental parties.

Additional differences are found when one turns to desired influence. In the Parliament both left and right feel that their clientele groups should have more influence than they feel they actually have, while the groups closer to rival parties should have less than they at present have. In the population this holds for perceptions of the labor unions, but—perhaps surprisingly—sympathizers of all parties seem to feel that the employers' organizations have about the amount of influence that they should have. Left members of Parliament would also accord less influence to retailers' organizations than would other MPs. Both within the population and Parliament a definite left-right distinction is apparent in attitudes toward action groups. Left parties are far more sympathetic towards action groups than either the religious parties or the right. Within the population a similar distinction is found for public opinion polls. This is not reciprocated at the level of Parliament where representatives of all parties are opposed to great influence of public opinion polls.

The religious-secular distinction emerges most clearly in attitudes toward the influence of the churches. This disagreement is not so evident in the amount of actual influence which the churches are

13. See, ibid., p. 169 ff.

felt to have. However, in the case of both the population and the Parliament, supporters of religious parties, understandably, think that the churches should have considerably more influence than they do.

The central position of the religious parties on the left-right dimension has made them crucial in cabinet formation. The Catholics have formed a part of the cabinet coalition in all cabinets since the war, and the Protestant Antirevolutionaries and Christian-Historicals have taken part with only rare exceptions.[14] Cabinet ministers from these parties have achieved considerable prominence, and some have enjoyed extremely long tenure. This has perhaps influenced the attitude of members of these parties concerning the amount of influence ministers should have upon decisions in the Lower House. In any case, there are differences in perceptions between the religious and

14. See the list of Dutch cabinets in Daalder, "The Netherlands," appendix 2, p. 418 ff.

secular parties. Especially, MPs from religious parties would assign more influence to ministers than would either the left or right parties. As the right-wing parties had ministers in the cabinet at the time of the survey, it is not surprising that they were more favorably disposed towards the influence of ministers on parliamentary decisions than the members of the left opposition parties who felt the impotence of their own position as if it were the influence of Parliament as a whole vis-à-vis the cabinet.

Finally, although voters of all parties agree on the level of actual influence which farmers' organizations have—which is in all cases lower than the desired level—the members of Parliament differ along this religious-secular dimension. Religious party MPs desire considerably more influence for farmers than do either left or right. This reflects the greater representation which farmers have within the religious parties, as well as the latter's more important rural base compared with the secular parties.

Interest Groups in the Republic of South Africa

By L. Pretorius and W. B. Vosloo

ABSTRACT: The South African interest group structure is in large measure determined by the racial and ethnic divisions within the population. The low degree of overlapping group membership can be attributed to three, partly coinciding factors: (1) voluntary establishment of associations to promote the interests of specific racial or ethnic groups; (2) government measures introducing racial segregation into associational life; and (3) the establishment of associations on an ethnic or racial basis as a result of clashes of interest within mixed associations. Despite these factors a number of racially or ethnically mixed associations do exist—for example, some trade unions—mainly as a result of the integrated nature of the economic system. Because most effective forms of formal political and economic power are concentrated in the hands of the white population groups, their organized interest groups are more influential than the respective nonwhite counterparts. There are indications, however, that nonwhite interests are increasingly articulated by institutional and nonassociational interest groups using the various communal councils as channels of access to the key points of decision making.

L. Pretorius is Lecturer of Political Science at the University of Durban-Westville and a graduate student of the University of Stellenbosch.

W. B. Vosloo is Chairman of the Department of Political Science and Public Administration at the University of Stellenbosch. Educated at Pretoria and Cornell Universities, he is the author of several publications and articles in the field of comparative government and administration, political theory and political behavior.

INTEREST groups have been neglected by most students of South African politics. Except for a number of monographs by Peter Harris[1] and surveys on trade unionism by Muriel Horrell,[2] most studies on South African politics contain only brief references to interest groups. Particularly lacking are analyses which show some sensitivity for theoretical frameworks and conceptual vocabularies that facilitate a comparative perspective. This paper is presented in the belief that it provides additional material for the purposes of reference and comparison and in hope that its omissions will stimulate much needed research.

THE PREPONDERANCE OF RACIAL AND ETHNIC DIFFERENTIATORS

The nature and activities of interest groups are strongly influenced by the sociocultural environment within which they exist. In South Africa this environment is a culturally heterogeneous society governed by a minority group in terms of a policy of differentiation which is justified with reference to this heterogeneity, but which reinforces it to the extent that South Africa is today virtually an ideal

type of the plural society as described by J. S. Furnivall and others.[3] The politically most significant lines of division are, of course, racial, dividing the population into four groups—that is, Africans, Asians, coloureds and whites (table 1).[4] Each of these groups, in turn, contains a number of ethnic groups.[5] Only the divisions within the white and African groups are important for the purpose of this paper. These divide the white group into Afrikaans—the majority group—and English speakers and the African population into ten ethnic groups (see table 3).

The principles and policies underlying the political system—generally known as apartheid or separate development—have been, and still are, extensively debated in forums varying from learned dissertations to the United Nations.[6] Hence, only the basic characteristics of the policy of separate development need be mentioned here. These include:

(1) the protection of the white man's control of the dominant European-type political sys-

1. P. B. Harris, *Interest Groups in South African Politics,* monograph no. 1 (Salisbury: University College of Rhodesia, 1968); P. B. Harris, *Studies in African Politics* (London: Hutchison, 1970), pp. 99–106; P. B. Harris, "Interest Groups in the South African Political Process," in *South Africa: Government and Politics,* ed. D. Worrall (Pretoria: J. L. van Schaik, 1971), pp. 253–284.

2. M. Horrell, *South African Trade Unionism: A Study of a Divided Working Class* (Johannesburg: South African Institute of Race Relations, 1961); M. Horrell, *South Africa's Workers: Their Organizations and the Patterns of Employment* (Johannesburg: South African Institute of Race Relations, 1969).

3. J. S. Furnivall, *Colonial Policy and Practice* (Cambridge: Cambridge University Press, 1948).

4. The term race is used here in accordance with the biological distinctions made in the South African Population Registration Act of 1950. On this act and other legislation affecting race relations, see, M. Horrell, *Legislation and Race Relations* (Johannesburg: South African Institute of Race Relations, 1971).

5. The term ethnic as it is used here refers to linguistic and cultural characteristics. Compare, M. G. Smith, "Pluralism in Pre-Colonial African Societies," in *Pluralism in Africa,* ed. L. Kuper and M. G. Smith (Berkeley, Cal.: University of California Press, 1969), pp. 103–104.

6. For a comprehensive bibliography on South Africa since 1960, see, H. Adam, ed., *South Africa: Sociological Perspectives* (London: Oxford University Press, 1971), pp. 301–332.

TABLE 1

SIZE AND DISTRIBUTION OF THE POPULATION

	WHITE AREAS	AFRICAN AREAS	TOTAL
Whites	3,730,951	20,377	3,751,328
Coloureds	2,005,325	13,128	2,018,453
Asians	616,995	3,441	620,436
Africans	8,060,773	6,997,179	15,057,952
Total	14,414,044	7,034,125	21,448,169

SOURCE: Adapted from M. Horrell et. al., eds., A Survey of Race Relations in South Africa 1971 (Johannesburg: South African Institute of Race Relations, 1972), p. 59.

tem by way of the exclusion of nonwhite—that is, Africans, Asians and coloureds—participation in the election of members of Parliament, provincial councils and municipal councils;

(2) the gradual and systematic disentanglement of white and nonwhite ethnic groups through a series of segregationist measures with respect to situations of intergroup contact, such as residential areas, schools, universities, occupations, hospitals, public transport, public amenities, churches and associations;

(3) the creation of separate opportunities for the progressive self-fulfillment of each major group in accordance with its own traditions and values by means of a series of developmental measures in the social and economic spheres and the provision of separate political tracks for each major group. For the blacks this track includes the possibility of developing independent states within their own territories. Since the coloureds and Indians have no traditional homelands of their own, they are apparently destined to develop parallel to,

but separate from, the whites within the geographical boundaries of the dominant political system.

It is thus not surprising that one of the primary characteristics of the South African interest group system is the ethnic and racial bases of a large number of interest groups.[7] Among the whites the Afrikaanse Sakekamers have their English counterparts in the chambers of commerce; the Afrikaanse Studentebond (ASB) is in constant conflict with the National Union of South African Students (NUSAS) which represents students on the English-speaking campuses. Similarly, there are Afrikaans and English womens associations, welfare associations and cultural associations.[8] Similar black associations include the Kwa-Mashu Traders Association, the South African Students Organization (SASO), the Natal Workshop for African Advancement, the Transkeian Womens Zenzele Association, the South African Bantu Social Workers Association, the Durban Indian

7. Harris, "Interest Groups," p. 260.
8. See, also, H. W. Van der Merwe and J. J. Buitendag, "Political, Ethnic and Structural Differences among White South Africans," in ASSA: Sociology in Southern Africa 1973 (Papers from the First Congress of the Association for Sociologists in Southern Africa, 1973), pp. 189–213.

Child Welfare Society and the Association for the Educational and Cultural Advancement of African People in South Africa (ASSECA).[9]

In many cases it is difficult to determine to what extent interest groups are voluntarily established on a racial or ethnic basis. It seems that three main, partly overlapping, patterns can be distinguished.

Associations are voluntarily established to promote the interests of a specific ethnic or racial group

During the 1930s and 1940s a number of associations were established with the purpose of promoting the political, economical and cultural interests of the Afrikaners. These included the *Afrikaner Broederbond*, the *Federasie van Afrikaanse Kultuurverenigings*, the *Reddingsdaadbond* and the *Blanke Werkersbeskermingsbond;* the last two associations are now defunct. Under the impetus of the black consciousness movement, a number of associations have recently been established to perform the same function for blacks. Examples are the Black People Convention (BPC), ASSECA and a variety of self-help, cultural and political associations.

Government measures introducing segregation into associational life necessitate the establishment of uniracial associations

The trade union movement provides the most obvious example of

government measures introducing segregation into associations, but this pattern is also evident in other spheres of associational life. Some professional associations, such as those representing the nursing profession, were forced by legislation to split along racial lines; others, including welfare and scientific associations, were forced to segregate by government threats to deny them financial aid.[10]

Clashes of interest within mixed associations lead to splits and the establishment of associations with a racial or ethnic basis

Initially, NUSAS represented white—Afrikaans and English—as well as black students; eventually, the students from Afrikaans universities and later black students broke away to form their own associations. Similarly, the *Suid-Afrikaanse Buro vir Rasse Aangeleenthede* (SABRA) was founded by Afrikaans intellectuals who left the South African Institute of Race Relations (SAIRR). In 1962 an all-white Psychological Institute was founded by psychologists who seceded from the South African Psychological Association when it decided to admit qualified blacks.[11]

The existence of ethnically and racially based interest groups reflects the clash of interests in a plural society, the structure of which is reinforced by segregationist legislation. In addition, it is important to keep in mind that the activities of certain interest groups reinforced racial and ethnic

9. Information on black interest groups is supplied in B. A. Khoapa, ed., *Handbook of Black Organizations* (Durban: Black Community Programmes, 1973); and B. A. Khoapa, *Black Review 1972* (Durban: Black Community Programme, 1973). Note: the term black is used here as a noun referring to Africans, Asians and coloureds collectively.

10. Compare, L. S. Thompson, *Politics in the Republic of South Africa* (Boston, Mass.: Little, Brown, 1966), pp. 145–146.

11. Ibid., p. 145. On student associations see, also, H. W. Van der Merwe and D. Welsh, eds., *Student Perspectives on South Africa* (Cape Town: David Philip, 1972).

cleavages and the structural rigidity of the political system.[12] Despite these factors, it is significant that a number of racially and ethnically mixed associations do exist. The forty-two mixed trade unions[13] are

examples of this apparent anomaly (table 2). This phenomenon is presumably a manifestation of the irrevocably integrated nature of the economic system which provides an "economic motive strong enough to hold together persons whose social interests seem to be disparate."[14] Other mixed associations, such as the Christian Institute of South Africa and the SAIRR are multiracial simply because of

12. Compare, S. Trapido, "Political Institutions and Afrikaner Social Structures in the Republic of South Africa," *American Political Science Review* 57, no. 1, pp. 75–87.

13. The term mixed trade unions refers to trade unions with Asian, coloured and white members.

14. Harris, "Interest Groups," p. 261.

TABLE 2

Trade Union Membership in 1969

	Number of Unions	Membership				
		White	Coloured	Asian	African	Total
White unions						
Confederation*	27	183,781	—	—	—	183,781
TUCSA	13	33,088	—	—	—	33,088
Unaffiliated	58	148,985	—	—	—	148,985
	98	365,854	—	—	—	365,854
Mixed unions						
TUCSA	25	46,297	62,749	20,784	—	129,830
Unaffiliated	10	13,869	4,699	1,525	—	20,093
	35	60,166	67,448	22,309	—	149,923
Coloured and/or Asian Unions						
TUCSA	23	—	14,524	9,036	—	23,560
Unaffiliated	16	—	26,240	1,310	—	27,550
	39		40,764	10,346	—	51,110
African Unions	14	—	—	—	16,040	16,040
Combined totals						
Confederation*	27	183,781	—	—	—	183,781
TUCSA	61	79,385	77,273	29,820	—	186,478
Unaffiliated	98	162,854	30,939	2,835	16,040	212,668
	186	426,020	108,212	32,655	16,040	582,927

Source: M. Horrell, *South Africa's Workers* (Johannesburg: South African Institute of Race Relations, 1969), p. 146.

* The South African Confederation of Labour includes three federal bodies: the *Koördinerende Raad van S. A. Vakverenigings*—thirteen affiliated unions; the Federal Consultative Council of South African Railways and Harbours Staff Associations—seven affiliated unions; and the Federation of Mine Production Unions—three affiliated unions. Three individual unions are affiliated directly with the confederation.

their aim to improve race relations by way of interracial contact.

ASSOCIATIONAL INTEREST GROUPS

The majority of South African associational interest groups are functionally specific organizations which promote and defend the goals of particular segments of the society. The most prominent commercial interest groups are the 250-odd local *Afrikaanse Sakekamers*, affiliated to the *Afrikaanse Handelsinstituut* (AHI), and the approximately 144 chambers of commerce, affiliated with the Association of Commerce of South Africa (ASSOCOM). These associations represent the interests of commerce as a whole.[15] The organizational structure of the AHI, for instance, includes cooperative[16] financial, industrial, mining and trading chambers which concentrate on dealing with the interests of members from these sectors; geographical representation is provided through the affiliated local *sakekamers* and thirteen regional committees. Industry and mining are also represented by the South African Federated Chambers of Industries (FCI) and the South African Chamber of Mines. In addition, there are virtually hundreds of associations articulating the interests of particular industrial and commercial undertakings. These vary from biscuit manufacturers associations to associations of bottle-store owners. Black businessmen are not as well organized as their white counterparts, but a number of local traders associations do exist.

The commercial and industrial interest groups are concerned with much the same issues as similar associations in other countries with a capitalist economic system. In addition, they take an active part in the ongoing debate about the economic aspects of the implementation of separate development. An important issue in this context is government attempts to induce the decentralization of industry. Policy making in this respect not only involves considerations of economic feasibility or attempts to satisfy competing regional interests, but is largely influenced by the government's determination to industrialize the areas bordering on the black homelands in order to limit the flow of Africans to the white cities[17] and to enhance the economic viability of the homelands. In this debate commercial and industrial interest groups, rather than unequivocally supporting or opposing the government, usually call for moderation. The president of the Transvaal Chamber of Industries, for example, warned against "the inflexible, dogmatic, and completely insensitive application of pressure on industrialists to move to the border industrial areas."[18] At present, *sakekamers* — chambers of commerce — agricultural associations and institutional interest

---

15. Of course, individual or groups of business concerns also act as interest groups. Compare, M. Savage, "Interlocking Directorships in South Africa," in *ASSA: Sociology in Southern Africa 1973* (Papers from the First Congress of the Association for Sociologists in South Africa, 1973), pp. 44–65.

16. The trading of a large number of South African farmers is channeled through agricultural cooperatives.

17. Compare, M. Arkin, "The South African Economy," in *South Africa: Government and Politics*, ed. D. Worrall (Pretoria: J. L. van Schaik, 1971), pp. 133–171.

18. Report by *Rand Daily Mail*, 28 January 1972, referred to in M. Horrell, D. Horner, J. Kane-Burman and R. Margo, eds., *A Survey of Race Relations in South Africa 1972* (Johannesburg: South African Institute of Race Relations, 1973), pp. 276–277.

groups, such as the homeland governments and local authorities, are also involved in the negotiations on proposals for the consolidation of the African homelands.[19]

The commercial and industrial associations also articulate the interests of employers in the private section. In 1963 there were 215 employers' associations representing 17,442 firms.[20] These are affiliated with a variety of coordinating bodies.

South African trade unions are not as powerful as those in the United Kingdom, but they nevertheless play a significant role in the political process. South Africa's trade unions—especially the mine workers unions—have always been concerned not only with the improvement of the wages and working conditions of their white members, but also with their protection against competition from unskilled and semiskilled African workers. The issue is not merely whether Africans should be allowed to do certain kinds of work, but also whether they should be allowed to join registered unions and whether African trade unions should be allowed to register. The continuation of mixed trade unions—that is, those consisting of Asian, coloured and white members—is also a major theme of the debate.[21]

At present, the right-wing white trade unions still have the upper

hand. To a very large extent this is so because they had the support of National-Labour pact government in 1924—when the first Industrial Conciliation Act was passed—and subsequently that of the National Party, which has since 1914 been the vehicle of Afrikaner political aspirations.[22] The history of the implementation of the National Party's labor policy over the past two decades abounds with examples of its extreme sensitivity to the sentiments and interests of the organized white workers. Despite certain restrictions imposed by the Industrial Conciliation Act of 1924, Africans were not completely excluded from registered trade unions before 1953. The Bantu Labour (Settlement of Disputes) Act of 1953, however, prohibited Africans from becoming members of trade unions and African trade unions from being registered. This excludes African workers from utilizing the machinery for collective bargaining created by the Industrial Conciliation Act. The Bantu Labour

19. On the consolidation proposals, see, M. Horrell, *The African Homelands of South Africa* (Johannesburg: South African Institute of Race Relations, 1973), pp. 10–37.

20. J. A. Lombard and J. J. Stadler, *Die Ekonomiese Stelsel van Suid-Afrika* (Cape Town: HAUM, 1967), p. 469.

21. On the history of trade unionism and the African labor question, see, Horrell, *South African Trade Unionism;* and Horrell, *South Africa's Workers.*

22. In 1923 the National Party (NP) under Hertzog and the Labour Party—established in 1919 as the political wing of the trade unions—under Cresswell entered into an election pact. The NP won the 1924 election and Cresswell became minister of labor. In 1933 the NP entered into a coalition with the South African Party (SAP) under Smuts, with a faction of the Labour Party—the Cresswellites—joining the coalition and the rest going into opposition. After the 1933 election the NP and SAP fused to form the United South African National Party (UP). In 1935 a group of Nationalists under Malan broke away to form the Purified National Party. In 1939 the UP cabinet split on the question of South Africa's participation in World War II, and Hertzog and his followers joined Malan. Hertzog became leader of the Reunited National Party, which he again left in 1941. He then established the Afrikaner Party. This party cooperated with the National Party which defeated the United Party in 1948. The Labour Party eventually disappeared from the scene.

Act provides machinery for industrial conciliation where Africans are involved, but it does not seem to be as effective as the machinery to which whites have access.[23] The Industrial Conciliation Act of 1956, as amended in 1961, stipulated that no further mixed trade unions providing for white, coloured and Asian membership would be registered. Mixed unions which continue to exist must have separate branches, and their executive committees must consist of whites only. This legislation precipitated a realignment of trade unions into three confederations: the Trade Union Council of South Africa (TUCSA), which included white and mixed unions; the South African Congess of Trade Unions (SACTU), which included unregistered African unions;[24] and the all-white South African Confederation of Labour. According to Muriel Horrell, there has not been as much splitting of individual registered unions along racial lines as might have been expected in view of the government's disapproval of mixed unions, but there has been a movement of whites into exclusively white unions to the extent that by 1969 the white membership of mixed unions practically halved. To a lesser extent, coloured and Asian workers also tended to join uniracial unions, but a majority are still members of mixed unions (table 2).[25]

The potential influence of the trade unions is limited because of the exclusion of Africans and the conflicting attitudes of trade unionists on this question. The effectiveness of TUCSA is particularly undermined because of its vaccilating attitude on the question of the affiliation of African unions. The Confederation of Labour is less prone to internal strains, but divergences do exist on matters such as the implementation of work reservation.[26] On the trade union movement in general, Muriel Horrell has remarked:

Trade unionism in South Africa is not only divided, but has failed to obtain support among large numbers of workers. It is estimated that of the economically active population at the end of 1968, only 30.3 percent of the white, 16.0 percent of the Coloureds, 21.2 percent of the Asians, and 0.3 percent of the Africans were members of unions.[27]

INTEREST GROUP TARGETS AND CHANNELS OF ACCESS

In South Africa, as in all political systems, interest group efforts are concentrated on the loci of authoritative political decision making. In South Africa these are the cabinet, deputy ministers and the bureaucracy.

The formal channels of access to the bureaucracy include a large variety of statutory boards, commissions and councils which not only provide a forum for negotiation between the bureaucracy and interest groups, but also form an integrated

23. Horrell, *South Africa's Workers*, pp. 66–68.

24. By 1953 SACTU represented approximately 50,000 African workers. It was, however, forced into exile by the detaining, banning or arrest of many of its leaders under the Suppression of Communism Act of 1950. In 1972 the Black Allied Workers Union (BAWU) was founded to serve as a coordinating body for African trade unions. Some of its leaders have since suffered the same fate.

25. Horrell, *South African Workers*, pp. 20–21, 24–25.

26. Ibid., p. 130.

27. Ibid., pp. 130–131.

part of the executive arm of the central government. These boards, commissions and councils are usually constituted in such a way that they are representative of relevant interest groups. Examples are the numerous control boards of agricultural commodities, the National Transport Commission, the South African Medical and Dental Council, the Electrotechnical Wireworkers Board, industrial conciliation boards, the Rent Control Board and the Welfare Planning Commission.[28] In addition, there is a large variety of councils acting in an advisory capacity on central and provincial government levels. On the central government level two types can be distinguished: councils advising the cabinet, in particular—for example, the Prime Minister's Economic Advisory Council—and councils instituted on the departmental level—for example, the Consumers Advisory Committee of the Department of Agricultural Economics and Marketing. The Transvaal Local Government Board is an example of such a body functioning on the provincial level.[29] Additional channels of access are provided through the media of correspondence, personal interviews and the attendance of government officials at the meetings or congresses of interest groups.

Another, though less important, target of interest groups is the national legislature, Parliament. The traditional channel of access is through the parliamentary lobby.

Some interest groups, such as the AHI, maintain permanent parliamentary committees to interact with legislators. Although various interest groups have spokesmen in Parliament, the effectiveness of lobbying seems to be limited where basic policy issues are concerned. This is due mainly to the fact that the basic policies of both parties are formulated in their respective caucuses, and rigid party discipline enforces a united front both in the House of Assembly and the Senate.[30] It is conceivable that interest group representations find their way to the caucus rooms, but it is virtually impossible to ascertain their impact on decision making. Parliamentary committees and commissions of enquiry provide additional opportunities for interest groups to bring their views to the attention of Parliament.

Generally, the channels of access described here are not typically available to black associational interest groups, although meetings with government officials do take place. Otherwise, they have to depend on white intermediaries. The inadequacy of the channels of access available to black interest groups contributes to the frequency of anomic outbursts among these groups. This is the case especially with black laborers, who are, in addition, not allowed to organize. Anomic modes of interest articulation have, however, not been limited to blacks. White South African students and workers have also participated in public protests and strikes, although these are more

28. See, also, B. Roux, "Central Administration, Provincial and Local Authorities and the Judiciary," in South Africa: Government and Politics, ed. D. Worrall (Pretoria: J. L. van Schaik, 1971), pp. 75–171; and J. J. N. Cloete, Sentrale: Provinsiale en Munisipale Instellings van Suid-Afrika (Pretoria: J. L. van Schaik, 1971), pp. 124–133.

29. Compare, Roux, ibid., pp. 104–105.

30. The two major political parties in Parliament are the National Party and the United Party. Only one other party is represented—that is, the Progressive Party which has only one representative in Parliament.

often than not expressions of organized anomie.

The much discussed tactic of civil disobedience is closely linked with the name of Mahatma Gandhi who founded the Natal Indian Congress (NIC) in 1894 to defend and promote the interests of South Africa's Indian community. The failure of the civil disobedience campaigns of the 1950s—sponsored by the African National Congress and the South African Indian Congress (SAIC)—contributed to the radicalization of African political movements and to the violence which shook South Africa in the early 1960s. The majority of associational interest groups, however, limit their modes of action to formal representation before officials and politicians, persuasion, negotiation and the like.

HOMELAND LEGISLATIVE ASSEMBLIES AND THE COMMUNAL COUNCILS AS INSTITUTIONAL INTEREST GROUPS

The implementation of separate development entails, *inter alia*, the creation of two main types of political institutions for the nonwhite population:

(1) legislative assemblies created for each of the African national units. The territorial bases of these are the various African homelands (table 3). The stated aim of the government is that these homelands should develop into politically independent territories.[31]

(2) communal councils created for the coloured and Indian population. These councils, the Coloured Persons Representative Council (CPRC) and SAIC have no clear territorial basis and are primarily community directed.[32]

The legislative powers of the assemblies and those of CPRC vary, and the SAIC has as yet no legislative powers. They serve, however, as potentially powerful structures for the articulation of the interests of the population groups for whom they were instituted. The demands made by the spokesmen of these institutions usually relate to issues such as the territorial aspirations of Africans, employment opportunities, the disparity between white and black wages and salaries, the lack of public amenities for blacks in white areas, influx control, housing and the proclamation of group areas.

As creations of the South African government, the assemblies and councils have certain channels of access to the cabinet, deputy ministers and the bureaucracy which may not be readily available to many black associational interest groups. Liaison meetings between cabinet members or government representatives and representatives of the councils and assemblies —usually members of the various executives—take place fairly regularly. In addition, the executive functions of the assemblies and councils are performed in coordination with various central government departments. This provides opportunities for virtually

31. On the African homelands, see, M. Horrell, *The African Homelands of South Africa*; and G. M. Carter, T. Karis and N. M. Stultz, *South Africa's Transkei* (Evanston, Ill.: Northwestern University Press, 1967).

32. See, W. B. Vosloo, "The Coloured Policy of the National Party," in *South African Dialogue*, ed. N. J. Rhoodie (Johannesburg: McGraw-Hill, 1972).

TABLE 3

ACTUAL AND/OR PROPOSED* COMPOSITION OF HOMELAND LEGISLATIVE ASSEMBLIES

NATIONAL UNIT	HOMELAND	NUMBER OF NOMINATED MEMBERS†	NUMBER OF ELECTED MEMBERS
Xhosa	Transkei	64	45
Xhosa	Ciskei	30	20
Zulu	Kwa Zulu	70	55
North Sotho	Lebowa	60	40
Venda	Venda	42	18
Shangaan	Gazankulu	42	26
Tswana	Bophuta Tswana	48	24
South Sotho	Basotho Qwaqwa	8	NIL
Swazi	Swazi	(No Legislative Assembly)	
South Ndebele	(No homeland as yet)		

SOURCE: Compiled from data supplied in M. Horrell, *The African Homelands of South Africa* (Johannesburg: South African Institute of Race Relations, 1973), pp. 44–61.

* Elections have not yet been held in all the African homelands.

† The nomination procedure varies; however, in terms of the various relevant constitutional provisions, the majority are recruited from the ranks of tribal chiefs.

continuous contact between white and black officials.

The assemblies and councils, in their turn, serve as potential targets for other types of black interest groups. Nonassociational interest groups, such as the tribal groups in the homelands, appear to be particularly effective in this area. Not only are the majority of the members of the legislative assemblies tribal chiefs (table 3), but where elections have been held tribal affiliations have generally been the decisive factor. Tribal interests are thus directly represented in the various legislative assemblies.

At present it is not clear whether the activities of associational interest groups have any significant impact on the political process in the black subsystems of government. In any case, associational interest groups in the homelands are limited in numbers, and political associations, such as the BPC and NIC, refuse to recognize the apartheid institutions. The potential influence of these institutional structures of interest articulation has not yet been fully realized, but there are indications that the government will find it increasingly difficult to resist pressure brought to bear on it by homeland leaders.

LEGITIMACY AND EFFECTIVENESS

The effectiveness of interest groups depends, *inter alia*, on their legitimacy; this, in turn, depends to a large extent on the "assumed compatibility of their claims with community values."[33] In a situation—such as that in South Africa—where major segments of the population adhere to different value systems, it can be expected that the legitimacy enjoyed by interest groups will vary dramatically from one community to the other. Even where the interest groups are regarded as legitimate, to a large extent this favorable attitude can be expected to be limited to those which articulate dominant interests.

33. H. W. Ehrmann, "Interest Groups," in *International Encyclopaedia of the Social Sciences* (London: Free Press, 1968), p. 488.

The crucial question is whether the members of the politically dominant community—that is, the whites in general and the Afrikaners in particular, in the case of South Africa—accept the legitimacy of the interest groups which speak for the subject communities.

Generally, it appears that groups whose aim it is to change fundamentally the political and social system or whose activities are perceived to be inimical to vested interests receive little sympathy. Evidence of this is seen in the lack of opposition from whites to government action against the leaders of organizations such as NUSAS, NIC, BPC, SASO and certain trade unions. Commercial, industrial, agricultural, welfare and professional associations do not usually incur public opprobrium, although there was a time when Afrikaners were extremely hostile to groups which they regarded as representing English capital. More overtly, political associations are generally viewed with hostility—depending, again, on the perceived goals of the association vis-à-vis the observer's interests. The English community and some *verligte* Afrikaners are, for instance, deeply distrustful of the *Afrikaner Broederbond,* while Afrikaners tend to view the Sons of England as the agent of British imperialism and the Black Sash with emotions varying from hostility to amusement.

Although a lack of legitimacy in the public eye—or, rather, the various public eyes—undoubtedly impairs the effectiveness of interest groups, the attitudes of ministers and bureaucrats toward them are of much more importance. The decisive criterion of legitimacy in this sphere is the compatibility of interest group goals with government policy. In this regard the pronouncements of the minister of labor on African trade unionism are instructive. He has repeatedly stated that he regards African trade unions as inimical to the interests of South Africa:

As far as the National Party Policy in regard to Bantu workers is concerned, it is our conviction that the organisation of Bantu wokers is neither in the interests of South Africa, nor in the interests of improving their own wage position, nor in the interests of promoting race relations.[34]

Particularly those associations which are, in the view of government, spokesmen endangering the stability of the state or aiming at a radical change in the social order are vigorously attacked. Very often they find that channels of access to the cabinet and bureaucracy are closed to them or that their representations are rejected out of hand. The present government has often been criticized for its actions against such groups. The most recent example is the spate of edicts banning the leaders of SASO, BPC, BAWU and other black associations.[35]

It is in this context that the homeland legislative assemblies and communal councils are of particular importance as structures of interest articulation. These institutions were created along the terms set by government policy, and their members are seen by the government as the representatives of the communities for whom they were

34. Quoted in Horrell et. al., *A Survey of Race Relations in South Africa, 1972,* p. 335. See, also, *Hansard 1973,* no. 1, cols. 50–56.

35. See, also, Horrell et. al., *A Survey of Race Relations,* pp. 52–54—on the "Parliamentary Select Committee on, and Commission of Enquiry into, Certain Organizations."

instituted. Hence, ministers and government officials are obliged to pay attention to the demands made by spokesmen of the assemblies and councils—even though they may not always accede to all their demands. The real and potential influence of these institutions is enhanced by the prestige of their leaders—such as Chief Minister Matanzima of the Transkei; Chief Buthelezi, chief executive officer of the Kwa Zulu Legislative Assembly; and Professor Ntsanwisi, chief councillor of the Gazankulu Legislative Assembly. In the long run, the demands made by them can only be ignored by the government at the price of further destroying the credibility of its policies.

With reference to the relationship between interest group legitimacy and effectiveness and government attitudes, Harris has observed:

Groups favoured by government are likely . . . to succeed in their endeavours, while those regarded with disfavour suffer from many disadvantages. This proposition applies equally to associations and groups in the broad field of economics as well as those more obviously "political."[36]

This supports our view with regard to the more overtly political associations, but the generalization should not be extended lightly to commercial, industrial and other associations which do not manifestly threaten the system. While there is evidence that the government "counter-presses the pressure groups,"[37] there is also evidence that the government has made con-

cessions which are not compatible with its traditional policies. The relaxation of restrictions on the use of nonwhite labor is a case in point. It is not easy to determine the extent of the influence of industrial and commercial interest groups in this area, but it is significant to note that the Prime Minister's Economic Advisory Council in 1963 "arrived at the conclusion that unless new efforts were made to supplement the available trained manpower, the future economic development of the country would be seriously hampered," and recommended "that greater use should be made. . .in the right ways and places, of trained non-white manpower."[38] The council includes representatives of the AHI, ASSOCOM, FCI, the Chamber of Mines, TUCSA and the Confederation of Labour.

CONCLUSION

It would be presumptuous to draw many conclusions on the basis of an incomplete and somewhat superficial description of certain aspects of the South African interest group structure. What should be evident is that a study of South African interest groups can in itself be an exercise in comparative politics. It may also be of some importance to students of political development to note that associational interest groups play an important role in the relatively developed white political system, while institutional and, to a lesser extent, nonassociational interest groups dominate the scene in the newly developing African homelands. It

36. Harris, *Studies in African Politics*, p. 104.

37. Ibid., p. 106.

38. Horrell, *South Africa's Workers*, p. 83.

appears that the development of South African politics will—unless a major upset occurs—largely be conditioned by the way in which the policy of separate development is implemented. This, in turn, will be influenced by the interest groups concerned. Future research should focus on the role these interest groups play in the shaping and implementation of government policy.

Interest Groups and the Consent to Govern: Getting the People Out, for What?

By THEODORE J. LOWI

ABSTRACT: The original Western liberal approach to government was that as long as there were multitudes of interests with no possibility of any interest becoming a permanent majority, the free interaction of these interests would provide a public good. Very probably, the most important feature of this early liberal approach to government by the consent of organized interests was the coupling of consent with regulation. In the process of aging and spreading, however, the original liberal view underwent drastic transformation. Under the new theory consent is to come from a genuine accommodation of government to the real interests of society; all twentieth century democracies seem to espouse this theory of consent in one way or another. Leaving aside the important issue of the morality of such a view, there is still the question of whether such an accommodation is possible; the closer one looks at this proposition, the more distant appears the possibility of consent by accommodation. One must question the point of view that the group is simply a way of looking at the individual and ask whether individuals are represented accurately or, heavily distorted. Three common distortions in group politics are discussed: (1) organization as distortion; (2) the artificial majority; (3) the illogic of collective action. Suggestions for the adoption of a view from the perspective of distortion and a return to the posture of regulation round out the analysis.

Theodore J. Lowi is University and John L. Senior Professor of American Institutions at Cornell University. Educated at Michigan State and Yale Universities, he received his Ph.D. in Political Science in 1961 and an Honorary D.H. from Oakland University in 1972. Awarded Post-Doctoral Fellowships by the Social Science Research Council and the Guggenheim Foundation, his research has been in the field of public policies and politics of governments in advanced, industrial societies. Professor Lowi's publications, which number over fifty, include: At the Pleasure of the Mayor, Private Life and Public Order, The End of Liberalism, The Pursuit of Justice _and_ The Politics of Disorder.

WESTERN democracies—in particular, the United States—pin an almost impossible amount of hope on a positive connection between interests and the consent to govern. One of the basic assumptions of modern mass democracy is that the free access of interests to the political system—expressed, if it helps, as inputs of demand and support—will produce a maximum of legitimacy and a minimum of raw force. Consent is simply an older and more efficient name for the same result. However, regardless of the preferred vocabulary, the results may or may not be produced by the identified conditions. The connection between interests and consent is entirely theoretical and problematic. Furthermore, unless that connection is more carefully examined than it has been in the recent past, untested assumptions about that connection produce nothing but mythology. It is the worst kind of mythology, because it is the mythology supported by the pseudo-scientific incantations of the social science profession.

EARLY VIEWS OF THE GROUP PROCESS

Early American thinkers, especially Madison, had a special and very creative outlook on the connection between interests and consent. Madison in his most famous essay, "Federalist 10," enunciated one of the most important and influential statements about this connection. It surely stands as an important expression of the original Western liberal approach to the problem. According to Madison, as long as there were multitudes of interests with no possibility of any one interest becoming a permanent majority, the free interaction of these interests would provide a public good. Interests organized in factions prevent tyranny by regulating each other and produce consent by relying upon government to provide temporary majorities. This interplay and counterpoise among factions or interest groups frees the government to be led by good men—in the Greek, not the snobbish, sense—within the framework of a fixed constitution.

Very probably, the most important feature of this early liberal approach to government by the consent of organized interests was the coupling of consent with regulation. Groups, lacking unilateral power over government, balance each other on the one hand and on the other hand seek through government to check each other by virtue of the sheer distrust each group has of the other. Consent is virtual, having been drawn from the same process rather than consciously granted. For, the same distrust which seeks regulative legislation is likely also to support a government which provides it. As Madison puts it: "The regulation of the various interfering interests forms the principal task of modern legislation."[1]

It was on this very basis that the original liberals found republics superior to democracies, as they saw the distinction. A republic was simply a government in which a scheme of representation takes place. Interests made up an intrinsic part of this definition; nevertheless, the indirectness of a republic offered a cure for those very same interests and factions: (1) representation would enlarge individual perspec-

1. James Madison, "Federalist 10," in *The Federalist on the New Constitution*, Alexander Hamilton, James Madison and John Jay (Philadelphia, Pa.: R. Wilson DeSilver, 1847), p. 34.

tives "by passing them through the medium of a chosen [elected] body of citizens; and (2) representation would produce government "more consonant to the public good than if pronounced by the people themselves," because it would be very difficult for even the most talented schemers to practice for long periods conspiracies or other "vicious arts" to impose bad judgments on all the others.[2] The interplay of interests in a republican form of government would make for better men in government, produce regulated interests and generate genuine consent—that is, the ability to govern on the basis of broad popular support.

It may well be that the American Constitution is the only government system built self-consciously upon those views. However, the theory and assumptions backing that view have been widely and increasingly shared as the advanced industrial societies emerged during the late nineteenth and early twentieth century.

CONSENT THROUGH ACCOMMODATION

In the process of aging and spreading, the original American liberal view underwent drastic transformation, even though the connection between interests and consent remained at the center of the theory. It is this changed version of the theory which has had such a tremendous influence in the United States and abroad. In this changed view, although consent was still to emerge from the interests, consent was no longer to be the result of competition, distrust and regulation among interests. Under the new

2. Ibid., p. 36.

theory consent is to come from a genuine accommodation of government, through its leaders and policies, to the real interests of society. All twentieth century mass democracies seem to espouse this theory of consent in one way or another. It may be expressed in the falangist method of incorporating all the effective interests inside one official party. Or it can be the Argentine variation, where loose coalitions are tolerated within an authoritarian governmental scheme. Or it can be the post-war French and Italian expression, where officially recognized interest groups are represented on actual government councils. Or it can be still newer forms of codetermination and participation. Or it can be some modern expression of Bonapartism, expressed in officially sponsored plebiscites. Or it can be the United States pattern of broad delegation to independent agencies on the assumption that the agencies and the interests will come into agreement.

That the more authoritarian democracies, rather than admit their authoritarianism, spend extraordinary amounts of time and concern manipulating, arranging or even deserving popular expressions of consent is a tremendously strong expression of their commitment to this particular basis for conducting a government. Now, it is distinctly not true to say that the Western European countries and the United States are authoritarian in the same sense. Nevertheless, their theory of state tends equally to stress consent of the same sort. This in itself is a measure of how far we have departed from the earlier liberal notion that consent and regulation are part of the same process. This fundamental change of perspective can be epitomized in the way in which Madison has come to be interpreted by the moderns. Take, for example, the treatment of Madison's definition of interest group—faction—by one of the United States' most influential and creative liberal political scientists. Madison's definition of faction was:

A number of citizens whether amounting to a majority or a minority of the whole who are united and actuated by some common impulse of passion, or of interest, *adverse to the right of other citizens, or to the permanent and aggregate interests of the community*.[3]

David Truman adopted Madison's definition, but eliminated the underlined part of the definition.[4] This leaves only the objective part; and the difference between two such treatments makes almost all of the difference in the world.

The change meant at least two things. First, it meant that in the modern liberal state—and in the theory generated by its support group, the scientific realism school of political science—all interests would have equal status. No moral ordering or judgment would be possible in the theory or practice of government. No choice could be made except through the process by which those demands and supports with the largest and most effective resources would win out over those with lesser political resources. Second—and most relevant here—this change of perspective meant that government was to gain its consent by discovering the real interests, by determining the strength and basis of the resources of each, and then accommodating to those interests by producing

3. Ibid., p. 33.
4. David B. Truman, *The Governmental Process: Political Interests and Public Opinion* (New York: Alfred A. Knopf, 1951).

policies and decisions which can be predicted directly by the political weight backing those interests.

Leaving aside the important issue of the morality of such a view, there is still the question of whether such an accommodation is possible. Note well: if such an accommodation is not possible, then description of interest group polities as though that were possible produces more myth than scientific realism.

At the outset we can say at least this much, that consent in a theory of accommodation to interests is a great deal more difficult to fulfill than consent in a theory of interest regulation. To regulate interests requires only that the state concern itself with activities, making sure that interests do not run rampant, behave illegally, violate the First Amendment freedoms of other interests or otherwise impose themselves on weaker interests except through the imposition of legitimately stronger resources. In contrast, accommodation means actual concern for the specific demands being made. This requires detailed information and knowledge about interests, and it requires a careful calculation among interests to determine whether the accommodations are sufficiently balanced and equitably distributed.

The closer one looks at this proposition, the more distant appears the possibility of consent by accommodation to interests. Yet, since the climate is so widespread and strong, politicians continue to try to accommodate and, of course, political scientists continue to describe the group process in terms of those efforts. Ultimately, if the politics of accommodation proves impossible, then Machiavelli—not Madison—is the father of the modern liberal state, despite our wish that this not be true.

This does not necessarily mean that every politician is a deceiver. There is a great deal of evidence to suggest the contrary, that sincere effort is made to accommodate. Some of that evidence will be found in the millions of dollars spent on sample surveys and on other cruder efforts to gain political knowledge. Even the most powerful leaders, especially in the United States, behave as though they prefer to operate within an active context of consent even when they could get what they want without it. It is the effort itself which creates the deception. "The medium is the message" may apply in modern politics to a far greater extent than in modern commercial communication. The politician deceives himself as much as he deceives those whose consent he seeks. His most sincere effort to find out all he would need to know about interests in order to accommodate them implies that he is going to find out something which he ultimately knows he cannot find out. What political leaders cannot actually discover about real interests they try to engineer into being and, that failing, try to control and suppress those who would report the news of their ignorance.

It might at first appear to be a good thing that politicians zealously seek to accommodate to interests and to be guided by organized publics. However, it is perilous to operate as if they can succeed in this attempt. Once we are given the strong impression that organized opinion can govern without "good men" and without independent lawmakers making independent choices about the laws which shall coerce us, then those same political leaders are stuck with the obligation to act as though they are actually governing by the real and continuing consent of the people, where the leadership is only a channel for the passageway of interests. Once this expectation is widespread, as it seems to be, a number of things follow naturally, imposing themselves heavily on political roles. First, as already suggested, politicians must employ deceit, however much they may sincerely desire to avoid it, because there will always be a tremendous gap between the independent decisions they are actually making and the channel of interests for which their role calls. Second, politicians must employ techniques of manipulation, shaping the consent they can neither find expressed spontaneously nor discover by the best sample survey research. Third, they are also led inexorably to suppress or misrepresent the dissensus which remains after they fail to accommodate a sufficient number of the interests of the society.

It is no coincidence that the knowledge industry and the scientific study of mass phenomena have risen in conjunction with the rise of mass democracies. Sample survey methods were tried as early as 1896 in presidential campaigns in the United States, but they were widely denounced as infringements on civil liberties and were not taken seriously by the most serious politicians. The knowledge approach to politics was not taken seriously by the most serious politicians until the latter part of the 1930s. This was not because it took that long to validate the idea and the methodology of sampling—such officially sponsored bodies as the Census Bureau had been doing this kind of work to good effect for years.

Willingness to invest millions of dollars in polling and to base billions of dollars of decisions on polling results came only as the need for more knowledge of mass opinions and mass behavior became desperately pressing. Scientific politics—especially polling—is as much a product of political and commercial need as it is a product of social science. Both the politician who uses this material and the social scientist who produces it are terribly aware of the incompleteness of the knowledge. Moreover, some of the best knowledge produced by social science research is negative knowledge—that is, knowledge which reveals the incompleteness of the interests expressed by organized groups and their spokesmen.

This entire scenario is produced in order to raise in its most dramatic form the original question of whether a system can actually be governed by the consent of organized opinions any better than it could be governed by the consent of more mythical public opinion or general will. Instead of studying the group process and then studying the policy outputs, we must take a step backwards and ask: to what extent do organized groups in society pull in enough of the total range of social interests to qualify as a source of public opinion or even to qualify for the full privileges and immunities of the First Amendment freedoms of speech and assembly? Indeed, to what extent can we justify Truman's early expression of the point of view that the group is simply a way of looking at the individual?[5] Groups

draw people and their interests into politics to a far greater extent than they would be drawn in without group activities; however, in being drawn in by groups, are they represented accurately or are they heavily distorted?

To anticipate the analysis, these same questions can be prejudiced still further. To what extent can groups ever be a proper medium for the messages which the people are seeking to convey to government? To what extent can organized groups ever represent any interests except those of the group oligarchy itself? To what extent can interests defined by objective situations—class, ethnicity, religion or anything else—be maintained when a few people seek to organize around them?

No matter how groups are organized, unless they are so small as to account for little, they are involved in at least three commonplace distortions—distortions which make a census of opinions through groups impossible and a

5. I have frequently given the wrong impression about my attitudes toward David Truman's classic work, *The Governmental Process*. I happen to consider it one of the most important works in modern political science, and I also feel the good it produced for political understanding far outweighs any contribution I might here or elsewhere have criticized. Actually, Truman frequently expressed grave concerns about the justifications and results of the group process and of specific organized groups. However, Truman comes into play frequently in a critique of group-based government because he was so explicit about the premises of group theory and the results of group activity. Truman's book is an extremely useful and efficient foil because of such explicitness. However, it should in fairness be said that his work is a kind of way station or transition point between earlier mythologies of formal democracy. He must be singled out for examples of the new assumptions, simply because the faith in the informal process is so great these days that few of these assumptions are articulated at all. That is a measure of how far these assumptions have been internalized.

consensus among opinions purely mythological. These distortions are systematic—that is, they are built into the nature of group organizations and are not a matter of accident or strategy. Consequently, the analysis of groups in politics cannot take place without first dealing with these distortions. Finally, these distortions make an objective analysis of groups impossible. Any approach to groups—their strategies, how they bring people in and how they affect government—which would pretend to be objective by not dealing with systematic distortions can never be anything more than a source of mythology.

THREE COMMONPLACE DISTORTIONS IN GROUP POLITICS

If one were searching for a single proposition to capture the relationship between groups and consent, it would be this: groups are one of society's most effective means of conquest. Such a proposition would, of course, be wrong by overemphasis, because some groups are organized to rebel—a raft of late 1960s groups, for example—and other groups upset consensus without intending to—for example, Jehovah's Witnesses. Nevertheless, this single proposition is closer to the truth about most standard self-interest groups than any other statement. To examine even the "most common and durable source of factions . . . the various and unequal distribution of property,"[6] is to find an equivalent number of laboratories for the discovery of the three commonplace and fundamental distortions. The fact that these distortions are commonplace will permit brevity in the treatment of each.

6. Madison, "Federalist 10," p. 34.

To organize is to distort

Organization begins with the individual, and one of the most important kinds of organization with which the individual must provide himself is an arrangement of some of his values into priorities. Priority ranking is the essence of organization, and it is just as painful for the individual as it is for a group. It is painful in the first place because priority ranking involves sacrifice. The cost to a student choosing Harvard Medical School is the sacrifice of Chicago and Yale. The choice of steak for dinner usually involves the sacrifice of lobster or some other attractive item on the menu.

To this particular kind of pain is usually added still another: a social or psychological pain which in many instances is far more difficult to bear than the material sacrifice of priority ordering, because the choice represents the individual to others. As Goffman would put it, the individual in his choices gives an impression and also gives off an impression. For one very commonplace example, the choice of decor for a house can be a desperate ordeal for an upper-middle class woman, because she can represent herself and her family in only one design to her friends and community.

The problem in contemporary social life can be understood best by observing in relief the situation in stable and traditional communities where persons can be known for themselves and their entire personalities. In societies of larger scale, such as modern urban society, few persons are known except through the choices by which they are represented. So much has this become the case that modern social science may quite accurately define the human being as a bundle of all of his roles and interests, not as a whole human being. One is known as a Democrat, or a lawyer, or a Protestant, or a liberal, or a swinger or a square. Few individuals, especially in political life, are familiar with many people across several of these roles and choices. These individual roles are, of course, not all that inaccurate as a means of anticipating behavior and acting accordingly. This may be one of the most powerful aspects of social science. It has its advantages in politics, because it is easier to treat interests as equal than it is individuals. Nevertheless, this is a distortion—however creative a distortion—since interests are not people, and people cannot be fully reconstructed from their interests and the priorities they themselves construct among their own interests. A few murders are indeed solved by reconstructing suspects from the interests that give them motives to murder. Even so, we require witnesses or some other corroborating evidence, because we realize that motives are not the fact itself.

Unfortunately, in politics reality requires that we go on treating interests and motives as persons. We could not otherwise operate. Yet, it is foolish to pretend that in so doing we are not operating this way, but operating some other way. One of the worst aspects of this is polling. Polling is a special problem in this context, precisely because it is far and away the most powerful and efficient way of getting reliable political knowledge. Polling does, however, involve tremendous distortions about individuals and their values and interests; this part of the process has not been brought adequately into political theory, as yet. One or two simple examples

ought to suffice. For one, every question on a sample survey which provides only a simple yes and no alternative is a profound distortion. Even those questions involving several alternative responses force the individual into the mold of the research agency, because the alternatives are still designed for only one dimension of the issue. This is a very poignant and special distortion precisely for the most knowledgeable people in the sample; before answering they must engage in a kind of internal dialogue and then provide the interviewer with a response which is, at best, "on net" from among several possible ones he would provide if the situation were spontaneous. Thus, the knowledge which the questionnaire is providing for the political planners is knowledge dictated and designed precisely for their needs by the questionnaire itself.

A second important example of the intrinsic distorting effect of polling approaches to knowledge about individuals is that the questionnaire or interview itself is an important variable in the knowledge which the individual members of the sample will turn back through the questions—that is, the questionnaire cannot take account of itself as a method of civic education. One of the most important concrete results of this is that the sample produces an impression of shared information which may deeply misrepresent the actualities among individuals prior to the introduction of the questionnaire. A second, and perhaps more misleading, aspect of this process is that the individual respondent gives off an impression of saliency about many issues which is simply not true. That is to say, when the interviewer asks the respondent for his opinion about anything from a neighboring housing project to capitalism versus socialism, the respondent, feeling his civic duty or whatever it is, is very likely to report some response inevitably indicating that he has already given the issue some thought and that the issue has a place on his priority schedule. Some of this problem can be faced by having a first round of permissive and open-ended questions allowing each respondent to identify for the researchers the issues which are most important. However, this is an extremely expensive form of double or triple re-interviewing. Moreover, it does not solve the problem entirely even then, because: (1) after the pilot study only a fraction of the issues so identified can be used on the full questionnaire; and (2) only one dimension of each issue is likely to be set up on the response alternatives provided in the final questionnaire. Much of the distortion, therefore, remains.

The artificial majority

Distortions of even greater proportion are involved when individuals try to combine their priority schedules and organize collectively. This particular source of distortion is almost completely beyond solution through polling and other social science research. In fact, the study of individual opinions within groups creates useful negative knowledge, in that it pierces through the innumerable false claims of leaders about speaking for the entire group. The more we learn, the more we see how consistently and completely minority opinions are suppressed in order to carry out interest group politics.

Even when only a husband and wife are involved in the joint effort of searching for a house to buy,

small differences in their respective priority schedules can cause painful differences in final decisions, unless each suppresses the differences or ultimately agrees to set the differences aside. Each individual added to the collective endeavor increases the complexity and the potential for suppression, probably at an exponential rate.

The suppression of minority interests is intrinsic to group politics. Of course, the membership can sit—as Quakers are supposed to do—until the spirit moves them. However, most studies of early Quaker and other communes in the United States suggest that there was always a good deal of minority suppression just the same. Even if that were not the case, most groups with a commitment to act effectively in politics will tend to use more decisive methods of decision making. They will vote on their choices and priorities, or they will seek some kind of arbitration, or they will agree to delegate the important choices to their leadership. In any of these cases, there will be a point beyond which dissenters must be silenced or purged. All groups operate on the basis of democratic centralism, even if they refuse to use violence in enforcing it.

There are many excellent works on interest group processes which reveal this kind of regular suppression of minorities. Grant McConnell's studies of agriculture and labor are filled with such incidents;[7] Robert Michels anticipated all of this sort of thing.[8] Probably the best

7. Grant McConnell, *Decline of Agrarian Democracy* (New York: Atheneum, 1969); and his *Steel and the Presidency* (New York: W. W. Norton, 1962).

8. Robert Michels, *Political Parties: A Sociological Study of the Oligarchical Tendencies of Modern Democracy* (Gloucester, Mass.: Peter Smith, 1960).

single statement of it, coupled with ample evidence, will be found in Truman,[9] where he calls the phenomenon "the democratic mold." From the standpoint of society at large, the suppression of minorities in groups is an extremely important form of social control. Groups must control their own membership in order to operate in politics, and that solves a lot of the problems of governing. However, this comes at a great cost; that cost is distortion. Government leaders or agencies which express trust in reports about membership opinion are usually engaging in whitewashes and subterfuges. Moreover, the prospect of voluntarily withdrawing from one group and forming the majority in another is most often another source of mythology. In an overwhelming number of instances, only one interest group is available to an individual through which to pursue a particular interest. Besides, it is considered bad sportsmanship to participate in the decisions of a group and then to object or withdraw simply because the individual member was on the losing side of the vote.

It was partly on this basis that Tocqueville appears to have compared Europe so unfavorably to America. He admired the "principle of association" in the United States, which appeared to him to be something like a peace-time version of the Minutemen, forming to act in concert on a given issue and then disappearing back into private life. This was, to Tocqueville, to be contrasted with "permanent and compulsory association" in Europe which "centralize the direction of their forces as much as possible and entrust the power of the whole party

to a small number of leaders."[10] This describes aptly the contemporary *syndicat* and *patronat* in France and the interest group in the United States. A permanent association is a distortion of its own interests, no matter how creative or effective the distortion may be.

The illogic of collective action

The first two types of distortion are actual distortions by suppression—real-world suppression dictated by the need to make choices. Every choice made by an individual or a collectivity represents the individual or collectivity incompletely, at the very best. In contrast, however, this third type of distortion is an artifact of collective life itself. It lies in the logic, or illogic, of group collective choice making rather than in the functional prerequisites of group life.

This is, of course, a reference to the "welfare function" as explored in many ways since Kenneth Arrow. What this means is that, totally aside from suppressing minority views on a given issue, there are some anomalies built into collective life which set the group majority against itself and set some goals in conflict with others. In other words, many decisions made by a group do not adequately represent any conceivable majority of the group or very much satisfaction to any of the members.

For the readership of such a journal as THE ANNALS, it is unnecessary to recount the logic of this problem. Yet, for the sake of understanding, perhaps a single story will suffice. A committee, so the story goes, is sent to the local

9. Truman, *Governmental Process*, chap. 5.

10. Alexis de Tocqueville, *Democracy in America* (New York: Random House, 1955), vol. 1, chap. 12 and vol. 2, chap. 5.

butcher shop to buy meat for the picnic. The butcher informs the committee that he has only chicken and beef available in large enough lots for their picnic. The committee goes into the corner and discusses the issue for a few minutes and returns to tell the butcher that they have decided to buy the chicken. But while they were deliberating, the butcher discovered that he also had turkey in large enough quantities; this means that the committee has to go back into deliberation. They then return to the butcher and report that since he also has turkey they have decided that they no longer want the chicken, but will take the beef.

This kind of outcome can—and does—happen frequently, because every majority on every choice can be different from the majority on every other choice. This can only mean that the majority already made artificial by the suppression of minority interests is all the more artificial because of the shifting membership of the majority and the unpredictable and inconsistent consequences of its decisions.

Groups adjust to these instabilities by imposing consistency on themselves. This they can do by leaving the agenda and most of the choices to the central oligarchy of the group. As Runciman succinctly summarized the case in his *Social Science and Political Theory*:

Arrow's argument shows that our intuitive criteria for a democratic decision cannot in fact be satisfied unless we are prepared under certain conditions to accept a social ordering which is either "imposed" or "dictatorial."[11]

This amounts to exchanging one kind of distortion for another.

11. W. G. Runciman, *Social Science and Political Theory* (New York: Cambridge University Press, 1972), p. 133.

SCIENCE AND CONSENT: INTEREST GROUPS IN THEORY AND PRACTICE

No amount or manner of improvement in the science of gaining political knowledge will ever eliminate the commonplace distortions in the interest group process. Quite the contrary, the more social science improves, the more we are likely to learn about distortion and the more distortion we are likely to discover. Rather than trying to eliminate distortion, we should instead be considering how to convert it into useful negative knowledge. This negative knowledge could improve modern political theory and political practice.

Almost every writer who seriously considered pluralist political theory has recognized distortion in one or more forms. Nevertheless, distortion has never been given a proper place in political science in general or survey research in particular. In order to live with the fact of distortion without allowing it to disorder theoretical viewpoints, political scientists have made one or more of the following tacit assumptions: (1) most people do not have strong interests anyway; (2) for those who do wish to pursue interests actively, there exists a sufficient number of alternative group channels to allow representation of the interests of suppressed minorities; (3) competition among groups prevents leaders from straying too far from members; (4) groups, which are by definition shared attitudes, are homogeneous enough to be adequately spoken for by their leaders or observed by politicians and analysts; and (5) there are other ways of getting knowledge about minorities suppressed within, or left entirely without, organized groups.

These assumptions might or might

not be confirmed by proper investigation. Left uninvestigated and unarticulated, they produce debilitating weaknesses in the empirical structure and normative implications of theories dealing with interest groups. To sum up the matter as briefly as possible, any study of interest groups which neglects these distortions or assumes them away can never escape the kinds of criticism hurled at political science all during the 1960s. To describe and assess interest group phenomena—coalition formation, group influences on government, group roles in increasing participation or citizen education— without giving full weight to distortion is to appear objective, but also to be a defender of almost any claims elites can make that they have popular consent. One of the commonplace pluralist positions would be that interest group politics works through coalitions and that coalitions are bargains among leaders of groups. Yet, leaders must distort in order to control their group resources and to use them effectively; also, they must be allowed maximum flexibility in order to develop a position which brings net gain to themselves and their groups. All this is good for the group as a corporate thing, and it may be better still for social stability in that, as a result, the leaders are more willing to support the regime if the government writes the coalition agreement into law. However, the relation of all this to consent, legitimacy, participation, citizenship or any of the other basic political values is not a great deal closer than monarchy. It is only more roundabout. Once members give their tacit consent to their leaders and their leaders give consent to regimes and regimes give

their consent to administrative agencies to deal flexibly with groups, one can begin to wonder whether all this is an improvement over a consent based on the claim of an ancient family to virtual consent based upon god or some other transempirical process.

A NEW PLACE FOR GROUPS IN POLITICAL THEORY?

A world view in which distortion is properly appreciated will not tolerate any political analysis which treats groups descriptively, accepts claims to consent lightly, defends support and obedience as facts. The truth that interest group is synonymous with distorted messages, suppressed minorities, ignorant analysts and deluded politicians does not wipe out established pluralist truths. Pluralism is likely to be the prevailing political view for a long time to come in industrial countries which are socially so pluralistic. The factor of distortion will merely serve to make pluralism more pessimistic. One can still conceptualize the political system; it simply will not always have a happy ending.

For both political scientists and citizens a proper appreciation of distortions and how commonplace they really are would lead to a very much altered focus on politics. This focus would at least begin to reduce the fascination with news, inside dope, personal opinions and motivations and the processes of coalition making. The focus would very probably shift to the level of policies and coercion. The basic questions of theory and practice would be: what was demanded and who is going to suffer for it?, rather than: how was it done? and who benefited? The shift would be from: is there consent and support?, to: for what was consent and support given? The stress in empirical science and in political practice would be upon the independence of legislature and executive rather than upon their intimate dependence upon the process. Furthermore, the conclusions would stress shortcomings, as well as functional fulfillment—theory—and consent —practice.

A view from the perspective of distortion would also stress a particular kind of reform. Reforms from this position would not attempt to eliminate distortions, but might instead: (1) somewhat reduce them by altering some of their most favorable conditions; (2) reduce the problem of distortion by stressing alternative channels of popular consent; and, meanwhile, (3) return to the posture of regulation, due to a recognition of the impossibility of accommodation. The following suggestions are offered not so much in the spirit of practice, but mainly in order to round out the analysis:

—Loosen up the grip that the oligarchy has on membership. (1) Limited liability: when groups incorporate, whether for economic profit or political advantage, the leaders and the members are shielded from most of the personal responsibility for results. There is no longer any reason to be absolute about the membership privileges which are gained by incorporation.
(2) Serious consideration should be given to the prospect of dusting off the use of injunctive power against the unions. Again, there is no reason why specific political misbehaviors by unions can take place without a public remedy.
(3) Slowly and carefully revise the constitutional doctrines applying First Amendment privileges to groups. Again, there seems to be no reason why courts cannot distinguish between groups and the context within which they are operating. For example, a National Association for the Advancement of Colored People (NAACP) chapter in southern Louisiana might require protection, as a corporation, from having to reveal membership records and other data, whereas the same type of organization in New York—having no fear of retaliation against its members—could be required to make membership lists, contributor lists and internal records public.

—Loosen the group coalition structure; make conspiracies against the public harder to achieve and maintain.
(1) Change labor law in order to make jurisdictional strikes possible under certain justifiable conditions. There may no longer be a compelling case in favor of absolute proscription of fights between groups contending for recognition in the same plant.
(2) Impose far heavier sentences against the leadership of corporations and trade associations found guilty of decisions to give on a corporate basis to political parties.
(3) Make provisions in regulatory statutes for private suits involving heavy damages where established groups are found guilty of interfering with insurgencies—for example, the case of Ralph Nader's report that General Motors tried to blackmail him. This should include much easier access by

members and nonmembers to the minutes and other private records of incorporated groups, including political parties.

—Provide independent and public alternatives to the present polling agencies. Most commercial polls are captives of the interests of the clientele they serve, and most commercially based media of communication make their most extensive decisions along these lines. Existing university polling agencies are either too narrowly based or too narrowly focused to serve broad public needs.

(1) The most important feature of this would be to establish at least one very large and independent polling organization that can operate as a kind of Tennessee Valley Authority (TVA) of public opinion. Its regular surveys would be designed to test the results in the national polls and to reveal oppressed minorities which are glossed over by claims made on behalf of groups by their spokesmen.[12]

(2) This same TVA of public opinion could be used to improve the electoral process through its capability to spend the kind of money necessary to provide a far larger number of open-ended questions which allow voters to define salient issues.

—Make governmental, especially congressional, decision-making

processes more independent of the group process. Since this was gone into at such great length in my book, *The End of Liberalism*, the treatment here will necessarily be brief and sparse.[13]

(1) The most important reform in the entire approach to interest groups would be the return to a more orthodox application of rule of law to the outputs of governments. In brief, this would mean applying a close approximation of the "Schecter rule" to government policy formulations. As I have argued, much of the present pluralist process depends upon policies which embody no actual rules; thus, agencies are left to deal directly, and without guidance, with organized clientele groups.

(2) Encourage a more open administrative process and a closer approximation to real agency rule making by provisions in the law which would make possible group and taxpayer suits enjoining agencies from further operation until they can provide the constitutional basis and rule upon which a decision or a line of decisions is being made. The legal notion of show cause is most profoundly needed in the relationship between government and citizen. In contrast, the present relationship between groups and government can be best epitomized by the old quip: "What's a constitution among friends?"

—Reassess abstention.

(1) Political scientists must begin to make distinctions

---

12. The concept of TVA which is employed here draws upon the theory in back of TVA that its output would operate as a yardstick regulating private activities in the same field. A yardstick method of regulation is essential in the field of interest groups and opinion, because more direct forms of regulation are almost certain to run afoul of the First Amendment.

13. Theodore J. Lowi, *The End of Liberalism* (New York: W. W. Norton, 1969).

among forms of participation. Not all participation is good. Not all participation improves citizenship, and some participation falls more easily into unlimited consent rather than the conditional and specialized consent that is the essence of democratic theory. Political scientists who study participation for its own sake are again greasing the skids toward popularly based tyranny.

(2) Of even greater importance is the need for recognizing and making distinctions among forms of nonparticipation. Some nonparticipation is a result of ignorance, apathy and satisfaction; however, a great deal of it is not. For example, every intelligent person ought to answer "it all depends" to questions about whether the president is doing his job well; and the same person ought to answer "don't know" to very broad and vaguely posed questions on busing or war and peace. In other words, very often it is the ignorant and the apathetic who do participate and the intelligent and highly motivated who do not. The first step is to admit that nonparticipation, either in the form of low levels of formally defined political behavior or lack of response on questionnaires, cannot be taken as an indicator of anything, least of all of acceptance.

(3) One step beyond the recognition of the possible meanings of nonparticipation is acceptance of nonparticipation as a bona fide and possibly effective form of political action. I would go so far as to urge the encouragement of that form of participation, but here I will rest only with its description. There is not even a word in the American vocabulary for such an action; we must borrow from the French: *abstentionism*. Abstentionism can involve an organized, willful and highly articulated act of refusal to vote or to belong to a group on the grounds that the refuser refuses to give consent. Participation merely in the form of voting against the incumbent amounts to an embrace of the system and consent to be governed by whoever wins. The only way to refuse to give consent and to imply that dissenters do not accept the regime is to refuse participation altogether, for reasons stated. To participate is to commit oneself to the outcome.

It should be patently clear by now that these reforms would, if adopted, bring about a closer approximation to the best ideals of pluralism, in theory and in practice. This, of course, amounts to an admission that however hard we try it is extremely difficult, perhaps impossible, to escape the pluralist political mold in a pluralistic and permissive society. However, the next step should also be taken: to confirm the hypothesis that the pluralism from which we get most of the good results attributed to it is not a natural phenomenon, but in large part the result of careful and deliberate arrangements made for groups—for example, by the original writers of the Constitution in the United States. As for the bad effects attributed to pluralism by its critics, these, too, come from deliberate cultivation of group support by bad legislation and weak and corrupt politicians. Taken together, all of this is intended also to support the concluding proposition that the only good pluralist is a pessimistic pluralist.

Interest Groups in Switzerland

By Dusan Sidjanski

ABSTRACT: This article is a general presentation of Swiss socioeconomic groups and associations and of the role they play in Swiss political life. While the main organizations were created before 1900, the evolution of the associations corresponds to the general trends of industrialization and division of labor. Swiss groups are characterized by a high concentration of their central bodies in Zurich and Berne and by federal structures reproducing the cantonal divisions of Switzerland. Consultation, based on constitutional provisions, is highly developed not only in internal politics, but also in foreign policy matters. One specific feature of this process is the existence of both the referendum and the initiative which constitute an element of the bargaining power of different associations. To illustrate this process, I draw on two examples: one related to the law on cartels and the other to the inflation policy. The last, but not the least interesting, aspect is the perception of this process by the public. In fact, our Swiss survey of 1972 gives a good idea of how the public perceives the influence of different groups and their capacity to defend its interests. It is clear that if the legitimacy of these associations and their activities is generally recognized, the Swiss voter condemns all violent forms of action and is reluctant even to approve demonstrations. On the other hand, normal activities of socioeconomic groups are supported by a large consensus.

Dusan Sidjanski is Professor of Political Science at the University of Geneva and Chairman of the Department of Political Science, Faculty of Economic and Social Sciences. Many of his works and studies contributed to the analysis of pressure groups and their influence; among others, he wrote Les Groupes de pression dans la Communauté européenne *in collaboration with Jean Meynaud and* L'Europe des Affaires.

The author wishes to express his thanks to the Swiss National Fund for Scientific Research for their grant for the study of Swiss groups and to Mr. M. Sliwinski and Mr. J. Nicola who constructed some of the tables for this study.

XCEPT for a few cases of closed decisions, the Swiss decision-making apparatus is characterized by extensive consultation of socioeconomic organizations. The progressive flowering of occupational groupings since the second half of the nineteenth century has transformed the structure of the Swiss economy and the decision-making process. No less than 1,100 socioeconomic groupings came into being between 1871 and 1972.[1]

1. *Liste des associations professionnelles et économiques de la Suisse*, 12th ed. (Bern: OFIAMT, 1968).

FIGURE 1

BREAKDOWN OF NUMBER OF SWISS OCCUPATIONAL ORGANIZATIONS IN ONE YEAR

Mean   : 10.68
Mode   : 8
Median : 9

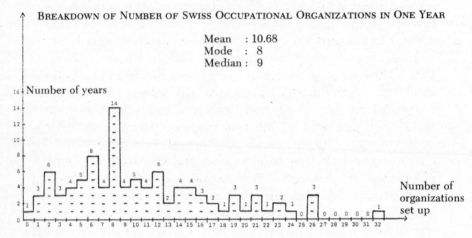

FIGURE 2

TWO-YEARLY AVERAGE NUMBERS OF OCCUPATIONAL ASSOCIATIONS SET UP

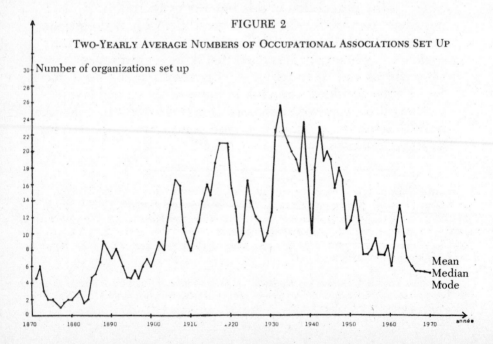

THE PATTERN OF INTEREST GROUPS

Development and numbers

As is shown in figures 1 and 2, this process was at first comparatively slow; the yearly average between 1871 and 1904 amounted to 3.5. The period from 1905 to 1922 witnessed a sharp acceleration— 264—with a yearly average of 15.5 and three peaks—21 new organizations in 1907, 23 in 1917 and, again, in 1919. For the period 1923 to 1931 the yearly number of new associations fell to an average of 13, but in 1932 an all-time high was reached with the formation of 32 groupings. That year marked the beginning of a period which, coming in the wake of the Great Depression, was the most active in terms of new organizational structures; no less than 336 groupings were formed over sixteen years—from 1932 to 1948—an average of 21 per year. From 1949 to 1972—the period for which data are available—the annual average was a more modest 8.8. For the entire period under review—1871 to 1972—the mean was 10.7 per year, with a median of 13 and a mode of 8.

The most important associations —above all, the big four which are central to the entire consultation process—all came into being during the initial period. Thus, *Vorort*— the Swiss Commerce and Industry Union—was set up in 1870 and was followed shortly thereafter, by *Union Suisse des arts et métiers* (USAM)—the Swiss Union of Arts and Crafts—in 1879 and the *Union syndicale Suisse* (USS)—Swiss Federation of Trade Unions—in 1880. Thus, from the very beginning, the rapidly expanding secondary and tertiary sectors had central organizations of their own on both the labor and the management side. Not much later, in 1897, the farmers were also to organize at the federal level. By 1900 the big four, which to this day have remained a constant factor in all consultations, had been established. Sectoral organizations were to develop later; the timing for the principal employers and workers organizations is shown in table 1. Once these major sectors of activity were covered, the development process followed a path of increasing specialization in line with the wide diversification of the economy. Table 1 also reveals a parallel between the establishment of employers and workers organizations.

The 1967 breakdown of the 1,081 occupational associations then in existence is shown in table 2. While these are only rough indications, they do give an idea of organizational density in relation to the size of the active population on a sector-by-sector basis, by revealing an over-all ratio of 1 organization for every 2,600 people as compared with 1 per 2,000 in the service sector—the highest density; 1 per 2,500 in agriculture; and the markedly lower ratio—substantially lower, in fact, than the general average—of 3,140 in industry. This is so because the large trade union organizations are found mainly in this sector, the outstanding example being the USS with its 440,000 members.

Main features

These groupings may be described in terms of, among others, the following four characteristics: (1) type of grouping, (2) geographical concentration, (3) network of affiliations and (4) federative structure.

Of the 1,081 associations: 728 are employers associations; 159 are wage earners or salaried employees

TABLE 1

FOUNDING OF EMPLOYERS AND EMPLOYEES ASSOCIATIONS

	Year	Employers Associations	Year	Employees Trade Unions
CENTRAL ASSOCIATIONS	1870	Vorort—Swiss Commerce and Industry Union		
	1879	Swiss Union of Arts and Crafts	1880	Swiss Trade Union
SPECIALIZED ASSOCIATIONS	1882	Swiss Society of Chemical Industries		
	1883	Swiss Society of Machinery Manufacturers	1888	Swiss Federation of Metal Workers and Watchmakers (FOMH) (Wage earners)
	1900 (1876)	Swiss Chamber of Watchmakers	1903	Textile, Chemical and Paper Workers Union
	1905	Swiss Employers Association of Machinery Manufacturers and Metalworking Industries		
	1906	Chemical Industries Employers Association		
	1912	Swiss Bankers Association	1917	Swiss Bank Employees Association (Salaried employees)
	1897	Swiss Society of Building Contractors	1922	Swiss Federation of Building and Wood Workers

TABLE 2

ECONOMIC AND OCCUPATIONAL GROUPINGS BROKEN DOWN BY SECTOR*

	AGRICULTURE, MINING AND QUARRYING	INDUSTRY AND CRAFTS	SERVICES	TOTAL
Number of associations in 1967	79	448	554	1,081
Active population in 1969 (thousands)	200 /2.5	1,421 /3.14	1,119 /2	2,740 /2.6

* No data showing the share of gross national product per sector are available.

associations; and 194 are of other types. The trade unions axiomatically try to mold themselves according to the structures of the employers organizations; however, the differences in number between employer and trade union associations reflect basic differences in membership, organization, degree of concentration and importance of the main sectors. By and large, the existing groupings may be said to cover essentially all of the needs arising within the Swiss community.

From the point of view of concentration, Zurich is the location of two-fifths—419, including 375 for the city of Zurich—of all associations. Bern comes next with 293—224 for the city of Bern. Together, these two cantons account for two-thirds of the total—712 out of 1,081. The reason for this concentration is the economic and industrial predominance of Zurich and the presence of the federal government in Bern. The remaining associations are disseminated as follows: 74 in Basle; 53 in the canton of Vaud, including 40 in Lausanne; 35 in Geneva; 32 in Aargan; 31 in St. Gallen; 26 in Neuchâtel; and 25 in Lucerne and Solothurn.[2] As for the network of affiliations, 184 national associations are affiliated with the USAM, 113 with the *Vorort*, 30 with the Central Union of Employers Associations,[3] 34 with the *Union Suisse des paysans* (USP), 15 with the USS, 13 with the Swiss Federation of Salaried Employees, 11 with the Confederation of Christian Trade Unions and 9 with the Federated Union of Staffs of Public Administrations and Enterprises.

If one were to draw a diagram, the USAM would be at the center of the diagram; it has both the largest number of affiliates and the most organic links with other organizations, which are made up of various handicraft units and small- and medium-sized enterprises. Although occupying a less central position, the *Vorort* (USCI) is most strategically placed. In addition to the 60 organizations exclusively affiliated to it, it has several common affiliates with the USAM, with *Fédération suisse des importatems et du commerce de gros* (FSICG)—Swiss Federation of Imports Business and Wholesale Commerce—and, of course, with the Central Union. Concurrent affiliation with others is less frequent. On the other hand,

the farmers (USP) and their network are more marginally located, while the USS constitutes a system of its own.

As do equivalent organizations in other countries, the four central organizations—the USCI, USAM, USS and USP—include vertical associations or occupational federations, as well as the regional groupings—including the associations of the French-speaking part of Switzerland—which, in turn, form regional central organizations. Typical of the Swiss system is the pattern of organizations at the level of the cantons, with each central canton section including canton sections of the socio-economic federations covering the main areas of economic and social activity in the canton. In many cases these organizations predated the setting up of the first associations at the federal level; they enjoy wide autonomy and have their own differentiated functions. This federative pattern, which reflects the diversity of the country and its political organization, influences the decision-making process within the national associations; for, in spite of the important part played by the permanent central secretariat and the leadership at the national level, the making of decisions and policies is often based on a consultation procedure involving affiliated associations and sections. The process may be modified, particularly in view of the urgency and concentrated character of certain economic and social issues; in such cases the influence of the national organizations and leadership is correspondingly strengthened.

Finally, two traits characterize the working of the organizational pattern under the Swiss political system: namely, the procedure for con-

2. *Liste des associations*, pp. 4, 8.
3. There are in Switzerland, as in Germany, two employers associations, one of which—the Central Union—is responsible for social affairs.

sulting socioeconomic groupings and the manner in which pressure groups use the initiative and referendum procedures. Provisions in the federal Constitution for the consultation of associations and the widespread practice of such consultation are—in addition to semidirect democracy—among the distinctive features of Swiss political life.

THE CONSULTATION PROCESS

The basis and the issues

The consultation procedure laid down in certain provisions of the Constitution—Articles 27ter, 32 and 34ter—has developed extensively.[4] In various fields the drawing up of legislative bills and, also, the preparation of many decisions are subject to the consultation process. Though based on the concept of contribution by groupings to public policy, this mechanism also affords scope for the play of interests by enabling the groupings not only to assist the authorities in their preparatory work, but also to influence their decisions. These aspects of the problem have been discussed in a number of political science studies.[5]

The interest of scholars in these matters is hardly surprising; what is more noteworthy is the increasing attention they are receiving from the Swiss political leadership.

Parliamentary reports and debates exhibit an increasing preoccupation with preventing occupational or economic groupings from acquiring such leverage over the preparation of legislative texts as might affect the National Assembly's freedom of decision. Signs of this are frequent in recent debates of the Council of States; its Management Committee, while for the time being endorsing the present separation of functions—as did the National Council—adds that:

This must not, of course, preclude paying close attention to each step of the preliminary procedure and making every effort to ensure that, from both a political and practical point of view, preliminary decisions are not irreversible.[6]

This is an important aspect of the influence of groupings, which by no means excludes the full range of pressures, both direct and indirect. This whole question of relations between pressure groups and the federal government was vividly highlighted by the Federal Council in the conclusion of its message to the Parliament; the Federal Council warned against the weakening of the public spirit in the following terms: "The main concern of individuals and groupings is to secure for them-

---

4. Article 32: "The provisions laid down in Articles 31bis, 31ter, second paragraph, 31ter and 31quinquies may be established only through laws or orders subject to the popular vote. For emergency cases arising in times of economic upheaval, Article 89, third paragraph, shall be reserved. The cantons shall be consulted in the drawing up of implementing legislation. As a general rule, they shall be charged with the execution of federal provisions. The economic groupings concerned shall be consulted in the drawing up of implementing legislation and may be called upon to cooperate in the application of implementing provisions."

5. Erich Gruner, *Die Wirtschaftsverbände in der Demokratie* (Zürich: Erlenbach, 1956); Jean Meynaud with A. Korff, *Les Organisations professionnelles en Suisse* (Lausanne: Payot, 1963); Leonhard Neid-

hart, *Plebizit und Pluralitäre Demokratie: Eine Analyse der Funktion des schweizerischen Gesetzreferendums* (Bern: Francke Verlag, 1970); Karl Meyer, *Verbände un Demokratie in der Schweiz* (Olten: Dietschi, 1968).

6. Report submitted to the Council of States by its Management Committee on the extension of administration control, ad. 9194, 12 February 1966, p. 13.

selves the largest possible share of goods and services." Clearly, the influence of pressure groups has become a public issue.

General consultations

According to Jean Meynaud,[7] the stages of consultation—once action on a matter has been initiated—may be summarized as follows: (1) inter-department consultation; (2) referral of the matter to one or more experts for preparation of a preliminary draft or for advice; (3) verbal contacts and discussions with canton governments and occupational groupings likely to be affected by the proposed legislation; (4) appointment of an expert commission if the issue is of national importance —in addition to independent experts, such bodies include experts from occupational organizations which are thus associated with the legislative process; (5) referral of the draft to canton authorities and the concerned occupational organizations for written consultation; (6) preparation of the final draft by the administration and transmission to other departments and to the Federal Council for decision. Once adopted by the Federal Council, the draft is sent to Parliament and sometimes submitted to popular vote.

During the first stage—steps (1), (2) and (3)—the administration prepares the preliminary drafts with occasional assistance from an outside expert, particularly where the subject matter is important or specialized. It then approaches the canton authorities and the socioeconomic groupings. This is the second stage—that of consultation proper. In view of the influence of consultative committees on the preparation of the final draft and, hence, on the decision-making process, the choice of the experts to serve on the commissions and their working methods are of particular importance. As has been stressed by Walter Buser, vice-chancellor of the federal government, the choice of commissioners has from the start been a controversial issue: so much so that on February 7, 1950, the Federal Office of Industry, Arts and Crafts and Labor (OFIAMT) substituted for its internal directives of March 1, 1939, exhaustive guidelines concerning the consultation of associations and the appointment of commissioners. This document makes it clear, albeit indirectly, that the administration is faced with more than gentle pressures in both their choice of groupings to be consulted and the selection of members to be appointed to commissions.

The major commissions include representatives of the federal department concerned and other federal services, as appropriate, the cantons, the scientific community, employers, workers, consumers and, possibly, other interested circles. The appointment of members is the responsibility of the competent federal administrations. It is not arbitrary. Under the OFIAMT guidelines—applied, by analogy, by the other offices and divisions—the cantons and groupings are invited to nominate a number of representatives exceeding, if possible, that of members to be appointed so as to give the administration a choice. Finally—and this is a typically Swiss constraint—the experts must be appointed with fair regard to regions and languages.[8]

7. Jean Meynaud, *Les Organisations professionnelles*, pp. 274–279.

8. Walter Buser, "Le rôle de l'administration et des groupes dans le processus de décision en Suisse," *Annuaire suisse de science politique*, 1969, pp. 122, 123.

According to the federal government's yearbook for 1971–1972, there are 142 commissions of which 32 were set up in 1971, with the following breakdown: Political Department, 8; Department of the Interior, 38; Department of Justice and Police, 5; Armed Forces Department, 38; Department of Finance and Customs, 10; Department of Economic Affairs, 28; Department of Transport and Energy, 15. By way of example, the 32 commissions set up in 1971 are composed of 487 members.

As may be seen in table 3, while

TABLE 3

COMPOSITION OF CONSULTING COMMISSIONS

	ADMINISTRATION	OUTSIDE	TOTAL
Full membership	136 28%	351 72%	487 100%
Chairmen	13 41%	19 59%	32 100%
Secretaries	25 78%	7 22%	32 100%
Other members	98 23%	325 77%	423 100%

only 28 percent of all members and 41 percent of the chairmen come from the administration, the latter provides the secretariat in a large majority of cases. About three-quarters of all members come from outside the government—that is, from private industry, occupational associations, independent experts; two-thirds of all the chairmen are also outside people.

In this process of consultation the federal administration is the main target of pressures and influences. These are brought to bear by the groups in several ways, initially through the expert commissions— members are, of course, in a privileged position from this point of view. At the same time, however, there may be parallel attempts to influence administration and government policies, particularly by groups having only minority representation on commissions. These attempts may take the form of direct contacts and exchanges—for example, special reports, visits and audiences—or more indirect methods, such as mobilization of opinion or demonstrations—a favorite form of action with farmers. They also provide a natural outlet for groupings which are not a part of the established consultation machinery.

The system of communications and influence at the federal level is supplemented by general consultation, usually in written form, with the authorities and, through them, with socioeconomic groupings in the cantons. This results in regional diversification by providing a framework within which regional organizations can express themselves and by allowing for differences among canton sections affiliated to a federal association. The opportunity enjoyed by such organizations to influence public policy at the canton level gives them, in effect, an indirect leverage over the federal administration and government.

Consultation in foreign policy matters

A similar process applies to foreign policy in the trade, economic and social fields. Roughly speaking, three stages may be distinguished in the drawing-up of economic and trade agreements: namely, consultation and preparation; negotiation; and conclusion of the agreements, themselves.[9]

9. Dusan Sidjanski, "Les groupes de pression et la politique étrangère en Suisse," *Annuaire suisse de science politique*, 1966, pp. 28–45.

In the preparatory phase the federal administration consults, in writing, various federal-level occupational associations, in particular the *Vorort* and the Swiss Farmers Union. This request for advice may be preceded by direct contacts with the social and economic groupings mainly concerned. In preparing its reply, each association takes soundings in accordance with its usual methods.

The views received from the various occupational organizations provide the initial basis for the formulation of the federal administration's official negotiating position which is determined through direct consultations involving, apart from the national bodies, those federations concerned by the proposed agreement. It thus represents the outcome of a concerted effort by the federal administration and the representatives of the circles mainly concerned. As in the other consultation procedures, a few especially important national organizations are always associated with the various stages of the process. Following this preparatory phase, a report is drawn up by the official in charge of trade agreements and transmitted to the Federal Council which, on the basis of this report, issues its instructions to the Swiss negotiators.

In the negotiations the Swiss delegation includes, in addition to the government officials, representatives of the *Vorort* and the Swiss Farmers Union or the Watch-makers Federation. These representatives are treated as government delegates: their travel and subsistence allowances are paid by the federal administration, and sometimes they are granted additional facilities—for example, office space for the *Vorort* representatives. As government officials, they must observe secrecy.

This practice, which has been formalized, is a peculiarly Swiss institution; if found in other countries—for example, the Netherlands or Central America—such instances represent exceptions to the rule of the administration, alone, negotiating on the government's behalf. In Switzerland, by contrast, interpenetration is such that it is impossible to assess the extent of mutual influences. What can be said is that in this case cooperation is substituted for pressure, all the more so because in the area of foreign relations a strong degree of convergence between the interests of the public and private sectors is a fair assumption. Such pressure as might be brought to bear at this stage could emanate from a federation which was not associated in the consultation process and had divergent interests of its own or simply from a business grouping or enterprise seeking to defend or increase its share in the anticipated benefits. This kind of action usually takes the form of direct contacts or attempts at persuasion supported by the most solid and convincing documentary evidence.

These relationships, whether of cooperation or pressure, are characterized by a substantial degree of trust and personal contact. In the small circle of political and socio-economic leaders involved, everyone knows everyone else and there can be no secrets. Conflicts and clashes of interests may arise, but the size of the Swiss community and of its network of leaders facilitates personal relationships and mutual watchfulness. Respect for established positions has nevertheless often stood in the way of fresher and more dynamic elements.

After the agreement has been negotiated, the public factor tends to reassert itself. Parliamentary control, in particular, is exercised at the time of ratification.[10] The chances of any changes being made at this stage are, however, slight; the Federal Assembly is unlikely to disapprove an international text upon which the Federal Council, which decisively controls foreign policy, and a foreign government have agreed. Therefore, it is a plausible assumption that, as a rule, pressures on Parliament will serve no purpose.

A system similar to that governing trade agreements operates in the areas covered by international economic organizations of which Switzerland is a member. In a multilateral setting, however, the work takes place at a more abstract level and is concerned with general rules, global concessions and over-all policies. In the case, for example, of the European Free Trade Association (EFTA), consultations before, and often after, international meetings have assumed a permanent character within an administrative agency, *Délégation économique*

permanente; *Ständige Wirtschaftsdelegation*—the Permanent Economic Delegation. It is made up of senior officials from the competent federal administrations and representatives of the *Vorort*, the Swiss Farmers Union, the Swiss Federation of Trade Unions and the Swiss Union of Arts and Crafts. It has a secretariat, under the responsibility of an official of the administration. Needless to say, for the more specialized matters, other occupational bodies are also consulted.

Extensive consultations also attended the preparation and negotiation of the free-trade agreement between Switzerland and the European Economic Community (EEC). The Swiss delegation included, in addition to the eight government representatives, four members of the *Vorort* and one from the Swiss Farmers Union. Among the matters on which negotiations were most arduous, two—namely, those concerning rules of competition and rules of origin—were dealt with especially by the *Vorort* representatives. Both matters were of quite special concern to the *Vorort*, and both had been the subject of a preliminary study. However, while the *Vorort* took a very active part in the preparatory work preceding the negotiations, it stayed pretty much in the background during the referendum campaign which preceded the vote of December 3, 1972.[11]

Resort to the popular vote

The Swiss system is characterized by the initiative and referendum procedures which afford further

---

10. Foreign agreements are concluded by the Federal Council, subject to approval by Parliament, in all cases entailing new international obligations for Switzerland. Such approval is, however, not necessary in the following cases, for which Parliament has delegated authority to the Federal Council: traffic in goods and payments—federal order of 28 September 1956, 28 September 1962—technical cooperation—federal order of 20 December 1962, 10 December 1964—protection and incentives for investment—federal order of 27 September 1963—and consolidation of debts—federal order of 17 March 1966. By far the greatest number of economic agreements are covered by the delegation of authority, although the tariff agreements based on the Swiss Customs Tariff Federal Act of 19 June 1959 constitute an exception. The free trade agreement with the European Economic Community was submitted both to parliamentary approval and to the popular vote.

11. See, M. L. Gänger and S. Burrus, "Action du Vorort durant les accord Suisse/ CEE" (Paper presented at Political Science Seminar II, conducted by Dusan Sidjanski, University of Geneva, Switzerland, April 1973).

scope for action by groups wishing to initiate legislation or considering themselves adversely affected by a decision. While these procedures enable groupings to appeal to the people, they also provide a means whereby decisions favoring them can be challenged. Whereas the negotiation process usually leads to accommodation and compromise, the outcome of referendum and initiative is a clear-cut, brutal choice: a matter of yes or no. This is why resort to optional referendum or initiative is comparatively limited (shown in table 4).

The optional referendum and initiative procedures are, in practice, open only to organized groups. As is often pointed out, the cost of any campaign on a reasonable scale comes to about half a million francs—a sum clearly beyond the means of the average citizen. Apart, however, from organized socioeconomic groupings, promotional action can be initiated by a committee enjoying the support of political parties or occupational organizations.

The popular vote has been used on several occasions—for example, by the Migros cooperative grouping which tried to secure a position in the Swiss economy against the opposition of the cartels and then to introduce certain innovations into the Swiss system. It could again be used in the future by marginal, but dynamic, groups bent on change and innovation. However, the results of past optional referendums and initiatives suggest that the people incline more often towards conservative solutions. Nevertheless—and in spite of the fact that their direct use is comparatively infrequent—these means can easily be turned into weapons which groups can use to exert pressure either on the authorities or on their peers.

THE ROLE OF INTEREST GROUPS

The framing of the law on cartels

The process which led to the adoption of the law on cartels affords

TABLE 4

REFERENDUMS AND INITIATIVES, POSITION AS OF JANUARY 31, 1974

INITIATIVES	INTRODUCED	WITHDRAWN	VOTED	YES	NO
1,891	108	36	without counter- proposal—48	6	42
			initiative and counter-proposal —7	1 5	6 2
			Counter-proposal only—7	5	2
Compulsory referendums—1,848	104			82	22
Optional referendums—1,874	73*			28	45

NOTES: Affirmative vote on initiative = antigovernment attitude; affirmative vote on referendum = progovernment attitude.

* From 1874 to 1970, 1,044 laws and orders were, in principle, subject to optional referendum, but only 73 were submitted to popular vote.

an example of the three successive stages of administrative preparation, parliamentary discussion and popular intervention. The preliminary phase—from 1937 to 1947—led up to the adoption of the new economic articles of the federal Constitution. Under these provisions the federal government is empowered, among other things, to order measures aimed at remedying the noxious effects of cartels. The first phase in the process proper included two separate cycles. The first was a round of preparatory work—1950 to 1957—which ended in the presentation of the report of the Commission for the Study of Prices; the commission's eight members included five university professors, three representatives of occupational organizations, an expert, a consultant and a three-member secretariat drawn from the administration. Thus, from the preparatory stage, consultation is provided through the participation of the major central employers associations, the trade union organizations and independent experts, with the widest possible regional representation designed to take account of the federative principle. While the experts' work was in progress, the Independent Alliance and the Migros Cooperative launched, in 1955, a popular initiative aimed at the prohibition of cartels. This was opposed by both the federal administration and the trade union and employers organizations. Though rejected in 1958, it had the merit of compelling the various groupings to define their positions. For example, in its campaign against the initiative the Swiss Commerce and Industry Union stated that its opposition was not unconditional and declared its readiness to support cartel legislation, provided that it was reasonable.[12]

The second phase began with the appointment of a commission of experts at the time of the campaign preceding the July 1957 vote. Its members were drawn from several categories and regions; they included, firstly, university professors, judges and government officials; and, secondly, representatives of occupational organizations.[13] The position of the members of the commission may be summarized as follows:[14] the USAM, the USCI and their affiliates wanted to restrict the scope of the law, while the other members tended to favor wide powers for the Federal Commission on Cartels. However, it may be presumed that occasional differences arose even within the employer group. For example, while the USAM and the small enterprises generally favored comprehensive controls including monopolies, the USCI and the large enterprises were by tradition opposed to such controls. On this, as on most of the issues, the commission adopted a compromise solution. For example, the commission compromised on the issue of boycotts; it met the demands

12. Claude Alain Burnand; "L'USCI et la législation fédérale sur les cartels" (Paper presented at the Political Science Seminar, University of Geneva, June 1964).

13. The thirty-three members included five academics, three government officials —including the director of the OFIAMT— three trade unionists and eleven employer leaders—representing more than one-third of the total membership—a representative of consumer interests and a delegate from Helvetia Union—salaried employees federation.

14. See, the study by Yvette Montangero, *Commission d'experts de la législation sur les cartels* (Geneva: University of Geneva, Department of Political Science, 1972).

of the employer groupings, who felt boycotts should be considered illegal, to the extent of providing for far-reaching exceptions.

In April 1959 the commission of experts handed in its report to accompany the bill. This marked the beginning of the consultation process proper which, under the federalist approach, associates both the canton authorities and the federal-level economic groupings.[15] According to the executive authorities, the views received from seventeen cantons, most of the associations concerned, certain political parties and a number of prominent jurists and economists showed that the experts' proposals represented an intermediate solution between divergent, although—from a political point of view—equally acceptable, conceptions. The executive authorities considered that there were no reasons for modifying the bill[16] which, in effect, represented a compromise resulting from a lengthy process of consultation in which the major occupational associations had taken part from the beginning. This phase ended with the adoption of the bill by the executive and its transmission to Parliament on September 18, 1961.

The third phase took place at the parliamentary level. Through either the political parties or their own, direct representatives, the groupings sought to secure modification before a hypothetical referendum—in this case, regarded as rather un-

likely—could be called. The Swiss Commerce and Industry Union, for example, succeeded in having a few minor amendments adopted. It appears that rather than risking a showdown it accepted the law as a lesser evil, while hoping for lenient application. It did not press for a referendum, preferring to abide by a compromise which reflected a general consensus. It could, moreover, hardly reverse itself after making various commitments during the campaign against the initiative launched by the independents and, later, during the consultation process. As Jean Meynaud points out, while consultation gives the participants an opportunity to make themselves heard, at the same time it implies certain constraints, since the positions to which they must commit themselves are bound subsequently to restrict their margin for maneuver.[17] The other groupings appear to have been similarly motivated. After the law of December 20, 1962, had been voted and after the expiry of the referendum deadline—the referendum procedure not having been used—the law came into force on February 15, 1964. The fifteen-member Application Commission was appointed at the same time. As a rule, experts having participated in drawing up the law also sit on the commission, thus guaranteeing continuity between the lawmaking and enforcement processes. The making of the decision and its implementation thus remain largely open.

Inflation policy

Decisions aimed at controlling an overheating economy are speedy,

15. These central groupings are to consult their affiliates—that is, industry federations and regional sections.

16. Federal Council message of 18 September 1961, p. 15. This is hardly surprising, since the groupings mainly concerned had already participated in the drafting of the bill within the commission of experts.

17. Jean Meynaud, *Les Organisations professionnelles*, p. 279.

but nonetheless open. For constitutional reasons—that is, lacking powers of intervention either explicitly laid down or implied—the federal executive cannot make decisions in isolation, as in France or England, but must seek parliamentary approval and resort to the referendum within the one-year deadline. The preliminary phase was marked by various control measures: the 1960 gentleman's agreement between the Central Bank and other banks, the financial decisions of 1962 and the 1963 order limiting the work force in enterprises. With economic crisis threatening at the end of 1963, the federal executive drew up a number of draft-legislative-texts to deal with the overheating economy. Considering the urgency of the matter, it carried out consultations from January 7 to 14; meetings were successively held with representatives of canton governments, employers, labor unions and banking circles. In so doing, the executive complied with its constitutional obligation to consult the main groupings concerned before taking an important and urgent economic policy decision. The draft was drawn up and sent to Parliament ten days later. The parliamentary phase, too, was shortened, because of the need for urgent action. In most countries decisions of this kind are closed ones, but in Switzerland they are, at present, open. The process was the same as that which, following consultations—vote of December 2, 1973, on the four federal orders respecting the economy—led to the imposition of controls on wages and profits, credit and construction. On the basis of the order of January 10, 1973, the Federal Council set up an Advisory Commission on Prices, Wages and Profits.

The official in charge of administering the control measures, Professor Leo Schurmann, is chairman ex officio. The commission further includes four representatives of the employers, three representatives of labor unions, two representatives of salaried employees and civil servants unions and one representative of the Swiss Farmers Union. Substitute members responsible for technical matters—which are dealt with at special meetings—are distributed in the same way, except for an additional representative of civil servants. In 1974 the commission drew up the draft of an agreement between central employers and workers associations concerning the control of prices, wages and profits and stipulating, among other things, that the total increase in social charges may not exceed 10 percent over a period of twelve months. This draft agreement will be submitted for consultation to the member organizations and their affiliates.

Observations

Studies on the part played by Swiss economic groupings show, by and large, that the main thrust of their action is aimed at the federal executive—that is, essentially the administration. It is clear from the foregoing that, through consultative commissions and the rest of the consultation machinery, occupational associations have an official channel of communication with the federal administrations. The importance which they attach to the Parliament as such seems to be declining, as evidenced by the decrease in the number of officers of occupational associations holding seats in the National Council; at present there are only seventeen of them, along with sixteen representatives of farming interests. It is significant that industry and commerce are largely underrepresented, with only 9 percent of the entire National Council membership. These groupings are noticeably less interested in seeing their members or representatives elected to the federal Parliament. This seems quite normal in light of the nature of the decision-making process: the decision-making process essentially takes place at the pre-parliamentary level, while Parliament confines itself, in most cases, to adopting the Federal Council's proposals with only minor changes —proposals which reflect a compromise between the views of the Federal Council's administrative apparatus and those of the major occupational organizations.

PUBLIC OPINION AND THE INTEREST GROUPS

Perception of influence

The Swiss electoral survey of 1972[18] provides a picture of Swiss public opinion with regard to the influence of groups and their effectiveness in defending the interests of the various sections of the citizenry (see table 5). The replies received implicitly suggest that the activities of the groups—occupational organizations—are accepted as normal. In other words, not only do the political leaders and those charged with political responsibilities consider interest groups as legitimate—on the basis of the constitutional provisions and the large extent to which consultation with groups is practiced—but so, apparently, does the public at large.

It is clear that the influence of big business is perceived as too great—60 percent—as well as, to a somewhat lesser extent, the influence of banks—46 percent; correspondingly, only 21 and 27 percent consider it to be just right. The situation in regard to the trade unions and the farmers associations is the reverse: only 15 and 16 percent feel that they have too much influence, compared to 39 and 30 percent who think that they have

18. This public opinion survey based on national random sample (N 1.917) was carried out by the Department of Political Science of the University of Geneva with collaboration of the University of Zurich and with the support of the Swiss National Fund for Scientific Research (Grant No. 1437/70).

TABLE 5

DEGREE OF INFLUENCE OF INTEREST GROUPS AS VIEWED BY VOTERS

INTEREST GROUP	TOO MUCH INFLUENCE (%)	JUST THE RIGHT AMOUNT (%)	NOT ENOUGH INFLUENCE (%)	DON'T KNOW (%)
Big business	60.0	21.0	2.0	17.0
Trade unions	15.0	39.0	21.0	25.0
Political parties	14.0	45.0	14.0	27.0
Farmers association	16.0	30.0	21.0	33.0
Churches	12.0	43.0	23.0	22.0
Federal Assembly	9.0	57.0	13.0	26.0
Banks	46.0	27.0	1.0	26.0

just the right amount and 21 percent who think that they do not have enough. This indicates indirectly that these two groups have much public support—60 percent for trade unions, 51 percent for the farmers associations—if it is accepted that people who answer "just right" and "not enough" can be considered as accepting the influence of, and being generally in favor of, those groups. If this interpretation is admitted, then it can be concluded, *a contrario*, that big business and banks have more limited general support—23 and 28 percent—and face a more hostile attitude in relation to their influence, which is thought to be exaggerated.

Finally, it will be observed that the influence of political parties and that of the Federal Assembly are considered as being just right by 45 and 57 percent, respectively. These answers concerning political parties have to be related to the opinion that their role is very important—28 percent—and fairly important—46 percent. Generally speaking, the public regards their role as being rather important—74 percent—as compared with 8 percent who regard it as not so important or not important at all.[19] Even compared to pressure groups, political parties are not considered to be very weak.[20]

Moreover, the judgment of the distribution of influence as rather satisfactory—with the exception of big business and banks—faithfully reflects the general support for the Swiss political system: 66 percent consider it to be a very or fairly good system and 25 percent, passable; subject to these qualifications, 91 percent express their support, as compared to those who consider

it not so good—3 percent—or bad—1 percent—and those who "don't know"—5 percent.

The degree of satisfaction with the government is lower, but still remains high. To the question: "how do you feel about the way the Swiss government runs the country?" 68 percent answered that they were very—12 percent—or fairly—56 percent—satisfied; 24 percent, that they were not too satisfied—21 percent—or not at all satisfied—3 percent (see table 6). As expected, the degree of satisfaction is still lower if the question refers directly to people's interests or problems. The voters were asked: do you believe that the federal authorities at Berne and the canton authorities are concerned with your problems; would you say that they look after your problems very much, somewhat, not much or not at all? The answers to these questions reveal a decreasing pattern in which general support for the system represents the highest point—91 percent—and satisfaction with the manner in which the people's interests are defended the lowest—46 percent (table 6).

Defense of interests

Furthermore, it is interesting to see how people react to the manner in which other organizations or representatives defend their interests. The question was phrased as follows: "to defend the interests of people such as you, on whom do you rely the most?" The answers to this question give one an estimate of the effectiveness of those organizations whose main task is defending people's interests (see table 7).

If we consider trade unions as occupational organizations in the broad sense, these come first with

19. Question number 55.
20. Question number 56 (4).

35 percent, as compared to 17 percent for elected representatives and only 8 percent for political parties. Even if parties are not considered as very weak compared to pressure groups, only 8 percent of the persons surveyed considered them to be effective, while elected representatives obtained a higher score—17 percent. If we distinguish between the answers of men and women, we observe two main differences: first, 48 percent of men rely on trade and professional unions, as against only 28 percent of women; secondly, the proportion of "don't know" answers, which is very low for men—8 percent—is fairly high for women—27 percent.

There appears to be a cleavage between members and nonmembers of occupational organizations. Out of the 1,906 individuals in the sample, 531 were members of occupational organizations—28 percent of the population, yet, only 111 women compared to 420 men. Among 1,375 nonmembers, 902 are women and 473 men, the percentage of women's rate of affiliation being 11 percent compared to 47 percent for men. Table 8 gives a more accurate picture of people's estimates of the organizations' effectiveness. Nonmembers predictably proved far more sceptical about the effectiveness of occupational organizations in the defense of their interests: only 26 percent of them designated occupational organizations, while 26 percent replied "none of these organizations." By contrast, a majority of the members designated the occupational organizations—53 to 69 percent. A similar difference was observed in the "don't know" group: 23 percent for the nonmembers as compared with only 5 to 9 percent of the members. On the other hand,

TABLE 6

DEGREE OF VOTER SATISFACTION WITH OFFICIAL CHANNELS

SUPPORT FOR THE SYSTEM (%)		SATISFIED WITH THE GOVERNMENT (%)		SATISFIED WITH FEDERAL AUTHORITIES (%)		SATISFIED WITH CANTON AUTHORITIES (%)	
Very good	11	Very satisfied	12 } 68	A lot	5 } 47	A lot	4 } 46
Fairly good	55 } 66	Fairly satisfied	56	Enough	42	Enough	42
Passable	25 } 91	Not too satisfied	21 } 24	Not much	30 } 37	Not much	30 } 37
Not so good	3	Not at all satisfied	3	Not at all	7	Not at all	7
Bad	1						
Don't know	5	Don't know	8	Don't know	16	Don't know	17

TABLE 7

TABULATED RESPONSES TO THE QUESTION: TO DEFEND THE INTERESTS OF PEOPLE
SUCH AS YOU, ON WHOM DO YOU RELY THE MOST

RANK ORDER	ORGANIZATIONS OR REPRESENTATIVES	PERCENT (TOTAL)	MEN (%)	WOMEN (%)
1	Trade unions Occupational organizations	35 $\begin{cases} 14 \\ 21 \end{cases}$	48 $\begin{cases} 18 \\ 30 \end{cases}$	25 $\begin{cases} 11 \\ 14 \end{cases}$
2	Elected representatives	17	16	18
3	Political parties	8	9	7
	None of these organizations	21	19	23
	Don't know	19	8	27

NOTE: N = 1,903; men = 893; women = 1,010.

there was no such difference in the case of parties and elected representatives: the political parties scored low among both members—7 to 9 percent—and nonmembers—8 percent. Elected representatives did better in all cases—10 to 21 percent—except among members of labor unions, where they scored only 8 percent.

Without overstressing the significance of this fact—which is confirmed by the replies concerning the influence of the various categories of groups—it may be observed that the members of labor unions also happen to be the ones who, in large majority—69 percent—rely on occupational organizations to defend their interests. By and large, these results confirm one fact: that those who join an occupational organization implicitly recognize its effectiveness, in that they look to it for better protection of their interests. Confirmation is also afforded of the soundness of the Swiss voters' assessment of the working of the Swiss political system, in which two forces occupy privileged positions: the authorities—government and administration—and the occupational organizations.

Considered by a large majority as a good political system, the Swiss democracy ensures, on the whole, peaceful change and manages to resolve political and social conflicts—social peace between employers and workers. This was confirmed by the answers to our question: "different groups sometimes resort to demonstrations, strikes, or civil disobedience—for example, sit-ins, refusal to pay taxes—in order to get what they want; in which situations do you think that such actions are justified? For each of the following situations, would you please indicate whether one of these three actions is justified or not (multiple responses allowed)." Results are listed in table 9.

Attitudes towards demonstrations, strikes and civil disobedience

The use of more or less violent means, such as demonstrations, strikes or civil disobedience, does not, by and large, seem to be condoned by Swiss citizens—a fact all the more remarkable in view of their frequency in neighboring countries, where they are a more or less normal occurrence. The proportion of those who reject them

TABLE 8

TABULATED RESPONSES BY SECTOR TO THE QUESTION: TO DEFEND THE INTERESTS OF
PEOPLE SUCH AS YOU, ON WHOM DO YOU RELY THE MOST

SECTOR	TRADE UNIONS (1)	PROFESSIONAL ORGANIZATIONS (2)	PROFESSIONAL ORGANIZATIONS (1 + 2)	POLITICAL PARTIES	ELECTED REPRESENTATIVES	NONE OF THESE ORGANIZATIONS	DON'T KNOW	TOTAL
Nonmembers	145	206	351	110	247	356	311	1,375
	11%	15%	26%	8%	18%	26%	23%	
Members of professional organizations	130	198	328	37	70	53	43	531
A + B + C	24.5%	37.3%	61.8%	6.9%	13.2%	10%	8.1%	
Employees A unions	114	59	173	18	28	28	25	272
Trade unions	42%	21%	63%	7%	10%	10%	9%	
Business B organizations	14	108	122	14	33	20	15	204
Professional organizations	7%	53%	60%	7%	16%	10%	7%	
Agricultural C unions	2	31	33	5	9	5	3	55
or organizations	4%	56%	60%	9%	16%	9%	5%	
Totals	275	404	679	147	317	409	354	1,906

NOTES: Row (var. 255; S. 19a): Would you tell me according to this list if you belong to a professional organization, to a union, or to any organization of these types?

Column (var. 119, Q.46): To defend the interests of people such as you, on whom do you rely the most?

altogether varies from 36 percent— Number 1, top of the scale—to 57 percent—Number 8, bottom of the scale. Admittedly, 7 to 19 percent gave "don't know" answers, while 15 to 25 percent answered "it depends"—which means that they could either approve or disapprove. However, even the total number of those who hesitate and those who express approval is only slightly in excess of a bare majority for items 1, 2, 3 and 4—49 to 53 percent—and well below it for the other items— 43 to 32 percent. As to the various forms of action—demonstrations, strikes and acts of disobedience— it is clear that demonstrations are most commonly felt to be justified, whereas strikes—although both legitimate and legal in most coun-

tries—and, above all, acts of disobedience are condoned by very low percentages.

Also, one may note that three out of the eight questions refer specifically to forms of trade union action— that is, dismissals, wage claims and participation. Not unexpectedly, it is in relation to these matters that strikes are most widely approved— by 13, 11 and 7 percent, respectively. Even so, the extent to which this form of action is supported in regard to issues of specific trade union concern remains surprisingly low. The years of social peace appear to have shaped the Swiss attitude towards strikes. As for acts of civil disobedience, they reach the maximum approval—4 percent—in regard to the protection of political,

TABLE 9

DEGREE OF PERCEIVED JUSTIFICATION FOR RADICAL TACTICS IN VARIOUS SITUATIONS

SITUATION (RANK OF a + b + c)	(a) DEMON- STRATIONS (%)	(b) STRIKES (%)	(c) CIVIL DISOBE- DIENCE (%)	SUB- TOTAL (a) + (b) + (c) (%)	(d) IT DE- PENDS (%)	NONE (%)	DON'T KNOW (%)
1) In order to prevent an undesirable building—for example, atomic energy plants or highways	28	2	3	33	20	36	11
2) In order to prevent dismissals	18	11	2	31	22	37	11
3) In order to put a stop to unjust treatment of a political, religious or other minority	25	2	4	31	18	38	13
4) In order to obtain a wage increase	12	13	1	26	25	42	7
5) In order to allow workers to participate in management decisions	11	7	3	21	22	44	13
6) In order to pressure public authorities or the Federal Assembly	18	2	3	23	15	48	14
7) In order to progress towards a more humane society	13	1	2	16	17	48	19
8) In order to limit the number of foreign workers	10	1	2	13	19	57	11
Average of eight issues	17	5	2	24	20	44	12

religious or other minorities. The question of the Jura may well have something to do with this.

These few indications confirm that the use of violent means by pressure groups would be unlikely to receive more than very marginal support. This is corroborated by the replies under item 6, which refers to pressures on the public authorities or the federal assembly: here only 18 percent are ready to condone demonstrations, 2 percent strikes and 3 percent acts of civil disobedience.

To illustrate the relative disparity of opinions concerning the various means of pressure on the authorities, we measured the spread between the opinions of individuals belonging to different parties or occupations and those of the average

Swiss citizen. This was calculated as a percentage, using the difference between frequency anticipated—based on marginal probability—and frequency observed—based on the actual breakdown of replies.[21]

The radical tendency is represented by the Socialist and Labour—*parti du travail*—party sympathizers, who favor mainly demonstrations as a means of pressure—11 percent more so than the average citizen. On the other hand, they are reticent as to the other two techniques. The supporters of the Independent Alliance also favor demonstrations—11 percent. The spread is too small in the case of most other parties. The Christian Democrats tend to be undecided; the Radicals and Liberals rather reticent; while sympathizers of the Agrarian Party are closest to the average citizen. The nonpartisan group, among whom the proportion of those failing to answer was highest, are less inclined to condone radical means of pressure and, in particular, demonstrations.[22] Table 10 illustrates the spread between the various occupations and the average voter.

Despite the lack of wide differences, it was most surprising to find the highest measure of approval for acts of pressure—demonstrations—among civil servants. The same tendency was observed, though to a lesser extent, in the professions and among senior execu-

tives and top management. Skilled workers and foremen did not emerge clearly, the spread here being insignificant. Middle management seemed most hesitant, with a higher incidence of "it depends" replies than other groups. Junior executives came very close to the average, although exhibiting a slight preference for strikes. Among craftsmen—a very small cell—disapproval of all of these means of pressure was more frequent than among the other groups. A large proportion of farmers—a small number—failed to answer. Finally, unskilled workers —day laborers—exhibited both the smallest proportion of answers favoring demonstrations and the largest proportion of failures to answer.

Two conclusions emerge: first, civil servants and senior executives are readiest to condone demonstrations; secondly, skilled workers, foremen and day laborers are very close to the average citizen in their reticence towards all of these methods; while junior executives, alone, show a slight preference for strikes.

CONCLUSIONS

The occupational organizations established at the national level have emerged as negotiating partners for the central government, supplementing the forces and authorities of the cantons. Since their very vocation is to think and to act in national terms, they have contributed not only partnership, but also support to the federal political process. Not surprisingly, the Federal Council has sought to stimulate the setting up of national occupational organizations and has even subsidized them in their beginnings. Nor is it surprising that these organizations should be concentrated mainly in Zurich, the industrial

21. Of the results obtained, only a limited part could be considered as valid, with a level of significance of $\alpha = 0.01$ (symbol +) and 0.05 (symbol ++). The other results could not be taken into consideration, either because the spread as compared with the average was too slight or because of the small number of party members or supporters.

22. The conclusions concerning the nonpartisans and the Socialists are more reliable in terms of statistical coverage.

TABLE 10

DEGREE OF JUSTIFICATION FOR RADICAL TACTICS AS PERCEIVED BY VARIOUS PROFESSIONS

PROFESSIONS	(a) PRO-DEM-ONSTRA-TIONS	(b) PRO-STRIKES	(c) PRO-CIVIL DISOBE-DIENCE	(a) + (b) + (c) PRO-RADICAL-ISM	IT DEPENDS	AGAINST	DON'T KNOW	TOTAL
Civil servants	30.6*	3.5	2.8	36.8	12.5	42.4	8.3*	
	+12.4	+1.2	+0.2		−2.2	−5.8	−5.6	144
	44	5	4	53	18	61	12	
Liberal pro-fessions, sen-ior execu-	23.6**	1.8	3.6	29.1	17.3	47.3	6.4*	
tives, top	+5.5	−0.6	+1.0		+2.6	−0.9	−7.6	220
management	52	4	8	64	38	104	14	
Skilled	20.3	1.4	3.1	24.7	12.8	51.1	11.4	
workers	+2.9	−1.0	+0.4		−2.0	+2.5	−2.7	360
foremen	73	5	11	89	46	184	41	
Middle	16.9	3.4	4.2	24.6	21.2*	47.5	6.8*	
management	−1.2	+1.0	+1.6		+6.5	−0.9	−7.2	236
	40	8	10	58	50	112	16	
Junior	15.1	4.4**	3.1	22.7	16.0	44.9	16.4	
executives	−3.0	+2.0	+0.5		+1.3	+3.5	+2.4	225
	34	10	7	51	36	101	37	
Others	17.0	2.1	0	19.1	18.1	52.1	10.6	
	−.09	−0.3	−2.7		+3.4	+3.9	−3.3	94
	16	2	0	18	17	49	10	
Craftsmen	15.1	0.8	1.6	17.5	15.1	54.0*	13.5	
	−3.0	−1.6	−0.8		+0.4	+.57	−0.5	126
	19	1	2	22	19	68	17	
Farmers	15.7	0.7	0	16.4	12.1	50.0	21.4*	
	−1.1	−1.4	−2.6		−2.6	+1.8	+7.4	140
	22	1	0	23	17	70	30	
Unskilled	12.0*	2.3	2.0	16.3	10.5	44.9	23.2*	
workers	−6.1	0.0	−0.3		−3.9	−1.8	+10.3	392
	47	9	8	64	41	176	91	
Total	18.1	2.3	2.6	23.1	14.7	48.2	14.0	N =
	347	45	50	442	282	925	268	1,917

Table constructed by M. Sliwinski.

NOTES: The percentage with + or − indicates the difference between expected value and observed value.

* Indicates the level of confidence equal to $\mathcal{H} = 0.01$.

** Indicates the level of confidence equal to $\mathcal{H} = 0.05$.

and economic center of the country, and in Bern, the seat of the federal government. Moreover, the network of Swiss organizations has developed mainly around the USAM and the *Vorort*.

Owing particularly to the growing demands placed on them and their comparatively limited administrative capacity, the federal authorities have striven to develop the con-stitutional concept of preparliamentary consultation. As the foregoing survey shows, this largely pragmatic process has become the kingpin of economic and social policy formulation. Resort to the popular vote, although it remains limited, nevertheless provides a kind of safeguard and means of action for minority groups. The examples given illustrate, albeit imperfectly, the manner in which the system works and, particularly, the interaction between referendum and initiative on the one hand and the normal law-making process on the other. However, they leave out of account one fundamental aspect: namely, that of implementation, a stage at which groups having accepted a compromise may try to block its application. Finally, it has been seen that the activities of interest groups in Switzerland are supported by a broad consensus of voter opinion. The evidence suggests that the average citizen tends to regard the normal activities of socioeconomic organizations as legitimate, while refusing, in principle, to condone more or less violent forms of action. There are, to be sure, signs of occasional challenges to this image of an ideally peaceful political and social order. The Swiss compromise is sometimes exposed to tensions, if not to outright conflicts.

Quebec: Interest Groups and the Search for an Alternative Political System

By Léon Dion and Micheline de Sève

ABSTRACT: Nearly fifteen years ago Quebec entered an active period of socio-political unrest. A people who had undergone considerable changes in their objective conditions of living without a corresponding change in their social consciousness suddenly found themselves forced, by their political leaders, to realize the extent of their maladjustment to a predominately urban and highly industrialized society and pressured to readjust their position. The *Union Nationale* Party was thrown into temporary disarray by the sudden deaths of Maurice Duplessis—uncontested master of the province—on August 30, 1959 and of his successor, Paul Sauvé, scarcely four months after he came to power. The Liberal Party under Jean Lesage was thus able to win the provincial election in June 1960. This event precipitated what has been labelled the quiet revolution. The Lesage program manifested a new desire to modernize the mechanisms of the state and to seize the initiative in policies of economic and social development. This set off a reform movement which, we can safely say, went beyond the ambitions of its initiators. The process of rationalizing the administrative mechanisms of a modern bureaucratic state created a wave of cultural shock which was felt at all levels of the society. Such changes could not occur without putting great pressures on the population or without having unexpected consequences, the most important being the rebirth of the Quebec nationalist ideology as a political movement and the formation of various kinds of popular movements.

Léon Dion received his Ph.D. in Political Science in 1954. He is Professor of Political Science at the Université Laval and President-Elect of the Canadian Political Science Association. His publications include: Bill 60 et la société québécoise, Les groupes et le pouvoir politique aux Etats-Unis, Société et politique: La vie des groupes, Fondements de la société libérale, Dynamique de la société libérale; *his* La prochaine révolution *is to be published in English by the University of Toronto Press.*

Micheline de Sève is Research Associate to Professor Dion. She received her M.S. in Political Science from the Université Laval in 1969. Currently completing her Ph.D., her thesis is on the Czechoslovak popular movement of 1968. De Sève's first interests are in political structural change and collective behavior.

The authors wish to thank Darlene Duern, who translated the article from French.

WE PROPOSE to retrace briefly the history of recent political developments in Quebec and especially to examine their repercussions with respect to the politicization of interest groups, both organic and nonorganic, in Quebec society during the 1970s. By organic collectivities we mean those social or political formations which are officially recognized by the established political system and which maintain relationships with its agents through institutionalized interaction mechanisms. By nonorganic collectivities we mean those social or political formations which operate without official recognition; they may be ignored or even censured by the political authorities, depending on their size and the forcefulness of their methods. Within each of these types we shall introduce a second criterion for classification—that is, the degree of acceptance or rejection of the established political system.

These collectivities can be separated into four distinct types. The first is comprised of unconditional organic collectivities—that is, those collectivities which are not only integrated with the mechanisms of the established political system, but also share its values and have similar objectives. The second type consists of conditional organic collectivities—that is, collectivities which are integrated with the established system and agree to act according to set rules, but which intend to change, more or less radically, the present system from within and aspire to set up an alternative political system. The third type includes conditional nonorganic collectivities which do not enjoy official recognition, but do not reject, in principle, the idea of their eventual integration into the established system in more favorable circumstances; their marginality is to some extent accidental and often temporary. Finally, there are the unconditional nonorganic collectivities—that is, collectivities which believe in an alternative political system. Convinced that they can never collaborate with the present system, they refuse to have any institutionalized connections with it and work outside the system towards its eventual overthrow, either with or without the recourse to violence and other illegal means. Table 1 illustrates the various positions adopted by these collectivities in relation to the controlling political system.

It must be noted that the establishment of parallel socio-political mechanisms could just as easily result from the incapacity of institutionalized channels to transmit specific demands, as from the marginal nature of the demands themselves or the impossibility of meeting them in the context of the

TABLE 1

DEGREE OF INSTITUTIONALIZATION OF COLLECTIVITIES

POLITICAL STATUS	POSITION IN RELATION TO THE PRESENT POLITICAL SYSTEM	
	Unconditional	Conditional
Organic	1) voluntary integration	2) tactical integration
Nonorganic	3) voluntary withdrawal	4) involuntary withdrawal

established system.[1] Nonetheless, it is essential that we not restrict the analysis to the present political system, but refer rather to the political system as a concept embodying multiple frames of reference. This allows for the perception of alternative political mechanisms and eliminates the association of deviance with irrationality or of marginality with the incoherence of expressed demands.

In order to better understand the climate of social unrest which has dominated Quebec for several years—the latest important incident being the one-year imprisonment of the leaders of the three large labor unions, the Confederation of National Trade Unions, The Federation of Quebec Labor (QFL) and the Quebec Teachers Federation (QTF), in February 1973—we shall try to outline the complex relationships between organic and nonorganic groups and the government. More specifically, we shall try to indicate how even organic collectivities can come to renounce their status as privileged spokesmen for established political agents[2] and to affirm a desire to break the system, with themselves as vehicles of a radical political alternative.

The increase in popular contestation and emergence of spontaneous protest movements is not a phenomenon peculiar to Quebec. In the 1950s the concept of polyarchy appeared to be gaining ground in many liberal societies.[3] According to this concept there is no real risk for individuals or groups in following the majority rule, because in the case of essential political questions—if not for all of them —there is no permanent majority or minority position. However, the system was, in fact, insensitive to the demands of the underprivileged levels of society. The harmony of interests of all social components as proclaimed by the political system was actually an illusion. The system, not equipped with mechanisms to articulate unorthodox or dysfunctional demands, refused to admit that there existed irreducible social conflicts. The expression the end of ideology—an expression coined during this decade—masked increasing tensions. This tension erupted in popular revolt against deep-rooted social injustices, not only in underdeveloped countries where such occurrences were considered normal, but in so-called advanced nations, such as the United States, Great Britain and Canada, which were supposedly safe from outbreaks of this kind.

The phenomenon is particularly interesting in Quebec, where its dimensions are even more complex. The difficulty in assuring the efficient functioning of interaction mechanisms—that is, interest groups, political parties, media of communication and advisory

---

1. Compare, Léon Dion and Micheline de Sève, *Cultures politiques au Québec* (Document de travail théorique, mimeographed, 1972).

2. Witness the official withdrawal of the QTF from all consultative committees on which it had participated in conjunction with various government agencies up to 1972.

3. Nonetheless, in Quebec the respect of the forms of polyarchical democracy was associated with the maintenance of a traditional mentality which was expressed by a benevolent paternalism with respect to citizens subject to the controlling authorities. Those who did not submit to the authorities were subjected to judicial punishment or moral reprobation.

bodies—between the social and political systems in a liberal regime is further complicated by problems arising from a sudden change in a people's social consciousness and reevaluation of their social and political identity. Certain tensions resulted from the realization that a liberal regime of the welfare state type is incapable of resolving recurrent social cleavages, such as the relative poverty of large sectors of the population. These tensions were increased by the revision of a secular nationalist ideology and redefinition of its political community by a people who had come to see themselves as a global society and not as an integrated part of a larger community. Thus, going beyond the concept of a purely cultural French Canadian community, there emerged a political concept of national identification: the "State of Québec."

Our study will be concerned with two basic questions. First, we intend to examine the origin and significance of the shifting of focus towards a *Québecois* identity. Second, we shall try to explain why, in this special case, one cannot speak of nationalism without simultaneously considering the social dimension, as well. To put it another way, we will consider how the primary interests of a large number of those in favor of Quebec's independence could develop from a conception of independence as an ultimate goal in itself to a strategic evaluation of independence as one step in effecting the change from one regime to another, not merely from one political system to another.[4]

4. By political system we mean the differentiated real organism, possessing its own legal existence, which specifies the organized political community—federation,

THE HISTORICAL CONTEXT: QUEBEC 1960-1973

We shall divide this period into three phases: phase one—1960 to 1965—during which the state became the promotor of social and economic development and the physical manifestation of the desire to modernize political and social institutions; phase two—1965 to 1970—wherein tensions developed between social groups formulating different demands and wherein the political system tried to return to a more passive role as arbitrator, rather than initiator, of social change; and phase three—1970 to 1973—during which one can trace the emergence of clearly polarized social movements, increasingly hostile to the existing political system and even to the political regime in its present form. Such a division can only compartmentalize real historical development; inevitably, these periods overlap.

---

republic and so on. By regime we mean global collective representations which legitimize and assign values to the system in the form of constitutions and other basic laws. See Léon Dion, *Société et politique: La vie des groupes; tome 1: Fondements de la société libérale,* (Québec: Presses de L'Université Laval, 1972), p. 117. Note: the contrast between *nation canadienne-française* in the first instance and *Etat du Québec* in the second is according to the distinction made in French and German usage. Thus, nation refers to a collection of individuals who have no political consciousness, but have a more or less intense sense of common cultural identity. The reference to *Etat du Québec* indicates that part of this cultural nation—that is, the *canadiens-français* of Quebec—have developed a political consciousness, as well. It is no longer a question of a collection of individuals, but rather a genuine political community that refers to *Québécois* specifically, not to French Canadians in general.

1960 to 1965: The quiet revolution

The sudden upheaval Quebec experienced at the beginning of the 1960s was not the result of rapid change in its social and economic environment. Rather, the explanation lies in the fact that political leaders and a growing proportion of the electorate were increasingly sensitive to the new exigencies of adapting to the administrative mechanisms of a modern economy. It was realized that the urbanization of the population had accentuated the repercussions of industrialization which, begun during the 1930s, had become predominant after World War II. The cultural frames of traditional society, which could not contain the rising middle class and its aspirations to modernity, were weakened by the rapidly growing number of urban dwellers, especially in the region of Montreal. Long before 1960 a new elite, trained in the social sciences at the university level, was making use of the new electronic media to break open the established order. When the Liberal Party under Jean Lesage and his *équipe du tonnerre* came to power in 1960, they were able to put into effect their ideas concerning the increase in governmental responsibilities, the direct intervention of the state in key sectors of economy and culture and the rationalization of the administrative process.

The constitution of a strong state apparatus, based on the professionalization of the civil service and adherence to the ideology of the welfare state, met the needs of concentration and control of the mechanisms of an advanced liberal society. Thus, the political system took on a motor-role with relation to the social system. Several important events indicate this fact: the nationalization of electricity in 1962; the creation of the *Bureau d'aménagement de l'Est du Québec* as a joint federal-provincial project in 1963—this being the first attempt in Quebec of planning at the regional level; the creation of a Ministry of Education in 1964 to replace the former *Département de l'instruction publique*, which had been under ecclesiastical control —thus, unifying the administration of a field of activity which in 1961 was scattered among thirteen different administrative agencies; the institution of a series of public economic corporations: *la Caisse des dépôts, la Société générale de financement* and later SOQUEM, SOQUIP and SOGEFOR. Finally, the government initiated a program of social welfare based on impersonal criteria of distribution, thus eliminating patronage which had previously been a major means of distributing government goods and services.

It is remarkable that during the euphoric period of the quiet revolution the government was not subject to organic collectivities which transmitted the inputs of the social system to the political system. In most cases political agents anticipated the demands which were usually expressed by organic collectivities. They took the initiative in developing policies designed to satisfy the needs of the people as the government saw them in its own analysis of the situation. These policies were no longer based merely on those demands expressed by social agents officially assigned to represent and articulate popular needs. This unprecedented dynamism of the Quebec political authorities was destined to shake the very foundations of the social order. It would breach the old protective shields of society, as is shown by the religious crisis which continues in Quebec to this day. It is related to the progressive lessening of the political authority of local traditional elites and to a breakdown of electoral conservativism which resulted from rural over-representation. Furthermore, there would arise unforeseen difficulties created by the effects of a large scale utilization of *animation sociale* — social activation techniques — along with the mobilization of new categories of social agents. Finally, Quebec would have to deal with the concomitant confrontation between federal and provincial levels of government on the question of jurisdiction.

Indeed, the "State of Québec" was to encounter serious problems caused by the division of power and duplication of functions between the two levels of government. The situation was further complicated because the federal government — which had invaded the field of provincial jurisdiction during the war years, 1939 to 1945 — continued to assert its authority from 1945 to 1960 and because the Duplessis regime lacked concerted economic and social policies. Some people interpreted this as indicating a structural imbalance in Ottawa's favor; the jurisdictional conflict thus contributed to the rebirth of a Quebec nationalist movement. First there was the *Alliance Laurentienne* at the end of the 1950s, then the nationalist movement was taken over by *Ralliement pour l'indépendance nationale* (RIN), founded in 1960 by a small group of former federal civil servants, professionals and intellectuals disil-

lusioned by their personal experiences in the English milieu.[5]

The first acts of terrorism by the *Front de libération du Québec* (FLQ) in June 1963 were a desperate attempt by a few dissidents from the official separatist movements to stir up a people largely indifferent to their colonial status.[6] Bombs were placed in Montreal mail boxes; some exploded. This display of revolutionary romanticism stirred up indignation against, rather than support for, the movement. Although it failed to mobilize mass support for the separatist cause, it nonetheless forced the emergence of separatism as a political issue. From that point the status of Quebec in the Canadian confederation has been a continuous concern of social and political leaders, as well as of politicized citizens.

1965 to 1970: The revival of nationalism and emergence of new social forces

Apparently, the transition from a laissez-faire-type political regime — strongly committed to traditional programs — to a welfare-state-type regime was easily accomplished. Such a transition was made even smoother by the fact that it alleviated the tensions which arose from the artificial maintenance of preindustrial political mechanisms and mores in a society which had in many aspects entered the industrial and even postindustrial age. However, clerical and local tradi-

5. See, Gilles Dostaler, "le R.I.N., parti de gauche?" *Parti-Pris* 4, 5 and 6 (January-February 1967), pp. 17–32.

6. A recent study of Quebec nationalism bases this normative evaluation on a scientific argument. See, Sheila H. Milner and Henry Milner, *The Decolonization of Québec* (Toronto: McClelland and Stewart, 1973).

tional elites were thrown into a state of panic by the sudden appearance of political elites who affirmed themselves as architects of collective values. Previously, this role of symbolic legitimization of all activity—political, as well as economic or cultural—had belonged to them. The new situation created a spirit of rebellion in the conservative milieu; they soon reacted against the "political giantism" which they considered a direct menace to the cultural integrity of the collectivity.[7] The rocketing popularity of the social credit movement in Quebec during the federal election of 1962 and the *Union Nationale's* return to power under Daniel Johnson in 1966 could be interpreted in the context of this resistance to change.[8]

The battle which raged around Bill Sixty and the creation of a Ministry of Education in 1964 were, however, the Liberal government's last attempt to assert itself as an agent of change. Beginning in 1965, the *équipe du tonnerre* was overwhelmed by the increasing burdens presented by the management of a more and more cumbersome administration. "*Opération 55*," undertaken by Minister of Education Paul Gérin-Lajoie, was intended to democratize public education at the secondary level; basically, it was more an administrative than a legislative venture. Henceforth, the Liberal government would concern itself with the implementation of its former programs rather than with instigation of new policies. The bureaucrats took over from the legislators and tried to reestablish normal interaction circuits between the social and political systems by means of consultative commissions and specialized councils.

Since we are more interested in tracing the emergence of a political alternative than in the evolution of relationships between the government and organic collectivities as such, we shall now trace the rise of popular movements in Quebec and the burgeoning of nonorganic collectivities after 1965. At a time when the Liberal government and its resolutely progressivist attitude was antagonizing organic collectivities anxious to maintain their privileges, underprivileged classes began to make their voices heard. In the working-class districts of the large cities, citizens committees sprang up determined to lay claim to the rights of the poorer classes to work, education and housing. As an indication of this fact, let us note that between 1960 and 1968–1969 the number of social welfare recipients jumped from 27,000 to 121,000.[9] The increase does not infer a sudden impoverishment of a great many people, but rather shows the state's willingness to assume responsibility for the socially and economically underprivileged classes.

7. The history of one of the most significant episodes of this rear-guard conflict is traced in Léon Dion, *Le Bill 60 et la société québécoise* (Montreal: Hurburtise, Editions HMH, 1967).

8. See, Vincent Lemieux, "Les dimensions politiques du vote créditiste au Québec," *Recherches sociographiques* 6 (May-August 1961), pp. 181–195; Maurice Pinard, *The Rise of a Third Party: A Study in Crisis Politics* (Englewood Cliffs, N.J.: Prentice-Hall, 1971); and Michael B. Stein, *The Dynamism of Right-Wing Protest: A Political Analysis of Social Credit in Quebec* (Toronto: University of Toronto Press, 1973).

9. According to the figures cited by Jean-Claude Leclerc in "Les milieux populaires de Montréal ont-ils un avenir politique? in *Le Québec Qui Se Fait*, ed. Claude Ryan (Montreal: Hurburtise, Editions HMH, 1971), pp. 239–244.

Citizens who had formerly been content to relegate to others the task of defending their interests, or who had been prisoners of their isolation and impotence, now found themselves awakening to a new kind of active political participation. Two important factors contributed to this new political awareness. First was the cultural change which accompanied the destruction of the frames of traditional society, in addition to the fact that poverty was no longer seen as destiny, but was considered an injustice and proof that the regime could not alleviate social inequalities. The appeal to Christian submissiveness —that formerly powerful weapon of both clerical and nonclerical elites —could no longer keep the citizens of Quebec in a state of passive subjection, as it had managed to do for so many generations.

This change went beyond attitude and became behavior as the result of the second factor: that is, the intervention of people specially trained in bringing about the participation of citizens who had previously been passive or indifferent. These *animateurs sociaux*, who had been more and more in evidence since the beginning of the 1960s, were responsible for bringing people to an acceptance of progressivist political measures. Their role was to cause the people of a given milieu to define their own situation and to come up with possible solutions to their common problems. These suggested solutions would then be passed on to government officials and experts at the upper levels of the political process.

This method was first used by the *Bureau d'aménagement de l'Est du Québec* (BAEQ) as a consultative technique for learning the actual popular needs before outlining a program for regional development. Soon other organisms adopted the *animation sociale* method; after 1965 they even hired their own experts trained in this technique of social activation. A few examples are the *Plan de réaménagement social et urbain* (PRSU), an organism for social research and action, the *Conseil des oeuvres* —both acting within metropolitan Montreal—the Company of Young Canadians and *Action Sociale Jeunesse,* whose volunteers went out to many localities.

Henceforth, their action of sensitivization of the working classes would take a new direction:

It was no longer a question of a context of planning or of regional development, but of an attempt to find an answer to the disorganization that prevails among the working-class in the large urban centres.[10]

Citizens groups, themselves, adopted *animation sociale* to their own needs, and to avoid the control of state-paid experts, they hired their own coordinators and learned to express their demands in their own way. Rather than using institutionalized channels, they formed new organizational structures which paralleled the network of interest groups and established organizations.

This new movement found additional support and even provoked a corresponding change in the position in the labor unions. The Confederation of National Trade Unions (CNTU) in 1968 began a second-front struggle in consumer affairs, indicating that labor unions were becoming aware of larger social problems; they had previously

10. Michel Blondin, "Animation sociale," in *Citizen Participation:Canada,* ed. James A. Draper (Toronto: New Press, 1971), p. 165.

been caught in a narrower conception of a business-oriented unionism rather than a syndicalism of control. However, one cannot speak of a radicalization of the labor movement at this stage. Rather, it was a case of apolitical politicization—that is, a "growing awareness of the political-economic dimension of social problems, combined with a desire to remain independent of the interplay of political forces, parties, and ideological doctrines."[11]

The creation of the *Associations coopératives d'économie familiale* (ACEF), designed to educate and protect consumers, resulted from this awareness of the problems faced by families in debt and of the difficulties of managing a budget in modern society. The lure of consumer goods and the general rise in the cost of living sent families into chronic debt—families from the new middle classes, as well as from the underprivileged sectors of society.

Between 1963 and 1968 citizens committees, tenants associations and parents associations multiplied in the working-class districts of Montreal, Quebec, Hull, Joliette and St. Jerome. On May 19, 1968 the militants of about twenty of these committees met in a school in Montreal's St. Henri district to discuss their common problems and to count their ranks. They opposed the establishment of a structured organization which might become more important than any single group among them, but they proposed to keep in closer touch in the future. Their aim was to develop a network of solidarity among

second-class citizens. They spoke of politicizing their action; yet, each group jealously guarded its individual autonomy, too recently won to be easily surrendered.[12]

These collectivities, although nonorganic, were not hostile to the established political system. They were clearly conditional nonorganic—that is, their goal was reformist, rather than radical, in intent. They demanded that they be included among the regular interaction mechanisms of the political and social systems and that they be recognized as were other governmental intermediaries. It was a movement to assert the rights of the poor, not a movement to overthrow the regime. However, these local struggles, basically defensive in nature, led to an over-all political project—that is, winning control of the municipal government in Montreal or at least electing councillors from the underprivileged districts of the city. This was the origin of *Front d'action politique des salariés de Montréal* (FRAP), a political party supported by the labor unions which were becoming increasingly interested in protecting the rights of all citizens.

Founded in 1970 after a year of deliberation and preparation, FRAP was a conditional organic collectivity which relied on several existing political action committees. It wanted to develop a network of political formations, at the level of each working class district, in close collaboration with the various citizens committees and other popular groups. Its objective was to change the political system from within by

11. Alain Touraine and Bernard Mottez, "Classe ouvrière et société globale," in *Traité de sociologie du travail*, ed. G. Friedman and P. Naville (Paris: Armand Colin, 1964), p. 263.

12. For a brief history of this period, see, François Lamarche, "Les comités des citoyens: un nouveau phénomène de contestation," *Socialisme* 68 (October-November-December 1968), pp. 105–115.

electing their own representatives; they had no intention of contravening the law, itself. With this in mind, FRAP partisans proposed integrative action methods,[13] such as presenting candidates in elections, and did not foresee the use of more divisive methods, such as the non-violent occupation of buildings, except in unexpected circumstances. Although certain confrontations went badly, it was less due to FRAP initiative than to the hastiness of the police to use their clubs in reply to verbal "provocation" or to the promptness with which the political authorities associated FRAP with any show of violence, even when the organization had nothing whatsoever to do with the event.

During this time a small group of FLQ terrorists succeeded in posing an endemic threat to the political system. Despite the fact that they were few in number, these amateur revolutionaries[14] promoted a generalized state of fear and brought "leftists" of all kinds under attack by an alarmed populace. Independently of the FLQ, various movements contributed to the maintenance of this potentially violent mood. Without actually throwing bombs, CEGEP and university students provoked bomb scares by pretending that explosives had been hidden in school buildings. Angered by the bureaucratization of

education and by their own dehumanization into computer statistics, the students occupied buildings, burnt academic records, ransacked documents and even destroyed a computer at Sir George Williams University in Montreal. This anarchical movement, climaxing in 1968, was part of the spontaneous student protest which led to the May 1968 crisis in France and shook Berkeley and other American campuses the same year.

Another confrontation occurred in the hinterland of the lower St. Lawrence River and the Gaspé Peninsula. The experts at the *Office d'aménagement de l'Est du Québec* (ODEQ) had decided to evacuate certain impoverished villages in these areas, relocating their citizens in small towns along the seashore. The villagers threatened to resort to violence. The *Opérations-Dignité* (O-D) resulted, as well as the popular movement for the construction of a cardboard factory at Cabano. Although these spontaneous groups are often confused with the citizens committees of the large cities, they differ from the latter in that they defended the integrity of their traditional social milieu and the right to preserve their cultural identity by remaining in their villages rather than expressed a desire to participate in a permanent manner in the decision-making process. The citizens of the O-D and Cabano were not so much trying to replace existing organic collectivities as trying to make their demands heard by the political authorities. The recourse to divisive action was thus a last resort, used only after a series of fruitless attempts to reach the administrative agencies or organic collectivities which had been deaf to their pleas. Furthermore, it must be noted that to date such methods

13. Integrative methods of action conform to the norms set up by the established political system; their immediate effect is to stabilize the system. Divisive methods contravene these norms; their immediate effect is to upset the established order. Léon Dion, Micheline de Sève, *Cultures politiques*, p. 304.

14. It is impossible to consider them professional revolutionaries. The lack of preparation and relative unimportance of their operations became clear during the trials which followed the events in question.

as roadblocks, marches on the provincial capital and ultimatums issued by angry citizens have been very effective in activating the mechanisms of the administrative machine or in forcing the allocation of government grants. The factory at Cabano is an example of this kind of negotiating between the government and a population which has no significant electoral power or financial means, but which does not hesitate to challenge the legitimacy of the established system by resorting to violence or, more frequently, by threatening violence in order to bring about the correction of a social injustice.

The issue of nationalism

Although the movement which we have just described—the activity of these social groups which carried new political demands—temporarily received the attention of the political authorities, it was never the government's principal concern. The question of nationalism, not the social issues, emerged as the dominant political issue during this period; this time the nationalist issue was not relegated to the fringes of the political system, but was at its very heart.

Daniel Johnson and the *Union Nationale* Party surprised everyone by defeating the Liberals in the June 1966 election. They found themselves confronted by contradictory demands, as well as by the problem of chronic unemployment and pressure to accelerate the growth of the Quebec economy. Although committed to a conservative and even reactionary election platform, they had to admit that the requirements of modern government necessitated the conscious recourse to the methods of bureaucratic administration. The technocrats whom they had attacked so vigorously during the campaign were allowed to continue their policy of rationalizing the administrative process at all levels, including the government's assumption of its full field of jurisdiction.

Quebec's desire to establish direct contact with France and other Francophone countries and to control, to some extent at least, its own international relations presented a particularly difficult problem. Quebec claimed the right to support *francophonie*—an expression embracing cultural affairs and external relations, which were under federal jurisdiction, and education, which came under provincial control—and refused to share its authority with Ottawa in this field.

The situation worsened relations between the federal and Quebec governments. The *Union Nationale* government under Johnson combined the views of a conservative party—up to this time opposed to any policy of state intervention in the sector of private enterprise—with a new insistence on the responsibilities of the provincial government in matters concerning socio-economic change. The inconsistency was to prove explosive. Nationalistic and socialistic tendencies found themselves closely connected. Because of their association with nationalistic trends, the concepts of social progressivism were able to assume a certain symbolic character which won the support of the masses. Reciprocally, social progressivism provided nationalist ideology with the concrete tools for its realization.

By the time of the 1966 election the RIN had gained popular support to the point that it obtained 7.3 percent of the vote. Daniel Johnson, the new prime minister of Quebec, saw potential support for his government in these nationalist feelings. The visit of President Charles de Gaulle in July 1967 and the General's famous *"Vive le Québec libre!"* were very opportune, giving Johnson the sanction he wanted to assume the initiative in cultural matters. The government capitalized on the event to pass from a defensive to an offensive position. It was able to blame the federal government and its lack of understanding for the failure of some of its own development policies. Thus, Johnson created a kind of political diversion by reversing the order of priorities—that is, putting the cultural before the socioeconomic issue. The Quebec government more or less shelved the socioeconomic problems caused by the abrupt transition from traditional to modern society to emphasize the promotion of *francophonie*. Moreover, Johnson was able to wield the strength of nationalist feeling in Quebec as a weapon in his negotiations with Ottawa concerning a revised constitution and a special status for Quebec. The rise in nationalistic feelings between 1965 and 1970 must therefore be attributed to the official political leaders, themselves, more than to the nonorganic collectivities. It was Daniel Johnson who proclaimed *"Égalité ou Indépendance"* in 1965; he had published a book under that title, thus giving official sanction to the aspirations to Quebec sovereignty.

The provincial Liberal Party, now in the Opposition, was also subject to the strains created by the different options concerning the division of powers between the federal and provincial governments. The quarrel between the federalist and nationalist factions of the party eventually led to an internal split[15] and the creation of the *Mouvement Souveraineté-Association* (MSA) in 1967 by René Lévesque; the MSA became the *Parti Québécois* the following year.[16] Thus, after 1968 there existed a conditional organic collectivity: a political party which was represented in the National Assembly by one member, René Lévesque, the former minister of natural resources in the Lesage Liberal government. The new political formation aimed at replacing the Canadian constitution with a new system based on a different association between the Canadian government and the government of a sovereign Quebec.

The sudden death of Daniel Johnson in 1968 brought about an abrupt transformation of the political situation. His successor, Jean-Jacques Bertrand, maintained a fairly aggressive attitude in asserting the rights of the provincial government with respect to Ottawa, but he could not hold the confidence of the nationalists who felt that under his leadership the Quebec government did not have the ability to protect their interests. In an indirect way Bertrand actually contributed to the growth of the *Parti Québécois* through, among other things, his failure to solve the particularly explosive issue of the status of the French language in Quebec.

15. A Liberal MP, François Aquin, became the first Independent member to sit in the National Assembly after General de Gaulle's inflammatory visit and proclamation—which the Liberal Party condemned as "untimely." Aquin retired from political life the following year.

16. The RIN dissolved itself and urged its members to join the new nationalist party; the Ralliement National (RN), composed of nationalist *Créditistes*, merged with the PQ.

In autumn 1969 he presented Bill Sixty-Three "to promote the use of the French language in Quebec."[17] The bill was designed only to encourage—not to oblige in any way—immigrants to send their children to French, rather than English, schools, as they had been doing in increasingly high proportions—up to 90 percent for some ethnic groups. Moreover, it was intended to legalize that which had previously been no more than privileges held by the English minority. The bill stirred up an enormous wave of protest among students, professors and intellectuals in general who rejected what they called the *protection dérisoire* —the mock protection—of a bill which favored linguistic transfers to English rather than to French. Nonetheless, despite an active press campaign against the bill and numerous popular demonstrations—one which brought more than 35,000 people to the Parliament buildings in Quebec City—the National Assembly, with the exception of what has been called the circumstantial opposition consisting of five members,[18] refused to give in to public pressure. At this point the enraged demonstrators and protestors maintained that in such circumstances the true

17. A similar bill had been presented the preceding year but had been withdrawn due to parliamentary opposition and unfavorable public reaction.

18. Three MPs, Yves Michaud (Liberal), Antonio Flamand and Jérôme Proulx (*Union Nationale*) refused to follow the official orders of their respective parties, but chose rather to declare themselves Independents. They were joined in the ranks of the Opposition by René Lévesque of the *Parti Québécois* and Gaston Tremblay, who had quit the *Union Nationale* and was the leader of the National Christian Party. Jérôme Proulx quickly joined the *Parti Québécois*, thus becoming the second *Péquiste* member to sit in the National Assembly.

political legitimacy lay in the public square and not in Parliament and that the members of Parliament (MPs) had betrayed the nation in refusing to protect the collectivity. Although they had been democratically elected, they were no longer considered to represent the will of the people. The bill was eventually passed with minor amendments, which served to convince many nonparliamentary opponents that it was useless to rely on the agents of institutionalized political control to protect the interests of the *francophone* majority—that is, of about 80 percent of the population. Thus, the *Front du Québec Français*, which had begun as a temporary nonorganic association, was forced by circumstances—that is, by the attitude of the government and the members of Parliament—to reorganize itself on a permanent basis. This was the origin of the *Mouvement du Québec Français*, of which certain Montreal factions became so radical that one could even classify them as unconditional nonorganic collectivities.

In brief, by the end of the 1960s two factions were emerging within the developing progressivist movement. On the one hand, there was the socialistic—*socialisant*—group, clearly reformist,[19] which relied to a large extent on conditional nonorganic collectivities favoring mainly integrative action methods. On the other hand, there was the nationalistic tendency which was split up among many conditional organic elements and some unconditional nonorganic groups. The

19. The term *socialisant* is comparable to the American expression pink socialism— that is, it is definitely leftist in orientation, but cannot be classified as communist, socialist or Marxist-Leninist.

conditional organic elements were united in the *Parti Québécois* or formed minority wings within other political parties or unconditional organic collectivities. The unconditional nonorganic elements were more radical; they favored the use of divisive action methods and foresaw the recourse to violence should the need arise to reverse the balance of power in favor of the *francophone* majority.

1970–1973: The October crisis and realignment of the progressivist movement

The events of October 1970 could not be fully understood without first examining the provincial general election of April 1970. In that election the *Parti Québécois*, which according to the tenets of equal representation should have constituted the official Opposition because it received 23.7 percent of the popular vote,[20] in fact won only seven out of one hundred eight seats. An unfavorable electoral map, a uninominal single-ballot voting system and a uniform distribution of the separatist vote across the province, instead of a concentration of its support in a few ridings, combined to explain this inordinate discrepancy between the number of votes cast in favor of the *Parti Québécois* (PQ) and the number of seats it actually won. The situation was considered a terrible injustice, especially by the young PQ militants who had worked enthusiastically during the campaign and had believed that victory

was near, despite the campaign gimmicks of the old parties to immobilize the PQ.[21] Their disillusionment was bitter, and the FLQ rose to popularity. The FLQ was able to justify its advocation of violence by pointing to the electoral failure of the nationalist movement. Consider the following passage from the FLQ Manifesto published during the October crisis:

We thought for a moment that it might be worthwhile to channel into the *Parti Québécois* our energy and our impatience, as René Levesque so well described it; but the Liberal victory clearly proves that that which is called democracy in Quebec is and always has been—the "democracy"[22] of the rich.[23]

The kidnapping of the British diplomat James Cross on October 5, 1970 by the *libération* cell of the FLQ and the subsequent kidnapping and assassination—in circumstances which are yet unclear—of the Liberal cabinet minister Pierre Laporte were intended, according to those responsible, to expose the weakness of the regime and to align the *Québécois* against their oppressors. Certainly, the Manifesto received a sympathetic response from the public. Its broadcasting on Radio-Canada—an autonomous

---

20. The *Union Nationale*, with 20 percent of the popular vote, obtained 17 seats; the *Ralliement des Créditistes* won 12 seats, with 11 percent of the vote; and the Liberal Party ended up with 45% of the vote and a comfortable majority of 72 of 108 seats.

21. The *Coup de la Brinks* (the Brinks affair) is the classic example of the demagogic tricks used to frighten the electorate and discredit the PQ by threatening the mass departure of foreign capital. Some days before the election a parade of armored Brinks trucks publicly filed out of Montreal, transferring to Ontario securities—stocks, bills, assets in general—which were supposedly endangered by the rise of separatism. The *piastre de l'indépendance*— the separatist buck—was another electoral gimmick of that campaign.

22. In English in the original text.

23. Translated from the text of the FLQ Manifesto printed in *Le Devoir*, 13 October 1970.

Crown corporation—was one of the only demands with which the federal government complied "for obvious humanitarian reasons." Everyone or almost everyone disapproved of the methods used by the terrorists, but many people did not take their threats seriously and could not help but feel that their social criticism rang true. Their concrete denunciation of social injustices and the direct tone of the Manifesto contrasted singularly with the highly intellectual analyses to which the readers of *Parti-Pris* and other left-wing Quebec publications were accustomed:

Oh yes, Monsieur Tremblay of Panet Street, and you, Monsieur Cloutier, construction worker in St.-Jérôme, there are many reasons why you can't afford "golden vessels" and all the fol-de-rol and pizazz that Drapeau the Aristocrat enjoys so much. Drapeau! —He is so concerned about our slums that he hides them behind painted fences so that the rich tourists cannot see our misery.[24]

The Manifesto ended with a call to strike and a general mobilization of the working class in preparation for armed struggle:

Carry on your own revolution in your neighbourhoods and at your jobs. . . . We must fight, not each one alone but all together, until we achieve final victory with all the means at our disposal, like the Patriotes of 1837–1838.[25]

Although these objectives of individual and collective equality coincided with the concerns of the more progressivist elements of society

and although the violent tenor of their language was similar to the analysis of the situation as proposed by political action committees and most other popular associations, this does not at all imply that there were organizational links or immediate connections between the FLQ and such groups. The political authorities, however, reacted as if this were the case. They did not hesitate to place the *Parti Québécois*, FRAP,[26] political action committees and even the social workers of the ODEQ and other governmental or paragovernmental agencies in the same category as the FLQ. Declaring that the country was in a "state of possible insurrection," the Canadian government invoked the War Measures Act, but applied it only to the province of Quebec. The army was called in to protect public buildings, and the police broke into private homes in the small hours of the morning to arrest bewildered people who had no experience of such situations—except in tales told about World War II. Although twenty people, at most, were involved in the kidnapping of Cross and Laporte, an unprecedented number of searches and more than 500 arrests shook the leftist milieu across the province.

The shock was brutal and to some extent beneficial to the nascent Quebec left, pointing out the need for political realism. Words and hard facts suddenly became one and the same thing. Repression

24. Ibid. The reference to *le vaisseau d'or*—the golden vessel—was an allusion to a restaurant of that name owned by the Mayor of Montreal, Jean Drapeau.

25. Ibid.

26. The municipal election of Mayor Drapeau was in full swing at the time, and, seconded by the unequivocal condemnations made by French-speaking federal cabinet ministers, Drapeau called his FRAP opponents "FLQ members in disguise." Several candidates of the new municipal party were arrested and held in detention under the War Measures Act.

took the concrete form of soldiers and police who patrolled the streets of Quebec and Montreal, searched cars at both ends of the bridge leading to a small city such as Rimouski, broke into private homes, read personal letters aloud and pillaged the libraries of "communists." Fear and a collective guilt complex stirred up by the assassination of a man whom the prime minister called "a typical Quebec politician, a man completely dedicated to the progress of his community"[27] led to a backlash of conservativism. FRAP in particular suffered a resounding defeat, with Mayor Drapeau winning more than 90 percent of the vote, and his Civic Party carrying the quasi-totality of seats in the municipal election.[28]

As far as the forces of order were concerned, the events of October 1970 brought the ranks of the "left" into the open, demobilizing its members and causing it to lose, in the short term, a good number of its potential supporters. The repressive action was efficient, illustrating the futility of violence in Quebec political context and at least temporarily silencing the FLQ. However, the lack of judgement shown by the application of repressive measures which struck out at partisans of reformist political measures,

as well as the truly extremist minority faction of the independence movement, had other, more dangerous long term consequences for the system and the established regime. On the one hand, the majority of leftist militants and nationalist partisans were locked together against the Bourassa government. In effect, the government attacked progressivists in general, suspecting them automatically of having FLQ sympathies, but did not worry about right-wing nationalist groups. Thus, the political authorities, themselves, forced those who favored social reform and PQ supporters to realize that technically they belonged to the same struggle.[29] On the other hand, it led many nonorganic or conditional organic collectivities to reconsider their strategy in favor of developing a genuinely radical alternative.

After the October crisis

Since the crisis of 1970 the polarization of social forces has continued. In the earlier phase, the pronationalist position in particular was characteristic of a more diffuse attitude which extended to organic, as well as nonorganic, collectivities. Since 1971 one conditional organic collectivity, the *Parti Québécois*, embodies the nationalist option. Under Daniel Johnson the *Union*

---

27. Taken from the statement of Prime Minister Bourassa, *Le Devoir*, 13 October 1970. Three years later the minister of justice, Jérôme Choquette, was to reveal that at the time of this speech the prime minister was aware of police reports indicating strong suspicions that there were connections between Pierre Laporte and the underworld with respect to the funding of the Liberal election campaign and the party organization during April 1970.

28. Two seats out of fifty-two went to independent councillors. No FRAP candidate was elected.

29. One of the principal FLQ members, Pierre Vallières, wrote at the end of December 1971: "To speak of a political division between a projected party dealing with the so-called 'social' front alongside of the Parti Québécois, which some tend to restrict too much to the 'national' front, would be to create a division within a single mass struggle. Such a division would compromise the chances for success of such a struggle and definitely reinforce the current regime." *L'urgence de choisir* (Montréal: Parti-Pris, 1971); reprinted in *Le Devoir*, 13 December 1971.

Nationale had considered separatism a possible last resort; today the party does not present a clear position concerning the issue of independence and, furthermore, has practically disappeared from the political map, if not from the political scene altogether. However, the *Parti Québécois* does not channel all the separatist vote because it presents a social-democratic program along with its political sovereigntist option.[30] This second part of the party program is enough to alienate the more conservative nationalists, since it identifies the *Parti Québécois* as the political formation which is farthest left on the current political scale. Thus, the PQ brings together the options of independence and social change; in the absence of a labor party, this has allowed it to gather at least the tactical support of most of the radical popular groups.

For some socialists—for example, Robert Burns, a PQ member of the National Assembly—the present choice is only a question of "going in cahoots with the *Parti Québécois*"[31] in the hope of causing the party to radicalize its position, giving more attention to the class interests of the Quebec workers in the party platform. For the time being at least, the dominant polarization is not between Marxist-Leninists and Social Democrats, but between those whose priorities are nationalistic and those whose priorities are socialistic. Spokesmen for both groups come from the middle class: civil servants, artists and writers, teachers or members of the liberal professions.

30. See, the party program, *Un gouvernement du Parti-Québécois s'engage,* (Montréal: *Parti Québécois*, 1973).

31. Statement made in an interview, *Québec-Presse*, 14 October 1973.

Nonetheless, the increasing politicization of the large labor unions could introduce a new factor into the political picture over the next few years. During the last two years violent conflicts have set the political authorities and the labor movement at odds. On October 29, 1971 a popular demonstration organized to protest the lockout at *La Presse*—which boasts that it is the "largest French-language daily newspaper in North America"—ended in savage repression; the Montreal police charged a crowd of 10,000 cornered in an alley. In May 1972 the legal strike of some 210,000 employees of the civil service and other related organisms—known as the Common Front, because the members of the three principal labor unions were involved—ended in the National Assembly's passing a special bill enforcing the return to work after the workers refused to obey several court orders. Infringement of this law led to the imprisonment of the three union leaders, as well as several union staff members, and heavy fines were imposed on strikers who refused to follow court injunctions. Because the conflict had been bitter and disruptive, the labor movement alienated many law-abiding citizens who were angered by the interruption of essential services, especially the hospitals, during the strike. Disagreement about the choice of methods and the political orientation of these labor conflicts led to a split within the CNTU. A new union, the *Centrale des syndicats démocratiques* (CSD), was formed; it adhered to the traditional concept of business unionism.

The major unions have nonetheless continued to work towards a radical unionism; it is already possible to discern an emerging class consciousness[32] within the ranks of the QTF and the QFL, as well as in the CNTU, which is the most combative of the three. Up till now, these groups had remained organic. They have not developed a strategy which could translate their new ideological analysis of the situation into efficient political intervention. Yet, the hostility of the established regime forced them from an unconditional acceptance of the present regime to a more mitigated position, definitely conditional. Traditionally these labor unions restricted their demands to those aspects which affected their immediate interests, but their political *weltanschauung* has now become global and they declare themselves in favor of a radical change of regime.

It is at the level of popular groups, especially in the Montreal region, that the October crisis had the most significant effects from the point of view of the development of a truly revolutionary movement, since it discredited simultaneously both terrorists and reformists. On the one hand, the hostile public reaction showed that the FLQ had obtained an end completely opposite to the one they had in mind. In the present context any terrorist action could only be the work of crackpots or of the police, itself.[33]

On the other hand, the failure of FRAP marked for many people the closing of the reformist channel for changing political and social institutions in Quebec.

The whole situation needed reappraisal. After due consideration, conditional nonorganic collectivities radicalized their options and became definitely unconditional; they redefined their objectives—excluding for the time being the use of violence—to set the foundations for a proletarian left-wing party. Deciding against the immediate formation of a mass party, the militants of political action committees and the more progressivist groups decided to infiltrate factories, offices and neighborhood associations in order to establish the bases of the political organization of the workers. They systematically undertook the setting up of collective services, such as free legal aid bureaus, day care centers and food cooperatives. They aimed at transforming the defensive struggles of social welfare recipients and underprivileged citizens into a political struggle which would denounce the regime and prepare the constitution of an autonomous political organization of the working class.

Although they are few in number and fragmentary in nature, these unconditional nonorganic collectivities now constitute an embryonic Marxist socialist move-

32. This realignment is indicated in the presidential reports of these three unions and in other political manifestoes during the last few years. See, *Ne comptons que sur nos propres moyens*, CNS 1971; *L'Etat rouage de notre exploitation*, FTQ 1971; and *L'Ecole au service de la classe dominante*, CEQ 1972. *Ne comptons que* and the *Deuxième front*, two documents edited by the CSN (CNTU), are published in English under the title *Quebec Labour* (Montreal: Black Rose Press, 1972).

33. Note the sarcastic comment which greeted the declaration of "Docteur Long-

tin," so-called leader of Groupe III, FLQ: "This message could have been the work of the police, indeed, they wouldn't have written it differently. In the first place it was sent to Montreal groups that had been branded 'pinko' by the authorities. Secondly, it reads like a literal translation from English to French—the work, perhaps, of an over-zealous young RCMP agent?" To our knowledge, no other paper even acknowledged Doctor Longtin's statement. *Québec-Presse*, 21 January 1973.

ment. In the first place, their frame of reference for interpreting concrete situations and analyzing sociopolitical problems is Marxist-Leninist theory. Secondly, they combine progressivist petit-bourgeois—that is, social workers, intellectuals, previously isolated white collar workers—with representatives of the underprivileged classes within the same organizations. Thirdly, although they are relatively safe from police harassment because they respect the letter of the law, their interpretation of the situation is intended to lead to a revolutionary praxis: they are engaged in a concrete plan to restructure society according to socialist values. Finally, they have the considerable support of a good many local unions and receive a certain sympathy from the union centrals, themselves. However, they have been unable to overcome the workers' mistrust of "Communists." They draw their members from the lumpen-proletariat and the middle strata of society rather than from the proletariat as such and are subject to the problems presented by a leadership which is too exclusively petit-bourgeois and by the ever-present temptation of that leftism which Lenin called the "infantile disease of Communism."

This properly revolutionary tendency, this beginning polarization at the very heart of the nascent Quebec left, does not at the moment constitute an important political force. On the other hand, the social-democratic tendency, which won 30 percent of the popular vote in the October 29, 1973 election, has so far advanced steadily.[34] The *Parti Québécois* has managed to

disassociate itself from extremist tendencies. It now presents itself as a middle-class party, a party of progressivist orientation. It hesitates even to take up the cause of the labor movement, because it is considered too radical. Taking its lead from the quiet revolution, the *Parti Québécois* proposes "quiet independence" as the tool for the socioeconomic development of Quebec. Thus, it is seen as a left-center formation whose credibility depends on the quality of the political team which it presents to the electorate. On the whole, its candidates are former high-ranking civil servants or former Liberal or *Union Nationale* MPs who have quit the ranks of their respective parties to join the PQ. More and more intellectuals rally to its cause; influential magazines, such as *Relations* and *Maintenant*, officially supported it during the last campaign.[35]

Only three years after the October crisis, then, the question of Quebec sovereignty has become a viable political alternative; in fact, its very viability frightened the majority of the electorate in the 1973 October election. The Liberals and the PQ offered clear programs; the other two parties, the *Union Nationale* and the *Créditistes*, were abandoned wholesale as the people voted for either the Liberal Party or the *Parti Québécois*. Satisfied with an efficient government administration, the majority voted in favor of the government party. With a single-ballot majority system of voting, this resulted in a landslide for the Liberal Party, which won the quasi-totality of seats—102 out of 110.[36] The very conclusiveness of

---

34. This is a gain of 7 percentage points over the results of the 1970 election.

35. Refer to their October 1973 issues.

36. The *Union Nationale* was wiped off the election map. It won only 5 percent of

their victory is embarassing, because it upsets the principle of equitable representation in a regime which calls itself democratic. The Opposition is reduced to six *Parti Québécois* members and two *Créditistes*, who do not even enjoy the status of a recognized party.[37] This imbalance could be conducive to extra-parliamentary forms of opposition. It could deteriorate relations between a government which is comfortable in the knowledge that it has the support of the majority and dissidents who are denied normal parliamentary channels for expression of their demands. Such a climate can only favor the emergence of popular movements which will mobilize active politicized citizens unable to articulate their positions in the National Assembly.

Although the Liberal Party won an overwhelming victory, its position is not necessarily stable. Until the next election Quebec finds itself with a two-party system; in such a situation the pendulum of power can easily swing against the ruling party. We might assume that any drop in popularity suffered by the present government would be accompanied by a corresponding rise in favor for the official Opposition.[38] To overthrow the

party in power would also mean to embrace an alternative political system. In such circumstances, a PQ victory would not result from a wave of nationalist sentiment based on an emotional evaluation of the status of *francophone* minorities within the Confederation, but would rather follow a positive evaluation of its program. Such an evaluation would take into account cultural interests, as well as social or economic preoccupations. If the *Québécois* should ever choose to vote for the *Parti Québécois* en masse, it would be to improve their living conditions and to increase their control over their own political system.[39]

Paradoxically, the possibility of independence for Quebec increases to the extent that the social issue takes precedence over the question of nationalism in electoral priorities.[40] It would then take

---

the vote and lost the seventeen seats it had held before the election. Although considerable *Créditistes* gains had been anticipated, the *Parti Créditiste* elected only two members out of one hundred ten.

37. In order for a party to be officially recognized in the National Assembly it must win either twelve seats or 20 percent of the popular vote. The *Parti Québécois* did not obtain twelve seats, but its 30 percent of the vote permits its recognition as the official Opposition.

38. After *fédéralisme rentable*—profitable federalism—the Bourassa government proclaimed *souverainété culturelle*—cultural sovereignty—a bizarre concept which leaves observers confused as to its future prospects.

39. In its *Premier budget d'un Québec indépendant,* excise financier 1975–1976 (Projet), Editions du Parti Québécois 1973, the PQ presents independence as a measure destined to favor the economic development of Quebec: "If we really desire to develop our society more rapidly, we must adopt the measures necessary to repatriate those powers which are out of our control. Only once these powers are concentrated in Quebec will we be able to even consider the sort of policy of economic expansion that is outlined in this budget"; ibid., p. 50. Independence during the campaign was discussed in economic terms such as these rather than on the symbolic level of national dignity or pride.

40. In his *La Prochaine Révolution* (Montreal: Leméa, 1973), Léon Dion presents an alternative hypothesis concerning the possibility of Quebec acceding to independence. This hypothesis must be given serious consideration. We think it plausible that in the event of a serious crisis in federal-provincial relations on crucial issues, a governmental party tired of throwing itself against the brick wall of the federal government and the other nine English-speaking provinces could declare an election. The

place as a preliminary step in changing the regime or as a corollary to the assumption of power by the party which currently carries the progressivist tendencies of the community, while at the same time demanding a new association with Canada. In the event that the PQ should be elected—and if its negotiations with the Canadian government concerning the restructuring of relationships between the two levels of government should prove fruitless—then political independence might be a primary step towards a more radical change of the regime itself.

issue of that election would be: secession. Carrying the hypothesis further, the party then receives a clear mandate from the electorate to separate Quebec from the rest of Canada. In 1967–1968, after President de Gaulle's visit to Quebec, Daniel Johnson toyed with this very idea.

British Pressure Group Politics:
The National Council for Civil Liberties

By ROBERT BENEWICK

ABSTRACT: This paper seeks to draw attention to a need to account for forms of pressure group activity which have become increasingly prominent in British politics. The focus is on groups that articulate demands of the disadvantaged or aggrieved in British society. This requires a pressure group framework, as well as the approaches used in studies of community action and political participation; it is argued that the literature on British pressure groups is inadequate in this respect. A typology is proposed to promote visibility in terms of relations with government. Groups can be seen to inhabit three worlds rather than one. The National Council for Civil Liberties is representative of third world pressure groups. It shares many characteristics and confronts similar problems, while possessing features which are peculiar to a group dedicated to the preservation and extension of civil liberties. The National Council for Civil Liberties has achieved effectiveness without acceptance.

Robert Benewick is Reader in Politics at the University of Sussex. He has taught at the University of Hull, Smith College and the University of the West Indies. He has published The Fascist Movement in Britain *(1972) and is joint editor of* Readings in British Politics and Government *(1968);* Direction Action and Democratic Politics *(1972); and* Knowledge and Belief in Politics *(1973). He is currently writing a book on the National Council for Civil Liberties for Cambridge University Press.*

The study of the National Council of Civil Liberties has been made possible through the support of the Social Science Research Council. Dr. Benewick is grateful to the National Council for Civil Liberties for making available their archives, papers and minutes. He is also indebted to Sandra Clark of Sussex University, Christine Jackson of the Cobden Trust and Dorothea King of the London School of Economics for their useful contributions to this paper.

IT IS the contention in this paper that the work of the National Council for Civil Liberties (NCCL) is representative of a type of group activity which has become increasingly prominent and important in the British political system. This group activity is not particularly new, although the range of issues formally articulated by groups has increased significantly, if not dramatically, over the last decade. An advantage in focusing on the NCCL is that, since it was founded in 1934, its relatively long history provides a better opportunity to study problems typical of what will be described as a third world of British pressure groups. A disadvantage arises in so far as the NCCL's stability sets it apart from some of the groups it is intended to represent; furthermore, unlike the NCCL, many of these groups have charitable status or receive government funds placing restraints on their political activities.[1] The approach does not deny the particular concerns and characteristics of different groups or those shared with more conventional or established groups, but emphasizes marked similarities which distinguish them for special consideration.

The adequacy of the literature on British pressure groups to account for recent developments will be discussed in the first part of the paper. The rest of the paper will be devoted to the specific example, the NCCL. In part two the study will be restricted to the organization's formative years, with an analysis of the consequences of its tactics for effectiveness and legitimacy. The study will be brought swiftly up to date in part three. An attempt will be made to compare the changes in tactics, targets and effectiveness of the NCCL between the two periods.

The measure for effectiveness is difficult to gauge when the NCCL's ethos is taken into account, for the preservation and extension of civil liberties implies an educative role. This is especially important in Britain where formal rights are not enshrined in a written Constitution. Public opinion is a direct, as well as an indirect, target; thus, a public campaign may not necessarily connote lack of access, although this may be the case. On another level this applies to groups engaged in the process of issue recognition, as well as articulation, and is compounded for a multi-issue organization, such as the NCCL, which has to dovetail issue recognition with group legitimacy. The absence of constitutional rights, the nature of the judicial system and of the legal profession combine to determine the second target for exerting pressure: the legislative process. This distinguishes the NCCL from the American Civil Liberties Union which pursues most cases and issues through the courts. Civil liberties clienteles also define a set of targets and cast the NCCL in a service and case work role. Representations on behalf of its clienteles are made in the courts and before tribunals, in Whitehall and local government, through Parliament and to the police. Since many issues involve civil liberties concerns, a fourth target is the pressure group worlds. Lobbying in this arena is reciprocal, although not necessarily a cooperative venture.

THE STUDY OF PRESSURE GROUPS

The literature on pressure groups in Britain is considerable. The

---

1. Benedict Nightingale, *Charities* (London: Allen Lane, 1973).

studies which are influential today, however, were generally written in the late 1950s and early 1960s when the rapid increase in pressure group activity was seen mainly as a response to the development towards a managed economy and the extension of the welfare state. What Samuel H. Beer has described as a persistent corporatism in British political development had, at least momentarily, peaked.[2]

The thrust of these studies taken as a whole is the regularization of relationships between groups and government. Pressure groups are accepted as an integral part of the political system, a component of a new constitutional trinity or one of three worlds comprising the structure of British government.[3] This description is more applicable to some groups than others, so that an early task for political scientists was that of classification. The pressure group world is bifurcated into sectional and promotional groups, to use S. E. Finer's and A. H. Birch's categorizations.[4] Sectional groups represent specific interests of well-defined clienteles, while promotional groups appeal to diffuse clienteles or society at large on broad social and moral grounds.

The structure of the British political system makes the executive the most important target for pressure group activity. It is the sectional group which most likely to achieve continuous access to Whitehall, and the establishment of

a sponsor-client relationship between a government department and a pressure group connotes the highest form of legitimacy. Promotional group activity is likely to be a one-off campaign, a matter of intermittent representations or a mix of tactics directed at a variety of targets, including the executive, Parliament, political parties and the public. The vertical dichotomies —sectional and promotional in this instance—are not intended to be rigid, for some promotional groups established sponsor-client relationships with the relevant Whitehall departments. Nor is effectiveness the prerogative of the trade associations, trade unions or the professions. Success is not guaranteed; sectional groups, too, have to rely on other channels of influence, while promotional groups—for example, those sponsoring social reforms—experienced considerable success under the Labour governments in the 1960s.

The acceptance of a managed economy and welfare state provides a climate congenial to pressure groups; however, it does not insure the legitimacy of all groups. The pressure group world is welcoming, but on its own terms. The requisite resources can be intangible, as well as tangible; ideological, as well as instrumental. Therefore, placing an issue on the agenda does not guarantee access to, and recognition by, decision makers. The representative nature of a group is an important consideration. Representativeness means that a group is recognized or, perhaps, created as an affected interest or that it is accepted as the aggregate voice of its clientele. It would seem to follow that actual or potential stability must be taken into account and, if so, this has implications for the new

2. Samuel H. Beer, *Modern British Politics*, 2nd ed. (London: Faber, 1969).

3. S. E. Finer, *Anonymous Empire*, 2nd ed. (London: Pall Mall, 1966); W. J. M. Mackenzie, "Pressure Groups in British Government," *British Journal of Sociology* 6 (June 1955), p. 218.

4. Finer, *Anonymous Empire*; A. H. Birch, *Representative and Responsible Government* (London: Allen and Unwin, 1964).

group and for the campaign. Allen Potter identifies responsibility as a criterion, the proof of which is past performance, adherence to the rules of the game and leadership style.[5] Legitimacy, then, cuts two ways, requiring that the parties to negotiation share a similar world view.[6]

PRESSURE GROUPS IN THE 1960s

Political scientists are beginning to revisit the pressure group world; for, there has been little systematic investigation of its changing character.[7] The early studies were influenced by the prevailing American literature. More recently, the questions posed by the elitist-pluralist debate current in the United States in the 1960s have begun to have an impact.[8] This does not mean that the work on British pressure groups constituted a celebration. There are warnings of a "closed circle," an "inner circle," a "new medievalism" and the development of a "corporate" state.[9]

The political system and the political culture impose restraints. These studies, however, are wedded to a particular era and are restrictive in their horizons. Whether a new body of theory will emerge or whether there will simply be a dressed-up version of the proposition that power is unequally distributed in the pressure group world, attention will have to be paid to another dimension of pressure group activity.

With the proliferation of issues articulated, there has been a correspondingly rapid expansion of the pressure group world. This mushrooming of group activity is as much a response to the extension of government activity in the economy and the growth of welfare services as were the pressure groups of the post-War period which prompted the research of political scientists. Modernization implies progress, but the new groups have demonstrated that all do not share in it. These groups can be seen as a negative response in that the disadvantaged are less well placed to exert pressure than when they constituted a majority.[10] Big government, too, has consequences for the relationships between the state and the individual which recent group activity has brought sharply into focus.

What has been described as the new politics of the 1960s represented for some a disenchantment with the major political parties and with the conventional channels for political expression and participation and search for

5. Allen Potter, *Organized Groups in British National Politics* (London: Faber, 1961), chaps. 11 and 12.

6. For a discussion of this point, see, Robert E. Dowse and John A. Hughes, *Political Sociology* (New York: John Wiley and Sons, 1972), chap. 12.

7. See, however, Benjamin W. Heineman, Jr., *The Politics of the Powerless: A Study of the Campaign Against Racial Discrimination* (London: Oxford University Press for the Institute of Race Relations, 1972); and, for community action groups, John Dearlove, "The Control of Change and the Regulation of Community Action, in *Community Work*, ed. M. Mayo and D. Jones (London: Routledge and Kegan Paul, 1974).

8. Geraint Parry, *Political Elites* (London: Allen and Unwin, 1969); Trevor Smith, *Anti-Politics* (London: Charles Knight, 1972).

9. Finer, *Anonymous Empire*; Allen Potter, "British Pressure Groups," *Parliamentary Affairs* 9 (Autumn 1956), p. 422; Mac-

kenzie, "Pressure Groups"; Jean Blondel, *Voters, Parties and Leaders* (Harmondsworth: Penguin, 1963), chap. 6.

10. Ben Whitaker, "Tentative Steps Towards an Anti-Poverty Programme," *The Times* (London), 24 July 1969, p. 9.

alternative forms and styles. The spin-off into group activity has not only affected many existing organizations, but has created new ones which contribute momentum and provide a great deal of the personnel. The new group activist does not fit into the old political network, public relations or the traditional do-gooder volunteer scene. Yet, the pressure group process is accepted even though many groups present challenges to it which may be inherent in the issues, in the manner in which they are articulated, as a consequence of ideological commitments or community involvement of the activists.

An account of the British pressure group world is no longer credible unless it includes the community action groups, voluntary agencies, service groups, consumer groups, advice and information centers, ecology and amenity groups, overseas aid organizations, minority groups, tenants associations, neighborhood councils, buffer organizations in the race and community welfare fields, community defense organizations and the dissident groups within professional associations. Some are protest organizations with a committed view; others provide aid or represent those unable to cope with or to confront government and its agents on their own behalf; still other groups strive to achieve a more traditional status of intermediary between government and citizen. Groups can be converted into agents of government services or even of government control. Some of the groups subscribe to a political position; others claim that they do not, although their activities contradict it; others cannot afford to, at least overtly.

It is not the novelty which commands attention; there have been similar, if more limited, growths in pressure group activity. During the period between World War I and World War II, for example, there was the formation of numerous internationally oriented organizations, as well as secular and religious groups which composed what was known as the peace movement.[11] Moreover, the militant tactics which characterize much of the recent group activity can be placed in a long tradition of political agitation. What is important is the examination of the impact these groups have on the political system and the evaluation of their effectiveness. This requires a pressure group framework, as well as the approaches adopted by the studies of community action and political participation.

In order to encourage systematic investigation it is necessary to revise the conventional typologies of British pressure groups which are proving inadequate in coping with the increasing number of articulated demands and the changes in political style where the distinctions between political movements and pressure groups and between political and charitable activities are blurred. The groups under consideration do not slot comfortably into either the sectional or promotional categories. A method is needed whereby these groups can be isolated individually and collectively to facilitate comparison not only with sectional and promotional groups, but also with each other. These groups can be seen to share characteristics which distinguish them from the more traditional groups, and there are considera-

11. Barry G. Buzan, *The British Peace Movement from 1919 to 1939* (Ph.D. diss., University of London, 1973).

tions which particularly affect their situation. Charity status has already been mentioned. As the gap-plugging rationales of the tradi-tional charities become less accept-able, they see their growth stocks in supporting group activity. How-ever, the group recipients can be placed in difficult positions, both in terms of financial dependence and the restraints imposed by charity laws. The government has also contributed to the development of this group activity by either creat-ing, encouraging or supporting groups. This can also be viewed as a neutralizing or containing process.

THE THREE WORLDS OF PRESSURE GROUPS[12]

It is proposed to view pressure groups as inhabiting three worlds rather than one which is seen as an integral part of the political system. The focus is shifted to the ways in which different groups stand in relation to government. The anal-ogy with the system of international stratification is limited, but sugges-tive, in that a global perspective can promote visibility for various groups and encourage empirical in-vestigation. The approach is sys-tematic in so far as it helps to account for the heterogeneous, dis-parate and dynamic nature of pres-sure group activity.

Within each world are groups whose position vis-à-vis the politi-cal system, kinds of resources and world views are markedly similar. At the same time this does imply a

12. An earlier version of this typology appears in Robert Benewick, "Politics With-out Ideology: The Perimeters of Pluralism," in Knowledge and Belief in Politics, ed. Robert Benewick, R. N. Berki and Bikhu Parekh (London: Allen and Unwin, 1973), pp. 130–150.

parity of resources, effectiveness or absence of intraworld conflict. In brief, the first world includes those groups whose relationships with government are institutionalized. They have continuous access through formalized channels and are likely to have established a working arrangement of sponsor-client with a ministry. Negotiations are largely routine, although a brief may extend beyond representation of a well-defined clientele. This may be the case because a group possesses commanding resources or because a particular issue also af-fects a wider public. The groups in the second world have also achieved a high degree of legiti-macy in terms of the norms of the political system. Access, however, is more likely to be intermittent and consultation at the departmental level is not guaranteed. Pressure group activity is expected and ac-cepted at several target points in the political system.

Sectional and promotional groups inhabit both worlds, and each world has its winners and losers. It is not the sectional and promotional character of groups that is important in the present context: first world groups are better placed to influence decision making than the issue-orientated second world groups. The claims of groups in both worlds are accepted as legitimate; in turn, first world groups have a stake in main-taining their advantageous position, while second world groups not only accept the norms of the pressure group worlds, but reinforce them through their activities.

The third world is an expanding and transitional one encompassing those groups, referred to in the preceding section, whose briefs in-clude: poverty, housing, education, urban renewal, transport, civic amenities, social services and welfare rights, civil liberties, penal reforms, drugs, minorities, immigration and race relations, sexual equality, the aged, the disabled, parenthood, overseas aid and development and the arts and communications. The problems confronting organizations operative in these areas are not peculiar to third world pressure groups, but are exacerbated by the nature of the issues, the approaches employed and a more radical world view which differentiates them from groups in the first and second worlds. For third world groups more may be involved than gaining issue recognition, establishing priorities and promoting resolutions. Many of these issues are recognized or at least not denied, and there have been and are other groups active in these fields. The issues are often articulated within a radical framework; this has implications for effectiveness and legitimacy not only in terms of government, but also in relation to clienteles.

Representativeness can be an acute problem either denying access or gaining access through the advocacy of an influential or an outsider, thereby challenging a group's identification and involvement with its clientele and questioning its radical pretensions. Resources are limited and limiting. A third world pressure group may possess valuable or exclusive information, yet not fulfill the requisites for responsibility by virtue of its being new or radical. Militancy and mobilization tend to be more legitimate as an option or last resort of first and second world groups than as a basic strategy for third world groups. John Dearlove has argued that in the context of local politics in Britain the means of such groups are not particularly effective, but that they may well be the only means available.[13]

The assumptions have been that decision makers are resistant to change, are selective in consultations and, where possible, will seek to transform third world groups into agencies of service, support and control. The latter is in part accomplished through charity laws and by government being a target for funding, as well as for more traditional rewards. Groups in the first and second worlds maintain a process which works to their advantage. This does not explain, however, the considerable success experienced by third world groups, such as the NCCL, Child Poverty Action Group or Shelter in housing. Nor does it take into account the various targets for exerting effective pressure within the political system. For example, in 1972 the Disablement Income Group, through the House of Lords, was successful in obtaining an agreement from the government to amend the Housing Finance Bill so that the chronically sick and disabled could claim larger rent rebates and allowances.[14] This example represents only a minor change in policy, although not for the group's clientele. It may well be that the impact of third world groups will be cumulative. However, more detailed research is needed on individual groups; for, success or failure may transform the nature of a group within the third world or be contingent upon it.

13. John Dearlove, *The Politics of Policy in Local Government* (London: Cambridge University Press, 1973), chap. 8.

14. Tony Lynes, "Wheelchair Power," *New Society*, 10 August 1972, p. 290.

FORMATION OF THE NCCL

The NCCL cannot be adequately described as either a sectional or promotional group. Its clientele extends beyond membership and, in the broadest sense, includes all of us. At the same time it is a multi-issue organization concerned with the interests of discrete minorities, as well as majorities. Nor are the issues necessarily exclusive to the NCCL; for, the dividing line between policy questions and civil liberties is often difficult to discern. For example, the NCCL receives many requests for aid and advice from prisoners—a clientele served by other organizations, including the Howard League for Penal Reform, Preservation of the Rights of Prisoners, Radical Alternatives to Prison and the National Association for Care and Resettlement of Offenders. Although its service, research and lobbying functions are similar to those performed by first and second world pressure groups, the nature of its representational, intermediary and watchdog roles brings the NCCL into continuous conflict with authority. This oppositional cast and radical world view aligns the organization with the third world of pressure groups.

The NCCL was founded by a group of literary figures, journalists, lawyers and liberal and left-wing politicians concerned with police treatment of hunger marchers and particularly with allegations of the use of agent provocateurs. The intention was to provide impartial observers to report on police behavior and to provide a deterrent by using observers with public reputations. The initial target, then, was the police; pressure was exerted directly and indirectly through publicity by tactics—which were extended to Fascist, anti-Fascist and pacifist demonstrations—singularly appropriate to a civil liberties organization. One month after formation the NCCL was involved in lobbying activities; for, the government announced the introduction of the Incitement to Disaffection Bill which imposed penalties for attempts to subvert members of the armed services. The bill as originally framed was seen to endanger previously accepted activities of political and pacifist groups.

The strategy of the new group with almost no resources was to enlist a number of influentials on an all-party basis to act as sponsors and vice-presidents. This would ease access and establish legitimacy, as well as aid recruitment and finance. Success was limited from a pressure group point of view; yet, a wider perspective is necessary, because the protection and promotion of civil liberties is not a neutral role. In the first place, the influentials were drawn from liberal-left circles—giving the NCCL a distinct political complexion—although the failure to recruit from a wider political spectrum cannot be attributed solely to the NCCL.[15] In the second place, those attracted to membership are likely to hold liberal or left sympathies, while those who avail themselves of NCCL services are in conflict with, or have run counter to, the state and its agents. In the third place, the political context of the 1930s must be taken into account. Although the decade has been romanticized, it was a time of high political commitment—at least among what could be described for convenience as a political class. It is

15. Letter of resignation from Vyvyan Adams, MP to Ronald Kidd (general secretary of the NCCL), 16 November 1934. Other Tory MPs were approached, but without success.

not surprising that, in this context or from a civil liberties viewpoint, the NCCL should become involved in the anti-Fascist struggle, thereby furthering its oppositional image in so far as the maintenance of public order was concerned. As a position, comparison is invited with the stands of the American Civil Liberties Union on the Vietnam War and the impeachment of President Nixon. The conflict between pressure group and political movement remains unresolved for the NCCL and for other third world groups.

METHODS AND TARGETS

The NCCL's first president, E. M. Forster, was aware of the dilemma. He lent more than his reputation and was active in steering the group on a course that would maximize its influence and effectiveness.[16] One method available to pressure groups was the deputation to the minister. It is significant that the attorney general was prepared to receive a deputation on the Incitement to Disaffection Bill which included the new and noisy NCCL, led by its president. The deputation was endangered by the NCCL's public and press campaign when its general secretary accused the attorney general of deliberate misrepresentation during the debate on the second reading of the bill.[17] The deputation was allowed to proceed only after a public retraction. The meeting was reported as acrimonious, but contributed to the pressure in Parliament for safeguards to the bill.

It is not clear whether the NCCL's credibility with the government was damaged, although no

deputation was received by the home secretary during the passage of the Public Order Bill in 1936.[18] Instead, the NCCL lobbied the Labour Party leadership and briefed sympathetic members of Parliament (MPs). The major preoccupation of the civil liberties movement in the 1930s was with police powers, and this centered on the Fascist/anti-Fascist clashes. Allegations of police partiality towards the British Union of Fascists or against the anti-Fascists were frequent.[19] Favoring government action to curb Fascism, the NCCL found itself in opposition to the Public Order Bill on the grounds that it placed too much power in the hands of the police and could be used against other organizations.[20]

Another method of exerting pressure particularly suited to a civil liberties organization and taken up by other third world groups was the NCCL-sponsored independent inquiry. The first has a contemporary significance in that the NCCL sent a commission to Northern Ireland to examine the workings of the Special Powers Acts of 1922 and 1933.[21] The next arose from allegations against the police in breaking up an anti-Fascist demonstration in 1936. In spite of a thorough and convincing report, the government and the police refused to reopen

16. Correspondence between E. M. Forster and Ronald Kidd, various dates 1934–1935.

17. Letter from Ronald Kidd, *Spectator* 6 (July 1934), p. 17.

18. A deputation organized by the NCCL on the right of asylum was received by the foreign secretary in October, 1938.

19. Robert Benewick, *The Fascist Movement in Britain* (London: Allen Lane, Penguin Press, 1972).

20. Ibid., p. 238.

21. National Council for Civil Liberties, *Report of an NCCL Commission of Inquiry Appointed to Examine the Purpose and Effect of the Civil Authorities (Special Powers) Acts (Northern Ireland) 1922 and 1933* (London, 1936, 1972).

the matter.[22] One reason for police refusal was their view of the NCCL as an organization devoted to attacking the police; thus, they did not want to afford it status or encouragement.[23] This was the police view of the NCCL throughout the period, and it persists today.[24] The difference now is that the NCCL has achieved status and is regarded more seriously.[25] In part this can be attributed to the NCCL's use of the inquiry, investigation and published report as pressure group weapons.

The courts were also an arena for NCCL activity. A panel of volunteer lawyers was maintained to defend civil liberties cases, and on one night a week the group's premises were transformed into what amounted to a free legal advice center. In 1937 the defense was arranged for striking miners who were charged with rioting. It was also through the courts that a notable success was achieved as a pressure group. The issue, in effect, was an attempt to place 16 mm. film under the same safety regulations that governed 35 mm. film. Opposition to the proposal came from several quarters, including educational institutions and associations, film societies, industrial firms and the NCCL. The opposition based its case on technical grounds, trade advantage and loss to numerous nontrade organizations and censorship. The home secretary announced that no new regulations would be brought in until the interested parties had been consulted.[26] Meanwhile, the police brought in a prosecution against a Durham Miners' lodge for showing a Russian film. The NCCL provided a solicitor and a number of expert witnesses and was successful in getting the summons dismissed.[27]

It is arguable that the most important achievement for the NCCL in the 1930s was securing its own organizational stability. Its political and oppositional character were shaped as much by the constitutional position of civil liberties as by political considerations. The NCCL gained recognition and support from liberal and left quarters. The hostility of the police cannot be equated with the views of government, although it has consequences for attitudes towards the NCCL.[28] The NCCL was able to survive two difficult decades and revive during a new period of political activism.

22. National Council for Civil Liberties, *Report of a Commission of Inquiry into Certain Disturbances at Thurloe Square, South Kensington on March 22nd, 1936*, (London, 1936); see, also, Benewick, *Fascist Movement*, pp. 203–209.

23. Robert Benewick, "The Threshold of Violence," in *Direct Action and Democratic Politics*, ed. Robert Benewick and Trevor Smith (London: Allen and Unwin, 1972), p. 57.

24. Ibid.; Benewick, "Politics Without Ideology," p. 144.

25. Examples range from invitations to the general secretary of the NCCL to lecture at the police college to frequent—thirty—references in *Police: Monthly Magazine of the Police Federation*, since its publication in 1968.

26. H.C. Debs 5s. (1 November 1934), col. 339.

27. The Cinematograph Advisory Committee of the Home Office was set up in 1938 and the NCCL submitted evidence. The committee report excluded nonflammable films from the Cinematograph Act of 1909, and the report was accepted by the government. A campaign was also successful in securing the exemption of noncommercial film shows from the Cinematograph Act of 1952.

28. For a discussion of Cabinet resistance to police demands, see, Benewick, "The Threshold of Violence," pp. 49–63.

The Development of the NCCL

World War II was a catalyst for NCCL activity. The need for an organization dedicated to the preservation of civil liberties is apparent in a situation where many traditional rights are restricted or sacrificed to wartime emergencies. Two conflicting tendencies emerged which influenced subsequent development. The first was an extension of the range of interests in a nonpolitical direction, a consequence of a changeover in the office of general secretary. The second was Communist pressure which damaged credibility not only as an intermediary and advocate, but as a liberal-left coalition. The NCCL regained stature only after a long campaign which contributed to the passage of the Mental Health Act of 1959.

The NCCL has considerably extended its brief from its early concerns with police powers, administration of justice and censorship to include the rights of prisoners, gypsies, immigrants, minorities, mental patients, servicemen, women and children and issues such as privacy, drugs and academic freedom. There has been a corresponding growth in resources. The NCCL claims an individual membership of 5,500,400 trade union and organizational affiliates and a annual budget of £40,000. Its professional staff has grown from three to seventeen and includes lawyers, case workers and a research arm in the Cobden Trust. Since 1963 there has been a Parliamentary Civil Liberties Group.

The methods developed in the 1930s have been carried forward. Observers attend demonstrations ranging from those of students on campuses to those in Northern Ireland. The inquiry, such as Samuel Dash's analysis of the Widgery Tribunal on the shooting of civilians in Londonderry in January 1972, remains an important part of NCCL work.[29] Research projects complement this approach and may form the basis of evidence to government committees.[30] Considerable success has been experienced in arranging deputations. There are at least three types: the periodic general discussion of a number of previously agreed upon issues, followed by a press conference; the private deputation for information; and the private meeting on a particular case or issue. The main point, however, is that the deputation is a form of limited access distinguishable from the institutionalized and intermittent negotiations of first and second world pressure groups with government.

The legislative process is important for the NCCL; yet, its attitude and approach seem ambivalent. No lobbyist is employed; no MP sits on the executive; there is a feeling that there are no natural allies, despite the Parliamentary Civil Liberties Group.[31] This is primarily a matter of resources, but the organization's history, image, multi-issue approach and the milieu of the third world of pressure groups have to be taken into account.[32] From the NCCL view

29. Samuel Dash, *Justice Denied* (London: The Defence and Educational Fund of the International League for the Rights of Man in association with the National Council for Civil Liberties, 1972).

30. Michael King with Christine Jackson, *Bail or Custody* (London: Cobden Trust, 1971).

31. At present one parliamentary candidate and one former MP sit on the executive.

32. For a discussion of the parliamentary links of the NCCL, see, Anthony Barker and Michael Rush, *The Member of Parliament and His Information* (London: Allen and Unwin, 1970), pp. 96–103.

there is little civil liberties consciousness among MPs, so that the parliamentary group consists mainly of members who have specialist interests in specific issues.

Lobbying by the NCCL takes a number of forms, including: (1) initiation of legislation through private members' bills—Independent Review of Police Complaints; (2) support for other private members' bills—Protection of Minors; (3) briefings on government legislation, including individual briefs to committee members—1971 Immigration Bill; and (4) wider circulation of MPs and peers on particular cases and issues—campaign to renew the right of individuals to petition the European Commission of Human Rights. Government committees invite the NCCL to submit evidence, although the organization has not been successful in getting its representatives onto committees. Since the NCCL was alone in undertaking research into bail, its evidence was crucial in contrast to its submissions to the Committee on Privacy where it was one of numerous organizations.

BOY SERVICEMEN

An example of NCCL effectiveness based on a combination of tactics is provided by their campaign to alter the conditions of service of teenage recruits in the armed forces. The campaign was in two stages. It began with representations on behalf of one serviceman in 1966, and subsequent publicity indicated the general nature of the problem. This was followed by a report to the minister of state for defense, questions and debate in Parliament, the announcement of a departmental inquiry, an all-party deputation and evidence submitted to the Lord Chancellor's Committee on the Age of Majority. The committee report boosted the NCCL campaign, but the government was slow to respond. When they did, it was in the form of minor concessions. The campaign entered the second round. Casework had reached a breaking point; however, the publicity was making an impact, with coverage spreading to those newspapers most likely to be read by school leavers. The Ministry of Defense response was an increase in its advertising campaign for recruits. The NCCL issued a second report, parliamentary pressure continued, and a further deputation was followed by the announcement that a committee to investigate the terms of engagement and other conditions of boy entrants was to be set up. The Donaldson Report,[33] published in 1970, was received by the campaigners as "a fantastic triumph for NCCL," but as amended by the government still left the young serviceman "as a second class citizen."[34]

The campaign illustrates how the NCCL successfully exerted pressure in three target areas: public opinion, the legislative process and that defined by its clientele—in this case the services. It has not been possible to convey the resistance to reform or to the NCCL in this instance. A former general sec-

33. *Report of the Committee on Boy Entrants and Young Servicemen,* (London: Her Majesty's Stationery Office, 1970), Cmnd. 4509.
34. Tony Smythe, *The Guardian,* 26 November 1970.

retary has assessed the position: "Our reputation and influence, as opposed to acceptance, rests on a determined response to evident injustices, the capacity to secure redress for victims and the ability to communicate."[35] How far this is applicable to other groups and to what extent it helps define a third world of pressure groups suggests the need for more research.

---

35. Tony Smythe, "The Role of the National Council for Civil Liberties," in *Direct Action and Democratic Politics*, ed. Robert Benewick and Trevor Smith (London: Allen and Unwin, 1972), p. 275.

Group Structure and Role Behavior

By ROBERT J. WOLOSIN

W HEN one person's behavior can be shown to depend on the behavior of another, a condition of behavioral dependence is said to exist. When, in addition, the second person's behavior depends on that of the first, behavioral interdependence emerges. Social psychologists have found it useful to deal with the regularities of human behavioral interdependence in a number of ways. The terms group structure and role behavior emphasize the relatively stable, organized features of behavior interdependence.

While it is perhaps true that no two persons in the world are entirely independent of one another's behavior, in practice, social psychologists have limited their studies of group structure and role behavior to more proximal social entities. Often, the groups which are studied are entirely ad hoc, consisting of two or more individu-als who spend less than an hour together. Indeed, at times the focus of study is the single individual. The assumption is that these subjects are somehow representative of the society from which they were drawn and that, therefore, the processes underlying their behavior are generalizable to that society.

It will be convenient to subdivide studies of group structure into three parts: (1) studies which measure or describe structure, whose goal it is to give an accurate picture of the anatomy of a group; (2) studies which deal with the concomitants of structural arrangements in groups, where group structure is the independent variable and some aspect of member behavior is the dependent variable; and (3) studies of the growth and change of social structure. The review covers the period 1965 to 1973 and emphasizes small group research.

Robert J. Wolosin is Assistant Professor of Psychology at Indiana University. Educated at Chicago and Michigan Universities, Wolosin received his Ph. D. in Social Psychology in 1968; also, he was a National Science Foundation and Rackham fellow during 1967–1968. A member of the American Association for the Advancement of Science, his area of research is social psychology and perception; group dynamics; and development of social concepts in children. Professor Wolosin's articles have appeared in scholarly journals.

THE MEASUREMENT AND DESCRIPTION OF GROUP STRUCTURE

The term group structure is applied to several distinct referents. Moore identifies five uses of the somewhat more inclusive term social structure: (1) patterns of action or observable uniformities in behavior; (2) structure as social system, emphasizing emergent properties of phenomena consisting of elements in interaction; (3) social differentiation or an uneven distribution of power, goods or services; (4) statistical categories or the distribution of any social characteristic of a population; and (5) orderly sequence or predictable change in events over time.[1] Each use might be applied to a social group. Thus, the observer of a group of individuals interacting with one another would be able to detect uniformities in the members' behavior—system properties such that events in one part of the group had an impact on events elsewhere in the group; differentiation of members into particular roles— such as leader and followers, status differentials and the like; distributions of age, sex or expertise; and, if the group were studied over sufficient time, an orderly progression of change in the above properties. These facts would constitute the group's structure. A definition which seems to include all of the above uses is that of Collins and Raven, who define group structure to be relationships among elements of a social unit; these relationships have to do with communication, attraction, dependence, power and prestige.[2]

1. W. E. Moore, "Social Structure and Behavior," in *The Handbook of Social Psychology*, ed. G. Lindzey and E. Aronson (Reading, Mass.: Addison-Wesley, 1969).

2. B. E. Collins and B. H. Raven, "Group

MATHEMATICAL TREATMENTS

Graph theory

Graph theory is derived from the mathematical theory of linear graphs. Structures are easily and naturally represented as collections of social or nonsocial entities— persons, roles, attitudes, tasks— and their relationship to one another—liking, authority, endorsement, assignment. Entities are treated as points, and relationships, as lines connecting the points. The advantages of this approach are its flexibility, the precision of its mathematical development generating unambiguous structural measurements and its visual clarity, particularly when small structures are involved. Its disadvantages are the cumbersomeness of its representation of larger structures and its implicit static nature. Change in structure is difficult to represent without using multiple graphs. Recent applications of graph theory to cognitive structures, roles and children's social-cognitive development are illustrative of its generality.[3]

Set theory

Closely related to graph theory is the description of group structure as a network of dyadic relations, such as A likes B. Using this nota-

Structure: Attraction, Coalitions, Communication, and Power," in *Social Psychology*, ed. Lindzey and Aronson.

3. N. T. Feather, "Organization and Discrepancy in Cognitive Structures," *Psychological Review* 78 (1971), pp. 355–379; O. A. Oeser and G. O'Brien, "A Mathematical Model for Structural Role Theory: III," *Human Relations* 20 (1967), pp. 3–17; S. Leinhardt, "The Development of Transitive Structure in Children's Interpersonal Relations," *Behavioral Science* 18 (1973), pp. 262–271.

tion, the distribution of relationships in a group can be described. The approach is often used to investigate perceived social structures. It has been found, for example, that people expect liking to be symmetric—A likes B implies B likes A—and influence to be asymmetric—A influences B implies B does not influence A—and transitive—A influences B and B influences C implies A influences C. How these findings bear on the actual distribution of liking or influence in a group is problematic, but Henley, Horsfall and DeSoto have argued that people feel uncomfortable in, and attempt to change, groups whose structure violates expectations.[4]

Another use of set theory has been developed to deal with the formal properties of actions. Actions are seen as concatenable to form strings, analogously with words and sentences. Groups can be characterized by strings admissible in given situations, and the analytic devices of mathematical linguistics can be applied.[5] One problem amenable to this type of analysis is that of gaining the floor—that is, legitimately capturing the group's attention. Parliamentary procedure is one instance of the organization of gaining the floor. The linguistic approach could be used to isolate floor-gaining mechanisms, which could then be related to other structural characteristics. In this connection, Duncan has isolated some of the mechanisms involved in dyadic turn-taking, although not through mathematical analysis.[6]

Matrices

In the matrix approach to group structure, aspects of groups are represented in matrices which can be manipulated to determine such properties as communication flow, clique formation and probability of runs of acts over time. Davis modeled the process whereby decisions at lower levels of an organization become represented at higher levels, finding that certain apparently reasonable group decision schemes—such as majority rules—might actually distort the information available to a centralized authority.[7] Raush[8] generated a model of aggressive interactions among delinquent boys, and Cohen,[9] using matrix algebra, studied group size in free ranging monkey tribes and nursery school children. Rosenberg[10] points out

4. N. M. Henley, R. B. Horsfall and C. B. DeSoto, "Goodness of Figure and Social Structure," *Psychological Review* 76 (1969), pp. 194–204; D. van Kreveld and R. B. Zajonc, "The Learning of Influence Structures," *Journal of Personality* 34 (1966), pp. 205–223; C. B. DeSoto and F. Albrecht, "Cognition and Social Orderings," *Theories of Cognitive Consistency: A Sourcebook*, ed. R. P. Abelson, W. J. McGuire, T. M. Newcomb, M. J. Rosenberg and P. H. Tannenbaum (Skokie, Ill.: Rand McNally, 1968).

5. M. Nowakowska, "A Formal Theory of Actions," *Behavioral Science* 18 (1973), pp. 393–416.

6. S. Duncan, Jr., "Some Signals and Rules for Taking Speaking Turns in Conversations," *Journal of Personality and Social Psychology* 23 (1973), pp. 283–292; A. W. Wicker, "Undermanning, Performances, and Students' Subjective Experiences in Behavior Settings of Large and Small High Schools," *Journal of Personality and Social Psychology* 10 (1968), pp. 255–261.

7. J. A. Davis, "Group Decision and Social Interaction: A Theory of Social Decision Schemes," *Psychological Review* 80 (1973), pp. 97–125.

8. H. L. Raush, "Interaction Sequences," *Journal of Personality and Social Psychology* 2 (1965), pp. 487–499.

9. J. E. Cohen, *Casual Groups of Monkeys and Men* (Cambridge, Mass.: Harvard University Press, 1971).

10. S. Rosenberg, "Mathematical Models of Social Behavior," in *Social Psychology*, ed. Lindzey and Aronson.

that mathematical learning theory, when applied to social interaction, has the important advantage of being able to follow changes in individual behavior as they occur over time.

When the cells of a matrix are used to represent interactional outcomes and the rows and columns are partitioned to denote possible actions of two persons engaged in interaction, motivational dependence and interdependence among the actors can be represented. Structural features of groups based on motivational interdependence, such as pure cooperation, pure competition and mixed-motive situations, are easily manipulated in the context of experimental games. While the initial thrust of gaming research was to document, often laboriously, how interpersonal behavior—for example, amount of cooperation—is changed as a function of outcome matrix, more recent work has focused on processes underlying and accompanying cooperative, competitive and other forms of interaction. Gallo, for example, found that gaming behavior was fundamentally different if real monetary rewards, rather than imaginary units, were employed as outcomes.[11]

NONMATHEMATICAL DESCRIPTIVE ACCOUNTS

More traditional accounts of group structure do not involve mathematical devices. Three important descriptive models which fall into this category are those of human ethology, behavior settings and systems theory.

Human ethology

Ethologists study, via naturalistic observations, specific relationships between an animal's innate equipment and its molar environmental context; attention has been paid to animal groupings and social behavior. The view is that certain innate releasing mechanisms elicit patterns of social behavior involved, for example, in mating or aggression. Applications to human behavior have appeared, including popularized accounts such as Lorenz' *On Aggression* and Morris' *The Naked Ape*.[12] The ethological approach highlights important, but subtle, aspects of group structure. Territoriality—the possession of space and its prerogatives—becomes personal space, which has been treated by Hall, Sommer and others. An important finding is that personal space is divided into regions at which different social functions are performed; violation leads to defensive maneuvers. The boundaries of the regions differ from culture to culture, with contact cultures re-

11. A. Rapoport and A. Chammah, *Prisoner's Dilemma* (Ann Arbor, Mich.: University of Michigan Press, 1965); P. S. Gallo, Jr., "Effects of Increased Incentives upon the Use of Threat in Bargaining," *Journal of Personality and Social Psychology* 4 (1966), pp. 14–20; C. G. McClintock, "Game Behavior and Social Motivation in Interpersonal Settings," in *Experimental Social Psychology*, ed. C. G. McClintock (New York: Holt, Rinehart and Winston, 1972); E. H. Burnstein, "Interpersonal Strategies as Determinants of Behavioral Interdependencies," in *Experimental Social Psychology*, ed. J. Mills (London: Collier-Macmillan, 1969); R. J. Wolosin, S. J. Sherman and A.

Till, "Effects of Cooperation and Competition on Responsibility Attribution after Success and Failure," *Journal of Experimental Social Psychology* 9 (1973), pp. 220–235.

12. K. Lorenz, *On Aggression* (New York: Harcourt Brace Jovanovich, 1966); D. Morris, *The Naked Ape* (New York: McGraw-Hill, 1967); I. Eibl-Eibesfeldt, *Ethology: The Biology of Behavior* (New York: Holt, Rinehart and Winston, 1970).

quiring smaller distances for trans-actions than noncontact cultures. On another level, seating arrange-ments in small groups have been shown to depend on the nature of the group task and the status of the members.[13]

Nonverbal communication shares with ethology an emphasis on the specific, although overlooked, func-tions of expressions. For example, eye contact between two interactors is a function of their physical prox-imity, intimacy level and mutual attraction. Moreover, staring at a stranger seems to produce a ten-dency towards flight.[14]

Behavior settings

Barker and his colleagues have developed a descriptive model of group-environment interaction known as the behavior setting model.[15] Behavior settings are things like grocery stores, high school classes or baseball games. They are characterized by regularly occurring behavior patterns which are coordinated with the charac-teristics of the physical environ-ment and which occur at specified times and places. Behavior settings are naturally occurring units; they exist and have physical, behavioral and temporal properties which are self-generated rather than artificially imposed.

One heavily researched variable within this model is the size of the behavior setting in relation to the available manpower. For example, where there are fewer people avail-able to perform the responsible roles in a behavior setting, a condi-tion of undermanning is said to exist. Research—conducted mostly on churches and schools—has shown that the average number of people available per setting is greater in large, than in small, organiza-tions and that members of small organizations enter a wider variety of settings, take responsible roles more often and report more experi-ences of challenge and obligation to participate as compared to mem-bers of large organizations.[16] Al-though the theory predicts that as organization size increases number of participants in settings increases, but at a decreasing rate, a recent test of this postulate showed that, in fact, participation increased linearly with organization size. Thus, the degree of manning should take into account the physical capacity of the

13. R. Ardrey, *The Territorial Imperative* (New York: Atheneum, 1966); E. T. Hall, *The Hidden Dimension* (New York: Double-day, 1966); D. E. Lott and R. Sommer, "Seating Arrangements and Status," *Journal of Personality and Social Psychology* 7 (1967), pp. 90–95; R. Sommer, "Small Group Ecology," *Psychological Bulletin* 67 (1967), pp. 145–152; J. P. Batchelor and G. R. Goethals, "Spatial Arrangements in Freely Formed Groups," *Sociometry* 35 (1972), pp. 270–279.

14. P. C. Ellsworth, J. M. Carlsmith and A. Henson, "The Stare as a Stimulus to Flight in Human Subjects: A Series of Field Experiments," *Journal of Personality and Social Psychology* 21 (1972), pp. 302–311; M. L. Knapp, *Nonverbal Communication in Human Interaction* (New York: Holt, Rinehart and Winston, 1972); A. Kendon, "Some Functions of Gaze-Direction in So-cial Interaction," *Acta Psychologica* 26 (1967), pp. 22–63; M. Argyle and J. Dean, "Eye-Contact, Distance, and Affiliation, *Sociometry* 28 (1965), pp. 289–304; S. Dun-can, Jr., "Nonverbal Communication," *Psychological Bulletin* 17 (1969), pp. 118–137; M. Weiner, S. Devoe, S. Rubinow and J. Geller, "Nonverbal Behavior and Nonverbal Communication," *Psychological Review* 79 (1972), pp. 185–214.

15. R. G. Barker, *Ecological Psychology: Concepts and Methods for Studying the Environment of Human Behavior* (Stanford, Cal.: Stanford University Press, 1968).

16. R. H. Moos and P. M. Insel, *Issues in Social Ecology: Human Milieus* (Palo Alto, Cal.: National Press, 1974).

setting, the number of applicants for various positions in the setting and the minimum number of persons required for the settings' activities to be undertaken.[17]

System theory

The system approach is becoming a dominant model of group structure and function. Berrien defines a system as a set of components surrounded by a boundary which accepts inputs from, and discharges outputs to, other systems.[18] This definition is general, encompassing cells, individuals and societies, as well as groups. Inputs to systems are of two varieties: (1) energic inputs provide the means whereby the system acccomplishes its tasks and maintains itself; (2) informational inputs guide the system through its environment. Outputs include formal achievements —what the system was designed to do—and wastes, or entropy.

Katz and Kahn maintain that social systems derive their quality from a structuring of events rather than of physical units.[19] Social psychological bases of social systems are members' role behaviors and the norms and values in which these behaviors are embedded. Since social systems are maintained by human beings, it is necessary to control potential variability of system maintenance. This is accomplished by the objective requirements of the system's environment, by shared values and expectations and by the enforcement of the rules.

CONCOMITANTS OF STRUCTURAL ARRANGEMENTS OF GROUPS

Size

The number of persons in a group has important implications for group functioning. McGrath and Altman report that relatively small group size is related to: (1) less perceived need for leadership and guidance, but also less perceived competence and ability; (2) fewer ideas expressed in discussion and less influence on others' attitudes; (3) fewer perceptions of the leader as exhibiting coordinating behavior, clarifying rules or delegating responsibility; and (4) greater perception of group task success.[20] Cartwright and Zander point out that as groups increase in size a smaller and smaller proportion of persons becomes central to the organization, makes decisions for it and communicates to the total membership. In discussion groups fewer members can attain the floor, the leader exerts more control over process, and more remarks are addressed to the group as a whole. Size also influences communication

17. A. W. Wicker, J. E. McGrath and G. E. Armstrong, "Organization Size and Behavior Setting Capacity and Determinants of Member Participation," *Behavioral Science* 17 (1972), pp. 499–513.

18. F. K. Berrien, "A General Systems Approach to Social Taxonomy," in *People, Groups, and Organizations,* ed. B. P. Indik and F. K. Berrien (New York: Teacher's College Press, 1968); J. Miller, "Living Systems: The Organization," *Behavioral Science* 17 (1972), pp. 1–82; K. Azumi and J. Hage, *Organizational Systems: A Text-Reader in the Sociology of Organizations* (Lexington, Mass.: D. C. Heath, 1972); D. P. Phillips and R. H. Conviser, "Measuring the Structure and Boundary Properties of Groups: Some Uses of Information Theory," *Sociometry* 35 (1972), pp. 235–254.

19. D. Katz and R. L. Kahn, *The Social Psychology of Organizations* (New York: Wiley, 1966).

20. J. E. McGrath and I. Altman, *Small Group Research: A Synthesis and Critique of the Field* (New York: Holt, Rinehart and Winston, 1966).

in that within larger groups it becomes impossible for members to maintain complete communication with one another; thus, consensus is harder to achieve, and there tends to be less satisfaction with group decisions.[21]

Indik explored the inverse correlation between organizational unit size and member participation rates.[22] He hypothesized that size operates indirectly through specific organization processes relating to communication, control, task specialization and coordination. These processes affect the individual's ties to the organization, such as his attraction and job satisfaction, which in turn affect performance. The critical mechanism involved communication; in larger organizations adequate communication was less often achieved, reducing attraction and resulting in decreased participation.

When size is related to available physical space, the variable of density is created. Stokols maintains that density is defined in terms of spatial parameters and is a necessary, but insufficient, condition of crowding.[23] Crowding is a motivational state aroused through the interaction of spatial, social and personal factors produced when, for example, coordinated activity is required but hampered by restrictions on movement. Some research on density effects is illustrative of this distinction. Freedman et. al. varied density and found no effects on simple and complex task performance, but they controlled for physical discomfort, restricted movement and high temperature.[24] Griffitt and Veitch manipulated effective temperature and density and found that both variables were related to subjects' mood, in that hot and crowded made for a bad time.[25]

Cohesiveness

A salient dimension along which groups differ is cohesiveness—the degree to which members desire to remain in the group. Cohesiveness is the resultant of the attractiveness of the group, as well as the attractiveness of alternative groups. Attraction to a group depends on four interacting sets of variables: (1) the person's motives for joining; (2) the incentives the group offers; (3) the person's belief that membership will lead to desirable or undesirable outcomes; and (4) the level of outcomes the person thinks he deserves. Group cohesiveness leads to several interacting consequences: (1) the ability of the group to retain membership; (2) the power of the group over its members; (3) the degree of participation and group loyalty engendered; and (4) feelings of security on the part of the members. At the present time cohe-

21. D. Cartwright and A. Zander, "Structural Properties of Groups," in *Group Dynamics: Research and Theory*, ed. D. Cartwright and A. Zander (New York: Harper and Row, 1968); I. D. Steiner, *Group Processes and Productivity* (New York: Academic Press, 1972).

22. B. P. Indik, "Organizational Size and Member Participation: Some Empirical Tests of Alternative Explanations," *Human Relations* 18 (1965), pp. 339–350.

23. D. Stokols, "On the Distinction Between Density and Crowding: Some Implications for Future Research," *Psychological Review* (1972), pp. 275–277.

24. J. L. Freedman, S. Klevansky and P. R. Ehrlich, "The Effect of Crowding on Human Task Performance," *Journal of Applied Social Psychology* 1 (1971), pp. 7–25.

25. W. Griffitt and R. Veitch, "Hot and Crowded: Influences of Population Density and Temperature on Interpersonal Affective Behavior," *Journal of Personality and Social Psychology* 17 (1971), pp. 92–97.

siveness is too global a variable to have much additional research utility; what is needed are studies which detail how specific types of cohesiveness, distributed variously among the group members, lead to particular qualities of interaction with particular outcomes for the group and its members.[26]

A start has been made in this direction. The development of interpersonal attraction has been conceptualized as a process of social penetration, which refers to overt interpersonal behaviors, as well as covert processes which take place in social interaction.[27] The scope of penetration includes the growth and deterioration of dyadic relationships through time as a function of rewards and costs to the dyad, individual personal characteristics of the members and situational factors. According to this theory, exchanges progress from the superficial to the more intimate layers of the actors' selves. Research in this paradigm points up the need to go beyond the typically short time span used to study attraction. For example, it was found that initially bad experiences can be overcome if the reward-cost ratio improves over time.

Another promising line of research involves interpersonal accommodation—the process whereby people are able to adjust to one another. Abrahamson maintains that this process is accomplished via selective attention to cues, vicarious learning and covert communication; he discusses social mechanisms operating at different stages of group development, for example, those engendered by the problems of absorbing new members into an on-going group. Norms and leadership facilitate accommodation.[28]

Control structure

Problems of reducing human variability confront all groups; the group's control structure constitutes its solution. Studies can be classified around the question: what kind of control is exerted over what group processes and by whom?

The first question is: what kind of control? Structural aspects of control include degree of centralization, span of control and formalization of rules. In industrial field studies Porter and Lawler found relationships between the structure of control and workers' attitudes and job satisfaction.[29] However, other structural variables bore stronger relationships with attitudes than did control structure. Answers to the ancient question of how to distribute control—centralized in the hands of the few or delegated

26. D. Cartwright, "The Nature of Group Cohesiveness," in Group Dynamics, ed. Cartwright and Zander; D. Byrne, The Attraction Paradigm (New York: Academic Press, 1971); A. J. Lott and B. E. Lott, "Group Cohesiveness as Interpersonal Attraction: A Review of Relationships with Antecedent and Consequent Variables," Psychological Bulletin 64 (1965), pp. 259–309.

27. I. Altman and D. A. Taylor, Social Penetration: The Development of Interpersonal Relationships (New York: Holt, Rinehart and Winston, 1973).

28. M. Abrahamson, Interpersonal Accommodation (Princeton, N.J.: D. Van Nostrand, 1966); H. H. Kelley, "Interpersonal Accommodation," American Psychologist 23 (1968), pp. 399–410.

29. L. W. Porter and E. E. Lawler, III, "Properties of Organization Structure in Relation to Job Attitudes and Job Behavior," Psychological Bulletin 64 (1965), pp. 23–51; J. G. Bachman, C. G. Smith and J. A. Slesinger, "Control, Performance, and Satisfaction: An Analysis of Structural and Individual Effects," Journal of Personality and Social Psychology 4 (1966), pp. 127–137.

among the many—have been heavily influenced by ideological considerations.[30] A more realistic approach is taken in Wood's model of power centralization and sharing.[31] Power sharing is analyzed according to the phase of the decision-making process—idea generation, evaluation and choice among alternatives—at which it occurs. Consequences of power sharing are seen in the quality, acceptability and riskiness of the decisions made and in organizational effectiveness. Variables such as the nature of the decision task and the individual motives of the participants mediate the effects of power sharing.

The second question is: control exerted over what group processes? Task activities are primary targets of control; however, as Katz and Kahn point out, social systems must maintain effective levels of motivation, must integrate members around norms and value systems and must maintain boundaries.[32] Thus, control tends to be exerted in each of these areas. The well-known and controversial studies of Milgram are striking examples of normative control over group process.[33] Subjects joined an experimental group consisting of themselves, an experimenter and a confederate. They were given the job of teaching the confederate a list of word pairs and of punishing the confederate with increasing levels of electrical shock for incorrect answers. Over half of the subjects continued shock—even when the confederate was in obvious pain—up to the highest level deliverable. Thus, the normative structure of the experimental situation—its legitimation of the procedure—was such as to overcome humanitarian values widely subscribed to in the extra-experimental culture.

Finally, there is the question: control exerted by whom? Hollander and Julian stress that leadership should be seen as a social influence process rather than a fixed entity.[34] The leader's role is characterized by legitimacy and is maintained by an exchange of rewards between leader and followers. The leader, who fulfills expectations and promotes group goals, is rewarded by status, esteem and greater influentiality. Gibb's interaction theory locates leadership in a wider context of role differentiation in groups.[35] Thus, leadership is a function of personal attributes and social system in interaction and exists in a group whenever the group's norms and structure allow the special abilities of one or a few members to be used in the interests of all. Effective leadership styles depend on the situation; when the situation is either highly favorable or highly unfavorable, authoritarian—task-centered—styles are more effective; democratic—group-centered—styles are more effective for situations moderately favorable to

30. D. Cartwright and A. Zander, "Leadership and Performance of Group Functions: Introduction," in Group Dynamics, ed. Cartwright and Zander.

31. M. T. Wood, "Power Relationships and Group Decision Making in Organizations," Psychological Bulletin 79 (1973), pp. 280–293.

32. Katz and Kahn, Social Psychology.

33. S. Milgram, "Some Conditions of Obedience and Disobedience to Authority," Human Relations 18 (1965), pp. 57–75.

34. E. Hollander and J. W. Julian, "Contemporary Trends in the Analysis of Leadership Processes," Psychological Bulletin 71 (1969), pp. 387–397.

35. C. E. Gibb, "Leadership," in Handbook of Social Psychology, ed. Lindzey and Aronson.

leaders. The last statement is the contingency hypothesis of Fiedler. This model has had considerable success in accounting for leadership effectiveness, although some of its recent evidence has been called into question.[36] The hypothesis of two types of leadership in discussion groups—task and social-emotional—has been clarified and confirmed by Burke, who found that dual leadership emerged only when groups were not primarily interested in keeping to the task.[37]

CHANGES IN STRUCTURE

Patterns of group activity change over time. Several observers have noted regularities in these changes. Tuckman finds four stages: (1) forming, characterized by anxiety and rule learning; (2) storming, involving conflict and emotional resistance; (3) norming, or coming together cooperatively; and (4) performing, or using structure to solve group problems. Phillips sees longer term changes as biphasic —working together and living together; and Slater has used T-group evolution to speculate about religious development.[38]

Changes in the status structure of groups have been studied by Bavelas et. al. and by Burnstein and his associates.[39] Bavelas et. al. found that rewarding an initially low status member's contribution increased his social standing. Burnstein and Katz reviewed studies in which status allocation— in the sense of responsibility for the group's outcome—was found to depend on task perception, as well as differential member performance. Thus, when the task was presented as important, it was harder for groups to achieve an optimal status allocation.

The development of contractual norms in game situations has received some attention.[40] Thibaut and Faucheux reasoned, and found, that the formation of bargaining norms in a mixed motive situation is a joint function of strong conflict of interest within the group—internal stress—and favorable alternatives outside the group—external stress. Other studies have shown that norms restricting the use of power develop in coalitions and as a response to potentially high conflict in mixed motive games. Thus, norms

36. F. E. Fiedler, "Personality and Situational Determinants of Leadership Effectiveness," in *Group Dynamics*, ed. Cartwright and Zander; G. Graen, K. Alvarez, J. Orris and J. Martella, "Contingency Model of Leadership Effectiveness: Antecedent and Evidential Results," *Psychological Bulletin* 74 (1970), pp. 285–296.

37. P. J. Burke, "Leadership Role Differentiation," in *Experimental Social Psychology*, ed. McClintock.

38. B. W. Tuckman, "Developmental Sequence in Small Groups," *Psychological Bulletin* 63 (1965), pp. 384–399; M. Phillips, *Small Social Groups in England* (London: Methuen, 1965); P. E. Slater, *Microcosm: Structural, Psychological and Religious Evolution in Groups* (New York: Wiley, 1966).

39. A. Bavelas, A. H. Hastorf, A. E. Gross and R. Kite, "Experiments on the Alteration of Group Structure," *Journal of Experimental Social Psychology* 1 (1965), pp. 55–70; E. Burnstein and S. Katz, "Group Decisions Involving Equitable and Optimal Distribution of Status," in *Experimental Social Psychology*, ed. McClintock.

40. J. Thibaut and C. Faucheux, "The Development of Contractual Norms in a Bargaining Situation Under Two Types of Stress," *Journal of Experimental Social Psychology* 1 (1965), pp. 89–102; H. A. Michener and R. Zeller, "The Effects of Coalition Strength on the Formation of Contractual Norms," *Sociometry* 35 (1972), pp. 290–304; P. Bonacich, "Norms and Cohesion as Adaptive Responses to Potential Conflict: An Experimental Study," *Sociometry* 35 (1972), pp. 357–375.

develop as substitutes for direct interpersonal influence when the costs of such influence would be great.

ROLE BEHAVIOR

Role behavior refers to that portion of a person's activity which is relevant to the social position he occupies. Again, it will be convenient to discuss three types of research: analytic and descriptive accounts of role activity, studies of the underpinnings of role behavior and the studies of change.

Analysis and description of role behavior

Biddle and Thomas set forth a formal analysis of role concepts based on partitions of persons, behaviors and persons and behaviors and systematize role variables in terms of behavior, position, role, interdependence and personal adaptation.[41] An analysis of societal roles derived from social structural characteristics was presented by Levy, according to which all societies differentiate roles on the basis of age, generation, sex, economic allocation—production versus consumption—political allocation—authority versus responsibility—and cognition—those who have basic knowledge versus those who have intermediate knowledge.[42] Goffman has presented an analysis of the ground rules of informal relations, or the field of public life.[43]

According to Sarbin and Allen, role enactment is evaluated according to three criteria: (1) is the actor's conduct appropriate for his social position; (2) does it meet the normative standards of observers; (3) is it convincing? Persons differ in the number of roles they perform, the intensity with which they perform various roles and the amount of time spent in different roles.[44]

Ruddock uses the term "role tree" to describe the organization of roles.[45] According to this useful concept, a branching network of roles is implied. Thus, the branches refer to general roles—for example, father, office worker—secondary branches to special roles belonging to the general roles—office worker's role with bosses, subordinates and clients—and the leaves the actual role enactments by which transactions are carried out.

Katz and Kahn see roles as the means whereby the individual is linked to the organization.[46] Each person in an organization is functionally linked with others on the basis of expectations. Expectations are linked to behavior using the concept of role episode. The role episode requires that the person's role others communicate to him regarding activities which he must perform is received so that they can perform their own. The person receives these role expectations—with more or less distortion—constituting the others' immediate control over his behavior; he acts or behaves in role, showing some degree of compliance with expecta-

41. B. J. Biddle, and E. J. Thomas, eds., *Role Theory: Concepts and Research* (New York: Wiley, 1966).

42. M. J. Levy, Jr., *Modernization and the Structure of Societies* (Princeton, N.J.: Princeton University Press, 1966).

43. E. Goffman, *Relations in Public: Microstudies of the Public Order* (New York: Basic Books, 1971); G. J. McCall, *Social Relationships* (Chicago, Ill.: Aldine, 1970).

44. T. R. Sarbin and V. R. Allen, "Role Theory," in *Handbook of Social Psychology*, ed. Lindzey and Aronson.

45. R. Ruddock, *Roles and Relationships* (London: Routledge and Kegan Paul, 1969).

46. Katz and Kahn, *Social Psychology*.

tions. This initiates a new round of the role episode.

Role analysis is a preoccupation of the interpersonal school of psychiatry and clinical psychology.[47] Books such as Berne's *Games People Play* and Harris' *I'm OK–You're OK* have an impact on how people view themselves and their social relationships. A good summary is found in Swensen. The main thrust of these studies is that communication takes place on several levels simultaneously and that the total meaning of an encounter must include the congruence or incongruence among these levels. De Berker presents case studies of role behavior in groups from a psychoanalytic framework.

Processes underlying role behavior

Processes underlying the enactment of roles include the individual's ability to understand what is required of him—reception of the sent role—and his willingness and ability to comply. Since role expectations are beliefs, they can vary in their clarity. Several types of unclarity are distinguishable: uncertainty and vagueness of expectations, perceived dissensus among role-others and perceived conflict between one's own and others' expectations. Generally, these are held to result in unsatisfactory role performance.[48] Expectations may be measured via the return potential, which relates a behavioral dimension to an evaluation dimension. Wicker made such measurements on church-going roles and found that the size of contribution was differentially evaluated among members of large and small churches.[49] Role expectations may not square with reality when one's own behavior is involved. Thus, Argyris found large discrepancies between values adhered to by executives and their actual role enactment in group meetings.[50]

The process whereby a person adopts a particular role in a given situation includes knowing what cues go with what positions in the social structure, noticing what cues are present, linking these up to determine the position of others and deciding to adopt complementary behavior. Inappropriate role behavior may stem from a failure in any of these components, but the most widely studied component is that of conformity with role expectations. Nord proposed an economic model of conformity based on social exchange theory.[51] The basic premise is that social actors trade conformity to norms for repute. Unlike economic exchanges, however, this

48. Sarbin and Allen, "Role Theory," in *Handbook of Social Psychology*, ed. Lindzey and Aronson.

49. A. W. Wicker, "Size of Church Membership and Members' Support of Church Behavior Settings," *Journal of Personality and Social Psychology* 13 (1969), pp. 278–288.

50. C. Argyris, "Interpersonal Barriers to Decision Making," in *Interpersonal Dynamics*, ed W. G. Bennis, D. E. Berlwe, E. H. Schein and F. I. Steele (Homewood, Ill.: Irwin-Dorsey, 1973).

51. W. R. Nord, "Social Exchange Theory: An Integrated Approach to Social Conformity," *Psychological Bulletin* 71 (1969), pp. 174–208.

47. E. Berne, *Games People Play* (New York: Grove, 1964); T. A. Harris, *I'm OK–You're OK: A Practical Guide to Transactional Analysis* (New York: Harper and Row, 1967); C. H. Swensen, Jr., *Introduction to Interpersonal Relations* (Glenview, Ill.: Scott, Foresman, 1973); H. L. Lennard and A. Bernstein, *Patterns in Human Interaction* (San Francisco, Cal.: Jossey-Bass, 1970); P. de Berker, ed., *Interaction: Human Groups in Community and Institution* (Oxford: Bruno Cassirer, 1969).

trade involves unspecified future obligations and interpersonal trust. Social approval is the money of social exchange; its value may depend on the giver, but it does reinforce conformity. People use it both to repay past favors and invest in future obligations. Moreover, the effects of conformity depend both on its supply and demand. Hollander and Willis cite current issues in conformity research as relating to the definition of conformity—agreement versus movement toward a norm; only the latter should be considered conformity—the motivational bases of conformity—desire to participate rather than the need for social approval—and types of response to conformity pressure, including, besides conformity, anticonformity—movement away from the norm—independence—agreement with one's previous decision—and variability—disagreement with one's previous decision.[52] Allen details some of the situational factors involved in conformity.[53] Thus, public behavior is more likely to conform than private behavior, and early commitment to conformity is likely to continue. Zelditch outlines conditions under which subordinates in a status hierarchy are more likely to be independent of their supervisors.[54] These conditions pertain to thinking that one can do a better job than can one's supervisor. Porter and Lawler's expectancy theory of job performance relates conformity to performance norms and to the instrumentality of acts—the subjective probability that effort will eventuate in accomplishment—as well as ability and role perceptions.[55]

It has long been recognized that nonconformity to one group's norms may be the result of conformity to those of another.[56] The concept of reference group incorporates this distant drummer notion and has recently been used in an analysis of delinquency. Thus, a person who in an ambiguous situation may be tempted to commit a crime will be more likely to do so if the perspective of a delinquent group is taken and if the chances of punishment are low.

Personality variables relevant to role behavior have been noted by Bass and by Williams,[57] who discusses general problems in merging personality with organizational research, including the inadequacy of most personality inventories for the purpose. Golembiewski cites interesting findings on birth order and the performance of functional roles in small groups, such as that the social specialist is more likely to be a later born,[58] while the "star" more likely to be a first born.

52. E. P. Hollander and R. H. Willis, "Some Current Issues in the Psychology of Conformity and Nonconformity," *Psychological Bulletin* 68 (1968), pp. 62–76.

53. V. L. Allen, "Situational Factors in Conformity," in *Advances in Experimental Social Psychology*, vol. 2, ed. L. Berkowitz (New York: Academic, 1965).

54. M. Zelditch, Jr., "Authority and Performance Expectations in Bureaucratic Organizations," in *Experimental Social Psychology*, ed. McClintock.

55. L. W. Porter and E. E. Lawler, III, *Managerial Attitudes and Performance* (Homewood, Ill.: Irwin-Dorsey, 1968).

56. H. H. Hyman and E. Singer, eds., *Readings in Reference Group Theory and Research* (New York: The Free Press, 1968).

57. B. M. Bass, "Social Behavior and the Orientation Inventory: A Review," *Psychological Bulletin* 68 (1967), pp. 260–292; L. K. Williams, "Personality and Organizational Behavior Studies," in *People*, ed. Indik and Berrien.

58. R. T. Golembiewski, "Integrating Small Behavioral Units into Large Formal Organizations," in *People*, ed. Indik and Berrien.

Whether these findings relate directly to earlier family roles or are mediated by personality dispositions is unclear.

An actor may have all the attributes indicating acceptance of role obligations and willingness to perform roles, but simply may not know how. Argyle and his colleagues have analyzed some of the components of social competence in various situations; general relationships with properties such as rewardingness and perceptual sensitivity are also noted.[59] Methods of training in social skill, such as sheer repetition of appropriate behavior, role playing and simulation, T-group experience and observation of models are discussed. So far, a combination of methods —for example, observation of models followed by role playing with feedback—seems to be most effective.

Changes in role behavior

Permanent changes in role behavior can come about as the result of changes in task structure, group composition and the structural properties of groups. They also come about as the result of changes in the individual through the life cycle. According to Clausen, the study of socialization focuses upon the development of the individual as a social being and participant in society.[60] A thorough review of this literature is given by Zigler and Child. Some of the issues they treat are active versus passive views of the child and positive versus negative approaches to human nature; socialization of specific behavioral syndromes, such as aggression and achievement, is dealt with at length.[61] These syndromes can be viewed as parts of the personal substratum from which role behavior flows—but they are not role behaviors, themselves—and particular socializing agencies must take over to refine the human material necessary for system functioning. Some of these agencies are discussed by Brim, who deals with socialization in occcupation, families and communities.[62]

While most studies of child socialization tacitly assume that influence goes from socializing agent to child, Bell has pointed out that correlational data can be read either way and that—as every parent knows—children exert specific and definite effects on parents.[63] Thus, a more appropriate model of child socialization would be an interactive one with multiple opportunities for feedback to occur.

Argyris and Harrison[64] present alternative models of changing role behaviors in organizational settings. Argyris advocates openness to feedback from subordinates, working with the decision-making

59. M. Argyle, *Social Interaction* (Chicago: Aldine Atherton, 1969); M. Argyle and A. Kendon, "The Experimental Analysis of Social Performance," in *Advances in Experimental Social Psychology*, vol. 3, ed. L. Berkowitz (New York: Academic, 1967).

60. J. A. Clausen, ed., *Socialization and Society* (Boston: Little Brown, 1968).

61. E. Zigler and I. L. Child, "Socialization," in *Handbook of Social Psychology*, ed. Lindzey and Aronson.

62. O. G. Brim, Jr., "Adult Socialization," in *Socialization*, ed. Clausen.

63. Argyris, "Interpersonal Barriers," in *Interpersonal Dynamics*, ed. Bennis et. al.; R. Q. Bell, "A Reinterpretation of the Direction of Effects in Studies of Socialization," *Psychological Review* 75 (1968), pp. 81–95.

64. Argyris, "Interpersonal Barriers," in *Interpersonal Dynamics*, ed. Bennis et. al.; R. Harrison, "Role Negotiation: A Tough-Minded Approach to Team Development," in *Interpersonal Dynamics*, ed. Bennis et. al.

group, going over group sessions for later reactions and T-groups for improving managerial role performance. Harrison advocates an approach to change involving a consultant: the consultant attempts to get organizational members to re-negotiate their power and to influence relationships explicitly and honestly—with emphasis on who does what, but without emphasis on understanding feelings.

ANTHROPOLOGICAL STUDIES

STUDIES IN ECONOMIC ANTHROPOLOGY

edited by George Dalton $7.00 cloth $4.50 paper

with essays by Karl Polanyi, Walter C Neale, Marshall Sahlins, Maurice Godelier, Philip Grierson, Shirley Birch, Larissa Lomnitz, Nelson H H Graburn, Hugh and Christina Gladwin, Allen W Johnson, Clifton R Wharton Jr, Irma Adelman and George Dalton

The essays in this volume show that economic anthropology is not a single topic but rather a wide subject containing very different fields of interest, some of which are shared by historians, economists, and other social scientists, and some of which are studied by anthropologists alone. Three things are clear: Those interested in economic anthropology can learn much that is important from neighboring subjects as well as from the use of statistical techniques. Writings on acculturation, applied anthropology, and (post-colonial) micro-development analyze change under markedly different historical and therefore economic and social conditions. The "substantivist-formalist" controversy is not capable of clear-cut resolution because more than one theoretical framework is required to analyze and measure the very different fields of interest studied in economic anthropology.

CULTURAL ILLNESS AND HEALTH
essays in human adaptation

edited by Laura Nader and Thomas W Maretzki $6.00 cloth $3.00 paper

with essays by Robert B Edgerton, James P Spradley, Michael Agar, Paul Bohannan, John W M Whiting and Beatrice Blyth Whiting, William Caudill, Margaret Clark, E Colson, E T Hall, Claudia Mitchell-Kernan and Keith T Kernan, Roy G D'Andrade, S L Washburn

Health is intimately connected with the way in which people construct reality; with the way in which communities function; with the way in which health expertise works in the context of the nation. This volume, which consists of papers presented at a recent conference on anthropology and mental health, challenges assumptions underlying concepts of health for individuals and for society and clearly points to the need for careful observation of human behavior. Part I deals with topics which on the American scene are viewed as "social problems" or crimes—mental retardation, drug addiction and divorce. Behavioral styles, including development and interaction, and human creativity and adaptation are covered in the life cycle section. Part III deals with theoretical questions pertaining to space, language, methods and cultural constructs, and evolution.

AMERICAN ANTHROPOLOGICAL ASSOCIATION

Publications Department
1703 New Hampshire Avenue NW • Washington, DC 20009

payment must accompany orders

WHO RULES THE POLICE?

Edited by Leonard Ruchelman

Drawing on a wide range of reading selections, Dr. Ruchelman seeks to probe the realities of the police officer's job in the context of community affairs. His essential interest is to examine the subject of civil accountability and control of the police. In his selection and ordering of case material, Dr. Ruchelman succeeds in illuminating a new political dimension which makes vital reading for police officers and citizens alike.

298 pages $11.95

OLD MEN DRUNK AND SOBER

Howard M. Bahr and Theodore Caplow

The first large-scale survey of skid row (the Bowery) to include two control groups of more "normal" populations. The major concern has been to compile and quantify the life histories of the Bowery with those of the control groups, attempting to systematically describe the Bowery population as a whole, and to assess the sociological theories of the origins and concomitants of homelessness.

407 pages   illustrated $12.50

SOCIAL DISABILITY
ALCOHOLISM, DRUG ADDICTION, CRIME, AND SOCIAL DISADVANTAGE

David Malikin

This book has arrived at a time when suitable classroom materials on this subject are not readily available. In fact, Dr. Malikin's concise and thorough treatment of the material, coupled with a modest price make this volume a must for all recommended reading lists. The book divides naturally into four sections—one for each of the disabilities considered—consisting of three chapters each. The first chapter is a comprehensive statement of the problem by an outstanding specialist; the second is a case history—one human being's story of his experience of disability—and the third chapter is a review and discussion of research and programmatic literature.

266 pages $9.75

IL PAESE:
VALUES AND SOCIAL CHANGE IN AN ITALIAN VILLAGE

Feliks Gross

IL PAESE is a study of an Italian community that has been caught up in the mainstream of contemporary social evolution. The once quiet and simple village has been the scene of significant change. Professor Gross has made a careful study of these changes—in social structure, in personal and collective values and goals, and in the life style of the people. Three times, in 1958, 1969, and again in 1971, the author journeyed to this rural Italian village to conduct his intensive field work.

298 pages   illustrated $12.50

MODERN ITALY
A TOPICAL HISTORY SINCE 1861

Edited by Edward R. Tannenbaum and Emiliana P. Noether

This volume is designed to give both the student and the general reader a full understanding of the quest of one of the world's oldest peoples for a meaningful place in the modern world. During the decade of the 1860s almost all of present-day Italy was brought under one government, but it took another hundred difficult years to become a modern nation. Fifteen chapters cover a wide range of topics, including statecraft, politics, ideology, foreign policy, regionalism, economics, labor, religion, education, and intellectual developments.

395 pages $12.50

Order Directly From:

NEW YORK UNIVERSITY PRESS

Washington Square, New York 10003

Book Department

INTERNATIONAL RELATIONS AND POLITICAL THOUGHT

HADLEY ARKES. *Bureaucracy, the Marshall Plan and the National Interest.* Pp. xiv, 395. Princeton, N.J.: Princeton University Press, 1973. $12.50.

The Marshall Plan has been widely viewed as an expression of realistic yet generous policy and thus a wise interpretation of the national interest in terms of community versus what Harold Nicolson called "tribal" concerns. But how did the blend of interest and generosity, of political strategy and humanitarian tactics, in the minds of its authors, fare in the process of bureaucratic elaboration? This is the central question which Professor Arkes addresses, and his study is an immensely stimulating one. With Herbert A. Simon leading the way with his essay on "Birth of an Organization: The Economic Cooperation Administration" in the *Public Administration Review* in 1953, Arkes concluded that a study in depth of the bureaucratic aspects of the Marshall Plan should produce a clearer understanding not only of American approaches to "getting the job done" but of American politics in a broad sense, including conceptions of national interest. This, indeed, is what emerges.

Diplomatic practitioners will find various observations and conclusions of the author at variance with their own. Practitioners of the time would not say that the United States "felt constrained to hold the program open to Soviet entry" (p. 23) but that we held it open in harmony with a policy pursued from 1933 on, consistent with the prevailing thinking in our government that Soviet participation in the international system was desirable. Nor would anyone involved in the drafting of the UN Charter construe that charter in federal terms (p. 43ff). While "Cold War" is the term commonly applied to the period after World War II, it had, in fact, begun in 1917, as the British and other governments of the Western world had been left in no doubt when they extended diplomatic recognition to the Soviet Union. It was implicit in the clash of two different political, economic, and ethical systems, one of which was determined to destroy the other by any means. "If I were writing this book again," Professor Arkes says in his preface, "I might give more attention than I did to the role of organized labor in the program, and particularly to its activities in Europe" (p. vii). This would have been well and might have spared the author the error of seeing the labor movements in Europe "as integrated into their political communities" (p.319). One of the disintegrating factors in Europe which the Marshall Plan was designed to redress was the teetering position of those movements in their political communities, and this, of course, was one of the reasons for the Soviet Union's bitter opposition to the plan.

The question of national interest is one of the central concerns of this study—national interest as conceptualized in and affected by a bureaucratic process. It usefully redirects attention to the understanding that began with the classics that the discipline of politics involves the application of general rules to individual cases; that individual cases may call the rules themselves into question; that the means pursued affect the ends one seeks; and hence diplomacy—a term Professor Arkes refrains from using—is a qualification, not simply an implementation, of foreign policy. Thus the "question of *how* to accomplish the ends of the program led back to the question of *what* those ends were" (p. 6); and, as we should have learned in the Vietnam business, the question of ends should lead to a consideration of *how* to accomplish them. All of which is by way of reinforcing what this reviewer said at the beginning: this is an immensely stimulating study, because it reaches for basic political concepts. It is not just another study of the Marshall Plan.

SMITH SIMPSON
Annandale, Virginia

DANIEL BELL. *The Coming of Post-Industrial Society.* Pp. vii, 507. New York: Basic Books, 1973. $12.50.

Last night at dinner I heard George Schultz diagnose—simply and masterfully—today's problems of the American society as rooted in the difficulties a society has in moving from long-established philosophical moorings to new realities and new values.

This is what Dan Bell's book is all about. We are moving, he says:
—from the goods producing industrial economy of the past to a service economy,
—to a society in which the intellectuals, the professionals, and technical workers will have unprecedented power and influence,
—to a time when theoretical knowledge will be the society's prime source of innovation and of policy formulation,
—to a time when the society can—as it cannot now—control technology and foresee its manifold effects,
—toward the creation of a new intellectual technology to guide decisionmaking.

Much of the book—chapters 2 through 6—is devoted to describing these five dimensions of the change that is underway, to explaining how these changes have come about, and to suggesting their implications. Then in a valuable concluding chapter entitled "Coda: An Agenda for the Future"—which might have been titled "The Consequences of Social Change"—Bell spells out the implications for the future. He forecasts what changes may be expected in the relative status of individuals and groups, in the bureaucratization of science, in the evolution of concepts of meritocracy and equality, in the development of strong adversary groups within a society concerned with the quality of life, and the difficulties to be expected in achieving consensus.

In painting a broad picture of societies past, present, and future, Dan Bell exhibits an encyclopedic familiarity with the literature of several disciplines and the trends in many segments of national life. He describes his work as "a venture in social forecasting," but by this statement he understates the breadth and depth of this intellectual enterprise; it is a tour de force.

Despite an undue length and the use of a profusion of sociological and little-used terms, *The Coming of the Post-Industrial Society* is eminently worth the effort required for its study. It puts together a multiplicity of diverse changes that have been taking place and gives meaning to their sum.

In the past, he reasons, most sociologists have "understood society as a unity of social structure and culture," but "what has been happening in Western society for the past hundred years is a widening disjunction between the social structure and the culture." Stated in other words, Bell is explaining that the changes in the economy, the expansion of knowledge and technology, and the growing concern with the externalities of science are changing the values men hold, the status they grant to classes within the society, and diminishing the influence of the corporation while the influence of the university and of government is increased.

JOHN J. CORSON
Arlington, Virginia

RICHARD B. DAY. *Leon Trotsky and the Politics of Economic Isolation.* Pp. vii, 221. New York: Cambridge University Press, 1973. $10.95.

Professor Richard B. Day of the University of Toronto has contributed a significant study to the better understanding of Marxism, Trotskyism, and the Soviet Union in general. This scholarly book is not aimed at the general reader; it is instead a highly specialized and complex review of the politics and economics of Bolshevik Russia, primarily addressing specialists in the field of Soviet and East European affairs. The volume is a fascinating supplement to earlier biographies of Leon Trotsky by Isaac Deutsher, Bertram Wolfe, and George Lichtheim. It is a revisionist approach to Trotsky's political career and literary output; the author's conclusions suggest that either Trotsky's theoretical positions were inconsistent or historians have failed to explain them because they have raised the wrong questions.

Professor Day offers clear and compelling evidence that Trotsky's hesitancy, inconsistency, and vacillation on major issues called for predetermined and disastrous results and conclusions. His opposition to Stalin's rising power was tactically erroneous while his insights usually appeared several years too late. Reviewing the exciting history of the 1920s in Soviet economics and politics, Day reaches the obvious but still dramatic conclusion that "The revolution had turned full circle: and the cataclysmic rush into political and economic totalitarianism was about to begin" (p. 178).

The book is divided into two parts, unequal in size. The first discusses the early 1920s, reviewing problems of the mobilization of Soviet labor, the evolution of the new economic policy, and the dubious "Search for a New Faith." The second part begins with an interesting analysis of the slogan of "Socialism in One Country," continues with a review of Trotsky's various alternatives prior to his complete fall from power, and ends with a discussion of "Integrationism" in defeat and exile, also offering a retroactive review of Trotsky's final judgments of the Soviet experiment.

To this reviewer, one of the more interesting highlights was Trotsky's leaning toward personal authoritarianism and out-and-out militarism. Although a professional civilian himself, Leon Trotsky seems to have insisted on strict military discipline. In terms of mobilizing the country's industrial workers, he preached their abrupt removal from place to place, the publicizing of a list of deserters, the creation of a penal work command out of deserters, and their internment in concentration camps. Thus the early Trotsky years of post-revolutionary Russia set the stage for the industrial and agricultural atmosphere of a later Soviet era.

In the latter part of his book, Professor Day examines the profound economic conflict underlying the succession struggle between Stalin and Trotsky. The main conflict-issue hinged on varying interpretations of the Soviet state motto of "Socialism in One Country." Trotsky's role gradually changed from protagonist to bystander; his alternatives were sharply limited. This is a sad story indeed, combining serious economic mistakes with a process of fundamental political degeneration. The end is both inevitable and depressing. Trotsky is more aggressive in his denunciation of Stalin as an "unprincipled intriguer who subordinates everything to the preservation of his power" (p.178) than in formulating his constructive political doctrines. Leon Trotsky had exchanged a lifetime for a few meager achievements. Future historians and biographers may well dispute the gloominess and pessimism of these conclusions.

ANDREW GYORGY

Institute for Sino-Soviet Studies
The George Washington University
Washington, D.C.

MORTON DEUTSCH. *The Resolution of Conflict: Constructive and Destructive Processes.* Pp. ix, 420. New Haven, Conn.: Yale University Press, 1973. $15.00.

Morton Deutsch opens up conflict situations to expose seeds of cooperation that lie within. This groundbreaking work in social-psychology does not deal with "pure" (zero-sum) conflict situations in which one side inevitably loses what the other gains. Rather, this coordinated series of essays and articles focuses upon "mixed" (variable-sum) cases of conflict made up of both cooperative and competitive elements that can result in mutual loss, mutual gain, or one party gaining more than another. Deutsch's basic question is: Under what conditions will participants evolve cooperative or competitive relationships in situations permitting either?

Deutsch's introduction is reminiscent of Anatol Rapoport's more charming *Fights, Games and Debates,* the former's struggle between two children over a water hose replacing the latter's

conflict between Tom Sawyer and the city dandy. Yet Deutsch goes well beyond Rapoport's contribution by providing experimental data that test conflict hypotheses posited in his theoretical essays.

Some problems emerge because of the author's unwillingness to spell out the reasoning and philosophical backdrop behind his basic assumptions. For instance, in warning the reader against committing the "group mind fallacy," Deutsch commits the fallacy of reification in trying to account for national behavior: "One should not ignore that nations as well as individuals have the capacity to act even though each unit cannot do the same kinds of things: a nation can declare war, a man cannot; a man can make love, a nation cannot." Individuals, of course, *do* declare war in the name of nations, and Deutsch's attempt to anthropomorphize the nation-state is all too representative of the dehumanizing tendency towards reification—or Whitehead's "fallacy of misplaced concreteness"—which dominates the literature of international politics. Yet here, as always, Deutsch *means* well; it just didn't come out clearly.

This example is symbolic of critical theoretical problems that crop up in socio-psychological treatments of conflict that neglect or ignore their philosophical roots. The roots behind the "cooperative process" assumptions of Deutsch—and Rapoport, too—come from phenomenology, though neither theorist seems to be explicitly aware of this fact in his writings. This hidden dependency upon phenomenology peeks out in spots: "Given the fact that the ability to place oneself in the other's shoes is notoriously underemployed in most people, and also given that this ability is impaired by stress and inadequate information, it is to be expected that certain typical biases will emerge in the perceptions of actions during conflict."

In sum, Deutsch has provided a hard-headed, fruitful examination of conflict at interpersonal, intrapersonal, and intergroup levels that posits testable propositions telling how to transform destructive conflict into cooperation, how to use third parties in the process, and how to compete more effectively from a relatively weak position.

ROBERT A. ISAAK
Department of Political Science
Fordham University
Bronx, New York

ANGUS M. FRASER. *The People's Liberation Army: Communist China's Armed Forces.* Pp. ix, 62. New York: Crane, Russak, 1973. $4.95.

This slim volume—57 pages of text—is the latest of the Strategy Papers published by the National Strategy Information Center and deals with the military strength and capability of the People's Republic of China. Angus Fraser, consultant for the Smithsonian Institute and the Historical Evaluation and Research Organization, was Senior Marine Adviser, MAAG, to the Republic of China prior to his retirement from the Marine Corps in 1964, and has the necessary credentials for writing this book.

Using the information available to him from "open sources," ranging from well researched monographs to undocumented newspaper reports and Defense Department statements, Fraser has provided a valuable, albeit brief, analysis of the composition and deployment of China's armed forces, its military spending and defense industry, and its nuclear weapons program. His conclusions are that China is modernizing its conventional capabilities, expending about ten percent of its GNP, and is prudently moving towards a stage when it will possess a limited nuclear deterrent against the United States and the USSR.

In a chapter that discusses the Peoples Liberation Army's strategic capabilities, Fraser postulates three general cases: "defense of the homeland; excursions beyond China's borders over continuous lines of communication; and excur-

sion over discontinuous lines." His well argued deductions are that China has impressive capabilities for defense of the homeland and will soon have the nuclear ability to make Japan (if China is attacked by the US) or India (if China is attacked by the USSR) a hostage country. In the case of an invasion by the USSR, China can also cut the vital Russian rail line at many places and isolate Vladivostok. Fraser does not see a possibility of China initiating action against bordering countries except in behalf of North Vietnam or North Korea if they are in dire need of such help. Even there it will have to first carefully assess reactions of Moscow and Washington. As far as military excursions beyond its borders are concerned, China's capabilities are extremely limited. China's military posture is basically defensive.

Analyzing China's strategic concerns, Fraser does not see any immediate threat to China from the United States, Japan, or other countries in South or Southeast Asia. "For the moment, China is preoccupied with the problem defined by a massive and threatening Soviet military presence along the border." Fraser suggests that the United States, while politically urging mutual restraint, must make it clear that it would not allow the extension of Sino-Soviet rivalry to third countries in Asia. At the same time the United States should maintain the "capability and will to retaliate against Mainland China should it initiate the use of nuclear weapons" against U.S. allies in Asia.

The scenario created by Fraser gives the current picture and is not intended to forecast future developments. If India develops nuclear capability or Japan emerges as a military power or if the pro-Moscow faction takes over after Mao's death, things may change radically.

The lay reader will find certain data—submarines: types "G", "W", "R", and so on—difficult to comprehend, and some parts of the work, particularly the first chapter, appear to have been written for the military specialist. Yet, the book is not a work of reference to be used only by specialists and scholars—it lacks an index, and the bibliography is rather limited.

RANBIR VOHRA

Trinity College
Hartford
Connecticut

GEORGE C. HERRING. *Aid To Russia, 1941–1946: Strategy, Diplomacy, The Origins of the Cold War.* Pp. vii, 365. New York: Columbia University Press, 1973. $15.00.

It can hardly be disputed that the dominant event of the years since the end of the Second World War has been the development of the Cold War and the ultimate achievement of détente. The foremost historical controversy has revolved around its origin, between those who consider that the Cold War arose from Soviet intransigence and those who blame the policies—or lack of them—of the Western powers. Any book which throws light on its origin and development is to be welcomed, for this is one of the darkest corners of modern historiography. Professor Herring has, in this respect, written a very welcome book—a concise, logical, and clearly written account of American lend-lease to the Soviet Union and of attempts to continue this into the years of peace which followed the end of the war in Europe, until deteriorating relations at last put an end to such collaborative activity.

When the Germans invaded the Soviet Union in June, 1941, the United States had already abandoned its position of neutrality. It was committed to helping the United Kingdom against the Axis powers, and was at once thrust into the improbable position of becoming an ally and backer of the Soviet Union. The decision to aid the Soviet Union was made with speed, and by the end of that summer the Office of Lend-Lease Administration was processing requests for supplies to be sent to the USSR.

Professor Herring traces skillfully both the diplomatic maneuvering and the reaction of American opinion to this generous treatment of a new-found ally whose credentials were not above suspicion. It is made clear that Roosevelt regarded lend-lease as a military weapon, that he thought that the war could be greatly shortened if the Germans could be effectively resisted on their eastern front, and that he feared—perhaps unnecessarily—some kind of deal between Hitler and Stalin. Roosevelt has been bitterly attacked for unnecessary generosity, for his naiveté in not demanding political concessions in return for military aid, and for contributing materially to the Communist domination of Eastern Europe.

The critics of Roosevelt, however, will find little consolation here. The author emphasizes the general wisdom of his policy. "His principal purpose was to furnish the maximum assistance to the Soviet Union and to build an effective alliance against Hitler, and he recognized that attempting to extract a *quid pro quo* from the Russians would only complicate the attainment of these immediate objectives . . . [he] correctly perceived that to require the Russians to make political concessions in 1941 would have been pointless." On his handling to lend-lease he is praised as "generally wise and realistic."

Difficulties were formidable enough in dealing with the Russians. It is implicit in Professor Herring's narrative that they never recognized the constraints imposed on American policy by the actions of Congress and the pressure of public opinion. It is no less clear that the Russians demanded supplies which they did not or could not use, and that much sophisticated equipment was just wasted. Nevertheless, as Khrushchev himself admitted, how would the Russians have advanced to the Elbe if they could not have moved on American vehicles? Professor Herring makes no exaggerated claims for the military importance of American supplies. "Lend-lease probably did not decide the outcome of the war in Russia, but the wartime statements of Soviet leaders make it clear that it helped to make the nation and the Red Army a much more potent fighting force."

How then did wartime cooperation turn to distrust, and alliance become transmuted into the Cold War? The author leaves us in no doubt that there was continuing opposition to the policy of lend-lease, and he traces the growth and ultimate success of this opposition as in the minds of an increasing number of people the concept of the Soviet Union as a suffering and deserving ally was transformed into one of a Communist aggressor bent on world domination. The turning point came for many in the conduct of the Russians during the Warsaw Rising of July, 1944, and the gradual fastening of Soviet control on the countries of Eastern Europe merely confirmed their suspicions and aroused their hostility.

So far the evidence supports the traditional view of the origins of the Cold War. Professor Herring makes it clear, however, that Truman and the more conservative of those around him had no realization of the Soviets' fear for their own security, and that their creation of a *cordon sanitaire* was something more than an act of naked aggression. But it was the clumsy and undiplomatic way in which lend-lease was terminated and the American failure—in deference, it is true, to the pressures of Congress and of public opinion—to give adequate economic aid which did most to arouse criticism and hostility in the Soviet Union. "It is indeed difficult," writes the author, "to defend American policy in the months after V-J Day." And so, amid recrimination and suspicion, the unstable structure of Soviet-American friendship collapsed in 1946–47.

Professor Herring has provided an admirable guide through these events, and if he has contributed significantly neither to the traditional nor to the revisionist points of view, this is perhaps a credit to his dispassionate handling of the evidence.

N. J. G. POUNDS
Department of History
Indiana University
Bloomington

MICHAEL H. HUNT. *Frontier Defense and the Open Door: Manchuria in Chinese-American Relations, 1895–1911.* New Haven: Yale University Press, 1973. Pp. ix, 281. $12.50.

The study of the Open Door policy has come a long way since Tyler Dennett and A. Whitney Griswold published their major works before the war. Historians such as Paul Varg, Charles Vevier, Thomas McCormick, Raymond Esthus, Marilyn Young, Jerry Israel, and Richard Challener have done much to explore the manifold meaning of the Open Door and to relate it to domestic concerns and intellectual currents in the United States. Another conventional study would thus be quite superfluous. But this book breaks fresh ground because the author has a linguistic competence to examine the Chinese dimension of the Open Door, a subject that has been all but ignored by other writers.

Basically, what Hunt does is to examine the Open Door policy in terms of its interactions with Chinese politics and foreign policy, in particular the Ch'ing dynasty's concern with frontier defense. The Open Door, according to Hunt, seemed to Chinese officials to be introduced to Manchuria as a counterweight to the power of other countries. For instance, Hsi-liang, governor-general of the Three Eastern Provinces, wrote, "Because China's power . . . is insufficient to hold back the advance of Japan and Russia, we must depend on the United States and Britain and on the policies of the open door and of the balance of power as a device to save ourselves from oblivion." Hsi-liang's thinking represented a mixture of the traditional tactic of playing barbarians off against one another with the awareness of the possibilities of *realpolitik* as well as railroad development in Manchuria for frontier defense.

Such ideas, the author argues persuasively, meshed well with the views of those American officials who pursued what he calls an activist, as opposed to a passive, traditionalist, Open Door policy. The dichotomy makes sense in the conceptual framework of this book. The activist strain, looking toward asserting American power and influence in China, became meaningful because it fitted in with the aspirations and thinking of frontier-conscious and *realpolitik*-oriented Chinese officials. The collaboration of Hsi-liang with Willard Straight, the epitome of American activism in the years following the Russo-Japanese War, was a perfect example of the marriage of convenience. Thus, for a brief period before the Republican revolution of 1911, China's frontier defense and America's Open Door policy became synonymous.

This is a fascinating story and a very imaginative interpretation. For the first time one is able to see clearly the interactions between American policy and Chinese politics. The interactions, as the author shows, were superficial, derived from the two peoples' vastly different traditions and modes of thought. Nevertheless, the very superficiality makes the study invaluable. The book is a landmark in the historiography of American-East Asian relations.

AKIRA IRIYE
University of Chicago

EDWARD SHILS. *The Intellectuals and the Powers and Other Essays.* Pp. xiii, 481. Chicago: The University of Chicago Press, 1972. $12.50

This is a collection of essays, almost all of them written in the fifties and sixties, dealing with a wide range of topics centering around the intellectual in Western and non-Western societies. The topics include: the definition of the intellectual, the traditions of intellectual life, alienation among intellectuals, the need for civil concerns among intellectuals, mass society, metropolitan and provincial culture, the problems of intellectuals in developing countries, and student rebellions. When the reader is confronted with such diversity, he is justified in going to the author for elucidation as to what *he* considers the central theme of his work. The reader will find this central theme stated clearly and at once in the Introduction. "Why," asks Professor Shils, "did the writers, historians, philosophers, and other intellectuals . . . feel such revulsion for their own societies, for the institutions through which they were ruled and the persons who ruled them?" The attitude of Professor Shils toward intellectual alienation, no matter where found, is unmistakeable; it puzzles and angers him. His essays are an expression of both attitudes.

Professor Shils' inquiry begins, logically, with a definition of the intellectual and an analysis of his relationship to society. Intellectuals are those "with an unusual sensitivity to the sacred, an uncommon reflectiveness about the nature of their universe and the rules that govern society." They have a "need to externalize this quest in oral and written discourse, in poetic or plastic expression, in historical reminiscence, in ritual performance and acts of worship." Intellectuals are dedicated to cultivating and transmitting those works of the past which have most nobly and validly expressed the sacred. But they are dedicated also to "the elaboration and development of alternative . . . potentialities" in the central value system, systematizing and rationalizing this value system and "adapting it to new tasks and obstacles." From this intellectual mission arise the supreme values of the intellectuals: the values of achievement, freedom, independent curiosity, disciplined inquiry and analysis, and criticism.

Nevertheless, the alienation of the intellectual from society and societal distrust of the intellectual remain, and for this unhappy situation, destructive both to intellectuals and society, Professor Shils prescribes a remedy; namely, "civility." Civility is defined as "the virtue of the citizen," the sharing of responsibility for self-government either as governed or governor. Civility demands that the intellectuals' concern with the transcendental be infused into everyday political and social life. It demands that intellectuals cease from the attempt to impose a single standard of valuation or a single solution on other spheres of life. It does not call for intellectuals to surrender their values, but it does demand their self-limitation out of respect for the good of the whole. It is only in these ways that some sort of balance between the intellectual and society can be achieved. If it is the intellectual who must do most of the shifting to achieve the balance, nevertheless the intellectual, thus self-limited, would have much to contribute to society; a demand for moral equality, a healthy distrust of unbridled authority and uncontrolled institutions, an insistence on justice. Even intellectual faith in a heroic existence and in an earthly paradise can have positive societal effects if it becomes infused into everyday life with all its imperfections, injustices, and irrationalities.

But Professor Shils does not believe that the prospect for a civil politics is altogether bright. A portion of the blame must be assigned to the low level of political life and to the "melancholy" experience of intellectuals who have tried to engage in civil politics. But the major trouble stems from the intellectual, and not only from his anti-political and anti-authoritarian traditions. The specialization of much modern intellectual work has removed the intellectual from the hurly-burly of politics. The triumphs of science have made ordinary politics seem mundane. The immensity of the problems that the modern world faces, such as the threat of nuclear destruction, makes politics seem puny by comparison.

That there are dangers for the intellectual in civil politics, Professor Shils is aware. There is always the danger that the civilly minded intellectual will become totally assimilated to the power with which he is seeking accommodation, that he will become a prop to the status quo. Indeed, says Professor Shils, "complete disavowal of every line of affinity between civility and ideology would turn civility into an ideology. Civility would become an ideology of pure politics concerned with no substantive values except the acquisition and the maintenance of public order. . . ." The ability of intellectuals to act civilly, in spite of these dangers, is exemplified by those atomic scientists who, though few in numbers, became concerned with the implications of nuclear energy.

A critical analysis of essays of such scope and erudition is not possible in a short review, but perhaps a few observations may be made here. As Professor Shils notes, the civilly minded intellectual may all too easily find himself subservient to men of power. Unfortunately, Professor Shils does not tell us how the intellectual, almost by definition the man without power, is to prevent this happening. Indeed, incidents from Professor Shils' own career might put us on guard here. Nor does Professor Shils explain the criteria which an intellectual should use in deciding whether to adopt an attitude of "civility" toward a given state; should all states be served "civilly," or all policies, or all regimes? Surely Professor Shils is not against the alienation of some Russian intellectuals; in fact, he admires them greatly. And what does it mean to be "civil-minded"? Were the intellectuals who were against the Vietnam war merely alienated, or were they being truly "civil" in terms of the interests of the society? Furthermore, is it not possible that the source of intellectual alienation lies not in the disparity between the values of the intellectual and the demands of society, but in the disparity between intellectual values and the *reality* of society; that precisely because the intellectual prizes rationality, criticism, and analyis he is capable of making a judgment that the reality of society does not coincide with human needs and that better societies could be conceived and possibly achieved. In short, is it not possible that alienation represents a series of rational judgments and decisions about the nature of the social worlds we inhabit?

EUGENE V. SCHNEIDER
Department of Sociology
Bryn Mawr College
Pennsylvania

C. L. SULZBERGER. *An Age of Mediocrity: Memoirs and Diaries, 1963–1972.* Pp. xii, 828. New York: Macmillan, 1973. $12.95.

C. L. Sulzberger, chief foreign correspondent of *The New York Times* from 1944 to 1954 and a syndicated columnist since 1954, has probably interviewed more of the world's rulers and statesmen, plus an assorted bag of other well-known personalities, than any other living person. He has collected his interviews and impressions in three huge volumes of memoirs and diaries—*A Long Row of Candles* (1969), *The Last of the Giants* (1970), and now *An Age of Mediocrity* (1973).

The title of his latest volume—which he insists will be the last of its kind—reflects his views of the quality of the statesmen of the past decade. The age of the giants has passed. In their footsteps "we find the technicians, a competent but uninspiring lot. . . . Efficient, competent, none is genuinely popular or charismatic in the least. . . . They are men of man's dimensions, [but they] may make for better government—and peace." Nixon, Heath, Brandt, and Pompidou are "fit men for the age of technocrats." Only a few giants, such as Mao and Tito, remain, but they are long past their prime and they seem to have no successors.

Mr. Sulzberger had his headquarters in Paris during the past decade, and he shows a special fondness for France and the French, which perhaps has led him to take an exaggerated view of the role of France in the modern world. He interviewed de Gaulle, Pompidou, Malraux, and other French leaders several times, and almost every time he was in Paris he golfed with Couve de Murville. His interviews with de Gaulle are among the longest and most fascinating in his book. He also often saw distinguished non-Frenchmen in Paris, including the Duke of Windsor, Caramanlis (a former prime minister of Greece), Bohlen, and Harriman. In 1971 he had "one of the most fascinating luncheons of my life" with André Malraux and Régis Debray. Of particular interest among his other interviews are those with Presidents Johnson and Nixon, Henry Kissinger, Robert McNamara, Gamal Abdel Nasser, Anwar El Sadat, Mohamed Heikal, King Hussein, Golda Meir, Indira Gandhi, Nguyen Van Thieu, Marshal Tito, Willy Brandt, Nikita Khrushchev, Aleksei Kosygin, B. J. (John) Vorster, Julius Nyerere, Salvador Allende, and Fidel Castro (from midnight to 6:00 a.m.). He seemed to be particularly interested in Greek affairs. He visited that country several times during the decade, both before and after the coup of 1967. He talked with most of the top political leaders, in and out of office, and he had several interviews with King Constantine in Athens and Rome.

A peripatetic observer, Sulzberger seemed to have an addiction for logging a continuous round of interviews with leading world figures. Few escaped his indefatigable approaches. Through his virtually non-stop interviews he presents portraits and summaries of the thoughts of most of the important statesmen and thereby throws light on most of the major developments of an entire decade. It is an episodic and rather superficial way to get a refresher course in recent history. While full of pungent stories and comments, the memoirs and diaries are less indiscreet than the author would like to believe; but even in describing "an age of mediocrity," he is never mediocre and never dull.

NORMAN D. PALMER
Department of Political Science
University of Pennsylvania
Philadelphia

AFRICA, LATIN AMERICA, AND THE MIDDLE EAST

NORMAN ASHCRAFT. *Colonialism and Underdevelopment: Processes of Political Economic Change in British Honduras.* Pp. ix, 180. New York: Teachers College Press, Columbia University, 1973. $8.50.

Eighth in a series of monographs sponsored by Teachers College's Center for Education in Latin America, Dr. Ashcraft's volume offers to many different readers a unique experience stemming from field investigations in the 1960s in British Honduras, for his purpose in attempting a marriage of the disciplines of anthropology and economics is unique in methodology. To an unsympathetic reader, the offspring of the marriage would appear to be something akin to sociology. The author is deserving of praise for experimentation; he specifically turns his back on the norms of historical research, makes intentional omissions—the immigration of Mexicans, the rise of political parties, the role of organized labor, and the border dispute with Guatemala—and rejects the areas explored by the political scientist. Whether the present volume will encourage others to adopt the interdisciplinary procedure of anthropology-cum-economics remains to be seen. The present example might frighten them away. For enthusiastic innovators, both pitfalls and opportunities are demonstrated by Ashcraft's formula.

The factors which have condemned British Honduras to underdevelopment are clearly set forth. There is sparse population and even more scarce capital investment. Most communication is by river canoe or by trucks and busses on rutted roads. Poverty is endemic. Commercial activity has shifted from dye woods to mahogany harvest which, in turn, have given way to concentration on sugar, then chicle, banana plantations, and ultimately to citrus. Describing rural education as "transfering to succeeding students a worn out, meaningless body of knowledge," the author's conclusion is that "there is little chance of education having an impact since the growth of underdevelopment continues unabated" (p. 108).

In his insistence that partial reforms will not solve the many deficiencies in the society of British Honduras, Dr. Ashcraft holds that "the system" must be changed. It is not clear whether it is the system of colonial political relationships, or the system of a capitalistic economy that must give way. Unhappily, there are many more complaints about poverty and illiteracy appearing in the pages of this book than there are positive recommendations or plans of action. Even aspirations for political independence are muted by fears that, bereft of British military protection, an infant country named "Belize" would fall victim to territorial encroachments by neighboring countries.

To evaluate such a novel approach to social problems, the reader is unusually dependent upon helpful footnotes, cross-references, and an index. Sadly, there are none. On the other hand, Dr. Ashcraft is to be commended for his diligence in searching out source materials, including items that are undated, unpublished, and dug out of an archives in which materials are not cataloged.

WILLARD BARBER
University of Maryland

LARRY W. BOWMAN. *Politics in Rhodesia: White Power in an African State.* Pp. 206. Cambridge, Mass.: Harvard University Press, 1973. No price.

Professor Bowman has written a depressing and realistic study—depressing for those who hope for significant political change in Rhodesia, realistic given the constraints on African political activities.

As the subtitle indicates, *Politics in Rhodesia* focuses on the small European minority—approximately a quarter million of the 5½ million total population—which has controlled the state since the British South Africa Company imposed its rule in 1890. The two other main participants in Rhodesian politics—the African majority and the British government—seem to stand, impotent, on the sidelines.

The impotence has been mutually reinforcing. African nationalist leaders, seeing the progress made toward majority rule and independence in British colonies during the late 1950s and early 1960s, felt assured similar progress could be theirs. Bowman calls this belief a "critical error": Black Rhodesians "presumed their struggle to be similar to that waged in other British colonies. In Rhodesia, however, the settlers controlled the political system, and this control was accepted by Britain" (p. 46). Given both the prolonged period during which the British government acquiesced in settler restrictions on Africans and its reluctance to use force when independence was declared by the white minority in November, 1965, African and British leaders alike were bound in joint frustration in their quest for majority rule.

Bowman sees the unilateral proclamation of independence as the outcome of increased white consolidation. Fear arose lest Great Britain use its paper prerogatives to achieve majority rule with unseeming haste—say, in a century or less. Though Rhodesian whites differed in tactics, they united in protecting their style of life. Their unity was expressed through the Rhodesian Front, according to Bowman "the first stable party structure in Rhodesian political history" (p. 94).

The only avenue for change in Rhodesia lies outside the current system. British leaders have blustered, but they always have been forced into granting further concessions to the minority; U.N.-mandated sanctions have significantly cut tobacco exports, but have scarcely brought the regime to its knees; Africans are united in rejecting minority rule, but are sorely divided between rival movements. Only guerrilla fighters infiltrated across Rhodesia's borders might effect change, for the regime's vulnerability arises from the relatively small number of Europeans in the country.

The 155 pages of text are well written and well documented. It is hard to pick fault with Bowman, for he has treated a complex subject with great skill. Several areas do need equally detailed attention, such as the debilitating struggles among Rhodesian African leaders, the conditions under which guerrilla warfare might be initiated and sustained, pressures from Commonwealth states on British leaders for majority rule before independence, the increasing coordination between the South African and Rhodesian governments, or the lobbying in the United States over the recently repealed Byrd amendment. Until these are examined, *Politics in Rhodesia* will remain the main current study of how a minority implements its control.

CLAUDE E. WELCH, JR.
Department of Political Science
State University of New York
Buffalo

ROBERT C. GOOD. *UDI: The International Politics of the Rhodesian Rebellion.* Pp. 368. Princeton, N.J.: Princeton University Press, 1973. $12.50.

The story of the Unilateral Declaration of Independence (UDI) in Rhodesia is emotion-laden—as stories bordering on race and color in contemporary world society generally are—and the height of emotion is often dependent on whose voice is heard, whether that of Ian Smith, the agents of the United Kingdom, the United States,

Zambia, South Africa and other African states, or the Organization of African Unity, or the United Nations. In this well-written volume, Robert Good, former U.S. Ambassador to Zambia and presently Dean of the Graduate School of International Studies and Director of the Social Science Foundation at the University of Denver, has made a great effort at objectivity, painstakingly and candidly presenting issues and events, and rising above deep emotional involvement.

The book opens with an account of early white settlement and British colonial rule in what is today known as Rhodesia and continues with the events surrounding the UDI. In discussing these events, Good emphasizes the high morale of the minority white settlers and their strong support for Ian Smith, the equivocal steps taken by the British Labor Government of Wilson, such as the decision to impose economic sanctions rather than military sanctions to quell what is considered to be a rebellion, Zambia's economic fears, the unsuccessful OAU diplomatic assault on Britain, and the threat of the break-up of the Commonwealth to which many African member states did not subscribe, the unsuccessful, dubious United Nations steps to deal with the issue, and a series of United Kingdom attempts to negotiate with Ian Smith, the last of which was conducted with the Tory Government in November, 1971. It was here that the story ended with Britain saying that the last settlement was the "end of the road." On the contrary, asserts Good, it was only another beginning, and he is right. Early in 1974, Ian Smith's white minority regime is still firmly in control of Rhodesia, defying all international pressures, and the "end" is not yet in sight.

UDI: The International Politics of the Rhodesian Rebellion is addressed to "many audiences, most importantly in Great Britain, as the book more than anything else is an account of, and a statement about, a British foreign policy problem. But the implications of the story touch many areas, not least the United States" (p. 11). It gives a good selection of important facts and historical events; but overemphasis on the role of Great Britain prevents a more comprehensive interpretation or analysis of the international politics of the rebellion. Here lies its main difficulty. Good could have done much better if he had gone a little deeper and explained, for instance, why the United States "became the only country in the world in explicit legislative defiance of its obligations under the Charter respecting sanctions" (p. 324).

Moreover, Good indicated the ignorance of many Westerners on events concerning Southern Africa and said that he often found himself explaining that Zambia was not the same as Gambia or Zanzibar (p. 11). A desirable improvement on his volume would, perhaps, be the provision of two maps—one of Africa and the other of Southern Africa—to help his readers. The map on page 91—the only map he provides—which deals with "Zambian Transport Routes" is not very helpful; in fact, it is confusing.

The sources of material for the book constitute its major strength. They are extensive, and Good demonstrates conscientiousness in selecting the most useful. It might have been better, however, if sources of information were shown in footnotes. The bibliographical notes for each chapter arranged at the end are meaningless in terms of specific information in the main text.

The journalistic style of reporting has some merit; it enhances the sequence of the story considerably. All said, Good's account of the Rhodesian rebellion is readable.

JULIUS EMEKA OKOLO
Howard University
Washington, D.C.

ALLAN HOBEN. *Land Tenure among the Amhara of Ethiopia: The Dynamics of Cognatic Descent.* Pp. xiv, 273. Chicago: University of Chicago Press, 1973. $9.50.

The Amhara of Ethiopia can trace their descent in both male and female lines through many generations; in theory the number of apical ancestors which could be named exceeds a thousand, but only a few lines are remembered—those recently articulated and the more prestigious. Territorial, religious, and political groupings are not primarily defined in terms of descent, but descent is basic to land holding. The Amharan man acquires land by inheritance from his parents; however, he may also claim land in the estate allocated to any of his apical ancestors, the extent depending upon his genealogical position, for in theory, the estate is subdivided equally per stirpes in each generation. The land so acquired is usually being farmed by someone else; it would appear, however, that those who thus lose land are not the poor, relying on a single plot for subsistence, but men who have too much land—who are unable to cultivate all their holdings or whose title claims are relatively weak.

Casual observers have presumed that land was held in some form of feudal tenure by a ruling aristocracy. Professor Hoben, in his study of villages in a remote area of the Ethiopian highlands, shows that this is not so. The society is relatively open. Influential men are able to acquire plots of land and so increase their power; but their position weakens in their old age and their own sons have to start afresh. In a study of quite exceptional clarity, the author spells out the rules governing the allocation of land and, with diagrams and case studies, describes its distribution. With case material from the local customary courts, he demonstrates how men pursue and defend themselves against these claims in enhancing their status in this community.

This is clearly an important book for social anthropologists, for it presents so succinctly the mechanics of a cognatic descent system. Students of Ethiopia will also be interested. But the book deserves a much wider readership, for in his final chapter Professor Hoben shows how the Amharan peasants violently resist new modes of taxation and are opposed to "progressive" plans for land reform. The outcome of the reforms, as they see them, is likely to be a perpetuation of the present inequalities, a threat to their fluid and competitive system.

At the present time there seem to be as many peasant rebellions against reforms conceived by radical central governments as against traditional injustices. This book indicates why—and emphasizes the need for close study of these traditional systems to correct our stereotypes of them.

P.C. LLOYD

The University of Sussex
Brighton
England

HELIO JAGUARIBE. *Political Development: A General Theory and a Latin American Case Study.* Pp. v, 603. New York: Harper & Row, 1973. $11.95.

In the last few years, a number of Latin American social scientists have published significant works in the United States. Now a prominent Brazilian political scientist has published what may come to be regarded as truly a major work in its field. Jaguaribe, who has previously written significant studies on political development, now presents his most detailed and systematic study in this field.

In the first two-thirds of the work, he gives a general analysis of the society, the polity, political development, and political change. This theoretical part of the work includes his detailed treatment of political models—a section that demands very careful reading, but is rewarding and seminal indeed. He uses an elaborate typology for classifying political systems and determining their levels of political development and their developmental potentials. The author's three basic models are national capitalism, state capitalism, and developmental socialism.

After laying this general foundation, the author devotes the final third of the book to a detailed examination of Latin America as a case study.

The region, in general, combines the characteristics of underdevelopment, social dualism—great concentration of wealth, education, and influence—population explosion, and inadequate amount and distribution of essential resources. In his structural analysis, Jaguaribe finds the area characterized by stagnation, marginality, and denationalization. Stagnation represents such a slow GNP growth as to widen the gap between the developed and the underdeveloped countries. Marginality—economic, social, cultural, and political participation —is seen in the gaps between a country's social strata and its regions, as well as between countries. Denationalization—economic, cultural, and political—comprises the transference of control over influence and decisions "from actors loyal or favorable to a nation to actors loyal or favorable to another nation."

This adds up to a future of "nonviability" for many of the countries of Latin America. The future alternatives he sees for Latin America are dependence on an advanced country or autonomy—to be sought by either the revolutionary way or the reformist way. The dependence alternative he feels "has confirmed the propensity of the Latin American dependent regimes to assume forms increasingly closer to the colonial-fascist model." This is a status quo regime of repression maintained by both internal and international forces. Jaguaribe presents this more lucidly for Brazil in another work—his chapter in Halper and Sterling's book Latin America (1972).

The final chapter of this outstanding book discusses trends in Latin America and in the United States.

WILLIAM P. TUCKER
Department of Political Science
Texas Tech University
Lubbock

JAAN PENNAR. The U.S.S.R. and the Arabs: The Ideological Dimension, 1917–1972. Pp. vii, 180. New York: Crane, Russak, 1973. $9.75.

The recent Arab-Israeli war and the subsequent Arab oil embargo have once again focused world attention on the Middle East. As the energy crisis becomes more serious, the significance of the Middle East as a possible source of conflict between the United States and the Soviet Union has increased. For both the United States and the Soviet Union, the importance of the Middle East derives primarily from global strategic and political considerations. But the struggle for power and influence is only one major aspect of the conflict. Deep-seated ideological and cultural antagonisms also are involved. According to Mr. Jaan Pennar the ideological competition between the capitalist West and the communist East has been relegated to a position of secondary importance by analysts viewing the struggle. To help correct this imbalance, Mr. Pennar has written a very readable book about the ideological dimension with regard to Soviet-Arab relations.

In developing theories of national liberation, Soviet theorists have adopted the "non-capitalist path" concept as their central theme. Applying this concept to the Third World in general and the socialist-oriented Arab states in particular has not been an easy task for Soviet theorists for a number of reasons. First is the question of religion, which is anathema to Marxism. The second obstacle is nationalism which, rather than class struggle, gave birth to socialism in the Arab world. Soviet scholars have tended "to play down the influence of these twin forces because Marxism's doctrinal restraints reject the far-reaching impact of these two forces." The author concludes that this failure to come to grips with the dynamics of nationalism in the Arab world has left Soviet theoretical formulations "somewhat incomplete."

Another very interesting observation the author makes revolves around the role of the Arab Communists. While their numerous bids for power have ended in failure, Pennar feels they are "once more becoming a factor in local politics, particularly in the Fertile Crescent."

The socialist concepts developed by Nasser in Egypt and the socialist doctrines of the Baath Party in Syria and Iraq are examined. Soviet enthusiasm for Nasserism, especially the post-Nasser variety of Sadat, has been tempered of late by the apparent tendency, quoting one Soviet theorist, of the "better paid Egyptian bureaucrats [to] link up with the private sector." According to the author, Egyptian socialism "may be on the verge of establishing doctrinal positions of its own." The ideological doctrine of the Baath Party is liberally laced with Marxist tenets, yet espouses nationalism and Arab unity. In Algeria, socialism has evolved in yet another direction.

Mr. Pennar's concluding remarks are worth noting, for he brings power politics and national interests into focus with ideology. Arab socialist doctrines in Egypt, the Fertile Crescent, and Algeria "will continue to guide the fate of those countries for some time to come." Soviet theorists, meanwhile, will continue their efforts to relate Arab socialist doctrines to Soviet "scientific socialism" as best they can. In short, the Soviets will continue to support Arab socialist development in order to protect their national interests in the Middle East as they see them.

E. ROBERT FRIES

Austin
Texas

STUART B. SCHWARTZ. *Sovereignty and Society in Colonial Brazil: The High Court of Bahia and its Judges, 1609–1751.* Pp. xxvii, 465. Berkeley, Calif.: University of California Press, 1973. $17.50.

KENNETH R. MAXWELL. *Conflicts and Conspiracies: Brazil and Portugal, 1750–1808.* Cambridge Latin American Studies, no. 16. Pp. vii, 289. New York: Cambridge University Press, 1973. $14.95.

No social process functions in a social vacuum. When one sets out to study a political event or a juridical institution,

therefore, it is well to realize at the outset its dynamic relation to other aspects of the social order; and it is even more commendable, perhaps, to investigate, in detail, this interdependence. Each of the above authors sets out to do just that.

Professor Schwartz' account of the *Relação da Bahia*—or High Court set up by the Portuguese government in 1609 in the capital city of its Brazilian colony—is a detailed, well-documented, and highly revealing account of the role, in these juridical processes, of personal, business, familial, kinship, and godparent relationships. The magistrates are viewed "not [as] disinterested protectors of the law standing above the dust of local politics, factional feud, and personal interest" (p. 279) but, instead, as men "of flesh and blood," with varying personalities and personal interests, interacting with other individuals in a colonial social order.

Sifting unpublished manuscripts, documents, and contemporary accounts in the archives and libraries of Brazil, Portugal, England, and Spain, as well as secondary works and also the literature on public administration and organization theory, Schwartz sets down, in an orderly and well-planned account, the original character of the Portuguese bureaucracy; the rise of magistrates as a political force in both Portugal and her colonies; the origin, structure, and function of the High Court at Bahia and the personal characteristics and professional experiences of its judges; the social order into which this High Court was introduced; and the subsequent impact upon that social order of the intimate, personal ties that developed between judges and other persons at Bahia, as well as upon the High Court itself, "often in ways neither desired nor intended by bureaucratic regulations" (p. 314). The longevity and the resilience of Portuguese political control in Brazil, facts which at times have puzzled scholars and researchers, are to be explained, the author maintains, by the penetration of primary relations into formal bureaucratic structures and procedures.

Appended, among other items, are a glossary, and data on the place of birth, class origin, education, and career of 168 magistrates of the High Court at Bahia, as well as the marriages to Brazilian women of a large number of these men, almost all of whom were from Portugal.

In a detailed and almost exhaustively documented volume, Kenneth R. Maxwell examines anew the conspiracy against the Portuguese government which developed in the Brazilian province of Minas Gerais in the latter part of the eighteenth century. While perusing unpublished manuscripts in the libraries and archives of Lisbon and London in Europe, and Rio de Janeiro and Belo Horizonte in Brazil, as well as relevant published works of the period and an extensive bibliography of secondary sources in these libraries and also in those of Chicago and Princeton, the author set out deliberately to broaden the context in which the political is viewed and "to determine [in this case] how social, political, and economic compulsions moulded policy and events, or were moulded by them" (p. vii). Among other things, he investigates Portuguese-Brazilian commerce and its important role in Britain; the emergence of a powerful commercial elite in Portugal, with interests increasingly incompatible with the more flexible mercantilism of the Portuguese minister Pombal and his successors; and the participation of local power groups in the mechanism of Portuguese political control in Minas, including Brazilians whose economic interests and motivations differed from those of the metropolis. The thesis is extensively documented that the Minas conflict emerged out of "socio-economic divergence" (p. viii) between Portuguese and colonial interest groups.

After examining the testimony given in court by individuals at the time, placing this testimony in a precise chronological sequence, and then testing the emerging hypotheses against evidence from business, fiscal, and administrative records and public and private correspondence, Maxwell concludes that the traditional account of the Minas conspiracy has been distorted. This distortion originated, he believes, in the testimony of the then Portuguese governor of Minas, the Visconde de Barbacena, whose reports to Lisbon, as well as to the viceroy in Rio de Janeiro, have long been accepted by historians as an accurate account of what happened. Pointing out that Barbacena was far from an unbiased and disinterested witness, Maxwell shows that his account is "open to serious qualification" (p. 165). With no intention of disparaging the role of Tiradentes, who "was clearly a catalyst of revolution in the troubled Minas of 1788" (p. viii), Maxwell points out that overconcentration on this role on the part of historians has tended to minimize the importance of the movement itself; and he proceeds to investigate further the emergence of the conspiracy; the personal characteristics of the several other conspirators, their motivation, and their planned and actual roles; the personal characteristics of the shrewd, diplomatic, but eventually ineffective Barbacena; the gathering crisis, the denouement, and the subsequent compromises.

Maxwell's analysis will be most easily followed by the serious student with some already-acquired knowledge of Portuguese, British, and Brazilian history, since, in dealing with so vast a context, individuals, organizations, movements, and events occasionally are referred to with their precise character and role left to implication. These few gaps might well be bridged in a new edition. One notes an occasional misunderstanding of local terms (p. 100). Whether or not we live—as some think—in "the age of ugliness" with reference to dress, personal grooming, art, and even music, certainly this is an age of careless proofreading. In this respect the University of California publication, with one or more printing errors every few pages—and these almost exclusively in English—compares unfavorably with the Cambridge achievement and its only occasional miscue.

DONALD PIERSON

Bloomington
Indiana

MAURICIO SOLAÚN and MICHAEL A. QUINN. *Sinners and Heretics: The Politics of Military Intervention in Latin America.* Pp. vii, 228. Urbana: University of Illinois Press, 1973. $8.95.

The authors of this slender volume undertake to explore the causes of the coup d'etat phenomenon in its Latin American setting. In the course of six chapters they assess existing interpretations found in social science literature, present a detailed analysis of the causative factors present in thirty post-World War II coups, and discuss the relationships between structural and cultural factors and the incidence of coups. The result is a closely reasoned volume that will be of greater interest to the sociologist or political scientist than to other categories of readers. Historians, for example, will note with appropriate amazement that the authors drew the bulk of their primary data from four journalistic sources, all of them U.S. based.

The core of the study is the analysis of the thirty coups which the authors offer as a representative sample of the sixty-three coups—by their count —which occurred between 1943 and 1967. The thirty coups are examined in the light of eight possible explanations, and statistical conclusions are presented about the significance of each one in terms of the presence or absence of related indicators. Since the construction of the sample obviously influenced the conclusions, it is difficult to take too seriously the quantitative value assigned to each indicator. One wonders why the authors did not extend their study to the entire universe of sixty-three coups. One also wonders at the reasoning that led to the inclusion in the sample of all the Bolivian and Venezuelan coups that took place in the 1943–67 period—a total of eight—and of half the Ecuadorian and Salvadorian coups—six out of twelve— but to the exclusion from their analysis of all but one of the seven coups which occurred in Argentina.

Fortunately the authors go beyond statistically based generalizations to analyze in qualitative terms the predisposing factors that are rooted in cultural traditions and levels of socioeconomic development. Their insights into the roots of political sectarianism so characteristic of Latin American politics are particularly useful as is their discussion of its basic modes. Their distinction between what they call a "primitive radicalism" which views political opponents as sinners and an "ideological radicalism" which views opponents as both sinners and heretics helps us understand the distinction between intraclass and interclass coups.

This volume was written before events in Chile and Uruguay removed them from the brief list of countries which have been free from coups. The authors' explanation for the ability of these two countries to withstand disruptive forces must now be re-evaluated in the light of recent developments. Still, few would quarrel with Solaún and Quinn when they insist that coups "must be seen from different perspectives and analyzed in the light of several interpretations" and that no single interpretation can adequately account for the coup phenomenon.

ROBERT A. POTASH

University of Massachusetts
Amherst

MARK STRAGE. *Cape to Cairo: Rape of a Continent.* Pp. 278. New York: Harcourt Brace Jovanovich, 1973. $8.50.

If there is a need in historiography for a talented Leonard Lyons, Mark Strage, an experienced journalist and facile writer, qualifies indeed. His colorful, thumbnail sketches of characters, his apt and laughable anecdotes, and his gift for irony—at times cynicism— make for easy reading. However, his penchant for frivolous detail sustains a work which, aside from insight into personalities, offers nothing that has not been presented before by way of historical data or interpretation. This is not to downgrade the usefulness of the book to professionals who will enliven their courses by using his amusing stories and footnotes or to high school students who are being introduced to the subject. But it casts no new light on the broad reasons for Europe's imperialism in Africa during the latter part of the nineteenth century.

The vehicle for much of the story is biographical, and the portraits of Rhodes, Lo Bengula, the Egyptian khedives, De Lesseps, Salisbury, the Mahdi, Gordon, Kitchener, Delcasse, and many others undeniably give a human dimension to what might seem an impersonal process. Strage does not believe that European intrusion into Africa was accidental, the result of "absence of mind." His shafts are deftly aimed at this selfishness, but his cynicism also encompasses the actions of Africans, leading at least one reader to question his choice of words and nuances.

Moving north from the Cape and south from Cairo, he chronicles the process of British expansion through Bechuanaland, Rhodesia, the Transvaal, Egypt, and the Sudan, ending with the Anglo-French confrontation at Fashoda in 1898. Surprisingly, he does not go into the thwarting of Rhodes' imperial dream by the German acquisition of East Africa, later Tanganyika—not even a paragraph. Having digressed so often and amusingly on secondary matters, he might have found time for the above. Battles, the diamond fields, and railroad building receive ample treatment. The book's other positive virtues include interesting photographs and an informative bibliography written with wit.

WALLACE SOKOLSKY
Bronx Community College
  of the City University
  of New York

ARYEH YODFAT. *Arab Politics in the Soviet Mirror.* Pp. ix, 331. New York: Halsted Press, 1973. $17.50.

The purpose of this work is both confused and over-ambitious. By focusing on selected aspects of the political system and international relations of only three Arab states—Egypt, Syria, and Iraq, 1946–71—the author undertakes "to describe the politics of the comtemporary Arab East as seen through Soviet eyes."

The most valuable part of this study is the first chapter, which summarizes post-Stalin revisions of Marxian theory that provide the ideological base for contemporary Soviet relations with the "third world," legitimating its aid and support of revolutionary, non-Communist regimes, including the three mentioned above, that persist in persecuting local Communists.

The remainder of this monograph suffers from at least six major defects:

1. There are no hypotheses, and the work thus leads to no generalizations, although the author sometimes offers "conclusions" which are supported only weakly, if at all, by the data that has been assembled.

2. There is no apparent conceptual scheme, logical or otherwise, to guide the author's selection of institutions or events that he chooses as objects for reporting Soviet comment. In consequence, he is vulnerable to severe criticism for having omitted many issues and events that are absolutely indispensable for understanding the nature and thrust of Arab politics. Only a few examples can be offered here: He is silent regarding Jordanian conflicts with Syria. The Lebanese civil war (1958) receives no attention. The work is barren of data and discourse on issues concerning the establishment of Israel, its subsequent teritorial expansion, and its numerous acts of violence that have elicited U.N. condemnation, censor, or calls for cease-fire. Nor is there mention of activities of Arab terrorists and other guerilla warfare.

3. The author has failed to cope

with a fundamental methodological problem that is identified in his preface. He notes that since 1953 "some Soviet publications . . . express views that can be ascribed only to the author . . . and do not represent an official position." He also indicates that certain publications seem to be "less in touch with shifts in the . . . official line" while others "can be taken, by and large, to represent the views of the Soviet Foreign Ministry. . . ." In the pages that follow, however, the author makes no distinctions and gives no more weight to the words of Khrushchev or Brezhnev than he does to an editorial from *Pravda* or an article in the *World Marxist Review*.

4. The events, institutions, national pacts, and alliances that were selected for comment are rarely explained, nor are they presented for analysis in the relevant domestic or international political milieu. The author proclaims that his "aim is not to provide a history of Soviet-Arab relations or of the Arab regions," and "no attempt is made to describe the actual policies and the course of relations between these countries and the Soviet Union; no details are given. . . ." In addition, he warns the reader that he has "avoided taking issue with controversial views, or correcting the factual data. . . ." In consequence, the nonspecialist will find the book's massive quotations from Soviet sources unrewarding, if not misleading, and he will have to dig elsewhere for essential explanation and analysis.

5. Although the author says that his aim is "to describe the politics of the contemporary Arab East as seen through Soviet eyes," he frequently digresses from this goal and makes extensive use of non-Soviet commentary. There are copious quotations from leaders of Arab Communist parties (for example, pp. 216–24, 237–45), and occasional use is made of British, French, and German party leaders. The author's awareness of these deviations is recorded in the preface, but his use of such sources—given the study's central purpose—seems unwarranted.

6. Finally, much of the material in this work is repetitious and otherwise badly organized. For example, the treatment of the "Egyptian Revolution" is broken down into seven subsections, by date, and for no apparent reason. Moreover, the three chapters dealing with Egypt, Syria, and Iraq take the story only to 1966, and much that is essential for understanding Arab politics during the time covered in these chapters is reserved for later sections of the book.

H. PAUL CASTLEBERRY
Washington State University
Pullman

ASIA

RONALD M. BERNDT and PETER LAWRENCE, eds. *Politics in New Guinea*. Pp. xiii, 423. Seattle: University of Washington Press, 1973. $15.00.

As New Guinea stands on the threshold of independence, it may pass through that portal as quite possibly the least developed country in the world—that is, least developed in Western terms. It may, however, have forms of society away from the coastal settlements which, in their total approach to life, are more satisfactory for their members than the disruptive consequences of what we are pleased to call modernization. This fact alone should give the proponents of change pause for thought; but it probably will not, nor is it much more likely to stop the encroachment of outside forces on presently isolated groups.

This volume is a collection of essays by fifteen anthropologists on the sociopolitical structure and behavior of communities in Papua and New Guinea, territories which have been under the trusteeship of Australia. Apart from their intrinsic merit, if these studies indicate anything it is the imperative need for interdisciplinary analysis of situations such as these, of the changes which are taking place, and of those which impend. The single discipline approach, so beloved by social scientists jealous of their exclusive disciplinary boundaries, can at best be only misleading and more likely downright wrong.

No two political systems could be farther apart than the ones in New Guinea. The traditional one is total in its approach to life and the role of man in life, and essentially supernatural in that it includes the spiritual as man in New Guinea perceives it. By contrast, the Western model now being imposed, at least in the coast settlements, is segmented, compartmentalized, secular, and still seeking legitimacy. It is also largely incomprehensible except to those individuals whose exposure to Western influences has been sufficient to alienate them from the traditional. If past experience is any guide, the course of events seems fairly predictable and less than auspicious. It seems a pity one part of the world cannot be left alone; if not, surely there must be some way of preserving something of the total approach to life which is so lacking in Western society and whose absence either causes or exacerbates many of our problems. Transitional disruption might be tolerable if it could be demonstrated—an unlikely proposition —that modernized man is any happier or more content than he was before he learned to wear shoes and take his squabbles to a court of law.

JOHN F. MELBY
University of Guelph
Ontario
Canada

SURINDER MOHAN BHARDWAJ. *Hindu Places of Pilgrimage in India: A Study in Cultural Geography.* Pp. xviii, 276. Berkeley: University of California Press, 1973. $12.00.

Despite its manifest importance as a feature of social and religious life in South Asia, pilgrimage has been the subject of few serious studies, and most of the available literature is summary and descriptive. Bhardwaj's book, therefore, is especially welcome. It is a geographer's reasoned and cogently presented analysis of the network of pilgrimage sites that define "a Hindu sacred space" and of the pilgrimage institution, the complex circulation mechanism that dynamically reaffirms the spatial, religious, and social dimensions of that sacred space.

Bhardwaj's study falls into two parts. In the first (chapters I–V), the author plots and analyzes the distribution of sacred sites throughout India according to accounts in traditional Sanskrit literature. Among other things, it is argued here that the general contour of India's sacred geography was established before the Christian Era and has persisted to the present; and Bhardwaj suggests that this sacred space was coextensive with the reach of secular, "Aryan," material culture.

In the second, and larger, part of the book, Bhardwaj orders and examines the substantial data he himself collected in 1967–68 at eleven pilgrimage sites in Himachal Pradesh, in the Himalayan districts of Uttar Pradesh and at Ujjain in Madhya Pradesh. Drawing on information from 5,454 interviews, he discusses pilgrims' perceptions of "levels of sanctity" of the sites, purposes of pilgrimage and distances traveled, caste composition and degree of interaction in pilgrim groups, priest-pilgrim relations, and pilgrimage as a diffusion mechanism for religious beliefs. Presentations are helpfully supplemented by more than 70 maps, charts, and tables.

Bhardwaj's rich thesis cannot be rehearsed in its entirety here. Essential to it are the well-supported arguments that there are different levels of pilgrimage sites—ranging from "pan-Hindu" to "local"—and that pilgrimage in India operates in two, distinct modalities—the pilgrimage at the "pan-Hindu" and "supraregional" levels that is motivated by general, "spiritual" needs and desires and the pilgrimage at the "regional," "subregional," and "local" levels that is sponsored by specific, "mundane" concerns. These two modalities, Bhardwaj argues, are respectively the pilgrimages of the

"Great" and "Little" traditional dimensions of Hinduism.

There is much here to stimulate inquiry in, and response from, several disciplines. Indologists, for example, will wish that Bhardwaj had surveyed more extensively the traditional literature. They will be astounded that the author ignores P. V. Kane's valuable discussion of pilgrimage (*History of Dharmaśastra*, IV: 552–825). And they will question Bhardwaj's somewhat uncritical subscription to the "Dravidian hypothesis."

But nothing is to be taken away from the significance of this book. A definitive study of pilgrimage in India awaits future investigations along the paths charted by Bhardwaj. Wherever those inquiries lead us, Bhardwaj's study will be an indispensable factor in the achievement.

GUY RICHARD WELBON

South Asia Regional Studies
University of Pennsylvania
Philadelphia

GEORGE A. DE VOS. *Socialization for Achievement: Essays on the Cultural Psychology of the Japanese.* Pp. ix, 612. Berkeley, Calif.: University of California Press, 1973. $20.00.

As its title suggests, this welcome volume deals with the cultrual psychology of the Japanese and their socialization of achievement motivation. Equally to be emphasized is its pertinence for a wide variety of readers concerned with economic development, personality, family, change, delinquency, and Asian and comparative studies. These essays report on some of Professor De Vos's—and his colleagues'—research over a twenty-five year period and reflect resourceful use of anthropological, psychological, and sociological approaches. They are grouped into three sections: Normative Role Behavior, Achievement Motivation, and Deviancy and Alienation. The latter section, in turn, examines three types or sources of deviance: juvenile delinquency during social change, minority status, and personal alienation.

The case histories of three leading novelists, for example, illustrate the peculiar alienating influences on Japanese intellectuals.

More than most American social scientists, Dr. De Vos has long appreciated the extent to which we are products of our own society. He has repeatedly called our attention to the unconscious ethnocentrism and outright bias which distorts many American scholarly writings on non-Western peoples. Since their authors focus on social factors and processes important to Western societies, they often fail to see other factors crucial to Asian cultures and the different ways even familiar factors interact. Thus, whether capitalistic or Marxist, numerous Western economists assume that economic behavior is instrumentally motivated. Still other investigators regard the Japanese family system as a serious obstacle to Japan's industrialization. Dr. De Vos, on the contrary, finds in the Japanese family important support for Japan's unparalleled rate of industrialization with relatively little societal chaos. Japan has become the world's third largest economic power, despite its lack of vital resources, which would seem to doom it to the status of an impoverished backward nation.

Dr. De Vos challenges those Westerners who facilely categorize Japan as a "shame" culture in contrast to American guilt culture. Japanese behavior he sees as "strongly motivated by guilt rather than by more superficial concerns with shame and 'face.' " Japanese feel they must "repay parents for the sufferings incurred in their behalf and must in a puritanical sense find self-justification in hard work." Assuming that the guilt factor must operate in familiar ways, these Westerners overlook it in Japan.

This book should be widely circulated, both for its intrinsic interest and as a contribution to the lessening of scholarly ethnocentrism. Future research, including the author's, will further change the problems, theories, and methodologies of Japanese and other Asian studies. In the meantime, we can benefit from his experiences, his efforts to see how, if at all, familiar research techniques can be used in other cultures, and his practice of continuously discussing his work with local colleagues.

T. SCOTT MIYAKAWA
Department of Sociology
University of Massachusetts
Boston

CHRISTOPHER HOWE. *Wage Patterns and Wage Policy in Modern China: 1919–1972.* Pp. xv, 171. New York: Cambridge University Press, 1973. $11.95.

This tight little book makes a valuable contribution to our knowledge and understanding of an area of the Chinese economy on which not very much has been written and in so doing throws light on economic policy during and after the Cultural Revolution. Using wage structures and policies and their relationship to economic development in a variety of economies as an analytic framework of reference, Dr. Howe assesses changes in the level and structure of wages in China since 1919 with particular emphasis on the period since 1949.

Starting with wage structure and development in an array of other economies and in China before 1949, the author then turns to his main task—taking the measure of wage levels and structures as well as policy since 1949. This he does in chapters on levels and structures, the effectiveness of wage policy, the process of wage determination, the limits of wage control, the overall incentive structure —wage forms, job tenure, emulation —and optimal incentive policy and China's economic future. The presentation is rich in selective quantitative data and analysis, and for this, students of China's economic life and development owe Dr. Howe a considerable debt since such data on wages, occupations, real earnings, and so on as he has uncovered, informed by his analytic acumen, have been quite difficult to come by.

Dr. Howe's conclusions focus on wage patterns, wage policy, and the incentive system as they have unfolded since 1919. Since that year, wage differentials have all tended downward; since 1949, differentials between industries have declined while those between skills and occupations grew in the 1950s, narrowed during the 1960s, and are now back to 1949 levels. The urban-rural gap grew in the 1950s and since has been stabilized or reduced. Real wages for nonagricultural workers have followed an upward trend at just under 2 percent a year from 1952 to 1972. As for wage policy, from 1949 to 1957 wage level and structure were utilized in a conventional manner to allocate labor and prod worker input. From 1957 on, direct controls on labor allocation were developed. The incentive system followed the Soviet model during the 1950s with emphasis on material inducements, but late in that decade such mechanisms as bonuses, premiums, and piece-rates were soft-pedaled or abolished. This tendency was reinforced in the 1960s as emulation campaigns were heavily politicized and further developed. Policy on wage levels has been successful while that on intersectoral and occupational differentials has not.

Several critical questions emerge from Dr. Howe's painstaking and useful descriptive analysis. First, though Dr. Howe takes notice that since the late 1950s labor allocation has more and more been by direct administrative process rather than by wage differentials, he persists in looking at China's labor market as if it were a conventional market when, in fact, the channeling of labor into various skills and occupations has been drastically changed. Not only are young people trained in skills without reference to wage differentials through a new educational selection process after graduation from high school, but the whole range of attitudes toward remuneration is being changed and the degree of internalization of values affecting work and living styles has been widened and is being reinforced by political indoctrination. In this context the negative or positive trends of wage levels and structures have to be interpreted in a different way than the usual one.

Dr. Howe's conclusion that wage differentials returned to their 1949 levels by 1972 rests on somewhat shaky grounds. The data from a Shenyang factory and apparently several other (1971) sources may not be any more representative than those this reviewer obtained in 1973 from Shanghai and Peking factories in which the intra-factory wage spans were about 3.5 to 4 to 1—similar to the spans in the 1960s—rather than 5 to 7 to 1 which Dr. Howe projects as currently representative. Whatever the wage reality is, it has to be viewed in a post-cultural revolution setting in which the internalized values of Spartan living have to be used as the framework within which money income is spent or saved.

CHARLES HOFFMANN
State University of New York
Stony Brook

MURRAY J. LEAF. *Information and Behavior in a Sikh Village: Social Organization Reconsidered.* Pp. 304. Berkeley, Calif.: University of California Press, 1972. $10.00.

Professor Leaf's book, *Information and Behavior in a Sikh Village: Social Organization Reconsidered*, is every bit as ambitious as its title suggests. "The principal claim this study makes upon the attention of social scientists is based not so much on the content of theory, method or fact alone, but rather on a broader and more general consideration of the pattern of relationships among them" (p.1). The findings of the six substantive chapters, each of which deals with a distinct subfield of anthropology, "taken together add up to a full-scale alternative theory of society and behavior" (p. 12), to which the work of "every major writer in almost every area of the discipline, and [writings] in philosophy, history and economics as well are relevant" (p. 13).

Communications theory provides the basic theoretical framework for the study, and the "message source," with its distinctive properties and relative value as a message, the key concept. Conceiving of village ecology, division of labor, economy, Sikh religion, kinship, and parties as information sources with varying degrees of specificity for determining behavior, Professor Leaf finds that the differences in the form and function between these spheres of activity and organization "are differences in their properties as message sources and not as some other sort of phenomena," thereby equating them analytically. In the place of a theory which selects a single order of phenomenon, be it religion, economics, kinship, or so forth, and argues that in a given society the others are subservient to it, Leaf's formulation enables him to add the apples of kinship to the oranges of village ecology to yield a "multisystemic" theory derived from the variety of messages as to possible courses of action ranging from land use to political affiliation, different and often competing identification of individuals, and so on, that actors must select, interpret, and respond to. The choices produce responses from the other constituents of the system—animate and inanimate—sanctioning or rewarding them, and thereby creating a stable though changeable social-cultural-economic structure. The interaction between individuals, groups, ideology, and environment—broadly defined in both physical and cultural terms—is continuous and dynamic, providing for individual choice and societal norms in a reciprocally influential process.

The substantive chapters contain a wealth of information on a Sikh village in the Punjab India, a subject which Leaf correctly feels is underrepresented in the literature. In addition to the customary ethnographical information, Leaf presents original research on each subject, indicating a remarkable range of abilities and interests. Just one example: his description of family farming, production, and consumption (pp. 116–137) and the implications of his model for developmental programs (pp. 250–258) will be of equal interest to anthropologists, agricultural economists, and students of rural health. In every instance, the material is, like his theoretical discussion, original, insightful, and provocative. But much of it is superfluous to the stated purpose of the work and he cannot devote enough attention to deal with it fully. And this is the general problem with the work. Its ambitious goal is not fulfilled because it attempts too much, making the theoretical argument difficult to accept on the basis of presented evidence, and difficult to grasp as a whole. What is clear is that Professor Leaf has made a major contribution to social anthropology, and a study of South Asia worthy of the attention of everyone in the field.

THOMAS G. KESSINGER
University of Pennsylvania

JAN LEYDA. *Dianying: An Account of Films and the Film Audience in China.* Pp. xiii, 515. Cambridge, Mass.: The MIT Press, 1972. $12.50.

This book is an ambitious attempt to write the history of the motion picture in China from the 1890s to the 1960s. The two characters in the title, *dian ying,* translate as "electric shadows," the term for cinema in Chinese. When Jan Leyda arrived in China in 1959, he neither read nor spoke Chinese, but he was a recognized scholar and critique of the cinema and his employment as foreign consultant in the Peking film archive gave him a unique opportunity to view old Chinese films and evaluate the state of contemporary cinema. In preparing this study he has drawn on his personal experience, supplemented by extensive reading of Chinese film scenarios and the existing literature in the field. He especially credits Cheng Chi-hua's *History of the Development of Chinese Cinema,* but this was available only in the original Chinese and was marred by ideological distortions.

Leyda seeks to relate the growth of Chinese cinema to the political and social revolutions convulsing that nation. But, unfortunately, the result is often episodic. It is difficult to follow his theme amid the numerous and detailed film scenarios which follow one upon another with occasional pause for historical commentary. On occasion, Leyda's method works well. He describes with enthusiasm the efforts of "undergound" left wing filmmakers in the 1930s, who conspired to voice social protest in spite of Kuomintang and later Japanese censorship. For example, *Wild Torrents,* in 1933, ostensibly described the flooding in the Yangtze Valley during the Japanese takeover in Manchuria, but the viewer's attention is drawn to the efforts by the landlord class to siphon off peasant relief funds. Films of this period, Leyda concludes, constituted the "most interesting and lasting" efforts of Chinese cinema.

Cutting the Devil's Talons, a Korean War propaganda film, combined traditional anti-foreign and anti-Christian feeling with pointed anti-American propaganda. The Catholic Archbishop of Shanghai was depicted as the head of a spy ring transmitting secrets to America through a hidden radio operated by a formidable nun. Leyda notes the direct adoption of certain Hitchcock techniques; but, he notes, the Chinese director added his own original touch.

In late 1956 and early 1957, the Hundred Flowers Campaign allowed for a brief period of experimentation. The first and last openly satirical film ever made in Communist China was produced. In *Before the New Director Arrives,* the foibles of bureaucrats, toadies, big planners, and "yes men" were exposed. Not until 1961 was there again a hint that some freedom of expression was permissible. Leyda records that, in a speech to filmmakers, Chou En-lai barely mentioned class struggle and urged more variety and quality in films. By 1964, a rigid conformity was reinforced. The filmed life of Norman Bethune was cancelled, since in a time of growing xenophobia no Westerner could be depicted as a friend. Deeply disturbed by the growing repression, Leyda left China in May, 1964.

From afar, Leyda records his bitter disappointment with a revolution gone wrong in the hands of the Maoist zealots of the Cultural Revolution. But, as was the case with his earlier historical commentary, he failed to appraise the deep-rooted internal and external causes of the Cultural Revolution. Tragic as it may be, freedom of expression is often the first casualty in a time of national peril.

In spite of such flaws, Leyda has produced a unique and useful study. Students of modern Chinese social history and film scholars will benefit by consulting this book.

EDMUND S. WEHRLE
Department of History
University of Connecticut
Storrs

GEORGE V. H. MOSELEY, III. *The Consolidation of the South China Frontier.* Pp. 208. Berkeley, Calif.: University of California Press, 1973. $10.00.

Along China's frontiers there are millions of ethnic minorities. Centuries of Chinese (Han) expansion and conquest had pushed them up to the mountains and into the ragged territories of the outlying frontiers where natural conditions are unbearable. During the heyday of imperial China, the minority people fell within the jurisdiction of China's imperial court and were subject to varying degrees of cultural assimilation.

But the events following China's modern contacts with the West have altered the situation. The weakening of central authorities and the subsequent feudalization of political power since the late nineteenth century had virtually dissipated most minority group ties with China. For many decades prior to the establishment of the Communist regime, they stayed effectively outside of Chinese political systems.

Thus, among the first order of business when the Communists came into power in 1949 was the reconsolidation of control over the frontier regions, heavily populated by the minorities and habitually claimed as Chinese territories. Professor George Moseley's present volume, originally a dissertation, is intended to account for one area of Peking's efforts in this regard, namely, to consolidate the minority areas in the Southwest-Kwangsi and Yunnan provinces. Moseley, a historian, is among a handful of serious scholars who have done research on this important but somewhat neglected subject. As such, his current book is a welcome contribution to knowledge on contemporary China in general and ethnic minorities in particular.

The central theme of this book deals with Peking's carefully executed policy to assert its power and authority in the Southwest as well as its efforts to induce socio-political changes to keep pace with China proper. In the process, Peking cautiously pursued stages of political and economic transformation with a deliberate intention of avoiding the minorities' accusation of "Great Han Chauvinism." During the 1950s, most minority groups were promised some degree of self-government, symbolized by the establishment of various levels of autonomous administrative units. Peking's cautious but determined performance succeeded in exerting control over these minority areas without the evidence of serious bloodshed.

To many social scientists, this pioneering work could be criticized for failure to pursue a more rigorous analysis of either China's minority policy or the minorities' sociopolitical changes. One might wish also that the book had properly up-dated its information to include whatever new data have been available since the completion of the dissertation research in 1967. Statistical data are sporadically cited in the book. Some of them do not reflect the latest information available.

These shortcomings are real; but they should not be allowed to obscure the positive contributions of the book. It has generally succeeded in presenting an informative and objective historical account of Peking's efforts to politically integrate the Southwest minorities, up to 1967 at least. As a pioneering work, the book clearly demonstrates its value in helping to lay the foundations for more detailed and perhaps even analytically oriented inquiry in the future.

HUNG-MAO TIEN
University of Wisconsin
Waukesha

KAZUSHI OHKAWA and HENRY ROSOVSKY. *Japanese Economic Growth: Trend Acceleration in the Twentieth Century.* Pp. xvi, 327. Stanford, Calif.: Stanford University Press, 1973. $15.00.

This work was ten years in the making. It is the product of an international collaboration extending over an even longer period of time. Happily, finally brought to fruition, it may well stand as the definitive work on Japanese economic growth over the period encompassed. Since K. Ohkawa is now professor emeritus at Hitotsubashi University and Henry Rosovsky has moved up to become Dean of Arts and Sciences at Harvard, it is unlikely that this prolific transoceanic combination will produce anything else that will modify or replace this careful and detailed study.

The book is divided into nine chapters and is so structured that if one is allergic to figures, statistics, and tables, reading the first two chapters and the last two tells the broad story. The details are available if one wants to pursue them deeply into the middle chapters, three through seven. Chapter one provides a historical introduction, an overview, the premodern background, the Meiji restoration, and the initial phase of modern economic growth in Japan. As the authors state: "The purpose of this book is to explain the growth of the Japanese economy during the twentieth century, with special emphasis placed on the years after World War II. It represents an attempt to fit Japan's experience into a historical growth model of the type familiar to economists."

Chapter two establishes the basic pattern of twentieth-century growth with an analysis of long swings and trend acceleration in private capital formation and a variety of other aggregate economic measures. It also contains a preview of the explanations, that is, a brief statement of major conclusions elaborated in later chapters. The study asks—and attempts to answer—three basic questions:

1. Why has long term growth been so rapid, and more particularly, why has the pace of growth been rising during the twentieth century?

2. Why has the post-World War II rate of growth been so much higher than earlier? Can it last? Despite the rising pace of growth throughout this century, the years following the war represent a sharp break, and this also has to be explained.

3. Why has Japanese growth taken the form of marked spurts or upswings followed by periods of relatively slower growth, and why have these spurts lasted a long time?

Chapter three introduces an aggregate production function restricted to private nonagriculture and measures the crude and refined input of capital and labor to arrive at crude and successively refined residuals. These residuals are considered at sectoral levels in chapter four where specific industries are analyzed together with the effects of intersectoral shifts, the role of agriculture, and some general considerations concerning technological progress. Chapter five studies the demand for and supply of labor, with special emphasis on the notion of "flexible supply" from 1900 through the 1960s. The role of aggregate demand in a gross national expenditure or resource allocation framework is treated in chapter six, which also contains an analysis of savings. Chapter seven is devoted to the impact of the foreign sector on Japanese growth, including exports, imports, the balance of payments, and resource constraints.

The first seven chapters conclude the part of the book focusing on empirical results; the last two chapters are both theoretic and speculative. Chapter eight presents the outlines of a historical model designed to explain long swings and trend acceleration in this century. The concluding chapter focuses on institutional innovation and Japan's rising capability to import and utilize advanced technology. It also explores and ventures a forecast of Japan's economic future.

The authors doubt that the Japanese rapid economic growth of the 1950s and 1960s can be sustained. A variety of constraints, such as world capacity to absorb the continued rapid expansion of Japanese exports, possible lack of raw material resources necessary to stoke Japan's productive machine, shortage of required skilled labor, and so on, appear to be converging to moderate the pace of Japan's decades of rapid growth. Indeed there appears to be a changing focus in Japan away from emphasis on economic growth toward concern with distribution of the product on more equitable terms and with greater attention to the amelioration of social and environmental conditions. The current exhortation now seems to be shifting to environmental improvement based on social investments. Indeed, the authors conclude their deeply intensive study on a hopeful note." There is no cause for pessimism in these conclusions. If the rate of growth is reduced for the right reasons, Japan may not surpass the West in aggregate income by the year 2000. It may, however, surpass it in aggregate happiness, and this might yet be the real meaning of the "Japanese Century" when it arrives."

JEROME B. COHEN
Professor Emeritus of Economics
    and Finance
The City University of New York

DONALD R. THURSTON. *Teachers and Politics in Japan.* Pp. vii, 337. Princeton: Princeton University Press, 1973. $14.50.

There have been few studies in English on Japanese interest groups, so this comprehensive analysis of the Japan Teachers' Union (JTU) is welcome both to scholars of Japan and to anyone interested in comparative education or interest group political activity. Because the JTU has been so controversial in Japan for its leftist political stance and constant support of the Socialist party, Thurston's ability to maintain a balanced view of his subject while pointing to its strengths and weaknesses is commendable. In short, this is one of the best doctoral theses turned into a book on postwar Japan and should serve as a model to others studying teachers' unions elsewhere and comparative pressure groups in any country.

Thurston begins with a very necessary chapter on pre-1945 Japanese educational patterns, especially the subservient role of the teachers to the national Education Ministry, their exclusion from political activity, and the contrast between pre- and postwar teachers' unionization. The next chapter details the impact of the liberal U.S. occupation reforms and the burgeoning unions after 1946, of which the JTU was one of the largest. He shows how the national union leadership began with a very radical posture opposed by many of the local and prefectural teachers, and the shift after 1960 toward more moderate national leadership. Ideological shifts are followed by a good analysis of the JTU organization and membership role, as the JTU tends to view its members as both workers, in a class struggle sense, and professionals entitled to special status in a society that has always valued its intellectuals.

The most interesting chapters, however, deal with JTU demands on the bureaucracy, regarded as hostile nationally but less so in local areas where the union can make itself felt more effectively. Thurston shows how the JTU, frozen out of the national power elite, was still able to modify the implementation of many conservative educational policies, such as the teacher efficiency ratings and student achievement tests. The related chapter discusses JTU participation in elections, where many of its officials serve in the national and prefectural legislatures, and its influence on legislation.

This supplements the previous chapter on JTU claims and policy demands, which is the climax of the book. Thurston concludes with a very useful summary chapter applauding the JTU as proof of the democratization of Japanese society and politics and an avenue through which Japanese public school teachers can make their professional demands known. There are eighteen charts and tables illustrating the author's major points, including some based on a written questionnaire survey he used to elicit teacher opinion in a few localities. An appendix gives the questionnaire in English and Japanese.

One aspect of the subject which Dr. Thurston omits is the attitude of the Japanese public toward the ideology and tactics of the JTU. This is not strictly germane to his project, but since a national survey of JTU members was not feasible the reader wonders how the public reacted to the JTU national leaders' promotion of foreign policy and other noneducational slogans, such as during the 1960 Security Treaty riots and the Japan-Korean treaty debate. This reviewer's work with Japanese surveys since 1945 suggests public ambivalence: great respect for the teaching profession, mild toleration of the political ideology espoused, but severe criticism of the use of force in any public movement.

DOUGLAS H. MENDEL, JR.
Department of Political Science
University of Wisconsin
Milwaukee

JEN YU-WEN. *The Taiping Revolutionary Movement*. Pp. xiii, 615. New Haven: Yale University Press, 1973. $19.50.

During the past few years, Western study of the Taipings has been placed on an entirely new footing as a result of the publication of two landmark works. The first of these, volumes II and III of *The Taiping Rebellion* (Seattle: University of Washington Press, 1971), by Franz Michael in collaboration with Chung-li Chang, supplies close to 1,600 pages of Taiping documents in English translation, each document fully annotated and introduced. The second landmark is the book under review.

The Taiping movement (1851–1866), although terra incognita to most Westerners even today, stands as one of the epic events of modern history. Had the Taipings been successful in their battle to oust the Manchus and in implementing their revolutionary program, Chinese history, and very possibly the history of the world, would have been substantially different. As it was, the human and physical destruction resulting from the insurgency and its suppression was staggering in scale, making the roughly contemporaneous American Civil War look like a Little League contest in comparison.

Jen Yu-wen's book, a synthetic condensation of a much larger work in Chinese, is the fruit of more than fifty years of inquiry into the Taiping movement. The book, like its subject, is of epic proportions, recreating all aspects of the movement's history and succeeding, as no other book in English, in bringing the Taipings, along with their opponents, to life. Important figures on both sides of the contest are portrayed in the round rather than as paper cutouts. Battles, minor as well as major, are reconstructed with a fullness of detail that has never before been achieved. And, most important, the story is told from the Taiping point of view: it is the Manchus, not the insurgents, who are "the enemy."

It is the Manchus, also, who are the final losers in Jen Yu-wen's perspective. For if the religious objectives of the Taiping movement—which Jen, unlike most Chinese historians, takes seriously—failed to lead anywhere, the movement's other major goals—radical transformation of the traditional order and the emancipation of China from alien rule—were embraced with fervor, even if only partly carried out, by the Revolution of 1911. Thus, if the Taipings, as rebels, served merely to confirm Manchu durability, as revolutionaries they marked the first stage in a historic process which ultimately consumed not only the Manchus but the imperial institution itself.

PAUL A. COHEN

Wellesley College
Massachusetts

EUROPEAN HISTORY AND POLITICS

JOHN E. DREIFORT. *Yvon Delbos at the Quai d'Orsay: French Foreign Policy during the Popular Front, 1936–1938.* Pp. vii, 273. Lawrence, Kansas: The University Press of Kansas, 1973. $10.00.

"One cannot be too much on his guard . . . lest his action be biased . . . by an undue regard for the opinions of men. Let him see that he does only what belongs to himself and to the hour."

Had Thoreau's warning been known and heeded by Yvon Delbos, France's foreign minister from June 1936 to March 1938, the course of events might have been significantly altered—particularly if we change "opinions of men" to "opinions of Englishmen." For what emerges most clearly from this study of Delbos' motives and decisions is his proclivity for showing an undue regard for the good opinion of Britain and a sad inability to judge what properly belonged to the hour.

The German invasion of the Rhineland occurred three months before Delbos took office; that of Austria three days before he left. In the twenty-one–month interim, France faced a series of crises in international affairs. In all cases but one she responded weakly and ineffectively, following policies supported by her foreign minister and at least partly of his invention.

Eager to keep the good opinion of Britain at all costs at a time when that nation was determined on fighting Bolshevism and "doing business with Hitler," Delbos led the French down the disastrous path of non-intervention in the Spanish Civil War. The same concerns helped keep France from giving military meaning to her pact with the Soviet Union during Delbos' tenure. French efforts to improve relations with Poland, Czechoslovakia, Rumania, and Yugoslavia—and, more importantly, to foster better relations and alliances among the Eastern European nations—came to naught, in part owing to Delbos' hesitancy to contradict British policies of appeasement.

In these and other instances Dreifort makes clear Delbos' failure to recognize and act upon Britains's equal need for French support. He points out the success of the one case in which Delbos acted forthrightly against both Italian belligerence and British recommendations: the Nyon Accords, which had the effect of stopping Italian naval attacks in the Mediterranean in the pre-war years. At the same time Dreifort never reduces his explanations to the level of uni-causality. Each successive debacle is discussed with the utmost effort to be comprehensive, objective, and fair. In the process a certain dullness pervades the text; Dreifort extends his caution to the point of eschewing evocative language, and only a few well chosen quotes add color to much of the narrative. But the end result is impressive. By the time Dreifort, indulging in altogether uncharacteristic alliteration, concludes that Delbos was "an honest man of courage and conviction, [but] miscast for dealing with the crescendo of crises that confronted France" we believe him—because he has shown us that is was so.

KAY LAWSON

San Francisco State University

KLAUS HILDEBRAND. *The Foreign Policy of the Third Reich.* Pp. vii, 209. Berkeley: University of California Press, 1974. $10.00.

CARL-AXEL GEMZELL. *Organization, Conflict, and Innovation: A Study of German Naval Strategic Planning, 1888–1940.* Lund Studies in International History. Pp. 448. Stockholm: Scandinavian University Books, 1973, Sw.Cr. 99:75.

Several German historians and political scientists have come to the conclusion that the year 1933 when Hitler came to power represents the beginning of a fresh chapter in the history of German foreign policy. This break was marked by the impact of the National Socialist ideology and by Hitler's concepts of progressive expansions. The author of the book under review, however, does not accept this view and has come to the conclusion that there is, indeed, a considerable continuity in German foreign policy from 1866–71, the founding period of the German Reich, to 1945. Hildebrand is of the opinion that there are political categories of a specifically German nature which remained determining factors throughout the period of Prussian-German history, from Bismarck to Hitler, and which can even be found at present among the political leadership in the Federal Republic of Germany.

Professor Hildebrand does not attempt to provide a comprehensive history of Germany's diplomatic relations but presents an analytical review of German foreign policy in order to provide enough background information to substantiate his position that German foreign policy from 1933 to 1945 contained both elements of continuity as well as indications of a break with tradition.

This position, at least on the surface, appears as a most reasonable statement because traditional attitudes of nations, as frequently represented by their leadership, have shown the tendency to survive even after dramatic political changes in the domestic sphere. These attitudes often re-emerged as an integral part within a new ideological framework. This is not only evident in German political developments but also can readily be seen in certain aspects of Soviet foreign policy, which contains some very ambitious foreign policy objectives noted also during the Tsarist regime. Part of the explanation is the interplay of domestic and foreign policy. Aims conceived in foreign policy consciously or unconsciously fulfill functions in domestic politics.

According to Professor Hildebrand, who stresses the unity of Prussian-German history, Bismarck's primary task was to stabilize the social and economic status quo. When the contradictions between different social groups rapidly increased, Bismarck resorted to open suppression of the Social Democrats in order to protect the bourgeoisie who had sided with the Emperor and the landed aristocracy. Slogans of nationalism and imperialism were used to win over the masses and to unite the nation, supplemented by state welfare legislation. The most powerful force for the integration of the German nation was World War I itself.

Also, the Weimar Republic was dedicated to maintaining the social status quo which had not been changed by the revolution of 1918. When domestic reaction against the parliamentary democracy threatened the social structure, the political Right supported Hitler's program of anti-semitism, anti-Bolshevism, and the conquest of *Lebensraum* as foreign political goals. These objectives were believed to be also of great importance for the domestic sphere because it was thought that they would protect society from changes. Professor Hildebrand, however, admits that Hitler himself might not have been conscious of the domestic implication of his megalomaniac policies. This interpretation of Hitler's policies is wide open to criticism because of the well-known Nazi hostility to the middle-class and the commitment to deep-seated social changes of the traditional bourgeois society with all its "decadent" values. Even Professor Hildebrand submits that the implementation of the Nazi ideology would have destroyed the existing society in the long run. He attempts to explain this apparent contradiction of one of his main theses by stating that Hitler's program had acquired an extreme and destructive form.

For Professor Hildebrand the continuity of Prussian-German politics which began with Bismarck is not over yet in spite of the collapse of the efforts of Hitler who "integrated all the political demands, economic requirements and socio-political expectations prevailing in German society since the days of Bismarck" (p. 146). The author observes that "the existing social order (including the industrial plants vital to survival) at least in one part of Germany" (p. 147) has survived. This observation explains his earlier statement that the political categories which emerged in the Bismarck era are still prevalent among contemporary political leaders in the Federal Republic of Germany where at present the most important issue faced by opposing groups is which of two courses should be followed. One group advocates domestic reforms and a realistic foreign policy while the other wishes to pursue "domestic reaction and revisionism in foreign policy." Even though the author does not clearly state his preference in the contemporary confrontation, it is not difficult to determine which of these two highly oversimplified alternatives he prefers.

In contrast to the socio-economic interpretation of foreign policy pursued by Professor Hildebrand, the work authored by Professor Carl-Axel Gemzell, published by the Department of History, University of Lund, Sweden, attempts to investigate the impact and interrelations of organizational structure, environmental influences, and attitudes toward innovation upon strategic policy planning. The author selected the German Navy and its planning between 1888 and 1940 as subject for his case study. The reason for his selection was the availability of exceptionally good archival material of this modern highly developed organization. The emphasis on naval strategic planning, that is, major changes in planning, was the result of the acknowledgement that strategic planning was a central product of the navy's work.

The author proceeded on the basis of three assumptions. First, it was assumed that the navy as an organization, normally assigned to narrowly defined tasks, would resist innovation. The second assumption was that the social environment would impose constraints on new naval activities but that in cases where innovation had been approved, the social environment would also be accepted. And finally, it was assumed that conflict situations would operate as major motivational factors. Furthermore, the conflicts would not necessarily have to be connected with conflicts between states but might also correspond to situations within the domestic realm.

Professor Gemzell studied the development of German naval strategic planning as a series of innovations and established their relationships with social conflicts, both of internal and external nature, over a long period of time. His findings verified his earlier assumptions. However, it must be admitted that at times it was difficult for the reader, who happened not to be entirely at home in the approaches and models used in cybernetic analysis, to follow the line of argumentation and the resulting conclusions.

ERIC WALDMAN

University of Calgary
Alberta
Canada

HAROLD MACMILLAN. *At the End of the Day, 1961–1963.* Pp. x, 572. New York: Harper & Row, 1974. $16.50.

This is the sixth and final volume of Harold Macmillan's political memoirs. The volume covers the last two years of his ministry, which came to an end with his resignation in October 1963. Owing to the ensuing lengthy illness, his political career came to an end with his resignation. Nearly ten years after the events occurred the former prime minister has published his record and recollection of them. In writing this superb set of memoirs, his method has been to rely on contemporary sources such as diaries, letters, speeches, and memoranda; and only rarely does he invoke the wisdom of hindsight to illuminate his array of events.

The set of memoirs is an embellishment of a long and distinguished career extending over fifty years of an active life, dating from the beginning of the First World War. Forty years were spent in the House of Commons, seventeen in different ministerial posts, and seven as prime minister. In his epilogue the prime minister recognizes that his ministry marks the end of an era; for the century of Victorian preeminence has passed. British supremacy in trade, industry, finance, and naval power has disappeared along with the dissolution of a vast Empire. As reluctant as Winston Churchill, Macmillan became the prime minister to preside over the disposition of the remaining vestiges of the Empire. This final volume of memoirs records the dissolution of the Federation of the West Indies, as well as the Federation of Central Africa, and the granting of independence to several of the countries formerly belonging to the federations. Independence also came to other countries of Asia and Africa, leaving behind only a loose confederation—the Commonwealth—held together by tenuous economic ties and cultural traditions.

Besides Commonwealth relations, Harold Macmillan devotes much of this final volume to foreign affairs, especially affairs affecting France and the United States. Many Americans will read with pleasure and profit the author's commentaries on Anglo-American relations. The prime minister allots an entire chapter of forty pages to the Cuban Missile Crisis. Throughout this harrowing ordeal, Macmillan was in close consultation with President Kennedy by a direct telephone line to the White House. After the Russians withdrew from Cuba, the prime minister praised the president for conducting the affair "with great skill, energy, resourcefulness and courage" (p. 219). The strong ties of friendship between the two leaders were severely strained during the negotiations over nuclear armaments. When the Americans abandoned the Skybolt project—or bomber rocket—in favor of the Polaris—or submarine weapon—the prime minister felt the Americans were trying to drive "Great Britian out of the nuclear business."

Though disappointed by the substitution of Polaris for Skybolt, Macmillan's diplomatic ventures with President Kennedy were more satisfactory than his negotiations with General de Gaulle over British entry into the Common Market. Although de Gaulle's veto was a humiliating defeat at the time, Macmillan outlived the general and ten years later was present at the signing of the Treaty of Brussels admitting Great Britain to the European Community. These and other significant events are amply and fairly recorded in this last volume of Macmillan's distinguished memoirs.

R. G. COWHERD
Lehigh University
Bethlehem
Pennsylvania

H. C. G. MATTHEW. *The Liberal Imperialists: The Ideas and Politics of a Post-Gladstonian Elite*. Pp. viii, 331. New York: Oxford University Press, 1973. $17.75.

This work in the *Oxford Historical Monographs* series is a traditional view of politics as a series of conversation pieces between gentlemen; it is polished and professional, as befits the work of a Christ Church scholar. We have been this way before, but it is a pleasure to traverse the ground again and to study the finer points. The book is essentially about four Liberal leaders—Rosebery, Asquith, Grey, and Haldane. Among them, the first was about the only British prime minister who never wanted to be a politician—and who could never make up his mind which party he wanted to belong to—while the other three were as hungry for office and power as anyone could be. It was an absurd combination, lampooned by John Morley as the "babies in intrigue." Yet for ten years they made a lot of the running in the Liberal Party.

Many English contemporary historians—I am one of them—are fascinated by the Strange Death of Liberal England. Was the disintegration of the historic Liberal Party a long-term phenomenon? Stephen Koss argues in *John Morley at the India Office, 1905–1910* (Yale University Press, 1969) that even by 1895 "the Liberal

Party, despite the freak recovery that awaited it, had ceased to be a viable ideological force and an effective tactical unit" (p. 41). Others believe that —give and take a lot of "ifs"—Lloyd George could have led a radical Liberal Party—"radical" in the Limehouse 1909 sense, not the Berkeley 1968 sense—to become what Gladstonian Liberalism had been: the predominant national party, commanding effective power. They argue that the political history of Britain since 1922, with Conservative governments as the norm and progressive governments as the exception, need never have happened.

How far does the present work illuminate the problem? It seems to show that the self-inflicted wounds, which have been a constant occupational hazard of British Liberals since 1915, were also a feature of the period 1895–1905; as also the irresistible urge to wash dirty linen in public, to substitute rhetoric for policy, to indulge in vain imaginings instead of grim realities. (I write as a slightly embittered former Liberal parliamentary candidate.)

Rosebery and Grey were hereditary Whigs; Asquith and Haldane were what the author calls intellectual Whigs. Only Asquith came from the small manufacturer or respectable artisan, non-conformist, hard-as-nails class that gave Liberalism its staying-power— and of course he was corrupted by the delights of high living. These so-called Liberal Imperialists tried to take over the party from the outside; they failed because they belonged to Westminster and Pall Mall and Mayfair, not to the world of chapels and co-ops and committee rooms. Lloyd George never forgot about that world, and neither did the seemingly easygoing Campbell-Bannerman, whom the Asquith-Grey-Haldane crowd badly underestimated. Dr. Matthew has so constructed his book that we learn nothing about the other Liberals—the Little Englanders, the Pro-Boers—who actually provided the raison d'etre of the Liberal Imperialists. Apart from an occasional glimpse of Campbell-Bannerman, we receive no impression of what is happening in the other camp—the camp of the gut Liberals, the folk Liberals, the Liberals of the lower class, and the gnawing conscience.

The historic Liberal Party, like Roosevelt's Democratic Party, was a coalition of minorities. Its strength was that, numerically, these formed a majority. But it needed a leader like Gladstone—or the Lloyd George that never quite was—to pull it all together. Rosebery could not see this; he complained that it was "an army of dervishes each carrying a separate flag." The message he delivered to this army was 'Efficiency' and a 'Clean Slate'—meaning, let's start again, without all the lumber of Irish Home Rule, and so on. Although they cheered the sporting earl, who could be both grave and debonair, they did not follow him; and at the critical moment, he was always far away in one of his great country houses writing with flair and insight about the statesmen of the past, but never putting precept into practice.

Asquith, Grey, and Haldane had to make their own way; in 1905 they concluded a pact—the Relugas Compact—which would have put Campbell-Bannerman on the shelf and delivered control of the new Liberal Cabinet into their hands. But when Campbell-Bannerman formed his government the Relugas Compact vanished into thin air; Asquith hastened to accept office without consulting his colleagues, and they tamely followed suit. As his Secretaries of State responsible for imperial affairs at the India Office and the Colonial Office, the new prime minister installed two Gladstonian valetudinarians, Morley and Elgin. Liberal Imperialism was a bust. More important, in significant ways, the historic Liberalism of Gladstone was a bust too.

Dr Matthew does not express his ideas in such a crude fashion; his conclusions are more sophisticated. He concludes that "their assumption that there were policies at the centre on which reasonable men could agree was an assumption which a democracy must make if it is to survive" (p. 295). But can a dynamic Liberal Party survive on that kind of assumption?

HUGH TINKER

Institute of Commonwealth Studies
University of London

ADAM B. ULAM. *Stalin: The Man and His Era.* Pp. vii, 760. New York: The Viking Press, 1973. $12.95.

Communist mythology has always given Lenin first place in its array of gods and rulers. But, in fact, it was Stalin who brought the real revolution to Russia and gave the regime its present character. The effects and horrors of his revolution and reign of terror are well known, but the actual role of Stalin as the prime mover remained obscure under the tightly woven veil of propaganda. Only after his death, Khrushchev, in seeking political advantage over his opponents, briefly and partially lifted this veil. Some of the details were revealed in Khrushchev's revelations to the party congresses in 1956 and 1961, in the clearing and rehabilitation of leading political prisoners sentenced in the great purges of the 1930s, in the memoirs of those who suffered at Stalin's hands, and in the new histories of the Stalin reign. In addition, the escape of Stalin's daughter to the West and her memoirs of her father give a human dimension not previously known. In spite of these revelations, however, the documentation is still far from complete, and with the veil again lowered over Stalin's role by Khrushchev's successors, there is little chance that additional material will be available for some time.

Making use of the new material, Professor Ulam of the Harvard Research Center has written a new comprehensive and analytical biography of Stalin and his role in Soviet history. The work is not a scholarly treatise which carefully cites and limits itself to the evidence. Rather it is a critical interpretation which evaluates Stalin's role from the Western point of view and tries to fill in gaps between the evidence, answering all the important questions about Stalin's personality and role and about the roles and personalities of those around him.

Professor Ulam explains Stalin as "a most reasonable and perceptive man—unless something touched off the inner springs of suspicion and rage" (p. 359). Also, like his fellow Bolsheviks but even more so, Stalin "was unable to distinguish between theoretical and factual reality, between the world of ideologically inspired dreams or suspicions and the world of hard facts" (p. 413). Ulam concludes that in the Soviet scene in the 1920s only a man with unusual suspicions and proneness to intrigue could have won the power struggle (p. 433). Equally important to Stalin's success was the inability of his opponents to organize against his intrigues and their ultimate willingness to prostrate themselves before him so that his megalomania would be appeased (p. 373). This view of Stalin as developed by the author from episode to episode is convincing, but without more evidence it has to be considered speculative. While the author's interpretation of Stalin's character is quite plausible, he seems less convincing in explaining why Stalin's associates, hardened by the revolution and the power struggle, continually debased themselves before Stalin.

As a critical biography and as a comprehensive and readable history of Stalin's rule, this volume is valuable for both the expert and lay reader. It both expresses the atmosphere of this crucial era in Soviet history and provides an interesting explanation for the success and the influence of one of the world's most skilled and cruel tyrants.

DAVID T. CATTELL

University of California
Los Angeles

GEORGE L. YANEY. *The Systematization of Russian Government: Social Evolution in the Domestic Administration of Imperial Russia, 1711-1905.*

Pp. xvi, 430. Urbana, Ill.: University of Illinois Press, 1973. $13.50.

One of the more common charges levelled against American historiography is that it is too largely taken up with political history, to the putative disadvantage of social, economic, or intellectual history. On the face of it, the charge has some validity. But when one is face to face with a work of genuine political history, questions arise about the categorization, for genuine political history does not tolerate any such artificial separation of history into specialities, any more than genuine examples of the other emphases do. Historical study is warranted to the extent that it explains something, and the choicer historical topics involve complex processes unfolding in many dimensions. One of these may be preeminently political, another economic, a third cultural; but all impose their own rules, and it is extremely rare that any one can be comfortably enclosed within one or another of the conventional rubrics. A genuine political history is one that centers on a political topic but recognizes no conventional boundaries and therefore enlists in its train any subject matter that helps to explain, thereby politicizing whatever materials fit the project and, in the process, enlarging the political rubric to its full extent. At this point the objection expires; there has never been a surfeit of good political history, or of any other kind—only a surplus of artificially restricted treatments, a superfluity of narrowly conceived studies. Politics, as Professor Yaney conceives of politics, can never be a narrowing or restrictive category but is rather a recognition of the pervasiveness of politics and of the full range of subject matter that properly belongs within that category.

The main axis of his investigation is the relationship between central authority in Tsarist Russia and the peasant countryside. His concern is with the aspiration toward system and with the efforts, inspired by the aspiration but not yet partaking of the attributes of system, that were made as a part of the process of creating the preconditions of systematization in Russian governance. Yaney's whole enterprise is, in one sense, a misadventure; his original aim was to introduce the agrarian reforms of the early twentieth century in Russia. His introduction turned into a book, an exemplary one if one considers what usually parades as the history of any domestic administration evolution. Presumably the original project is still to come, but we have meanwhile gained a quite original insight into the process that underlay twentieth century reform efforts. It is, as the author properly acknowledges, not the only way of looking at the process; but it is both a detailed and fully conceptualized presentation of what it took, phrasing the matter all too epigrammatically, to bring Russia into the twentieth century.

There should be no question that this is a major contribution to the interpretation of modern Russian history. That will be noticed quite readily by the appropriate specialists. I think it more important to emphasize the contribution Yaney has made to an understanding of the process we usually label modernization. That label tends to become a residual category, welcoming any putative explanation of how a society got from one point to another. Yaney has chosen a much more concrete focal point, the introduction of system into an unsystematic social order, as a way of tracing social and political change, taking into account the multitude of blunders and missteps that characterize the process without resorting to ineptitude or stupidity as explanations of failure but instead depicting these missteps as features of an evolutionary process and making them comprehensible as necessary compromises on the part of those who wish to systematize but are also charged to govern. The process is not peculiar to Russia, and a proper understanding of it could save us untold woe in our own time.

LYMAN H. LEGTERS
University of Washington
Seattle

NEW FROM ILLINOIS

NATIONAL PARTY PLATFORMS, 1840-1972
FIFTH EDITION

Compiled by Donald Bruce Johnson and Kirk H. Porter
The answer to virtually any question about national party platforms from 1840 (the year of the first platform) to 1972 can be found in this up-to-date volume, a standard reference book which presents authenticated copies of the platforms of all the major parties and the principal minor ones.

Reviewers' comments on earlier editions include: "There is a little something for every political researcher in this book, be he Democrat, Republican, Communist or Greenback."— *Washington Post and Times Herald*. ". . . an essential book for political science and government collections."— *Library Journal*. ". . . an important addition to the documentation of our past and a practical guide to political development in the United States."— *American Notes and Queries*. 890 pages. $15.00

RECENTLY PUBLISHED

THE SUPREME COURT AND SOCIAL SCIENCE

Paul L. Rosen
"In times of stress and rapid change, when many persons look to the courts to make needed reforms, it is especially important to understand how the courts apply knowledge about social conditions and customs in articulating constitutional law. . . . Professor Rosen considers the pressures exerted on the Supreme Court to expand civil rights by tracing the court's use of social science knowledge, by exploring the limitations inherent in its use, and by suggesting some areas of public law which might be improved by its systematic application."— *The Annals*. ". . . well-written and extensively researched."— *The Journal of Politics*.
272 pages. $9.50

LAWYERS BEFORE THE WARREN COURT
CIVIL LIBERTIES AND CIVIL RIGHTS, 1957-66

Jonathan D. Casper
A study of the recruitment and goals of attorneys in private practice who argued civil liberties and civil rights cases before the Supreme Court during that period of rapid change from 1957 to 1966. ". . . a careful, scholarly, often provocative analysis of a neglected subject."— *The Annals*. ". . . an important addition to our knowledge about the lawyer's role in the policy process."— *American Political Science Review*.
232 pages. $9.50

UNIVERSITY OF ILLINOIS PRESS   Urbana Chicago London

UNITED STATES HISTORY
AND POLITICS

GORDON FELLMAN and BARBARA
BRANDT. *The Deceived Majority:
Politics and Project in Middle
America*. Pp. 265. New Brunswick,
N.J.: Transaction Books, 1973. $9.95.

RICHARD E. RUBENSTEIN. *Left Turn:
Origins of the Next American Rev-
olution*. Pp. ix, 286. Boston: Little,
Brown, and Company, 1973. $8.50.

There is a familiar reader's experience: one sits down with a new book
and, after a dozen pages or so, spins it
into a corner, never to retrieve it.
Sometimes it is a mistake. Social scientists have rarely appreciated the point
of the journalist's seductive lead, and a
good many books that begin turgidly,
foolishly, stupidly, or merely annoy-
ingly, have a great deal to say. On the
other hand, the twelfth page impulse
can spare a body a terrific waste of time.
Here we have an example of each.

The trouble with the introductory
parts of *The Deceived Majority* is the
authors' truculent and vexing refusal to
define the terms on which the book is
based. This is a book about "class" and
"classism, . . . discrimination by
members of one social class against
members of another." So, what *is*
"class"? The authors cannot say. "Class"
has to do with "power, wealth, education, occupation, and general values
and lifestyle" and it *has* "yet-to-be-
understood connections" with racism
and sexism. But these are not to
be explored here and "for this book,"
the authors continue, they "shall not
define class in a way that can be
considered universally useful or true
for all purposes. [That is, they shall not
"define" it at all.] Indeed, we do not
believe that class can be defined that
way at all."

But this is a book *about* class, is it
not? So, where is the reader left after
page fourteen? Should he spin it into
the corner?

It would be a mistake to do so. For, if
Gordon Fellman and Barbara Brandt
are befuddled by the concept of

"class"—their new names for classes
are no help, just jargon—they are
meticulous and open-minded observers
of political and social behavior. They
have provided a valuable insight into
one specific power struggle in contemporary America—the controversy, dispute, and competition over the building
of a freeway through a working-class
district of Cambridge, Massachusetts.
The Brookline-Elm Inner Belt became
a live political issue in the middle
1960s. Alignments on the question
proved complex and shifting, the more
so because of the existence of alternate
routes. State and federal highway agencies, state officials, industrial corporations, elected local officials, state legislators, powerful and articulate institutions such as Harvard and M.I.T., anti-
Belt neighborhood groups, and, finally,
the amorphous majority of the neighborhood affected—generally hostile to
the destruction of their neighborhood
but also apathetic—all these bore in
some way on the final resolution of the
issue.

This came in December, 1971, when
the governor of Massachusetts announced that the Inner Belt was cancelled. A happy ending for the neighborhood. Or was it? This is the topic of the
book, and in it Fellman and Brandt
touch on the real problems of decisionmaking and power in our society
as well as on the attitudes of citizens
towards the efficacy of their equality.
They say nothing about class in the end
because they said nothing about it in
the beginning. Nor, despite a final
chapter entitled "Toward New Forms
of Participation," is *The Deceived Majority* a program for establishing the
genuine democracy which the authors
find wanting and to which they are
explicitly committed. But the book is
also, in microcosm, a well-done and
depressing account of the dichotomy
between the rhetoric and reality of
democracy in America.

In *Left Turn*, the terms are defined
precisely and unambiguously; Richard
E. Rubenstein is a felicitous stylist,
perhaps, indeed, too felicitous for the

good of his book; the absurdities and distortions of its first part are neither blurred nor disguised by jargon and evasion. The author has set out to systemize American historical development scientifically. He posits ruthless and inevitable rules of political coalition, disintegration, realignment through six cycles, the six periodic consensuses being the Federalist, the Jeffersonian, the Jacksonian, the Republican, the Progressive, the New Deal, all neatly characterized by the fact that they were "all-bourgeois" alliances against "the underclass."

Such schematizations can, of course, be honest pedagogical tools when accompanied in the lecture hall by the caveat that they are tools and not laboratory formulas. In *Left Turn* it is formulas that they are, and forcing two centuries of unruly political history into such a symmetrical mold results in all the predictable vagaries. Rubenstein contends with historical figures from Jefferson to Aristotle, from Lincoln to Montaigne, as if they and the author are seated on folding chairs in an auditorium, the latter making short work of his opponents with sneers, innuendo, and extended index finger. The "relationships" which Rubenstein draws in order to establish his schema reduce to something like the numerology that connects Lincoln and John F. Kennedy—both elected in '60, seven letters in the names of both, and so on. Thus: "clearly . . . there seems to be a relationship between liberalism and racism" and readers are asked solemnly to note that all the great liberal presidents were war presidents.

Then there are the errors, gross and minor, the sloppiness inevitable in forcing not entirely malleable facts into an unyielding form: Jefferson's "disciples formented the War of 1812 in an attempt to grab Canada by force" (a sophomore who has read his Amherst pamphlet knows better than to wax too glibly on that subject); the masses of Gilded Age urban immigrants were "mostly Irish Catholics"; the Republican Party controlled both White House and Congress from 1861 to 1913; William Jennings Bryan resigned as Secretary of State in 1917, after Wilson's decision to enter the war, and he was an anti-big business secretary. Finally, related to the factual errors, the absurdities: "it was generally impossible to distinguish labor violence from racial violence"; Lincoln was called "a traitor to his class" (à la FDR) by Republican Party plutocrats. And so on.

If this sort of thing sounds familiar, yes, Professor Rubenstein does acknowledge his schooling in the Socialist Workers Party. He has benefitted from the more intelligent radical historiography of the 1960s but, in the end, not very much. *Left Turn* is the same old outdated irrelevance gussied up with a little art nouveau. The author heroically resists mentioning Leon Trotsky and the Red Army until page 160, and through the whole, he awkwardly interjects credentials of his grooviness: "our political culture so closely links economic success and political power with sexual potency"; Rubenstein's characterization of the exploitation of women as "particularly brutal."

One thinks of depleted forests and pulp mills. One recalls one's impulse after the first dozen pages.

JOSEPH R. CONLIN
Department of History
California State University
Chico

AMY M. GILBERT. *Executive Agreements and Treaties, 1946-1973: Framework of the Foreign Policy of the Period.* Pp. x, 213. Endicott, N.Y.: Thomas-Newell, 1973. $10.00.

DAVID P. CALLEO and BENJAMIN M. ROWLAND. *America and the World Political Economy: Atlantic Dreams and Realities.* Pp. xii, 371. Bloomington, Ind.: Indiana University Press, 1973. $12.50.

Amy M. Gilbert's monumental effort to examine the expansive usage of Executive Agreements as the framework for American foreign policy since World War II is to be applauded. Her significant achievement rests in her categorization of these agreements into four distinct types: Class I—those agreements concluded by the Executive pursuant to a Treaty (NATO); Class II—those concluded to implement the intentions of Congress (Reciprocal Trade Act); Class III—those supported or confirmed by a Joint Congressional Resolution (Tonkin Bay Resolution); and Class IV—those not submitted to or confirmed by Congress involving administrative and/or housekeeping matters.

The author's scholarly development of the Bricker Amendment provides an added dimension to the emerging power struggle between Congress and the president, but whether this Great Debate was a truly "educational experience" is questionable since the vital controversies over the Imperial President and foreign affairs arose afterward.

What is, perhaps, most disappointing in an otherwise Herculean treatise is the author's extreme caution in her analysis of the "creeping commitments" issue. Her tacit acceptance of past administrations' interpretations of the Geneva Accords (1954), the Kennedy "commitment" to Vietnam under the rubric of SEATO, the tortured description of the Tonkin Bay episode as such and the consequent Tonkin Bay Resolution is hardly compatible with rigorous scholarship. Moreover, the cursory look at *The Pentagon Papers* is most distressing, especially in light of the author's value judgement that by 1967 the "Administration had not made clear its rightness or necessity, and had not explained to the citizens how the [Vietnam] war was an expression of national need and sentiment to which they could respond wholeheartedly."

The lack of a rigorous conceptual framework is further illustrated in the author's cautious perceptions of the Nixon "New Eras" which are, in short, mere descriptions of the scenarios surrounding the Cambodian intervention and of the recurrent peace proposals— Hanoi versus/and Nixon—with not tight-knit analysis of the October 1972 to January 1973 Paris Agreements.

Finally, more intensive scholarship should have included an analysis of such "secret" agreements as the US-Thailand arrangements, categorized as Class III, and the earlier Pact of Madrid (Spain) up for renewal in 1975.

However, over all, Amy Gilbert has provided a significant contribution to such subsequent studies still to be made on executive agreements.

The truly brilliant analysis by co-authors Calleo and Rowland of America's post-World War II international economic-political policies will and should establish a sound framework for additional in-depth studies as the 1970s unfold.

The American design—that is, 1) the geopolitical Atlantic Alliance; 2) the (Cordell) Hull trade liberalism; and 3) the federalist theory to encourage an emerging Atlantic Community—is subjected to a rigorous, scholarly examination with the aid of voluminous statistics, charts, and graphs. Our postwar trade policies—that is, liberalization, deflation, parity changes, and the Special Drawing Rights—are evaluated, both their successes and failures, in terms of rhetoric versus the reality of the "American hegemony" until the recent, ever-changing power realities forced a painful reappraisal, as yet incomplete.

Attention is focused upon such dichotomies as (1) the conflicting concepts of "economic efficiency" and the creation of a "broadly humanitarian society" and (2) the shibboleth of "perpetual growth" with its counterproductive effects, including the environmental issue. The authors' sober examination of the impact of international corporations which operate not within Ricardo's "free-market" but within the Keynesian version of "mercantilism" adds a dimension whose total impact is, as yet, unknown.

Especially instructive is the chapter on Japan's postwar economic development as a great "mercantilist state" whose resistance to "liberalization" is due to its unique interpenetration of business with government. Therefore,

Japan "will follow a more lonely course."

Diagnosis of the Third World is, perhaps, the least satisfying aspect of an otherwise significant study. Yet the forewarning that "the prospects for a peaceful, steady and non-revolutionary transformation" of these countries is "not bright" is, certainly, most apt.

In the final chapter, the co-authors project their major thesis—that is, the ingredients for a "True Basis of a Liberal World Economic System" through the development of a loosely related series of national and regional systems based upon the "planned democratic welfare state." But, where are the Soviet Union and China in all of this?

ALFRED J. HOTZ

Augustana College
Sioux Falls
South Dakota

C. ROBERT KEMBLE. *The Image of the Army Officer in America: Background for Current Views.* Pp. vii, 289. Westport, Conn.: Greenwood Press, 1973. $10.75.

It is no mystery why a self-styled "military careerist" would investigate how past generations have regarded their military men. One result of Vietnam has been the U.S. Army's obsession with its image. Nor is there any question about Kemble's world view. Rather like a knee-jerk hawk, he blankets several disparate critics of the military with the label "pacifist," without precision. For example, he calls T. W. Higginson, abolitionist and Civil War hero, a "semi-pacifist." A what?

The book is perplexing in scope. It is purportedly the first of two parts, and in fact 85 percent of it deals with the 1800s. But then an extensive epilogue, admittedly an afterthought, races through the 1900s right up to "distasteful guerilla warfare." The author himself indicates that he was unprepared to analyze the modern era when he alludes to a certain trend which will not be "fully completed until World War I,

if then [itals added]." Since his judgments are so tenuous and his bibliography incomplete, the epilogue should have been left unwritten. Kemble says he wrote it for "relevance."

The sources are also curious. No one could survey every contemporary reference ever made to the military, and it seems fair enough to borrow general ideas from such authorities as Hofstadter on social Darwinism. But it is a major defect to cite Millis, Cunliffe, Schlesinger, and others alongside legitimate primary materials in the mainstream of the book's argument.

One might also question the theme. The title suggests there is a single "image." But throughout we are told that it was "anything but sharply defined," and even that there were "painfully contrary reactions" to the figure of the military officer. Actually, two "images" seem to recur: one, that military men were "refined virile patricians," such as Washington and Winfield Scott; and two, that "regular" officers were dandies, outclassed by non-establishment types like Jackson and Zachary Taylor. But there are so many exceptions to these general attitudes that "it turns out that America's view of the Army officer . . . never has been . . . a single image at all, but rather . . . several diverse, if related, figures." Was Kemble really surprised that "it turns out" that way? Americans are, after all, pretty pluralistic.

In that bewildering twentieth century, Kemble decries the fact that the modern officer is ridiculed in Heller's *Catch-22* and CBS-TV's *M*A*S*H*. He argues that the military "desperately" needs a new image that "must come from the people as a whole." Yet here again, he seems to miss the obvious. One view of the military held in the post-Tet era by many people in pluralistic America who are not pacifists is that Army officers are sometimes ridiculous. This book does nothing to correct that unfortunate fact.

WILLIAM T. GENEROUS, JR.

The Choate School
Wallingford
Connecticut

ROBERT JAMES MADDOX. *The New Left and the Origins of the Cold War*. Pp. ix, 169. Princeton, N.J.: Princeton University Press, 1973. $7.95.

In recent years the New Left historians have produced a flurry of works in which they challenge the traditional views regarding the roots of the Cold War. These revisionists argue that the Cold War must bear the stamp "Made in the USA," placing blame for it primarily upon the bumbling statesmanship of the Truman administration or upon American capitalism's insatiable demand for growth. Robert James Maddox, a diplomatic historian at Pennsylvania State University, has written a critique of the revisionists, not of their interpretations but of their scholarly methods. His conclusion is that they simply fail to "measure up to the most elementary standards of good scholarship."

Taking the works of seven of the most prominent revisionists—William Appleman Williams, D. F. Fleming, Gar Alperovitz, David Horowitz, Gabriel Kolko, Diane Shaver Clemens, and Lloyd C. Gardner—Maddox compares the evidence they use to substantiate their findings with the sources they rely upon. He finds that *"without exception"* these books are "based upon pervasive misusages of the source materials." He indicts the authors for making assertions without evidence, misuse of evidence, distortion of evidence, and exclusion of negative evidence. Indeed, "the most striking characteristic of revisionist historiography," according to Maddox, "has been the extent to which New Left authors have revised the evidence itself."

His indictment is compelling. His examples of distortions of context, misuse of quotations, and general abuse of sources should be required reading for all graduate students so they will know what pitfalls to avoid in order to assure good historical craftsmanship. But Maddox is so consumed with distaste for the revisionists that his book is marred. He focuses intensely on the faults of the revisionists and vilifies them for their poor scholarship, but he fails to scrutinize at all the scholarship of the traditional historians of the Cold War. He does not respond to the fundamental interpretation of the New Left authors, yet by his vitriolic exhortations he draws the reader inexorably into the implication that they are not only sloppy scholars but that they are wrong. For a critique of the New Left view one would be better served by Robert W. Tucker's *The Radical Left and American Foreign Policy* (1971).

Maddox's pervasive hostility to the New Left historians is certain to invite a round of replies and countercharges. This is unfortunate, not only because Maddox's book would have been better had he been more reserved in making his assertions, but because it is time to call a halt to this academic war over the Cold War and move, as Lisle A. Rose suggests in *After Yalta: America and the Origins of the Cold War* (1973), into a post-revisionist interpretation.

ROBERT DETWEILER
California State University
San Diego

ERNEST R. MAY. *"Lessons" of the Past: The Use and Misuse of History in American Foreign Policy*. Pp. xvi, 220. New York: Oxford University Press, 1973. $6.95.

This excellent little book has three major theses: that foreign policymakers are often influenced by what they perceive to be the lessons of history; that they ordinarily use history badly; and that they could use history more accurately with help from professional historians. Ernest R. May, professor of history at Harvard, contends that the framers of foreign policy frequently use false analogies from history because their knowledge of history is inaccurate or incomplete. But "potentially, history is an enormously rich resource for people who govern" (p. xiv).

May devotes a large part of the book to analyses of previous periods where such misuses of the past have occurred:

World War II, the early Cold War, Korea, and Vietnam. In the case of Vietnam, he points out that "here one can see men who would have been scandalized by an inelegant economic model or a poorly prepared legal brief making significant use of historical parallels, analogies, and trends with utter disregard for expertise or even the inherent logic of their assertions" (p. 121).

May then examines the decision to bomb North Vietnam in 1965 to illustrate how historical thinking could have been more comprehensive and systematic. Considering six historical precedents in which bombing was used for political purposes, he arrives at generalizations which would have contraindicated the bombing of North Vietnam. May does not presume to have all the answers; in fact, he considers alternative courses of action and allows the possibility that the decisions made were ultimately the best available choices. But the decisions could have been informed by reasoned historical judgments; instead they were usually based on superficial analogies of dubious applicability. This section of the book is distinguished by the careful historical research and balanced judgments for which May is justly known.

After a marginally effective foray into history's predictive powers, May suggests ways for historians to aid in the formulation of America's foreign policy. Along with a number of useful and tightly reasoned ideas, he includes a somewhat controversial scheme in which "some outside historians might be authorized to use [Government] records not yet generally open" (p. 185)—a plan which could well lead to "court historians" who would write only what bureaucrats wanted to hear and who would, in any event, incur the resentment of their less-favored colleagues. He closes with a plea for greater use of professional historians by the government. Yet within his own text May provides examples of how historians have been unable to transcend the conventional wisdom at any given point in time—page 101, for example. Can historians free themselves from prevailing prejudices well enough to provide meaningful guidance to policymakers? They did not do so during the Cold War, with one or two notable exceptions. Although May's diagnosis of the misuse of history appears accurate, it seems unlikely that his prescription will provide a cure for the affliction he has so ably described; it may, however, be a step in the right direction.

FREDRICK J. DOBNEY
Department of History
Saint Louis University

DONALD R. McCOY and RICHARD T. RUETTEN. *Quest and Response: Minority Rights and the Truman Administration.* Pp. ix, 427. Wichita: The University Press of Kansas, 1973. $12.00.

To read this book is to help realize how far, how very far, this nation has travelled since the 1940s toward a multiracial society. During President Truman's administration, to take only one example, blacks could not attend Washington's National Theatre—then the only show in town. (Truman, by the way, walked through a CORE picket line to attend a play there.) In 1973, not only in Washington but throughout the country, there are growing signs of assimilation of members of that ten or eleven percent of Americans who were fated to be born without the shade of sallow pink so highly prized by WASPS and other ethnic minorities who have controlled the country since the beginnings of the republic.

For whatever reason, Harry Truman —a reluctant warrior at best—was the first president to try seriously to further the cause of the black Americans. F.D.R. was dragooned into accepting Fair Employment Practices under government contracts. It is one of the more unfortunate accidents of the American political process that found Dwight Eisenhower in the White House at the very time that affirmative national leadership was so badly needed. Had Ike built on what Truman started, the problem of race—which seems so intractable today—might have been further alleviated. For with all the progress of the past quarter-century, race still remains the nastiest of all internal social problems. The white American is still not ready to accept in any reasonable complete sense his brothers and sisters who are not white.

Truman did as much, I suppose, as one could expect a border-state ward politician to do during the 1940s. For that he deserves full marks, as the authors of this careful study indicate. When placed against the reactionary racial tendencies of the Nixon adminis- tration, the Truman period stands out clearly as a high point in American history.

This book is chronology as history. It is not a deep analysis or really an assessment of the Truman years and how the president responded to the growing demands of black Americans. Even so, it is a useful book for one major point: it shows that it was the chief executive, much more than the legisla- ture and even more than the courts, who was primarily instrumental in ad- vancing the cause of civil rights. Perhaps the authors did not mean to leave that impression, but surely that is so. In the American system of govern- ance, in this year of the Watergate and energy crises, the presidency still stands as the most important of the organs of government. The president can do much, as did Lyndon Johnson and to a lesser extent Harry Truman; or he can do little, as witness Eisenhower and Kennedy; or he can actively coun- teract the desires of black Americans, as witness Richard Nixon. The essential point is that it is the chief executive who sets the moral, and thus the legal, tone for the nation.

Professors McCoy and Ruetten are to be commended for this study. The hope is that they will continue their efforts and plumb deeper into the American psyche, so as to place historical facts within a more meaningful context.

ARTHUR S. MILLER

National Law Center
George Washington University
Washington, D.C.

ARTHUR M. SCHLESINGER, JR. *The Im- perial Presidency.* Pp. x, 505. Boston: Houghton Mifflin, 1973. $10.00.

Arthur Schlesinger's latest book on the American presidency is, like its predecessors, both thoroughly re- searched and strongly opinionated. His major historical theme, pursued from Washington's day to Nixon's, is the encroachment of presidential power upon the constitutional power of Con- gress. This has come about primarily through the assumption by presidents, at times of real or supposed crisis, of the right to initiate acts of war. This process has accelerated in the last thirty-five years, and in the Nixon ad- ministration has been carried over into nonmilitary areas. Occasional assump- tion by earlier presidents of the power to take warlike measures without con- sent of Congress was usually followed in each instance by a reassertion of power on the part of Congress, as after the Civil War and World War I; but the aftermath of World War II brought a rapid succession of crises—the Cold War, Korea, Vietnam—which tempted Presidents Truman, Kennedy, and Johnson to exercise powers never in- tended for them by the Founding Fathers. President Nixon, inheriting war in Vietnam, extended it without legislative sanction to Cambodia and Laos. Meanwhile, as portrayed in Schlesinger's scenario, he undertook to expand the presidential prerogative to cover a large area of domestic affairs. This he accomplished, or attempted to accomplish, by impounding funds ap- propriated by Congress, abusing the pocket veto, downgrading the cabinet, intimidating the media, professionaliz- ing the army, and building a powerful White House staff composed of men dedicated to his success and troubled by few scruples. The apparent goal, whether or not deliberately sought, was a revolutionary conversion of the con- stitutional executive into a "plebiscitary presidency" ruling largely by decree between presidential elections. The trend in that direction, as Schlesinger sees it, was halted only by Watergate.

It is refreshing to find Schlesinger

acknowledging that he and other liberals were fascinated by the idea of a "strong" presidency when the office was occupied by such men as Roosevelt and Kennedy, only to view similar exercise of power with intense alarm when in the hands of Johnson and Nixon. The remedy is not, in Schlesinger's opinion, a "weak" presidency such as would be produced by some of the legislation sponsored by Senator Ervin and others, but rather a presidency which, while strong, would be kept within constitutional bounds by the reestablishment of "comity" between the president and Congress. The fact that the closing chapter deals at length with impeachment and other possible ways of legally removing an incumbent president suggests that the author sees little hope of such "comity" developing between Congress and the present occupant of the White House.

JULIUS W. PRATT

Medford
New Jersey

JOSEPH M. SIRACUSA. *The New Left Diplomatic Histories and Historians: The American Revisionists.* Pp. viii, 138. Port Washington, N.Y.: Kennikat Press, 1973. $6.95.

During the 1960s a group of historians emerged who shared the view that the United States historically has been an expansionist nation and that, since the 1890s at least, the principal objective of its foreign policy has been the establishment of a worldwide commercial empire. Such a policy, they maintained, has been a rational expression of the dictates of a capitalist political economy whose agents have prescribed unhampered American access to the world marketplace as the key to continued domestic prosperity and stability. In pursuit of this policy the United States went to war with Spain in 1898, entered World Wars I and II, precipitated the Cold War, and generally acted as a counterrevolutionary force in the world for most of the twentieth century.

The writings of these scholars have evoked a plethora of critical articles and at least three book-length scholarly critiques. Of the latter, Robert Tucker's *The Radical Left and American Foreign Policy* (1971) is the best logical analysis of their main ideas and conclusions while Robert Maddox's controversial *The New Left and the Origins of the Cold War* (1973) is a comprehensive and somewhat polemical attack upon the scholarship of those who have focused on the Cold War.

Broader in scope than the works of Tucker and Maddox, Siracusa's volume not only examines New Left scholarship on the Cold War but also surveys New Left interpretations of American foreign policy in general, American expansionism in the 1890s, United States involvement in the two world wars of the twentieth century, and American diplomacy between the wars. In the process Siracusa examines the works of William Appleman Williams, whom he regards as the principal living mentor of New Left historians, and Walter LaFeber, Thomas McCormick, N. Gordon Levin, Jr., Arno Mayer, Carl Parrini, Lloyd Gardner, Robert Freeman Smith, Gar Alperowitz, and Gabriel Kolko. Charles A. Beard and Karl Marx, he asserts, are their most prominent "nonliving heroes." His basic thesis is that most of these scholars wrote for the purpose of promoting "the replacement of America's capitalistic political economy . . . with a near self-sufficient democratic socialism."

Siracusa's treatment of the historiography of these scholars is more descriptive than analytical, for although he carefully delineates their views and conclusions, he refrains from giving an extended personal assessment of the logic of their arguments or the efficacy of their methodology. He offers instead a summary of the views of established traditional historians, whose comments range from outright rejection of the ideological assumptions and scholarly methods of the New Left historians to varying degrees of praise for their insights and contributions to historical dialogue, modified in most instances, however, by a reluctance to accept a monistic economic explanation for historical developments. In basing his conclusion that "In sum, much of the New Left diplomatic historiography that emerged in the 1960s lacked intellectual validity" on the criticism offered by the traditional historians, Siracusa neglects to inform us on precisely what points he personally finds New Left scholarship suspect.

Siracusa's chief contribution, then, lies in providing us with a very readable exposition of recent radical historiography and in showing how its practitioners hoped to use it to inspire change in United States policy abroad through fundamental reform of a capitalist political economy at home. One must look elsewhere, however, for evidence to support his implication that their goals and their ideological assumptions were inconsistent with the canons of good scholarship.

ARNOLD H. TAYLOR
Department of History
Howard University
Washington, D.C.

CUSHING STROUT. *The New Heavens and New Earth: Political Religion in America.* Pp. v, 400. New York: Harper & Row, 1974. $12.50.

This is an erudite and ambitious study of the relationship between religion and politics from the colonial period to the present. Discussing groups as diverse in time and outlook as the New England Puritans, pre-Civil War abolitionists, adherents of the Social Gospel, and the Black Muslims, Cushing Strout attempts to explore how religious movements in America shaped and underpinned the development of republican institutions and ideals; in his words this is a study of "the political consequences of religion."

Well written, though the discussion at times becomes exceedingly technical and condensed, this is nonetheless a disappointing effort. What makes it so derives from its overly ambitious scope and its narrow focus, its deficiencies lying in two areas. First, at best Strout discusses the ideas of dominant Protestantism, concentrating almost exclu-

sively on the major Protestant religious thinkers. He fails to explore in sufficient depth the contributions of non-Protestant movements, treats sketchily the periodic upsurge of dissident and utopian sects, and almost totally ignores the intolerance—religious, racial, and political—of American Protestants. Particularly glaring is the paucity of his discussion of the Know Nothing movement, the movement for immigration restriction during the late nineteenth and early twentieth centuries, and the anti-radical and nativist movements of the World War I years and the 1920s. Second, Strout's account is essentially narrative. Despite his intention of studying the relation of religion and politics, Strout fails to analyze American Protestant thought as an ideology, a coherent if changing set of ideas and how this related to political republicanism and libertarianism. Nor does he explore how American religious movements were shaped by technological, bureaucratic, and other social and economic changes.

As such, *The New Heavens and New Earth* is a modest contribution to our understanding of the factors influencing American republicanism. What it does best is to provide a comprehensive summary of the major religious leaders, the dominant political movements, and the principal religious questions surfacing since colonial times. It does not, however, adequately address the more significant questions of how religious movements shaped and were shaped by political forces and, most disappointingly, does not even attempt to assess the transformation of formerly dominant religious ideals—libertarian and ethical—given the sweeping social changes resulting with the emergence of a modern bureaucractic society.

ATHAN THEOHARIS
History Department
Marquette University
Milwaukee
Wisconsin

HARRY M. WARD. *Statism in Plymouth Colony.* Pp. viii, 193. New York: Kennikat Press, 1973. $9.95.

This little volume is concerned with the seventy-year history of Plymouth colony before its incorporation into the state of Massachusetts in 1692. It is written with clarity and is important as a contribution to historical knowledge. Moreover, it is extraordinarily well documented. Out of the 168 pages of the basic text, 46 are devoted to footnote references. The bibliography at the end of the volume extends over 18 pages.

The Plymouth colony, launched in the 1620s, drew up a unique code in 1636. This was, indeed, the first time that American colonists had organized themselves without the right of incorporation from a higher authority. In assuming this right the Plymouth colonists enacted what was the first American constitution.

Plymouth began to build its institutions under primitive frontier conditions. The settlers recognized that the state they were establishing was to provide justice rather than to wield power. Concerned with the authority which their state must exercise, they were fortunate to have men of wisdom and moderation as leaders of the colony. Plymouth provides a supreme example of men in a state of nature constructing a free political society.

In addition to being a political organization, Plymouth was also a religious community, conceived as having an external relationship with God and conforming to the will of God. Yet religious affiliation was not a specific condition for exercising rights. Religion may, however, be rightly regarded as the basis for certain moral requirements and restrictions in the personal conduct of Plymouth settlers. For example, they deemed it necessary to restrain pleasure and licentiousness in individual lives. They strongly disapproved of disrespect for executive officers. They recognized the need for constant military preparedness, for they were confronted continually with Indian restlessness and periodically with neighboring warfare. On the other hand they did not themselves indulge in military aggrandizement.

Toward their own political and religious dissenters the Plymouth colonists occasionally exhibited intolerance, but the long-run effect of dissent was for them to create a pluralistic society. They virtually separated civil and religious affairs. While they maintained a strong sense of community, the individual liberty permitted in Plymouth had a remarkable breadth for the time. Unlike the Puritans of Massachusetts, the Plymouth fathers adhered to English ideas of government as they saw them and they did not repudiate the English monarchy. Their experiment was at once idealistic and realistic.

The foregoing summary exemplified the attributes of Plymouth on which Mr. Ward expounds.

WILLSON H. COATES
Emeritus Professor of History
University of Rochester
New York

RAYMOND E. WOLFINDER. *The Politics of Progress.* Pp. xii, 416. Englewood Cliffs, N.J.: Prentice-Hall, 1974. $10.95.

In the context of pluralism-elitism comes this case study of the city of New Haven, the administration of Mayor Richard C. Lee, and the urban renewal efforts which are among the most successful in the nation. Arising out of a doctoral dissertation completed in 1961, it went unpublished by the local university press because it contained "embarrassing material," until a commercial press, deciding it contained healthy disclosures and revelations, accepted it for 1974 publication.

The author gathered much of his material while he was worker in the New Haven city hall for a year, during which time he often worked closely with the mayor, who had first been elected to that office in 1953, finally retiring in 1969. Gathering data from elite interviews, survey research, voting and census data, content analysis, and participant observation, Wolfinger found the policy achievements under Mayor Lee were atypical, that he had the opportunity, skills, and incentives to accomplish much, particularly in the area of urban renewal.

New Haven is an old manufacturing city and home of Yale University, with a declining population. Residents are working or lower middle class Catholics, Jews, and Negroes, so ethnicity is a major political factor. The author's mobilization theory proposed that the "strength of ethnic voting depends on both the intensity of ethnic identification and the level of ethnic relevance in the election," with the best sign of ethnic relevance being the presence of a fellow ethnic's name on the ballot. Ethnic voting is greatest in the second and third generations when the group has produced a middle class; mobility, however, can dilute ethnic salience. The city has a mayor-council form of government, thirty-three aldermen, bipartisan municipal elections, and frequent ethnic voting patterns. There is a bifurcated elite with multiple interaction systems.

Patronage has been a useful technique in the power politics of the city, and Mayor Lee used it in getting support from other politicians, the electorate, and specialized local publics such as businessmen. However, in important areas he acquired experts. In addition, he used symbolic gratifications, advertising and public relations publicity well in his policy coordination. The Redevelopment Agency nominally planned the renewal programs, but actually Lee himself made the major decisions, and the Citizens Action Commission was initially a front organization of prominent community leaders to sell renewal to others. Wolfinger concluded with the view that innovation and expansion of public programs will appear more frequently as cities hire professional managers.

This is a competent case study of a particular issue—renewal over a particular time period. The book describes how a certain policy can be successful, though situations may be different in other cities. Most mayors do not get to serve for sixteen years, many do not have a patronage system which the mayor can make quick use of, and many do not have the type of mayor-council, mayor-businessmen, and mayor-community relationships which the author observed in New Haven.

ORA W. EADS, JR.
Tennessee State University
Nashville

SOCIOLOGY

KATHRYN WATTERSON BURKHART. *Women in Prison*. Pp. 465. New York: Doubleday & Company, 1973. $10.00.

This is a book of personal experiences, the writer's and also those of the prisoners and a few of the prison-keepers about whom she writes. There can never be any doubt of her sympathy with the prisoners, but she tells us she has learned also to see the jailers as "just people." It is the "system" on which she turns her anger and which she wishes to see abolished, partly on the grounds that it does not work—which means, she says, that it does not reform or make responsible citizens of those it imprisons—but more because she feels that it is barbarously cruel to people who have committed crimes because of social injustices of which they have been the victims and that it is demoralizing to those whose business it is to impose its cruelties.

The central section is composed entirely of nineteen short chapters, each titled with a woman's name, such as "Susan," "Proud Mary," "Aletha," and each reporting an interview by Mrs. Burkhart with the named prisoner. These, again, consist chiefly of direct quotations from the prisoners, telling of their sufferings and resentments, their longings, and their outlook on life, and are interspersed with descriptions of the women and extenuating, often admiring, comments by Mrs. Burkhart. This section also has pictures of ugly jail settings and of prisoners looking through bars, working at prison tasks, sometimes enjoying comradeship with each other, and sometimes lying in postures of despair. Also, throughout the other two sections there are inserted between each two chapters similar but briefer monologues by individual prisoners. These chapters and monologues bring many an accusation against the functionaries who have mistreated the prisoners and recount the endless hardships, prejudice on grounds of race or social class, meaningless restrictions and regulations, unnecessary indignities, neglect, and callousness to which they have been subjected. These vignettes are very effective and do enlist the sympathies and responsive distress of the reader.

The book as a whole, however, is difficult to review for two reasons. Its main effort is plainly to awaken sympathy and arouse urgency in the reader to reform the "system" of criminal justice in the nation. Yet it gives essentially a prisoner's-eye view of the system, and only that of perhaps weak, but essentially good, prisoners. There are no prisoners depicted who are callous or deviously self-interested. The present writer constantly feels the lack of a more objective stance. It would be pleasant to share unreservedly the prisoners' and author's indignation at the refusal to let the prisoners embrace and hold their children when they visit and at the prohibition against the prisoners' taking of food into their cells. But are these restrictions really "meaningless"? The smuggling in of drugs and even of weapons through the agency of children is not unthinkable, and prisoners' need to cache food when an escape or prison revolt is being planned is obvious. Even some of the more unpleasant ways of searching prisoners when they enter may have similar reasons, apparently not known to the prisoners who resent them or imagined by the author; yet these reasons may be vividly present to the minds of prison superintendents and guards whose very lives may depend on their vigilance.

Mrs. Burkhart also seems to condone violent crimes too readily and to give too little heed to the interests of the victims. She remarks justly that the poor and the underprivileged are not in a position to commit the bloodless, almost abstract crimes of high-level swindlers and highly educated financial manipulators who may steal hundreds of thousands yet be treated leniently, while the poor man or woman who strikes or shoots as he or she robs is condemned unmercifully. This seems entirely true, but still, to be shot or stabbed or even just knocked down and left unconscious, perhaps with permanent brain damage or disfigurement, to have burglars enter in the night, or to be mugged in the street is truly more to be feared than to be mulcted even of much property; we fear it more, and rightly.

Personally I should like to concentrate on one issue which she faithfully raises but allows to be overshadowed by her seeming rejection of all imprisonment as inhumane per se. This is the presence in our prisons of many who have not been convicted, not given the speedy trial which elementary justice demands, yet are often subjected to as much harshness and indignity as those judged guilty. In many prisons the overcrowding their presence causes increases the misery of all the prisoners and encourages the mistreatment of some prisoners by others. The reason for this injustice seems to be the insufficient provision of courts, judges, and other elements necessary for trials. These lacks, in turn, are caused and allowed to persist by public resentment against criminals, and apathy and uncritical, generalized resistance to paying taxes. If those of us who want reform of our system of criminal justice can convince the public that such expenditures are absolutely required by justice since they will protect the innocent and that their absence is a violation of civil rights second to none, we might gain support for the necessary tax increases. But even this step cannot be taken unless an important part of the public is won over. Equally eloquent but less total exoneration and championship of prisoners are more likely to win credence than what can easily be interpreted as intemperate partisanship or airy impracticality.

ELIZABETH LEVINSON
Counseling Center
Bangor
Maine

EVELINE M. BURNS. *Health Services for Tomorrow: Trends and Issues.* Pp. i, 226. New York: Dunellen, 1973. $15.00.

Health is wealth. If you have your health you have everything. These "sayings" I have heard and have learned to appreciate through my troubled years of life in wavering health. Helping us maintain health, our real wealth, are a wide array of social and professional services, ranging from physicians to medical schools to hospitals, drug companies, insurance companies, the government, and others. These are "health services" in the author's terminology.

The emphasis here is on trends, issues, and problems in American health services, a critical area of concern given the nature and importance of the services, the rapid changes in such services, the many new plans for action, and the rising disgruntlement of patients who are no longer quite so patient with what is perceived as deteriorating services, or a set of unfulfilled rising expectations, or a combination of both. This book, by a long-standing expert in the field, is a collection of some of her previously published works. The writings analyze health service problems, trends, and legislation, and provide critical insights and judgments. Much data is drawn from health services in other nations.

The writings are collected to help plan for health services for the future, for tomorrow as the title states. The problems, issues, and options are presented in the hope that an informed body of specialists, politicians, and citizens can better choose new forms of health care services through knowledge of defects inherent in our present system and options available for change. Why worry about tomorrow when health services today are in drastic need of improvement? "Today is the tomorrow worried about yesterday." Since we did not pay enough attention yesterday, today is upon us now. Tomorrow will be here only too soon. And, although this saying is applicable to chronic worriers such as your reviewer, it can also stand as a warning; we must consider tomorrow today lest we find tomorrow here, with continuing problems, and then wonder foolishly why we did not make an effort for improvement yesterday.

This is not an exciting book, nor an original one, and it is scholarly in the technical sense rather than literary in style, approach, and appeal. It is meant for a small, specialized audience of technicians, such as social workers, policy planners, and critics in the field broadly designated as public policy in health services. Hospital administrators and physicians may find the criticisms of current health care hard to swallow, but they can well treat these as bitter medicine for remedial purposes.

HARRY COHEN
Department of Sociology
Iowa State University
Ames

JONATHAN R. AND STEPHEN COLE. *Social Stratification in Science.* Pp. xiv, 283. Chicago: The University of Chicago Press, 1973. $12.50.

Treating science variously as a social system, an institution, and a community, Jonathan and Stephen Cole argue that it has a stratification system—that is, an hierarchically arranged distribution of prestige and power—best explained by functionalistic theory, in which universalistic criteria determine positional assignments of scientists and in which those positions which fulfill the most important functions enjoy the most generous rewards.

The book is a curious combination of methodological sophistication and theoretical naiveté and ambiguity. Science is neither a social system nor an institution nor a community, but a loosely structured category of social and cultural forms and practices or, in the terminology of the late Pitirim A. Sorokin, a congeries of social and cultural institutions variously organized into social and cultural systems. Since science is not a single coherently organized social system, the statistical manipulation of figures on the citations to the works of scientists, the receipt of scientific awards and honors, the distribution of I.Q. scores as between the more and less pretigious universities have results comparable to the tortured "demonstrations" of the early chemists of the properties of phlogiston which was also a non-existent entity.

There is also ambiguity as to the meaning of "universalism" as the criterion for the assignment of significance to scientific discoveries and to the individuals who make them. In Talcott Parsons' original version, the universalism-particularism pattern variable referred primarily to the evaluation of social persons on the basis of objective achievements rather than on the basis of ascribed properties—such as belonging to a good family. One wonders why there should be any controversy over the basis for the determination of scientific truth and importance; traditionally, scientific truth means "established in accordance with the rules of logic and the technical norms of scientific method" and importance means "having major implications for the ever changing body of empirical truths." Thus, in the conventional view of science, only so-called universalistic criteria should apply.

However, during the course of their argument the Coles abandon universal standards for the determination of truth and importance. They argue:

Science is universalistic to the extent that all scientists are evaluated according to the quality of their scientific contributions. . . . There does appear to be a relatively high level of consensus as to what constitutes outstanding work, what are important problems to be addressed, and what are acceptable empirical techniques for

testing scientific theories. . . . The basic message of Kuhn is that consensus determines truth, not truth consensus. . . . One of the primary mechanisms through which consensus is maintained is the practice of vesting authority in elites. . . . The stars in a particular field determine which ideas are acceptable and which are not (pp. 77,78,79).

At a critical point the argument of the Coles becomes quite circular, and it seems that far from the truth and importance of scientific findings being the foundations for the appearance of a scientific elite, the elite determines truth and importance. In the end, a particularistic criterion determines position in the so-called stratification system. This brings to mind Walter Bagehot's salty observation that too often by the time a man of science becomes an authority on a subject he becomes a nuisance on it.

The Coles have not studied science; they have examined a few aspects of the practice of theoretical physics. They have not demonstrated that theoretical physics is a social system ordered by a stratification subsystem which neatly allocates physicists to proper positions of comparative importance on the basis of the significance of their discoveries; they have demonstrated what everyone already knew—that the high culture of theoretical physics is primarily a product of a relatively few centers which monopolize most of the awards and prizes, disproportionately attract the more promising students, and possess access to the best laboratory and research facilities.

The book is fascinating, both for its data and its snarl of ambiguities and problems, only a few of which it has been possible to trace in the brief space of the present review. For the rest:

The faithful reader here will find
A book, indeed, to blow the mind,
To lift him high beyond the air,
To plunge him into deep despair
To haunt him—and it's all because
It treats a world that never was.

Don Martindale
University of Minnesota
Minneapolis

HORATIO FABREGA, JR. and DANIEL B. SILVER. *Illness and Shamanistic Curing in Zinacantan: An Ethnomedical Analysis.* Pp. xvi, 285. Stanford, Calif.: Stanford University Press, 1973. $10.95.

This welcome new volume to the medical anthropology literature immediately places among the leading contributions of this interdiscipline which is now influencing medical school curricula, comparative studies of the world's medical systems and understandings of the ecology of health and the evolution of disease. Fabrega and Silver present an in-depth study of the traditional medical practitioners, illness conceptualizations, and treatment sequences in a Mayan community in southwestern Mexico which reflects a strength of perspective possible through coordinated medical and anthropological expertise. They document a vividly contrasting system of medical care by using several analytical approaches, research techniques, and levels of explanation. The meanings of illness in Zinacantan are shown with materials from the cultural analysis of informants' accounts, elicited texts, questionnaires, and through biomedical analyses of symptom configurations. Psychological characteristics of the curers are investigated with projective tests. Local capabilities for identifying levels of illness severity are illustrated with responses of practitioners and laymen to sets of photographs of diseases. Pressing research needs in medical anthropology are explicitly drawn out of the study's findings. Contrary to the title, the book is much more than an ethnomedical analysis.

The unusual diversity of the volume will, however, leave the specialist reader wanting regarding some topics. For example, providing the data on extent of political participation, frequencies of transactions with Ladinos, and frequencies of visits to cities might have been preferable to stating whether practitioners and laymen were similar or different in these respects. Some information on disease patterns and causes of deaths could have further highlighted the rich materials on illness conceptualizations. The level of cultural analysis could have been broadened with observations on concepts of health and preventive practice and perhaps some ethnoanatomy, ethnopharmacology, and so on through the contingent systems, including ethnosociology. One particularly unfortunate omission is that apparently none of the study samples included a woman medical practitioner even though roughly 30 percent of the traditional practitioners in Zinacantan are women. The few typographical errors and bibliographic omissions of cited references do not detract from the overall accomplishment.

The authors give considerable attention to discussing the ways in which an inquiry such as theirs can contribute to solving problems facing both medicine and anthropology, such as understanding and explaining the persisting diversity of the world's many medical systems. Here their work is certain to generate discussion and debate. Indeed, their hope that this volume may stimulate further studies seems to be an expectation with good prospects for fulfillment.

EDWARD MONTGOMERY
Department of Anthropology
Washington University
St. Louis
Missouri

ROBIN FOX. *Encounter With Anthropology.* Pp. 370. New York: Harcourt Brace Jovanovich, 1973. $8.95.

Robin Fox first encountered anthropology while enrolled in the bachelor of science degree program at the London School of Economics, followed by the Department of Social Relations at Harvard. He did field work on the Irish island of Tory and in Cochiti pueblo, New Mexico, and has taught at Exeter, London School of Economics, and Rutgers. He took extended excursions into zoology, philosophy, and literature. His book is a series of essays, some previously published, reflecting this background and his reactions to it.

In the lengthy introduction, "Anthropology as a Vocation," in the final chapter, "The Cultural Animal," and in the epilogue, "Anthropology Tomorrow," he argues that anthropology is sick if not moribund and advances his prescriptions to revive it. His arguments are often devastating, provocative, and entertaining, but they seldom stand up to close analysis.

As one example, Fox attacks anthropology for its espousal of behavioralism, relativism, the "superorganic," and field work as an end in itself. In each case he gives the most extreme views of a few anthropologists and presents them as characteristics of all. Anthropology, he claims, has abandoned biology and the search for human nature, untouched by the "amazing" discoveries in endocrinology, primatology, genetics, ethology and other biological fields.

The remedy Fox advances is an integration about a Darwinian evolutionary framework with emphasis on the evolution of behavior. This is not a new idea. It was advanced by A. L. Kroeber in 1928 in his paper on "Sub-Human Cultural Beginnings" (*Quarterly Review of Biology* 3:325–342). The second chapter of the fourth edition (1971) of an introductory textbook I wrote with H. Hoijer is titled "The Evolution of Man and His Behavior," and the theme runs through much of the book. The point here is that I could not have written the part on the evolution of behavior in the first edition in 1953 because most of the data were not extant. Fox's strictures on anthropology suggest that if he were a physicist he would condemn Sir Isaac Newton, whom he mentions, for not utilizing advanced particle physics.

Most of Fox's book consists of a number of unexceptionable essays, covering topics upon which many anthropologists have written. Three, "The Evolution of Sexual Behavior," "Comparative Family Patterns," and "Kinship and Alliance" apply Fox's evolutionary approach in interesting ways, although he extrapolates from primate and mammalian behavior to a much greater degree than I think most anthropologists will think justified at present. Fox says that the previously published "Abolition of Race" aroused the most violent criticism from extremists of all types and skin colors, but I doubt that much if any came from anthropologists. Seven essays on various topics are based primarily on his field work. The essays are well written, urban, often witty, and quite suitable for public lectures. They also have some original and stimulating ideas and interpretations.

In his epilogue, "Anthropology Tomorrow," Fox pursues his theme of the importance of a Darwinian evolutionary framework but adds to his pantheon Marx, Freud, and Lévi-Strauss. He plunks for an activist anthropology that will indulge in social criticism and that will be oriented toward showing how culture and society are either based upon or warp man's human nature. He considers himself a true radical anthropologist but disassociates himself from the current so-called "radical anthropologists" in a few brief and scathing words.

Despite the somewhat negative character of this review, I recommend the book. Anthropologists will find some stimulating suggestions in it as well as some perhaps healthy irritation. Non-anthropologists will find some pleasant reading about current anthropology as well as abundant ammunition with which to needle any anthropologists they know.

RALPH L. BEALS
University of California
Los Angeles

GEORGE F. GILDER. *Sexual Suicide.* Pp. vii, 308. New York: Quadrangle Books, 1973. $7.95.

For those who like old chestnuts warmed over and served with a patina of "chic-sauce," George Gilder's *Sexual Suicide* will be just their dish. For thoughtful readers, however, it will be hard to swallow.

The old chestnut in this case is the notion that "the world is going to hell in a hand basket." This fact, asserts Gilder, is exemplified by many aspects of contemporary American society: the sexual revolution, open marriage, divorce, abortion, violence, crime, the disintegration of the black family, welfare, day care, equal pay for equal work, affirmative action programs for women, androgyny, homosexuality, and masturbation. Because Gilder treats all of these phenomena as negative and tends to lump them together in a monolithic evil, it is difficult for discriminating readers to know where to put themselves if, for example, they are against crime and for masturbation.

Gilder, a writer, ex-editor (*Ripon* and *New Leader*), and "adviser . . . for a number of leading government officials," sees the above mentioned social "ills" as symptoms of the disintegration of our "sexual constitution," a disintegration which will lead to "sexual suicide."

Gilder's failure to clearly define these two crucial terms renders his thesis a bit fuzzy. However, it goes something like this. The "sexual constitution," a primary pillar of civilization, is rooted in sexual differentiation. Women have a richer, more self-confident, superior sexuality which is inextricably linked to procreation and, hence, to the family. Men, on the other hand, have an inferior sexuality: shallow, intermittent, fragile. They are not naturally family-oriented. They must be socialized—by women—to commit themselves to families and to the jobs that provide for families. If such male socialization should be weakened, males would literally run wild—raping women, abandoning families, prompting police repression, and ultimately destroying civilization. In fact, says Gilder, this already is happening in our sexually suicidal society.

What is the reason for this terrible state of affairs? In Gilder's devil theory, the blame lies with the "sexual revolution" and the "women's liberation movement," both of which encourage women to abandon their natural sexuality.

Gilder even "demonstrates" that the seemingly most straightforward, reasonable, and benign of feminist requests, equal pay for equal work, is really a subversive threat to male sexuality, and hence to the sexual consititution. Unequal pay for equal work, it turns out, is necessary for the maintenance of civilization. (See c. 6, p. 96 ff. and p. 247 ff.)

Finally, on page 249, Gilder takes up the question that thoughtful readers have been asking since page one. "If woman's role is so great, why don't men want it?" Well, they really do, says Gilder, one "proof" being that "more men than women turn transvestite." But men resign themselves to the fact that only women can have the "superior" role and that they must be content with the "inferior" role. In order to assuage this inequality, of course, many men will have such compensations as jobs, money, power over women and children, and so on. And this arrangement is necessary for civilization, and so on. And if it changes, all hell will break loose, and so on. If this sounds familiar, it may be because it evokes echoes of distressingly similar arguments in pro-slavery and pro-colonial literature. Gilder's old chestnut turns out to be a very old and very wormy one.

Gilder's level of argumentation and prose style are exemplified by the following sentence. "It [the present era] has been a time when fashionable psychologists proclaim that all orifices were created equal ('I'm okay, you're okay'), and the 'missionary position' [which we are all presumed to know means the man upstairs] is casually dismissed as the way squares peg round holes" (p. 2). One could forgive Gilder this sentence if it were not so disconcertingly typical. When faced with a choice between accuracy and entertainment, Gilder goes for the latter.

Gilder purports to deal with an important subject: some big, risky, revolutionary changes that are taking place in American society today due to a number of factors, including the complex phenomenon called feminism. But, an author should not be congratulated merely for writing about an important subject. Rather, he should be criticized when, like Gilder, he brings to his enterprise a level of argumentation that would make Rona Barrett blush.

If we want to review a broad and balanced spectrum of literature relating to feminism—and we should—why turn to Gilder, with his slick, self-serving rationalization of male chauvinism? Why, instead, do we social scientists not more widely review such work as John Money and Anke Ehrhardt's *Man and Woman, Boy and Girl* (Baltimore: The Johns Hopkins University Press, 1972)? This collection of Money's studies at Johns Hopkins constitutes a rigorous investigation of some biological bases of sex differentiation, it has profound implications for social science, and it is sufficiently provocative to be cited by feminists and anti-feminists alike.

Gilder is right about one thing. Feminism is a revolutionary movement. It is bound to have some negative, dislocating effects. Anticipating, and possibly ameliorating, negative effects, while developing the positive possibilities, is an enterprise that will require all the intelligence, ingenuity, and humanity we can muster. *Sexual Suicide* cannot be considered a contribution to such an enterprise.

JOY HUNTLEY
Department of Government
Ohio University
Athens

GERALD N. GROB. *Mental Institutions in America: Social Policy to 1875.* Pp. 476. New York: The Free Press, 1973. No price.

Professor Grob has performed a valuable service in documenting the historical development of social policy toward the mentally disabled in America, from the early colonial days to the last quarter of the nineteenth century. His main theme is that social, economic, and political factors were as important as medical considerations in the emergence of mental institutions. In early colonial days the family was principally held responsible for the welfare of any of its members who became "mentally distracted." Society was involved only to the extent that the behavior of lunatics threatened the public safety or resulted in the person or his family becoming public charges because of the disabling consequences of mental illness. The attitude of the public in colonial times toward the mentally ill is reflected in the law passed by the General Court of Massachusetts in 1676 that directed town officials to provide for the care of distracted persons so that "they do not Damnify others." During the eighteenth century, community care of the mentally ill was mainly subsumed under the existing poor law system which obligated society to assume responsibility for the aged, the indigent, and the incapacitated. The sick, the destitute, and the disturbed were confined in alms houses, county poor houses, and correctional institutions. Under the impetus of the reform movement, imported from France and England, moral treatment was introduced into America during the early decades of the nineteenth century. For a time, it appeared that the small family-type hospital would provide the answer to the social problem of mental illness. The initial high hopes regarding the curability of mental disease were quickly shattered with the growth of the large, impersonal public mental hospitals. Professor Grob has given an interesting account of the early origins of the medical speciality of psychiatry in America. His scholarly review of the progressive and periodically regressive shifts of social policy toward the mentally ill provides a historical perspective to current issues.

JAMES D. PAGE
Department of Psychology
Temple University
Philadelphia

LYN H. LOFLAND. *A World of Strangers: Order and Action in Urban Public Space.* Pp. ix, 223. New York: Basic Books, 1973. $9.50.

This book, according to its preface, seeks to explain how we live as we do, especially how urban dwellers manage to cope with strangers. This is done largely by avoiding having dealings with them. The argument is to the effect that city life is tolerable for the urban dweller in accordance with what he knows about people living around him. How he acquires and uses that knowledge to gain privacy and the contents of such knowledge are what the book is about. The relationships among urban dwellers take place mainly in public places. These are defined as nonprivate locations of all kinds to which people have legal access, such as stores, banks, and restaurants, as well as parks and libraries. The urban dweller's aim, then, is to maximize the prospects of privacy in these surroundings. "A stranger is anyone personally unknown to the actor of reference, but visually available to him" (p. 18). An individual's capacity to recognize a stranger and act on that recognition, it is averred, depends upon an elaborate process of information and experience coding which the individual will have learned in growing up. The only things an individual is likely to know about particular strangers are the things he perceives visually. A useful coding system, in these circumstances, is one evoking whatever kind of behavior is likely to assure some privacy from strangers who have been visually identified and sized up. Without some means of making public space private, urban society, in the author's view, could not escape chaos.

The book divides into two sections. The first traces the transformation of the city from ancient times into the industrial era, with a brief discussion of the stranger's standing at various times and places. The second primarily treats the current urban scene with attention focusing on the means by which public spaces are rendered private by the urban dweller. In the preindustrial city the stranger was, in the main, appearentially identifiable by his clothing, language, body markings, and the like. The infrequency of strangers and a widespread heterogeneous use of public space in urban places meant that strangers could circulate among the local citizenry without difficulty of identification or accommodation. As cities expanded spatially and in population, and as travel became easier, this state of affairs changed. Industrialization increased job opportunities, which brought more people into cities.

The wealthy could escape close association with strangers by locating their residences away from those of the lower classes. The middle classes, including the *petit bourgeoisie,* were less favored. They had to rely on their political strength to secure segregative-type protection from the proletariat. This protection took the form of spatial-type controls affecting strangers—zoning, building codes, more specialized uses for public space, and so on, not to mention police forces and humanitarian services. As a result, restrictions on the uses of public space mounted: bans of loitering, soliciting, and the like. Strangers in the modern urban scene came to be known by where they stood, not by what they wore (p. 82). Race, socio-economic condition, and, in some instances, occupation and religion became the bases for spatial ordering of people. Moreover, the untoward connotations attributed to various occupations and kinds of people have been culturally transmitted by the family, the media, and other socializing forces. The urban dweller is not without understanding of the who or what is a stranger according to his own social class, occupation, or race. Public space is transformed into private by other means, too, through creating home territories, as in an individual or a group "taking over" a particular location and adapting it repeatedly to its own use; through creating urban villages, in which the entire round of life can be lived out by one person or a group in a narrowly defined locale, that is, a neighborhood; and through traveling in packs, by which a group of intimates enjoys the advantage of mobility but the simultaneous aloofness from strangers. An especially interesting chapter attempts to delineate some of the specific steps utilized in transforming public space into private—taking a reading, reaching a position, styles of waiting, and so forth. A number of "principles" are offered to explain how the transforming process is accomplished, as in minimizing expressivity and/or body contact, looking before one sits, minimizing eye contact, and in cases of doubt, how to flee the scene.

The usefulness of this book lies in its introduction to the subject. It brings together in a simply presented manner some of the literature on the subject of how the urban dweller accommodates strangers. Portions of this subject undoubtedly merit further in-depth investigation, especially as to the implications of the material referred to in the immediately preceding sentences. Much of what the book covers, nevertheless, is known experientially to most who live among unfamilar faces in cities. Further research in appropriate areas of this broad subject will hopefully engage the scholar's skills more while retaining the flavor of the taxi driver's insights.

HARRY W. REYNOLDS
School of Public Affairs and Community Service
University of Nebraska
Omaha

ARMANDO MORALES. *Ando Sangrando (I Am Bleeding): A Study of Mexican-American Police Conflict.* Foreword by U.S. Senator Fred R. Harris. Pp. x, 142. La Puente, Calif.: Perspectiva Publications, 1972. $7.95.

When bleeding, one may presumably cry out in anguish, without regard for good grammar or scientific rigor. This, however, does not excuse parading academic titles and presuming to speak to academic colleagues, when in reality the author speaks for Los Angeles' Chicanos and addresses his plea for reform to the holders of white power.

Actually, Morales' "book" does contain some valid evidence of brutality and racist behavior on the part of representatives of Los Angeles' law en-forcement establishment. Unfortunately, the worthwhile bits and pieces are scattered among heaps of rubble. While one can endure poor organization, duplication, and artificial infla-tion—for example, some of the au-thor's letters are quoted within the text in their entirety, inside address and all—other practices are likely to offend the serious reader.

For example, at one point Morales confuses facts with conceptual schema and value judgments and presents them all in a single oversized table (pp. 113–115). Even worse, he quotes from the President's Commission's report on police reaction to drunkenness and pro-ceeds to confuse drunkenness with driving under influence, failing to men-tion that his recommendations on this problem are in direct opposition to the Commission's argument (pp. 53–54, 56). (See The President's Commission on Law Enforcement and Administra-tion of Justice, *Task Force Report: Drunkenness.* Washington, D.C.: U.S. Government Printing Office, 1967, esp. pp. 2–4.) Similarly, his quoting of a procedure to calculate area crime rates is followed by tables in which a vital part of the quoted procedure—as-signing different weights to felonies and misdemeanors—is omitted, re-sulting in an inaccurate picture of police development practices (pp. 50–52). Finally, Morales indulges in numerous unwarranted generalizations, for example, "Mexican-Americans live in a totalitarian-like atmosphere which is part of a larger community system which functions as a democracy" (p. 124)—which show him to be as care-less a stereotyper as any representative of the "establishment" he attacks.

Not only do the defects obstruct the positive message concerning the legiti-mate gripes of Mexican-Americans, but the message that does filter through is a negative one which is quite likely to harm the minority-rights cause. Publications of this genre remain living testimony to an unpleasant and oft-ignored aspect of the turbulent dec-ade just behind us, namely, the emergence among America's suppressed minorities of vociferous leaders, whose usefulness to their respective constituencies is, at best, questionable. Armed with a degree of literacy, but with a much higher dose of aggressiveness, these leaders apparently did very well for themselves. For example, our author managed to inch himself into a fairly comfortable position, to a point that when legitimate publishers rejected his manuscript, he managed to set up his own publishing house and even succeeded in coaxing one of the more intelligent members of the U.S. Senate into writing an approbatory foreword to his so-called study. It would hardly be fair or reasonable to imply that the phenomenon of these operators is the chief factor responsible for the failure of their alleged constituents to significantly improve their position. However, it is certainly not implausible to suggest that a relationship between the two might exist.

In short, the Chicano cause merits far better treatment than it has received in *Ando Sangrando*.

ISRAEL RUBIN
Department of Sociology
Cleveland State University
Ohio

JUNE SOCHEN. *Movers and Shakers: American Women Thinkers and Activists, 1900–1970.* Pp. xi, 308. New York: Quadrangle Books, 1973. $8.95.

Dr. Sochen calls her book "a modest effort in the area of twentieth-century women's history," yet it deserves more than modest applause. As she notes, those who write history are shaped by cultural values. Thus we find that various groups—one hopes that blacks and women are now conspicuous examples—have generally been slighted in our history books. And, all too frequently, when they do appear, it is secondarily, in relation to "dominant" figures or groups, or as afterthought, not as "movers and shakers." For both its compensatory and intrinsic value, *Movers and Shakers* has merit.

The women Sochen deals with are those "whose participation in the life of their time was significant and worthy of recognition," who illustrate her underlying and explicit assumption that in all periods of time a minority of individuals march to the tune of a different drummer. Her book attempts to inform us, then, of a number of women thinkers and activists who concerned themselves with the position of women, who applied themselves in word and/or deed toward understanding and exposing or changing the condition of their sisters, and who experienced conflict with the cultural expectations and standards of the society of which they were a part.

Movers and Shakers begins by elucidating briefly the basic precepts of feminism. It continues with generally concise descriptions of "the few American women, the movers and shakers, who found their purpose in life less than satisfactory and defined the problem as a woman problem, rather than a personal one," and their work and lives. Chapters correspond with temporal periods: 1900–1920, 1920–1940, 1940–1960, and the 1960s. As Sochen maintains that cultural attitudes are central to women's position, material relating to the context of the times in which her subjects lived and moved is provided. In addition, while these women are treated as the admirable people they are, Sochen does not shrink from calling some of the movers and shakers occasionally short-sighted or in error.

The relatively few criticisms of *Movers and Shakers* do not jeopardize the book's value. The first relates to style: while, on the whole, the book is lively, it is at times choppy, without transitions between the discussion of one person or event and the next. Secondly, the author takes the time to define three categories of feminists, general, radical, and pragmatic, yet utilizes this tripartite classificatory scheme only for the first two periods covered. No explanation is given for the absence of such classification in the remainder of the book. Lastly, *Movers and Shakers* is a selective view and assessment of the female thinkers and activists of this century. This is, however, for all intents and purposes inevitable. Further, the author makes such a demurrer in her preface and articulates her minimal criteria for inclusion in this account of movers and shakers.

Thus, while not a complete accounting of all female movers and shakers, this well-researched book succeeds in opening the reader's eyes to some true American heroines, to contributions women have made to our society, and further provides some perspective on the current women's movement. To a woman, these strong individuals who are the subjects of the work questioned the culture's definition of them and, believing that women share problems, roles, conditions *qua* women, tended to be comprehensive in their criticism of American society and to stretch boundaries, extend limits. In sum, although *Movers and Shakers* is but a small part of women's lost history, one is grateful to June Sochen for it and hopes that others will continue the work.

PATRICIA BAYER RICHARD
Government Department
Ohio University
Athens

GEORGE S. STERNLIEB and BERNARD F. INDIK. *The Ecology of Welfare: Housing and the Welfare Crisis in New York City.* Pp. xi, 292. New Brunswick, N.J.: Transaction Books, 1973. $9.75.

GEORGE STERNLIEB and ROBERT W. BURCHELL. *Residential Abandonment: The Tenement Landlord Revisited.* Pp. 444. New Brunswick, N.J.: Rutgers University, Center for Urban Policy Research, 1973. No price.

Professor Sternlieb is director of the Center for Urban Policy Research at Rutgers University. He has assembled a first-rate interdisciplinary research syndicate. Professor Indik, for example, is professor of social work. Sternlieb also has apparently unlimited access to a computer. He has addressed himself in a series of studies on what he calls "the low-end sector" of urban housing. This

is a field of great concern, of violent opposition of viewpoints, of stereotypes upon which public policy is to be based—and of a dire absence of hard facts, hard to come by. Sternlieb and his associates have tried to assemble these facts by extensive open-ended interviews with hundreds of slum dwellers, by the manipulation of data from diverse sources, and through the cooperation of public and private agencies.

The study of abandonment is based upon the inner city core of Newark, New Jersey, which Sternlieb's team has surveyed twice, in 1964 and 1971. He concludes that the basic issue is "disinvestment of private capital in core cities." The combination of risk, decreased profitability, and loss of potential for capital gains has substantially restricted the kinds of professional owners who are willing to invest in slum properties. The studies lead to the conclusion that the "slumlord" is a convenient myth. Nobody is raping these properties for high return. Indeed, in the virtually stagnant market, the only visible purchaser is the city. This is why two-thirds of the abandonments are preceded by failure to pay taxes, an "avenue of illegal credit." The city unwittingly encourages owners to destroy through non-improvement.

Sternlieb analyzes in detail the experiences of those who remain—the new minority landlords. Their buildings are better maintained, but the new landlords' hopes for the future are fast ebbing; their investment is at a dead-end. How can society cope with this?

The other volume describes the welfare families, their housing, their attitudes toward the housing and its setting, their hopes and fears, and policy implications. More than 400 welfare families were interviewed. A basic analytic tool was the Cantril Self-Anchoring Striving Scale: Where does the tenant think that he stands today in relation to the best life as he has defined it and the worst life as he has defined it? Sternlieb's team has detailed data on the recipients of welfare—their place of origin, ethnicity, age, household size, family composition, employment. The team has cross-tabulated the data in every conceivable way. Some of the resulting subgroups are so small that the authors themselves cannot offer meaningful statements about the subgroup.

Of the seven specific housing facets about which the welfare recipients were asked, safety was rated lowest and the one most needing improvement. "It is difficult to do justice to the bitterness and fear that pervades many interviews." (The authors noted that the intensity of these feelings does not come through in the computer printout.) The welfare respondents characteristically see their personal past as better than their personal present and their personal future as considerably better than either. (This seems to be characteristic of the Cantril scale when used elsewhere.)

As in the Newark study, there is little to corroborate the wide-spread assumption that buildings largely tenanted by welfare families are more frequently owned by large-scale professional landlords, "slumlords," than other structures.

This whole series of volumes provides indispensable reference tools for those concerned with the problems of the central city—for those who prefer facts to stereotypes and myths.

CHARLES S. ASCHER
Institute of Public Administration
New York City

SISTER FRANCES JEROME WOODS. *Marginality and Identity: A Colored Creole Family through Ten Generations.* Pp. xvi, 395. Baton Rouge: Louisiana State University Press, 1972. $15.00.

This is a study of the development of identity among the colored Letoyant Creoles of Louisiana who are a marginal ethnic group in the total American society. About ten thousand descendents of one couple have been traced through ten generations over two centuries from colonial times to mid-twentieth century, and a comprehen-

sive and intensive analysis of the total situation has been made in a natural environment, and not in an artificial laboratory setting, through the case study approach, with evidence derived from a multiplicity of sources.

Two hypotheses have guided this study: (1) A people who possesses a marginal ethnic status in society and is geographically isolated for a long period of time will develop a unique sense of identity and strong bonds of group solidarity; this identity will be maintained through the institutionalization of what is most important to identity; and (2) As individuals move from isolation into the larger society, their sense of identity will be weakened and they will gradually become assimilated into other groups. These hypotheses have here been largely verified.

Unlike the Negroes in the United States and many other minorities elsewhere, the Creoles are found to have a clear concept of themselves as a distinct people as well as of a homeland, which has followed from their familiarity with their own history and culture and has also, in turn, promoted psychological security. However, the author also indicates the gradual dilution of their ethnicity by continual migration, increasing identification with other racial populations, and out-group marriages. The detailed findings of this study appear in four sections on "Establishing an Identity," "Maintaining an Identity in the Southland," "The Diaspora," and "Epilogue."

Ever since Park and Stonequist, studies on "marginality" have rendered a distinct contribution to the understanding of inter-group and intra-group relations, especially through replacement of the biological emphasis of human behavior of a sociological one. Yet, some of the generalizations of earlier writings were vague and impressionistic; they rested on the questionable assumption of the inevitable conflict between marginal groups and the dominant population and were also overly preoccupied with psychological aberrations among marginal individuals. In this respect, the study under review appears to be a valuable contribution to a more consistent sociological inquiry into some hitherto neglected and misunderstood aspects of the marginal situation and marginal personality.

Besides dealing with alienation and identity, this study explains majority-minority relations, and racial attitudes and discriminatory practices among American minority peoples themselves. It also provides further insights into questions of concern to the greater society.

SANTOSH KUMAR NANDY
Toronto
Canada

ECONOMICS

PHILIP H. BURCH, JR. *The Managerial Revolution Reassessed: Family Control in America's Large Corporations.* Pp. 195. Lexington, Mass.: D.C. Heath, 1972. No price.

This is a major work in the field of corporate control and power. Burch has done a heroic amount of digging in an effort to rehabilitate an alleged prematurely interred family as opposed to management control of the larger U.S. corporations. His discussion of sources of information on corporate control and his assemblage of facts is invaluable. His critique of earlier work in the field also has merit, although Burch's own methodological weaknesses vitiate some of this critique as well as his substantive findings and conclusions.

Burch's main theme is that management control has been overrated, that family control of big business is still of major importance—42 percent or more of the 450 large firms examined were found to be under family control in the mid-1960s—and that the "managerial revolution" is consequently far from complete. Burch does concede that management control is very important, perhaps more important than family control overall, and that its trend is upward. He makes a good case that family, or owner, control is still of

consequence, but his findings are weakened by the inadequacies of both his criteria for establishing control and his specific concept of family control.

Despite the importance of the control concept, Burch defines it in a footnote, and he makes no distinction between requirements for initially attaining control and for maintaining it once strategic position has been established. He asserts that "it is now generally agreed in most major business circles that working control of any large company can usually be obtained through possession of something like 4 or 5 percent of the voting stock. . . ." (p. 25). This crucial statement is not supported by any serious argument or evidence, and the reviewer's work on the subject has convinced him that Burch's statement is quite wrong.

Furthermore, Burch's figure, if true, would indicate the urgent necessity of incorporating into his analysis the holdings of institutional investors, as the Patman study of 1968, for example, indicated that bank trust departments alone held over 5000 "control" size holdings—5 percent or more. But, curiously enough, Burch carries out his analysis essentially disregarding this body of data, merely suggesting disconcertingly that institutional investors' "influence over certain aspects of corporate affairs . . . has, no doubt, sometimes been . . . quite substantial" (p. 17). Jean-Marie Chevalier, in his comparable study of corporate control (*La structure financière de l'industrie américaine,* Paris, Cujas, 1970), is more consistent, applying his stock ownership criterion of control across the board, with the result that he arrives at a radically different picture from that of Burch; that is, a great deal of banker control and greatly reduced familial control. Chevalier is also more sophisticated than Burch in distinguishing between the stock ownership needed to preserve control (5 percent) and that required to obtain it de novo (15 percent)—even though Chevalier's particular figures are debatable.

Burch's concept of "family control" is also vague. He obviously has in mind the durable, ownership-based control position of a wealthy clan like the DuPonts, but his criteria—4 to 5 percent ownership by a family or group of families, plus a long-term inside or outside representation of the family on the board—is a very imperfect measure of continuity of owner-based family power. With this definition, "family control" could be read from 4 percent ownership and management status on the part of a single individual, which takes the "family" out of family control and reduces it in this case to residual minority ownership plus possible continued power based on strategic position. Since the 4 percent criterion is defective, as indicated earlier, this standard can be met where control has been lost as a result of family disinterest, inactivity, and disagreement, paralleling the common gradual divestment of family stock holdings. Furthermore, family domination can occur without Burch's criteria being met—for example, A.P. Giannini dominated Transamerica and Bank of America and passed along the reigns to his son Mario while holding under 4 percent of the stock of both organizations. Burch never seriously discusses the question of whether family and management control might not be based entirely on strategic position, with the stockholdings irrelevant as a control device, where the latter are as small as 4 or 5 percent, or less.

Despite the serious defects of this study Burch makes a good case that ownership and familial control of the classic variety—Sun Oil, DuPont, M. A. Hanna—is still strong and is possibly underrated in significance. In the process of developing this theme he has many interesting and illuminating comments on corporate facts and research problems. It is evident, however, that a number of conceptual and theoretical issues have to be resolved before Burch's kind of empirical effort will bear full fruit.

EDWARD S. HERMAN
Wharton School
University of Pennsylvania
Philadelphia

NEIL H. JACOBY. *Corporate Power and Social Responsibility: A Blueprint for the Future.* Pp. x, 282. New York: MacMillan, 1973. $10.00.

Dr. Jacoby's book is less a "blueprint for the future" than a primer for the defenders of the contemporary character of U.S. capitalism. It undertakes to examine and refute a series of criticisms of U.S. business institutions put forward by the "Radical Left" of which Charles Reich's *Greening of America* is taken as an adequate summation. Its principal shortcoming is that in the relatively little space which is available to cover a series of complex issues Dr. Jacoby can do little more than summarize his views in the briefest way and provide rebuttals which rest on his authority as a former Dean of the Graduate School of Management at the University of California, Los Angeles, as a member of the Council of Economic Advisors during the Eisenhower Administration, and as the author of a number of books on economic matters rather than on detailed evidence and argument.

The topics examined include the trends in the number of size of business corporations, the degree of economic and financial concentration in corporate enterprise, the dangers, or the lack of them, posed by conglomerate enterprises, multinational corporations, and the existence or nonexistence of a military complex. The most original data offered has to do with the number of corporate enterprises created and "extinguished" over a twenty-five year period, offered as a picture of trends in the "corporate population of the United States." Other data, such as the percentage of the national income realized as corporate profit, the relative number of corporations in certain size classes, the share of all wealth owned by corporations, all plotted over time, is more familiar. It is more or less alarming depending on whether corporations are viewed as a single class or as differentiated according to the degree of market power or financial power which may be concentrated in the leaders of particular lines of business.

One aspect of the book which makes it a somewhat original defense of the business system is the emphasis given to the contemporary character of management education which is viewed as creating new possibilities both of business effectiveness and of corporate social utility. In particular, the defense of corporate conglomerates rests on the proposition that there are transferable management skills so that apparently unrelated businesses benefit from a pool of management talent and practice that no one of them could assemble individually. Similarly corporation management is given credit for recognizing the interdependence of the individual enterprise and its social and political environments and for incorporating various social utilities into the calculus of management decision. The general world of politics and economics within which corporations function is seen as pluralistic, the influence of government, labor unions, and consumers acting as checks on the unilateral self-regarding decisional dispositions of corporate managers.

Dr. Jacoby's conclusions about the future of corporations and corporate managers as business citizens are optimistic. He assumes that growth trends in wealth and income will continue to be greater for the less developed part of the world so that the gap between rich and poor nations will diminish, that governmental regulation of the economy will be steadily extended without eliminating the competitive character of American business, that business managers will be more concerned than in the past with the social costs and profits of their activities, that multinational corporations will create a base for new international institutions, and that shareholders will play a more active role in the policymaking of business enterprises, challenging the pretensions to autonomy of corporate managers.

Extensive literature on all of these topics is cited in the footnotes—the work of those who oppose Dr. Jacoby's position as well as of those who support it. However the text is primarily devoted to conclusions rather than the weighing of opposing arguments and evidence. This is a good-natured work of advocacy. Those who are well informed will find little new; those who are naive will find only an introduction to a complex controversy. It is of interest to social scientists because it marks a shift in the thinking of at least some supporters of corporate business; governmental and labor union intrusions into the autonomy of corporate enterprise are accepted as evidence of the creation of a distinct kind of pluralist polity in which institutional competition offsets the imperfections of the contemporary market economy. It is a document, therefore, on the character of social thought which is presently offered as sound doctrine to at least some elements of our business-managerial elite and as reassurance to the rest of us as to the health of a most important social institution.

PHILLIP MONYPENNY
University of Illinois
Urbana

STUART BRUCE KAUFMAN. *Samuel Gompers and the Origins of the American Federation of Labor, 1848–1896.* Pp. ix, 274. Westport, Conn.: Greenwood, 1973. $11.50.

Contemporary historians have not treated Samuel Gompers kindly. With exception of the Wisconsin School—John R. Commons and Selig Perlman—Gompers has typically been deprecated as the embodiment of "pure and simple" unionism and of "more" as the ultimate aims of trade unionism. In general, labor commentators have been out of sympathy with Gompers' "narrowness" of purpose.

Now comes Stuart Bruce Kaufman, an assistant professor of history at the University of Maryland, with a sort of rehabilitation of Gompers. The rehabilitation consists of a demonstration that Gompers was basically a Marxist-socialist in his insistence that the unionism which was most effective was the one which adhered to its working-class base. In this respect he was more socialist and Marxist than his seemingly more radical critics, including the Knights of Labor who sought to dilute the essential working-class character of unionism by rich versus poor populist panaceas.

Unlike the Knights, whose reformism sought to arrest industrial capitalism's development, Gompers, like Marx, saw trade unionism's development tied in with capitalism's development. Gompers stopped short, however, of accepting Marx's logic that socialism was the necessary consequence of trade union development. At first he hedged on the question; then he explicitly rejected socialism.

Kaufman examines Gompers' unionism as it worked itself out in the Cigar Makers Union, in the founding of the American Federation of Labor, and in its predecessor, the Federation of Organized Trades and Labor Unions. The self-supporting dues, the benefit structure, economism as the central union aim, and lobbying are the pieces which make up the Gompers model. Gompers' advocacy of industrial union organization and nondiscriminatory admissions policies indicate that his reputation as a reactionary is not justified.

Kaufman considers the possibility that Gompers' socialism was an act of expediency and resolves the question in favor of Gompers' motivation by a "deeply held commitment to radical change." This is not unreasonable; neither is it unreasonable, however, to suggest that socialism so pervaded the intellectual atmosphere in which the younger Gompers moved that it was necessary for an aspiring trade union leader at a minimum to maintain socialist sympathies.

The details of Professor Kaufman's case are not altogether new. What he does well is to re-create the historical setting—the social laboratory, so to speak—in which Gompers and his associates evolved and sharpened their analysis. In any case, Professor Kaufman's work is a well-researched, well-written, and useful modern interpretation of Gompers and the sources of his ideology.

JACK BARBASH
University of Wisconsin
Madison

NATHANIEL S. KEITH. *Politics and the Housing Crisis since 1930.* Pp. 232. New York: Universe Books, 1973. $8.50.

This book has the flavor of a very good after-dinner speech. The author saw and sat in on Washington politics where housing was the issue for four decades. His language is colorful and direct. The message is partisan, but knowledgeable and perceptive; it is also dated.

Mr. Keith was the first head of the Federal Urban Renewal Program, though he had not much interest in urban renewal per se. His book and his "commitment," to use a current catchword, have to do primarily with public housing—subsidized, government-built, and government-run low-rent urban housing. The book is largely a collection of personal reminiscences, often in the first person, about the personalities and points of view which affected federal housing legislation.

Keith's book opens the door on how legislation on that subject evolved. He was around—as a reporter—and he was wholeheartedly on one side of the sharply drawn public housing issue during the thirties, a kind of volunteer lieutenant. In 1940 he became a public relations man for the Federal Housing Administration and then a speechwriter for the first head of the National Housing Agency (NHA), the grandparent of the Department of Housing and Urban Development. When he became NHA special assistant for congressional relations he was at last in the role he identifies with in this book. His task was to scout and lobby on behalf of administration housing measures and to marshall verbiage and pressures. He continued this role after leaving government employment, primarily through the National Housing Conference, a clearinghouse for support of progressive housing legislation.

The book provides a concise but readable chronology of major federal housing legislation from 1933 to 1973 and an inventory of the people and groups who played significant roles in drawing up proposals, introducing and managing bills, and developing counter-ploys, mostly in connection with public housing but with major reference also to the establishment of a permanent "umbrella" agency for housing functions in 1949. It is readable because there is a very clear plot—in more than one sense of the word. Public housing comes across as a symbol of concern for the less fortunate, which a surprisingly narrow list of "liberals" seem to have sewn onto their sweatshirts, while the "reactionary real estate lobby" was bent on keeping the poor in their hovels. Keith's personal emotions are reflected in his habitual epithets. The few people who cannot easily be classified as liberals or reactionaries, including William Zechendorf, Daniel Moynihan, and Wilson Wyatt, the man Truman chose to head up the veterans' housing program, are dismissed as "flamboyant."

Keith's point of view does not prevent this book from being a useful document, nor does it diminish the sincerity or judgement of the "housers" he admired and helped. An author's strong bias tempts the reader to be the devil's advocate, however, and that is not a difficult role in this case. Giving the devil his due, the conservative forces, that is, Republican administrations, turn out to have a reasonably good record in advancing the goals which Keith attributes to the other group. It was not until Eisenhower, for instance, that provisions were made for relocation housing in urban renewal projects; George Romney pushed the output of federally assisted housing well beyond the best levels achieved by Democratic administrations; rent supplements were proposed early and often by conservative groups; the same groups sensed the basic unworkability

of the "model cities" approach and anticipated the high unit cost debacle of public housing construction. Perhaps the sorriest admission is Keith's tribute to former Attorney General John Mitchell for his long service to the National Housing Conference.

Not many people now will be quite as willing as Keith to see the course of housing legislation in the United States in terms of Good and Evil. Legislation is not equivalent to housing, and the reality seems to confound the intent and strategems of true believers. Urban renewal, for example, had an appeal to liberals who reasoned that by tearing down slums there would arise an inescapable necessity to build public housing—where else would the slum dwellers go? The conservatives, on the other hand, liked urban renewal per se, and at last came around to accepting the idea of public housing so slum land could be cleared for other purposes. The physical goals were the same; why worry about whose motives were more noble? As it turned out, public housing and urban renewal competed for the same appropriation dollar, despite being philosophically complementary. In the Eisenhower years, as urban renewal spending went up, public housing expenditures went down. This might sound like a bad thing for the displaced families, but Keith so far paints himself into a partisan corner that he must proclaim as unfounded the criticisms of urban renewal relocation, which became so loud in the Kennedy-Johnson years, to say, in effect, that public housing was not so necessary after all.

The book is a history of partisan debate. It is not informative about the housing inventory of the country or the housing industry. For an insight into the politics of housing at the national level, however, it does not have a close rival.

WALLACE F. SMITH

Department of Business
    Administration
University of California
Berkeley

RAYMOND H. MILKMAN et al. *Alleviating Economic Distress: Evaluating a Federal Effort.* Pp. xxiv, 407. Lexington, Mass.: D.C. Health, 1972. $17.50.

This book, focused mainly on "devising a practical approach to program evaluation," is a historical and evaluative study of Economic Development Administration (EDA) programs.

The book contains two major parts. The first, chapters 1 through 5, evaluates the EDA programs in a historical setting. The primary influence in preparing EDA legislation was the experience gained from the operation of the Area Redevelopment Administration (ARA). In spite of the relative success of the ARA in its goal of encouraging private enterprise in depressed areas, it was beset with problems of inadequate funding, general economic recession, and unrealized expectations. Faced with these and other troubles, the ARA was replaced, for reasons of political expediency, by the Economic Development Administration. The EDA legislation was signed into law on August 26, 1965.

During the first year of EDA's history, the time constraint governing evaluations and the pressure to expend the appropriation before June 30 overshadowed any attempt to develop an effective system for evaluating project applications. However, the period between October 1966 and January 1969 witnessed several significant changes in the EDA, including reorganization of the staff and identification of some specific guidelines. As an interim measure, a strategy for giving first consideration to the "worst areas—those with the highest unemployment rates and lowest incomes" (p. 30) was adopted. Such a policy won political support in the Congress; but the critics were quick to point out the futility of funding areas with extremely limited potential for economic growth. Many factors, such as the inability of depressed communities to contribute their proportion of project costs, the stringency of administrative regulations, and the lack of initiative and resources in the "worst" areas, resulted in a gradual relaxation of this policy.

The second part of the book, chapters 6 through 13, describes the evaluation approach that was developed and presents the results of its implementation. Project-oriented and program-oriented evaluation approaches are briefly examined in chapter 6, and chapter 7 provides a summary of initial results and conclusions derived from the evaluation of several projects under the EDA. Chapters 8, 9, and 10 are directed to the question of "growth centers" and their role in the development of depressed areas. A rather simple, but eminently practical, model for the identification of growth centers is presented in chapter 9.

The growth center strategy is based on Francois Perroux's principle of "development poles," that is, the idea that the best way to assist residents of a depressed area is to accelerate the development of nearby growth centers to which they can migrate or commute to work. The growth center is expected to provide infrastructure, jobs, and services not otherwise available to residents of the surrounding distressed hinterland. Chapters 11, 12, and 13 discuss economic development of Indian reservations, evaluation of EDA's training-related projects, and prognosis for the future, respectively.

The authors, in evaluating EDA's impact, conclude that, in most cases, the agency has been successful in its mission of stimulating the development process in economically depressed areas. The book is a much-needed and valuable addition to the nontheoretical literature on program evaluation; it deserves the attention not only of academicians but also of policymakers and politicians involved in programs for economic development.

P. I. MATHEW
Department of Economics
Westfield State College
Massachusetts

ROBERT A. PACKENHAM. *Liberal America and the Third World: Political Development Ideas in Foreign*

Aid and Social Science. Pp. xxii, 395. Princeton, N.J.: Princeton University Press, 1973. $15.00.

From ten years of investigating government policy at all levels and analyzing theory, Robert Packenham concludes that both U.S. officials and scholars have "significantly" projected into international political development "excessively dogmatic liberalism." Thus, he faults the ethnocentric tendency to export specifics of U.S. policy, institutions, and methods common to all developers whether in education, industry, or transport. He thinks that by looking at their political parochialism, Americans can "better understand and relate to political development in the Third World."

During the 1947–68 period, Packenham notes that economic-dominant aid to postwar Europe helped insure economic recovery, forestall Communism, and as the political product, maintain stability and democracy; but that both operators and scholars acted inappropriately on much the same policies and theories for twenty-five years toward a highly different Third World. While a political development approach was but one factor, he says that although few countries went Communist the economic gap widened in and between countries and U.S.-standard democracies declined.

Of three major U.S. political development doctrines, Packenham finds: "The *Economic*—strong, especially in aid agencies; *Security*—most influential in Eisenhower years; and the less influential *Explicit Democratic* expanded," particularly in the Kennedy Latin American "Alliance"; and in the "Title IX Amendment to the 1966 U.S. Foreign Assistance Act." The Amendment was labeled: "Utilization of Democratic Institutions in Development." He found aid agencies at odds with the State Department over its emphasis on aid for short-run political purposes: winning friends, punishing enemies, and influencing elections. Among examples of official liberal excesses, Packenham offers: Kennedy's

policies toward Peru, British Guiana, and Vietnam; and Johnson's toward the Dominican Republic and Vietnam.

From a cross analysis of the three doctrines and three categories of theories, Packenham concludes that officials listened little to social scientists—at least partly because theorists had little concrete to offer on specific situations. He has uncovered no innovator able to synthesize useful political development guides between the extreme hard-core liberalism and "vulgar Marxism."

Meanwhile, what prescriptions? Packenham:

concludes that most Third World countries do not want, at this stage anyhow, exclusively, or even mainly, democratic systems, especially the U.S. type. They want less ambitious systems, with enough authority to achieve economic development and social-economic justice—with personal freedom.

urges more tolerance toward radicals and radical regimes—and, in extreme cases, even toward revolution.

thinks that diplomats are apt to be more effective and less ethnocentric than development advisors in exporting political development.

advises Americans to learn more about themselves and Third World countries and people from parallel problems among blacks, Chicanos, Indians, and other groups at home.

DANA D. REYNOLDS

President, International Center for
   Dynamics of Development
Arlington
Virginia

STERLING SPERO and JOHN M. CAPOZZOLA. *The Urban Community and Its Unionized Bureaucracies: Pressure Politics in Local Government Labor Relations*. Pp. xvii, 361. New York: Dunellen, 1973. $12.50.

One of the great administrative and fiscal dilemmas facing the cities in the 1970s is the emergence of strong, militant, and effective public employees unions. Public employees are about a sixth of the nation's work force, and municipal employees are the most rapidly expanding segment. More than three million state and local workers hold union or association membership cards. Municipal employees unions— including craft and industrial unions, professional associations, and others— have organized public school teachers, police, firemen, social workers, office workers, sanitation and transportation workers, and every other category of municipal employee. In the 1960s, we saw basic functions of cities virtually paralyzed by strikes, which were unusually effective. Wages of city employees rose dramatically in the 1960s, sometimes to levels higher than their counterparts in private employment. This is an important factor in the urban financial crisis where operating costs are rising exponentially while revenue collecting potential is declining.

Spero and Capozolla, who are professors of public administration at New York University, have written a definitive analysis of the relations between municipal unions and local government. The authors have brought vast knowledge and many years of experience to their subject. They augment and deepen their analysis of the contemporary situation with a historical perspective that traces the development of pertinent labor law to the present. They examine the evolution of collective bargaining in six case studies— Philadelphia, Detroit, Cincinnati, Milwaukee, New York City, and Hartford.

The authors examine every aspect of the collective bargaining process, both the formal and informal tactics, union lobbying, and pressure tactics. They give extended consideration to the significance of greater union voice in public policymaking and assess the impact of union power on future public policy. The fiery issue of the right to strike by public employees is soberly examined, and the authors conclude that it is by no means an easy issue to take sides on.

Spero and Cappozolla have made a valuable contribution to the record as well as to analysis. The book is rich in detail with many case histories, actual events, and personalities. Every chapter is copiously documented, and there is a twenty-page bibliography. As a sociologist of cities and their problems, this reviewer found the book instructive and useful. Any general urbanist would find the book a positive addition to the book shelf, both for reading and reference.

IRVING LEWIS ALLEN
University of Connecticut
Storrs

OTHER BOOKS

ADIE, ROBERT F. and GUY E. POITRAS. *Latin America: The Politics of Immobility.* Pp. v, 278. Englewood Cliffs, N. J.: Prentice-Hall, 1974. $5.95. Paperbound.

AKENSON, DONALD HARMAN. *The United States and Ireland.* Edited by Edwin O. Reischauer. Pp. vii, 311. Cambridge, Mass.: Harvard University, 1973. $12.50.

ALEXANDER, GARTH. *The Invisible China: The Overseas Chinese and the Politics of Southeast Asia.* Pp. xi, 264. New York: Macmillan, 1974. $7.95.

ALLENDE, SALVADOR. *Chile's Road to Socialism.* Pp. 208. Baltimore, Md.: Penguin, 1973. $2.45. Paperbound.

ANDERSON, CHARLES H. *The Political Economy of Social Class.* Pp. v, 340. Englewood Cliffs, N.J.: Prentice-Hall, 1974. $9.95.

ARNDT, WILLIAM B., JR. *Theories of Personality.* Pp. iii, 493. New York: Macmillan, 1974. $10.95.

BARROS, JAMES and DOUGLAS M. JOHNSON. *The International Law of Pollution.* Pp. xii, 476. New York: The Free Press, 1974. $14.95.

BELL, R. E. and A. J. YOUNGSON, eds. *Present and Future in Higher Education.* Pp. v, 192. New York: Barnes & Noble, 1974. $12.00.

BINKIN, MARTIN. *U.S. Reserve Forces: The Problem of the Weekend Warrior. Studies in Defense Policy.* Pp. 63. Washington, D.C.: The Brookings Institution, 1974. $1.95. Paperbound.

BISH, ROBERT L. and VINCENT OSTROM. *Understanding Urban Government: Metropolitan Reform Reconsidered.* Pp. 111. Washington, D.C.: Enterprise Institute for Public Policy Research, 1973. $3.00. Paperbound.

BLAKEY, ARCH FREDRIC. *The Florida Phosphate Industry: A History of the Develop-*

ment and Use of a Vital Mineral. Pp. x, 197. Cambridge, Mass.: Harvard University Press, 1973. $13.00.

BREALEY, R. A. and C. PYLE. *A Bibliography of Finance and Investment*. Pp. 361. Cambridge, Mass.: MIT Press, 1973. $18.50.

BROWN, HARRISON et al., eds. *Population: Perspective 1973*. Pp. 284. San Francisco, Calif.: Freeman, Cooper & Co., 1973. No price. Paperbound.

BUREAU OF PUBLIC AFFAIRS, DEPARTMENT of STATE. *Foreign Relations of the United States, 1948–The Far East: China. vol. VIII*. Pp. III, 986. Washington, D.C.: U. S. Government Printing Office, 1973. $9.30.

BYARS, ROBERT S. and JOSEPH L. LOVE, eds. *Quantitative Social Science Research on Latin America*. Pp. 272. Urbana, Ill.: University of Illinois Press, 1974. $8.95.

CALVEZ, JEAN-YVES. *Politics and Society in the Third World*. Pp. 327. Maryknoll, N.Y.: Orbis, 1973. $6.95.

CANNEL, WARD and JUNE MACKLIN. *The Human Nature Industry*. Pp. 306. New York: Doubleday & Co., 1974. $3.50. Paperbound.

COHEN, MICHAEL D. and JAMES G. MARCH. *Leadership and Ambiguity: The American College President*. A General Report Prepared for The Carnegie Commission on Higher Education. Pp. xi, 270. New York: McGraw-Hill, 1974. $10.00.

CONVERSE, JEAN M. and HOWARD SCHUMAN. *Conversations at Random: Survey Research as Interviewers See It*. Pp. v, 111. New York: John Wiley & Sons, 1974. $7.50. Paperbound, $3.50.

CORD, ROBERT L., JAMES A. MEDEIROS, and WALTER S. JONES. *Political Science: An Introduction*. Pp. 673. New York: Meredith Corporation, 1974. No price.

COTTRELL, LEONARD S., JR., ALBERT HUNTER, and JAMES F. SHORT, JR., eds. *Ernest W. Burgess On Community, Family and Delinquency*. Pp. 337. Chicago, Ill.: University of Chicago Press, 1974. $13.50.

COX, FRED et al., eds. *Community-Action, Planning, Development: A Casebook*. Pp. v, 218. Itasca, Ill.: Peacock, 1974. $4.25. Paperbound.

COX, FRED et al., eds. *Strategies Of Community Organization: A Book of Readings*. 2nd ed. Pp. v, 464. Itasca, Ill.: Peacock, 1974. $7.50. Paperbound.

CRIST, RAYMOND E. and CHARLES M. NISSLY. *East from the Andes*. University of Florida Social Sciences Monograph, no. 50. Pp. iii, 166. Gainsville, Fla.: University of Florida Press, 1974. $4.00. Paperbound.

CUNLIFFE, MARCUS. *Soldiers & Civilians: The Martial Spirit in America, 1775–*

1865. Pp. vii, 499. New York: Free Press, 1973. $4.95. Paperbound.

DAY, STACEY B., ed. *Proceedings 1973: Ethics in Medicine*. Pp. iii, 72. Minneapolis, Minn.: Univ. of Minn. Printing School, 1973. $4.50.

DE BLIJ, HARM J. *Systematic Political Geography*. 2nd ed. Pp. vii, 485. New York: John Wiley & Sons, 1973. $13.95.

DEL VAYO, J. ALVAREZ. *The March of Socialism*. Pp. 426. New York: Hill & Wang, 1974. $12.50.

DILLON, MARTIN and DENIS LEHANE. *Political Murder in Northern Ireland*. Pp. 317. Baltimore, Md.: Penguin, 1973. $1.75. Paperbound.

DONELAN, M.D. and M. J. GRIEVE. *International Disputes: Case Histories, 1945–1970*. Pp. v, 286. New York: St. Martin's Press, 1974. $12.95.

DONGHI, TULIO HALPERIN. *The Aftermath of Revolution in Latin America*. Pp. vii, 149. New York: Harper & Row, 1973. $12.00. Paperbound, $2.95.

DOWD, DOUGLAS F. *The Twisted Dream: Capitalist Development in the United States Since 1776*. Pp. vii, 314. Cambridge, Mass.: Winthrop, 1974. No Price.

EDEN, JEROME. *Planet in Trouble: The UFO Assault on Earth*. Pp. 214. New York: Exposition Press, 1973. $7.50.

THE EDITORS OF *CHANGE*. *On Learning and Change*. Pp. 256. New Rochelle, N. Y.: Change Magazine, 1973. $2.95. Paperbound.

EINAUDI, LUIGI R., ed. *Beyond Cuba: Latin America Takes Charge of Its Future*. Pp. vii, 250. New York: Crane, Russak, 1973. $11.50. Paperbound, $5.95.

EISENSTADT, S.N. *Tradition, Change, and Modernity*. Pp. v, 367. New York: John Wiley & Sons, 1973. $14.00.

EVERITT, ALAN, ed. *Perspectives In English Urban History*. Pp. 271. New York: Barnes & Noble, 1973. $16.50.

EVERS, HANS-DIETER., ed. *Modernization in South-East Asia*. Pp. vii, 249. New York: Oxford University Press, 1973. $19.75.

FELD, WERNER, ALAN T. LEONHARD, and WALTER W. TOXEY, eds. *The Enduring Questions of Politics*. Pp. v, 336. Englewood, N.J.: Prentice-Hall, 1974. $5.95. Paperbound.

FERRO, MARC. *The Great War 1914–1918*. Pp. vii, 239. Boston, Mass.: Routledge & Kegan Paul, 1973. $11.75. Paperback, $5.25.

FILMER, PAUL and MICHAEL PHILLIPSON. *New Directions in Sociological Theory*. Pp. 246. Cambridge, Mass.: MIT Press, 1973. $3.95. Paperbound.

FROHOCK, FRED M. *Normative Political*

Theory. Pp. vi, 118. Englewood Cliffs, N.J.: Prentice-Hall, 1973. $6.50. Paperbound, $2.95.

FRUTKIN, SUSAN. *Aimé Césaire: Black Between Worlds*. Pp. iii, 66. Washington, D. C.: University of Miami, 1973. $3.95. Paperbound.

GHEDDO, PIERO. *Why is the Third World Poor?* Pp. iii, 143. Maryknoll, New York: Orbis, 1973. $3.95. Paperbound.

GILBERT, JOHN H. *The New Era in American Foreign Policy*. Pp. 216. New York: St. Martin's Press, 1973. $8.95. Paperbound, $3.95.

GOLDMAN, PERRY M. and JAMES S. YOUNG, eds. *The United States: Congressional Directories 1789–1840*. Pp. 417. New York: Columbia University, 1973. $20.00.

GORDON, CYRUS H. *Riddles in History*. Pp. 188. New York: Crown, 1974. $7.95.

GROSSMAN, JONATHAN. *The Department of Labor*. Pp. v, 309. New York: Praeger, 1973. $10.00.

HAAS, MICHAEL. *International Systems: A Behavioral Approach*. Pp. vii, 433. New York: Chandler, 1974. $14.00.

HAMPE, KARL. *Germany Under The Salian And Hohenstaufen Emperors*. Pp. 315. Totowa, N.J.: Rowman and Littlefield, 1974. $15.00.

HANDELMAN, JOHN R., HOWARD B. SHAPIRO, and JOHN A. VASQUEZ. *Introductory Case Studies for International Relations Vietnam/The Middle East/The Environmental Crisis*. Pp. ix, 100. Chicago, Ill.: Rand McNally, 1974. $4.95. Paperbound.

HEREN, LOUIS et al. *China's Three Thousand Years*. Pp. v, 252. New York: Collier Books, 1974. $3.95. Paperbound.

HERNDON, JAMES F. and JOSEPH L. BERND, eds. *Mathematical Applications In Political Science, VII*. Pp. 84. Charlottesville, Va.: University Press of Virginia, 1974. $9.75.

HIDEN, MIKAEL. *The Ombudsman in Finland: The First Fifty Years*. Institute of Governmental Studies. Pp. v, 198. Berkeley, Calif.: University of California Press, 1973. No price.

HILDEBRAND, KLAUS. *The Foreign Policy Of The Third Reich*. Pp. v, 209. Berkeley, Calif.: University of California Press, 1974. $3.95. Paperbound.

HILL, MICHAEL. *A Sociology of Religion*. Pp. 285. New York: Basic Books, 1974. $10.00.

HILLS, WILLIAM G. et al., eds. *Conducting The People's Business: The Framework and Functions of Public Administration*. Pp. vii, 491. Norman, Okla.: University of Oklahoma Press, 1973. $19.95. Paperbound, $7.50.

HIRO, DILIP. *Black British, White British*. Pp. vi, 346. New York: Monthly Review Press, 1974. $8.95.

HOFFMAN, HEINRICH and HENRY PICKER. *Hitler Close-Up*. Pp. 223. New York: Macmillan, 1974. $9.95.

HUGHES, HELEN, ed. *Prospects For Partnership: Industrialization and Trade Policies in the 1970s*. Pp. v, 289. Baltimore, Md.: Johns Hopkins, 1973. $10.00.

JACOBS, JERRY. *Deviance: Field Studies and Self-Disclosures*. Pp. iii, 190. Palo Alto, Calif.: National Press Books, 1974. $3.95. Paperbound.

JOHNSON, ELMER H. *Crime, Correction, And Society*. 3rd ed. Pp. vii, 671. Homewood, Ill.: The Dorsey Press, 1973. $11.50.

JONES, WHITNEY R. D. *The Mid-Tudor Crisis 1539–1563*. Pp. 226. New York: Barnes & Noble, 1973. $13.00.

KRAEMER, HAZEL V. *Youth And Culture: A Human-Development Approach*. Pp. v, 670. Monterey, Calif.: Brooks/Cole, 1974. $6.95. Paperbound.

LA ROCHELLE, PIERRE DRIEU. *Secret Journal and Other Writings*. Pp. vii, 81. New York: Howard Fertig, 1973. $8.00.

LAUDICINA, PAUL A. *World Poverty and Development: A Survey of American Opinion*. Pp. iii, 126. Washington, D. C.: Overseas Development Council, 1973. $2.50. Paperbound.

LEMON, NIGEL. *Attitudes and Their Measurement*. Pp. 294. New York: Halsted Press, 1974. $11.50.

LEONHARD, WOLFGANG. *Three Faces of Marxism: The Political Concepts of Soviet Ideology, Maoism, and Humanist Marxism*. Pp. v, 497. New York: Holt, Rinehart and Winston, 1974. $15.00.

LEVISON, ARNOLD B. *Knowledge And Society*. Pegasus Traditions in Philosophy Series. Pp. ix, 188. Indianapolis, Ind.: Bobbs-Merrill, 1974. $4.95. Paperbound.

LICHTHEIM, GEORGE. *Europe In The Twentieth Century*. Pp. ix, 409. New York: Praeger, 1974. $5.95. Paperbound.

LIGHTFOOT, KEITH. *The Philippines Nations of the Modern World*. Pp. 251. New York: Praeger Publishers, 1974. $10.00.

LINDSEY, BEN B. and WAINWRIGHT EVANS. *The Revolt of Modern Youth*. Americana Library 28. Pp. v, 364. Seattle, Wash.: University of Washington Press, 1974. $9.50.

LITTWIN, LAWRENCE. *Latin America: Catholicism and Class Conflict*. Pp. vii, 135. Encino, Calif.: Dickenson, 1974. No price. Paperbound.

LUNDIN, ROBERT W. *Personality: A Behavioral Analysis*. 2nd ed. Pp. 484. New York: Macmillan, 1974. $10.95.

Man, Materials, and Environment. Environmental Studies Series. Pp. x, 236. Cambridge, Mass.: MIT Press, 1973. $3.95. Paperbound.

MARKEL, LESTER. *What You Don't Know Can Hurt You.* Pp. v, 288. New York: Quadrangle, 1973. $2.95. Paperbound.

MASOTTI, LOUIS H., and JEFFREY K. HADDEN, eds. *Suburbia In Transition.* Pp. 345. New York: New Viewpoints, 1974. $4.95. Paperbound.

MAXWELL, JUDITH. *Energy From The Arctic.* Pp. iii, 125. Washington, D.C.: National Planning Association, 1973. $4.00. Paperbound.

MCLELLAN, DAVID. *Karl Marx: His Life and Thought.* Pp. vi, 498. New York: Harper & Row, 1974. $12.50.

MCLENNAN, BARBARA N., ed. *Political Opposition and Dissent.* Pp. i, 393. Cambridge, Mass.: University Press, 1974. $15.00.

MIDDLETON, DREW. *Where Has Last July Gone?* Pp. ix, 284. New York: Quadrangle, 1974. $7.95.

MILGRAM, JOEL I. and DOROTHY JUNE SCIARRA, eds. *Childhood Revisited.* Pp. v, 364. New York: Macmillan, 1974. No price.

MILLS, NICOLAUS, ed. *The Great School Bus Controversy.* Pp. ix, 356. New York: Teachers College Press, 1974. $10.95.

MOYNIHAN, DANIEL P. *Coping: On the Practice of Government.* Pp. 430. New York: Random House, 1974. $10.00.

MURPHY, WILLIAM T., JR., and EDWARD SCHNEIDER. *Vote Power. How To Work for the Person You Want Elected.* Pp. vii, 224. New York: Anchor Press, 1974. $1.95. Paperbound.

NISBET, ROBERT A. *The Sociology of Emile Durkheim.* Pp. 293. New York: Oxford University Press, 1974. $9.95.

PANGLE, THOMAS L. *Montesquieu's Philosophy of Liberalism: A Commentary on The Spirit of the Laws.* Pp. vii, 336. Chicago, Ill.: University of Chicago Press, 1974. $10.00.

PARKER, DONALD DEAN. *Gabriel Renville Young Sioux Warrior.* Pp. 173. Jericho, N.Y.: Exposition, 1973. $7.00.

PETERSON, GEORGE E., ed. *Property Tax Reform.* Pp. v, 188. Hartford, Conn.: University of Hartford, 1973. $4.95. Paperbound.

PETRAS, JAMES, ed. *Latin America; From Dependence To Revolution.* Pp. viii, 274. New York: John Wiley & Sons, 1973. $8.95. Paperbound, $5.95.

PREET, ERNEST H. *Economic Blocs And U.S. Foreign Policy.* Pp. vii, 202. Washington, D.C.: National Planning Association, 1974. $7.95. Paperbound, $3.50.

PURCELL, THEODORE V. and GERALD F. CAVANAGH. *Blacks in the Industrial World: Issues for the Manager.* Pp. 358. New York: The Free Press, 1973. $3.95. Paperbound.

RAMSEY, JOHN. *Concepts of Politics: A Working Book in American National Government.* Pp. v, 198. Columbus, Ohio: Charles E. Merrill, 1974. $5.95. Paperbound.

RODNICK, DAVID. *Man's Quest For Autonomy: A Background for Modernization.* Pp. ix, 365. Lubbock, Tex.: Caprock Press. 1974. $9.95. Paperbound.

ROLFE, SIDNEY E. and JAMES L. BURTLE. *The Great Wheel: The World Monetary System.* Pp. vii, 279. New York: Quadrangle, 1974. $9.95.

ROSE, PETER I., STANLEY ROTHMAN, and WILLIAM J. WILSON, eds. *Through Different Eyes: Black and White Perspectives on American Race Relations.* Pp. xii, 453. New York: Oxford University Press, 1973. $12.50.

ROSENFELD, ERWIN M. and HARRIET GELLER. *Afro-Asian Culture Studies.* Pp. 401. Woodbury, N.Y.: Barron's Educational Series, 1973. $3.95. Paperbound.

ROSS, NORMAN A., ed. *Index to the Expert Testimony before the Indian Claims Commission.* The Library of American Indian Affairs. Pp. v, 102. N. Y.: Clearwater, 1973. No price.

ROSS, NORMAN A., ed. *Index to the Decision of the Indian Claims Commission.* The Library of American Indian Affairs. Pp. 158. N.Y.: Clearwater, 1973. No price.

RUDOFSKY, BERNARD. *The Unfashionable Human Body.* Pp. 288. New York: Doubleday, 1974. $5.95. Paperbound.

SALOMON, JEAN-JACQUES. *Science and Politics.* Pp. 277. Cambridge, Mass.: M.I.T. Press, 1973. $15.00.

SARAN, RENE. *Policy-Making in Secondary Education: A Case Study.* Pp. 282. New York: Oxford University Press, 1973. $14.50.

The Second Newman Report: National Policy and Higher Education. Report of a Special Task Force to the Secretary of Health, Education, and Welfare. Pp. vii, 227. Cambridge, Mass.: MIT Press, 1973. $3.45. Paperbound.

SCHUBERT, GLENDON. *Judicial Policy Making.* American Government Series. Pp. 239. Glenview Ill.: Scott, Foresman, 1974. $3.95. Paperbound.

SCOTT, ANDREW M. and EARL WALLACE. *Politics USA: Cases on the American*

Democratic Process. 4th ed. Pp. v, 556. New York: Macmillan 1974. $5.95. Paperbound.

SEIBEL, HANS DIETER. *The Dynamics of Achievement: A Radical Perspective*. Studies in Sociology Series. Pp. 53. Indianapolis, Ind.: Bobbs-Merrill, 1974. $1.50. Paperbound.

SHIBUTANI, TAMOTSU, ed. *Human Nature and Collective Behavior: Papers in Honor of Herbert Blumer*. Pp. v, 404. New York: E. P. Dutton, 1973. $4.95. Paperbound.

SLATER, PHILIP. *Earthwalk*. Pp. 230. New York: Doubleday & Co., 1974. $7.95.

SOHN, LOUIS B. and THOMAS BUERGENTHAL. *Basic Documents On International Protection Of Human Rights*. Contemporary Legal Education Series. Pp. iii, 244. New York: Bobbs-Merrill Co., 1973. No price.

SOHN, LOUIS B. and THOMAS BUERGENTHAL. *International Protection of Human Rights*. Contemporary Legal Education Series. Pp. v, 1402. Indianapolis, Ind.: Bobbs-Merrill Co., 1973. $19.50.

STEINBERG, STEPHEN. *The Academic Melting Pot: Catholics and Jews in American Higher Education*. Pp. xiii, 183. New York: McGraw-Hill, 1974. $8.95.

SUCHESTOW, MARCEL. *Econognosis: A Revised Economic Knowledge*. vol. 1, Pp. 332. New York: Vaton Book Press, 1973. $18.00.

THAYER, FREDERICK C. *An End To Hierarchy! An End to Competition! Organizing the Politics and Economics of Survival*. Pp. vii, 232. New York: New Viewpoints, 1973. $2.95. Paperbound.

Toynbee on Toynbee: A Conversation between Arnold J. Toynbee and G.R. Urban. Pp. 113. New York: Oxford University Press, 1974. $5.95.

TRETICK, STANLEY and WILLIAM V. SHANNON. *They Could Not Trust The King*. Pp. 197. New York: Macmillan Publishing Co., 1974. $12.95. Paperbound, $4.95.

TSIPIS, KOSTA, ANNE H. CAHN, and BERNARD T. FELD, eds. *The Future of the Sea-Based Deterrent*. Pp. vii, 265. Cambridge, Mass.: MIT Press, 1973. $3.95. Paperbound.

TUGWELL, REXFORD G. and THOMAS E. CRONIN, eds. *The Presidency Reappraised*. Pp. 320. New York: Praeger, 1974. $8.95. Paperbound, $3.95.

UNWIN, JAMES O. *The Future of Religion*. Pp. 126. Jericho, N. Y.: Exposition Press, 1973. $4.50.

WALTON, JR., HANES. *The Study and Analysis of Black Politics: A Bibliography*. Pp. v, 161. Metuchen, N.J.: Scarecrow Press, 1973. $6.00.

WALZER, MICHAEL et al, eds. *Regicide and Revolution*. Pp. v, 219. New York: Cambridge University Press, 1974. $12.50.

WARTH, ROBERT D. *Lenin*. Twayne's Rulers and Statesmen of the World Series, no. 21 Russia. Pp. 198. Boston, Mass.: Twayne Publishers, 1973. $5.95.

WEAVER, THOMAS, ed. *Indians of Arizona: A Contemporary Perspective*. Pp. vii, 169. Tuscon, Arizona: University of Arizona Press, 1974. $3.95. Paperbound.

WECHSLER, JAMES. *Revolt on the Campus*. Americana Library 26. Pp. v, 458. Seattle, Wash.: University of Washington Press, 1974. $9.50.

WEYL, WALTER EDWARD. *American World Policies*. Americana Library 27. Pp. vii, 307. Seattle, Wash.: Washington Press, 1974. $9.50.

WHITE, CARL M. et al. *Sources of Information in the Social Sciences*. 2nd ed. Pp. vii, 702. Chicago, Ill.: American Library Association, 1973. $25.00.

WIEGAND, G. C., ed. *Toward A New World Monetary System*. Pp. iii, 204. New York: McGraw-Hill, 1973. $8.95. Paperbound.

WILLEMSEN, ELEANOR W. *Understanding Statistical Reasoning: How to Evaluate Research Literature in the Behavioral Sciences*. Pp. 223. San Francisco, Calif.: W. H. Freeman, 1974. $10.00. Paperbound, $4.95.

WINNIK, HEINRICH Z., RAFAEL MOSES, and MORTIMER OSTOW. *Psychological Bases of War*. Pp. 261. New York: Quadrangle, 1973. $9.95.

WOLF, WILLIAM B. *The Basic Barnard: An Introduction to Chester I. Barnard and His Theories of Organization and Management*. Pp. v, 140. Ithaca, New York: Cornell University, 1974. $9.00. Paperbound, $7.50.

WRIGGINS, W. HOWARD and JAMES F. GUYOT. *Population, Politics, & The Future Of Southern Asia*. Pp. vi, 402. New York: Columbia University Press, 1974. $8.50. Paperbound, $2.95.

YOUNG, RALPH A. *Instruments of Monetary Policy in the United States: The Role of the Federal Reserve System*. Pp. v, 196. Washington, D.C.: International Monetary Fund, 1973. $1.25. Paperbound.

ZAX, MELVIN and GEORGE STRICKER. *The Study of Abnormal Behavior*. 3rd ed. Pp. v, 582. New York: Macmillan, 1974. $5.95. Paperbound.

THE AAPSS

½ PRICE

Inventory Clearance Sale
of THE ANNALS

$3.00 paperbound—now $1.50
$4.00 clothbound—now $2.00

Due to an overstock, the following ANNALS issues are available for a limited time at the special sale price.

Number
of Copies
paper   cloth

How Wars End
Nov. 1970, vol. 392, paper & cloth

Collective Violence
Sep. 1970, vol. 391, paper

A New American Posture toward Asia
July 1970, vol. 390, paper & cloth

Political Intelligence for America's Future
Mar. 1970, vol. 388, paper & cloth

The Sixties—Radical Change in American Religion
Jan. 1970, vol. 387, cloth

The Protagonist Powers and the Third World
Nov. 1969, vol. 386, paper & cloth

Evaluating the War on Poverty
Sep. 1969, vol. 385, paper & cloth

America's Changing Role as A World Leader
July 1969, vol. 384, paper & cloth

Progress in Family Law
May 1969, vol. 383, paper & cloth

The Future of Corrections
Jan. 1969, vol. 381, paper & cloth

Resources and Needs of American Diplomacy
Nov. 1968, vol. 380, paper & cloth

The Changing American People: Are we Deteriorating or Improving?
July 1968, vol. 378, paper & cloth

The Ombudsman or Citizen's Defender: A Modern Institution
May 1968, vol. 377, paper & cloth

Women Around the World
Jan. 1968, vol. 375, paper

Number
of Copies
paper   cloth

Social Goals and Indicators for American Society, Volume II
   Sept. 1967, vol. 373, cloth

Realignments in the Communist and Western Worlds
   July 1967, vol. 372, paper

National Character in the Perspective of the Social Sciences
   Mar. 1967, vol. 370, paper

Americans Abroad
   Nov. 1966, vol. 368, paper & cloth

The New Immigration
   Sep. 1966, vol. 367, paper & cloth

American Civilization: Its Influence on Our Foreign Policy
   July 1966, vol. 366, paper & cloth

The Peace Corps
   May 1966, vol. 365, paper

Ethics in America: Norms and Deviations
   Jan. 1966, vol. 363, paper

Nonalignment in Foreign Affairs
   Nov. 1965, vol. 362, paper

Political Socialization
   Sep. 1965, vol. 361, paper

Latin America Tomorrow
   July 1965, vol. 360, paper & cloth

The Negro Protest
   Jan. 1965, vol. 357, paper

The Non-Western World in Higher Education
   Nov. 1964, vol. 356, paper

Africa in Motion
   July 1964, vol. 354, paper

Urban Revival: Goals and Standards
   Mar. 1964, vol. 352, paper

The Changing Cold War
   Jan. 1964, vol. 351, paper

Communist China and the Soviet Bloc
   Sep. 1963, vol. 349, paper

- Quantity and wholesales discounts cannot be applied to this special offer.
- Shipping charges additional if payment is not received with order.
- Watch for other sales in future issues.

Please send me the volumes as indicated above.

☐ Enclosed is $———
☐ Please bill me

Name————————————————————————————————

Address—————————————————————————————————

City————————————————State————————————Zip———

THE AMERICAN ACADEMY OF POLITICAL AND
SOCIAL SCIENCE

3937 Chestnut Street   **Philadelphia, Pa. 19104**

INDEX

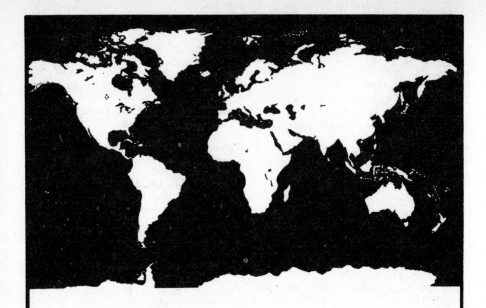

THE DEATH OF COMMUNAL LIBERTY
A History of Freedom in a Swiss Mountain Canton
BENJAMIN R. BARBER

For centuries the group of alpine villages that make up modern Canton Graubünden has managed to maintain its remarkable political tradition of direct democracy. But assimilation into the wider context of Switzerland and Europe has brought this tradition of communal liberty into violent conflict with the forces of modernization. Combining political theory and history, Benjamin Barber's multifaceted study traces the growth, maturity, and decline of a political and social life-style that may offer a communitarian alternative to the Anglo-American experience of representative government as an increasingly alienating and stifling bureaucracy. $12.50

THE RULES OF RIOT
Internal Conflict and the Law of War
JAMES E. BOND

Riots, insurrections, guerrilla movements, civil wars—all forms of internal conflict are increasing throughout the world. There are laws to protect human rights in peacetime and during international conflicts, but no body of law protects those caught up in civil strife. James E. Bond focuses on this major question: How can we regulate civil guerrilla warfare? "A fine piece of work on a critically important problem."—Richard A. Falk $11.50

PEOPLE'S CHINA AND INTERNATIONAL LAW
A Documentary Study
JEROME ALAN COHEN and HUNGDAH CHIU

Professors Cohen and Chiu provide an extensive introduction, notes, and commentary to supplement this comprehensive study of the views of the People's Republic of China on all the major questions of public international law. The material chosen includes official acts and statements from every level of the Chinese government, the writings of Chinese scholars, and the speeches of China's leaders. *Studies in East Asian Law, Harvard University* 2 vols., $60.00

Origin and Purpose. The Academy was organized December 14, 1889, to promote the progress of political and social science, especially through publications and meetings. The Academy does not take sides in controverted questions, but seeks to gather and present reliable information to assist the public in forming an intelligent and accurate judgment.

Meetings. The Academy holds an annual meeting in the spring extending over two days.

Publications. THE ANNALS is the bimonthly publication of The Academy. Each issue contains articles on some prominent social or political problem, written at the invitation of the editors. Also, monographs are published from time to time, numbers of which are distributed to pertinent professional organizations. These volumes constitute important reference works on the topics with which they deal, and they are extensively cited by authorities throughout the United States and abroad. The papers presented at the meetings of The Academy are included in THE ANNALS.

Membership. Each member of The Academy receives THE ANNALS and may attend the meetings of The Academy. Annual dues for individuals are $15.00 (for clothbound copies $20.00 per year). A life membership is $500. All payments are to be made in United States dollars.

Libraries and other institutions may receive THE ANNALS paperbound at a cost of $15.00 per year, or clothbound at $20.00 per year. Add $1.00 to above rates for membership outside U.S.A.

Single copies of THE ANNALS may be obtained by nonmembers of The Academy for $3.00 ($4.00 clothbound) and by members for $2.50 ($3.50 clothbound). A discount of 5 percent is allowed on orders for 10 to 24 copies of any one issue, and of 10 percent on orders for 25 or more copies. These discounts apply only when orders are placed directly with The Academy and not through agencies. The price to all bookstores and to all dealers is $3.00 per copy less 20 percent, with no quantity discount. It is urged that payment be sent with each order. This will save the buyer the shipping charge and save The Academy the cost of carrying accounts and sending statements. Monographs may be purchased for $4.00, with proportionate discounts.

All correspondence concerning The Academy or THE ANNALS should be addressed to the Academy offices, 3937 Chestnut Street. Philadelphia, Pa. 19104.